James Turnbull

Fine FRENCH WINES

Flammarion

CONTENTS

Note

There is no Finest Vintages list for the champagnes featured in this book that are non-vintage (i.e., those produced from the crop of more than one year)

Most estates can be visited; be sure to make a courtesy call prior to arrival. The demand for the best wines is so strong that some estates rarely have any stock in their cellars to sell, and readers are best advised to buy the wine through retail outlets. Those outlets likely to carry the wines appears at the end of the book.

Prices indicated correspond with the wine photographed and are those asked at the property, except in the case where on-site sales are not available, in which case they represent the average price charged by the sales outlets. At the time of publication, one euro was equivalent to one U.S. dollar and to 0.64 British pounds. The star notations represent the following price brackets:

★	Less than 15 euros
★★	from 15 to 30 euros
★★★	from 30 to 60 euros
★★★★	from 60 to 120 euros
★★★★★	In excess of 120 euros

Metric measurements are used throughout the book, their equivalents are as follows:

1 hectare = 2.471 acres
1 liter = 0.227 gallons US, 0.22 gallons UK
1 kilometer = 0.62 mile
1 gram = 0.035 ounces

INTRODUCTION

Margaux, Musigny, Le Mesnil, Montrachet… The great names in French wine hold an irresistible fascination for the wine lover, triggering memories of fine bottles enjoyed in the past—and of the context and with whom they were enjoyed—or otherwise stimulating the imagination of he or she who has not yet had the luck to taste the wine. France is the quintessential wine country, producing an extraordinarily wide variety of styles of the highest quality, and its influence on wine making in other countries is widespread. Its wines provide the yardsticks by which many foreign wine makers judge their own work; its grape varieties are planted abroad in the hope of producing similarly successful wines; and French enological know-how is much in demand in both hemispheres, a situation which has given rise to the "flying wine-maker" genus.

The country's long-established pre-eminence stems from a number of factors. The first is geographical: French vineyards lie roughly between latitudes 43° and 49° north, and mostly enjoy a temperate climate conducive to the slow, protracted ripening of grapes. They are never far from water: the Atlantic and Mediterranean coastlines and the numerous rivers which traverse the country play an important role in moderating local vineyard climates, and protecting them from the occasional hazard that nature throws their way. Then there is France's remarkable quantity of high-quality grape varieties, which are capable of producing every style of wine including the luscious "noble rot" wines and the oxidized *vin jaune*. There is the varied geological composition of the soils and sub-

soils: the chalk of Champagne, the schist of Anjou, the iron-rich clay of Pomerol, the gravel of Graves, and the pudding stones of Châteauneuf-du-Pape, to name but a few, make possible the production of wines of great character. And France has history: centuries of wine production and observation have enabled growers to identify the ideal grape variety for each *terroir*, and time has refined the pairing by acclimatizing each grape to its soil. Another significant asset are the country's large forests of oak, which supply the raw material for the barrels in which most "serious" wines are matured. Varied soils, noble grape varieties, suitable microclimates, natural phenomena such as *Botrytis cinerea*, and local tradition—put all of these together and one has France's extraordinarily diverse catalog of fine wine.

Ask a man in the street to name a French wine, and he will in all likelihood cite Bordeaux. The high profiles of its world-famous châteaux, the sheer quality of their wines, and the relative ease in buying Bordeaux at all quality levels thanks to the region's huge output and well-oiled distribution, ensure that there will always be a ready market for these wines. At over 289,100 acres (117,000 hectares), Bordeaux is France's largest wine region. Lying near the Atlantic coast, it enjoys both a temperate climate—influenced by the ocean, the Garonne and Dordogne rivers and their shared estuary, the Gironde—and soils perfectly suited to viticulture that enable its growers to make wines of many styles, of which the best examples have unrivalled finesse and breed. Bordeaux are generally blended wines made from several different grape varieties: Cabernet-Sauvignon, Cabernet Franc, and Merlot are the main red-wine grapes in use, Sauvignon and Sémillon the main white-wine grapes, and the sum of these almost always makes a more interesting and satisfying wine than the individual constituent parts.

Burgundy is more the province of the connoisseur—not because its wines are harder to appreciate, but because of the extreme fragmentation of its vineyards due to inheritance laws that require equal vineyard distribution to each child. Nearly all are under multiple ownership, entailing very differing quality levels of what appear to be the same wine. What is more, there are over one hundred different appellations. The consumer can find this very confusing. The industry is made up of small family businesses, a number of big *négociant* (wine wholesaler) firms and some cooperatives. The name of the producer, not the vineyard, is what counts. Lying in eastern central France, Burgundy's vineyards cover some 61,780 acres (25,000 hectares), and comprise four entities: Chablis and its neighboring vineyards, the Côte d'Or (subdivided into the Côte de Nuits and the Côte de Beaune), the Côte Chalonnaise, and the Maconnais. One sole grape, the Pinot Noir, produces all the red wines of quality, and one, the Chardonnay, all the whites. Burgundy is above all defined by the *terroir*: the Pinot Noir and the Chardonnay brilliantly convey the compelling personalities of the region's heterogeneous soils with, at their best, absolutely spellbinding wines.

The Rhône Valley's viticultural zone is second only to Bordeaux in size and production. It covers some 177,900 acres (72,000 hectares), and is made up of two parts, each having distinctly different climatic and geological characteristics. The northern part has a conti-

nental climate and is, like Burgundy, a region of small, family-run businesses and a handful of *négociant* firms. This is a land of terraced vineyards hewn out of granite, of the mighty Syrah and perfumed Viognier grapes, of the famed Côte-Rôtie, Condrieu, and Hermitage wines. The southern part, stretching from Montélimar down to Avignon, has a Mediterranean climate. A whole panoply of grapes are permitted, giving generous, heady wines of complexity. The best is Châteauneuf-du-Pape, made in a region of arid vineyards strewn with quartzite pudding stones, in which there are many large estates that recall those of the Médoc in Bordeaux. Generic Côtes-du-Rhône is better known, being produced in enormous quantities, and can represent excellent value for money.

The Loire Valley entrances the visitor with its *douceur de vivre*, and the food and wines of the region are a major attraction. The majestic Loire river and its many tributaries play an important role in warming riverside vineyards, making viticulture viable in a region where grapes would otherwise have trouble ripening. This is a large region: the river has its source in the Ardèche and flows northwards and then westwards for some 620 miles (1,000 kilometres) before reaching the Atlantic coast at Nantes. There are a little over 123,600 acres (50,000 hectares) of vineyard, and four broadly definable vineyard entities: the Centre, Touraine, the Anjou-Saumur region, and the Pays Nantais. The varied types of terrain, the many grape varieties, and the cold chalk cellars of Touraine and Saumur enable the Loire Valley to produce all styles of wine. Most are simple and of limited interest, yet the better wines are capable of surprising those not in-the-know by their dimension and complexity. The resilient Chenin Blanc produces the best dry and sweet white wines in Anjou and Touraine, while Sauvignon makes the whites of the central region; all the great red wines from Anjou and Saumur are made principally, if not entirely, with Cabernet Franc, while the best reds from the central region are made from Pinot Noir.

Sandwiched between the Vosges mountains and Germany lies Alsace, which has been making wine since time immemorial. The Vosges are important because they precipitate the rain in the clouds blowing from the Atlantic towards the continent, which makes Alsace a remarkably dry region, with hillside vineyards that can become extremely hot in summer. Alsace has some 35,830 acres (14,500 hectares) under vine, and on splendid vineyard sites of varying geological composition, four noble grapes—Riesling, Gewürztraminer, Muscat, and Pinot Gris—are planted producing aromatic wines of great elegance and refinement. A handful of other varieties are also permitted on less revered sites. Over ninety percent of Alsace wine is white, and in favorable years glorious late-harvested *Vendanges Tardives* and *Sélection de Grains Nobles* wines are produced.

South of Alsace and east of Burgundy lie the Jura mountains, in which some of France's most characterful wine is made. The Jura's speciality is its *vin jaune*, a dry, oxidized wine from the Savagnin grape which is capable of extreme longevity. The region's 4,448 acres (1,800 hectares) of vineyards also produce red and rosé wines from the local Trousseau and Poulsard grapes respectively. Burgundy's Pinot Noir sometimes finds its way into the reds, and the growers make dry whites well worthy of interest with Chardonnay and Savagnin. The exquisite loft-dried *vin de paille*, one of France's best-kept secrets, is also made here. Jura wines are food wines *par excellence*.

Provence is much appreciated by French and foreign tourists alike, for whom it is synonymous with summer holidays and the thirst-quenching rosé after a day at the beach. Provence produces a handful of great wines, albeit in tiny quantities: the wines of Bellet (above Nice) and Palette (just outside Aix-en-Provence) are made by only a handful of estates, but are well worth making an effort to find; Bandol produces rosés and above all reds of structure and complexity, which can develop splendidly with age; and Les Baux-de-Provence also produces serious red wine. As almost everywhere within range of the Mediterranean, the principal red-wine grapes are Syrah and Grenache, with Cinsault and Mourvèdre also present in many vineyards, and Cabernet-Sauvignon progressively appearing. Mourvèdre is at its very finest around Bandol, where it is the dominant variety.

The vineyards of Languedoc and Roussillon, the most ancient in France, have, without a doubt, shown the greatest progress in recent years. Stretching across the Gard, Hérault, Aude, and Pyrénées-Orientales *départements*, the common denominator is the Mediterranean climate—one of scorching heat, violent storms, and little rain. Yet there are great differences in microclimates due to factors such as wind and altitude. Some regions are dried by hot winds blowing down towards the sea, others enjoy cooling sea breezes blowing inland. Mountain vineyards have greater rainfall and far cooler nights than those on the plain, giving better acidity levels and finer aromatics to the grapes. Soils, as might be expected in such a large area, are very varied. The great progress has come through replanting with nobler grape varieties and better-adapted clones, through the adoption of ecological practices in the vineyard, through painstaking efforts to keep yields down, and through careful wine making at controlled temperatures followed by reasoned maturation in wood. The region is full of excellent value-for-money wines.

The southwestern corner of France comprises wines as disparate as Cahors, Jurançon, Bergerac, Irouleguy, and Gaillac, between which there is no real common denominator, apart perhaps from the growers' Gascon spirit and legitimate pride in their "country" wines. These vineyards are also among France's oldest, and the Southwest is a veritable museum of long-forgotten indigenous grape varieties found nowhere else. The whites may be either dry or sweet and the reds either easy-drinking or serious wines perfectly suited to the region's gastronomy. Several estates today produce wine of extraordinary quality, rated as highly as the top wines of Bordeaux and elsewhere, and without a trace of the region's traditional rusticity.

Finally there is Champagne. Sold in almost every country in the world, Champagne has become an international symbol of French savoir-faire and refinement. Champagne's greatest asset is the chalk subsoil of its *falaises* (hills), which were formed following an earthquake some eleven million years ago. There is hardly any topsoil, and vines' roots quickly come into contact with this chalk, *Belemnita quadrata*, which contains marine sediment from the period when the Paris basin was covered by the sea. Combined with the region's cold climate, the chalk enables the production of wine of great finesse and complexity. The celebrated monk Dom Pérignon discovered the virtues of blending wines of different localities and grape varieties here in the seventeenth century, which has been the technique used ever since. The Champagne vineyards are grouped in four principal regions—Montagne de Reims, Vallée de la Marne, Côte des Blancs, and Côte des Bar—and cover a little over 74,130 acres (30,000 hectares). They are planted with three grape varieties: Pinot Noir, Pinot Meunier, and Chardonnay. The best-known labels are produced in large quantities and sold around the world; they are produced by the Champagne houses, with their own grapes and those supplied by contracted growers. There are also some five thousand growers who make and market their own Champagne, which is invariably less expensive and can be delicious. Finally ten thousand other growers deliver their crop to one of the 140 cooperatives in Champagne.

Today France is going from strength to strength, with progressively more of its growers using eco-friendly methods to produce even greater wines from her hallowed appellations, and superb wines are coming from regions that not long ago gushed oceans of coarse, low-grade produce. Communication and globalization are having their effect, stimulating wine makers to excel in order to maintain their market share and to keep the competition—foreign or from fellow countrymen, at bay. Which growers produce the finest wine—the most authentic, the most harmonious—and in which regions? Which grape varieties are used, what do the wines taste like, do they improve with age, and what sort of food do they best suit? This book presents the best estates, and reviews their growing and wine-making techniques, and the styles of wine achieved. Bottles from these châteaux and domaines will in all likelihood satisfy the most discerning wine lover. The selection was made on the basis of two criteria—quality and regularity—assessed over many comparative tastings. The estates are classed by region and are listed in alphabetical order within their different appellations or sub-regions.

JAMES TURNBULL

BORDEAUX
A.O.C. Saint-Estèphe

- *Wine selected:*
  Château Cos d'Estournel
  Deuxième Cru Classé

- *Grape varieties:*
  Cabernet-Sauvignon 60%, Merlot 40%
- *Average vine age:*
  35 years
- *Vineyard size:*
  65 hectares
- *Soil type:*
  Gravel over limestone
- *Production:*
  350,000 bottles

Finest Vintages:
1996, 1995, 1993, 1990, 1989, 1986, 1982

Château Cos d'Estournel
33180 Saint-Estèphe
Tel. (0033) 556 73 15 50
Take the D2 north of Pauillac towards Saint-Estèphe. After a couple of minutes those unmistakable pagodas loom up ahead. Such a curious sight they are that many visitors forget to look to their left to admire Lafite-Rothschild!
- *Owner:* Michel Reybier
- *Managing Director:* Jean-Guillaume Prats
- *On-site sales:* Yes
- *Visits:* By appointment
- *Price:* ★★★★

CHÂTEAU COS D'ESTOURNEL

In 1811, Louis Gaspard d'Estournel recognized the gravel and limestone plateau from which the vines of Cos d'Estournel look over those of nearby Château Lafite as an ideal vineyard site. Unfortunately, having acquired a number of plots totaling a dozen hectares, he encountered financial problems and was forced by his creditors to sell his estate that same year—yet subsequently managed to buy it back ten years later. Over the following thirty years he increased the vineyard size to fifty-seven hectares, and his wine was rapidly recognized by the brokers in Bordeaux as being of *Deuxième Cru* quality.

A temple dedicated to wine

Inspired by his business trips to the Orient, d'Estournel built an eye-catching Chinese-style edifice to house his wine, which remains to this day one of the region's most famous landmarks. The magnificent carved door previously gave access, it is said, to the harem of the Sultan of Zanzibar; it is fitting, perhaps, that in its new role it should give access to a temple dedicated exclusively to wine, in which—contrary to the custom in most grand Médoc châteaux—no space has ever been taken up by living quarters.

D'Estournel did not live to see his wine's official recognition as a *Deuxième Cru*, for he died two years before the 1855 classification. The property changed hands four times before being acquired by Fernand Ginestet in 1917. After a long and prosperous period it was sold in 1998 by his grandsons Jean-Marie, Yves, and Bruno Prats

to Groupe Bernard Taillan, already proprietor of Châteaux Gruaud-Larose, Chasse-Spleen, Haut-Bages Libéral and others. It has since been acquired by Monsieur Michel Reybier. Since 1998 the estate has been run by Jean-Guillaume Prats, son of Bruno.

A soft, elegant, and stylish Saint-Estèphe

Cos (pronounced Coss) d'Estournel is not typical of the wines of Saint-Estèphe, which can for the most part be described as dense, tough, and rather unyielding, usually as a result of the large proportion of Cabernet-Sauvignon used in their blends, and also because of the predominance of clay in the soil. This wine has more softness, style, and elegance, thanks no doubt to the high percentage of Merlot used and to the largely gravel soil.

Remarkable consistency

Cos d'Estournel has been remarkably consistent over the decades. It invariably exhibits a depth and richness of fruit underpinned by a structure of fine ripe tannin which enable it to develop well over long periods. Since the beginning of the 1980s it has gained notably in refinement. The lighter less tannic vintages can be delicious young, yet the great vintages really need two decades in bottle to show what the wine is all about

When they finally reach maturity, vintages such as the fleshy, leathery, and slightly spicy 1978 are highly suitable partners for winged game dishes: teal, prepared *en civet*—in a red-wine, bacon and vegetable stew—would be an excellent choice.

BORDEAUX
A.O.C. Saint-Estèphe

- *Wine selected:*
  Château Haut-Marbuzet

- *Grape varieties:*
  Cabernet-Sauvignon 50%, Merlot
  40%, Cabernet-Franc 10%
- *Average vine age:*
  30 years
- *Vineyard size:*
  55 hectares
- *Soil type:*
  Günz gravel over limestone and clay
- *Production:*
  300,000 bottles

Finest Vintages:
1996, 1990, 1989, 1988, 1982

Château Haut-Marbuzet
33180 Saint-Estèphe
Tel. (0033) 556 59 30 54
Take the D2 north of Pauillac towards
Saint-Estèphe. After a couple of
minutes one finds the unmistakable
Cos d'Estournel on one's right. Turn
right and proceed to the village of
Marbuzet. Haut-Marbuzet is well-
indicated. (Do not confuse it with
Château de Marbuzet!)
- *Owner:* Henri Duboscq
- *General Manager:* Jean-Guillaume
  Prats
- *On-site sales:* Yes
- *Visits:* 9–12 a.m., 2–6 p.m.
- *Price:* ★★

CHÂTEAU HAUT-MARBUZET

In the entire Gironde there can be few *grands vins* so individual, so brilliant and widely admired as that produced at Château Haut-Marbuzet, in Saint-Estèphe. Flying in the face of conventional wine-making wisdom, Henri Duboscq creates a one-off that is invariably one of the top wines of the commune, despite being on paper a humble *Cru Bourgeois*. Not for him the advice of the professional enologist, and the predictability that often results! Let all wine lovers be thankful!

Innate intuition and profound self-confidence

The story of Haut-Marbuzet's meteoric rise to greatness started in 1952, when Hervé Duboscq, Henri's father, purchased the seven-hectare vineyard—at the time almost naked of vines—and with no experience or training, simply an innate intuition and profound self-confidence, started making wine. It was excellent from the start, and his equally great talent at selling enabled him to rapidly build a clientele of private wine lovers and to ask, and get, the price of a *Troisième Cru*. It was evident very soon that more land would be needed to satisfy growing demand, and he started buying up neighboring parcels—and in so doing rebuilt a large domain split up a century before into twelve parts by the MacCarthys.

Hervé's son Henri joined him in the adventure in 1962, and by 1994 the latter, in charge since 1973, had 55 hectares at his disposal. Enough (for the moment) to satisfy the demands of 20,000 regular clients, including top politicians and public figures, prestigious restaurants and the European Parliament.

The Duboscq method

The Haut-Marbuzet vineyard is made for great wine. But it is above all the wine-making techniques which give Haut-Marbuzet its individual character. Duboscq delays harvesting until the grapes are almost over-ripe, and then works rapidly, leaf-stripping until 10 a.m. and starting to pick only when all dew has evaporated. He uses a high proportion of Merlot, which gives his wine softness and flesh.

The grapes are entirely destemmed, and after fermenting at as high a temperature as is possible, the wine macerates for a long period. It is then matured in oak barrels, which are renewed in their entirety every vintage—Haut-Marbuzet is the only *Cru Bourgeois* to allow itself this luxury. And Duboscq does not blindly buy the same wood every year, but tailors his purchases as a real connoisseur of wood, precisely to the type of wine to be aged. This is an important factor, since it masks the normal Saint-Estèphe hardness and austerity, and contributes opulence and complexity.

Exotic, exuberant, and exciting

What results is a wine of great sensuality, soft and fleshy, exotic, exuberant, and exciting; eminently drinkable in its youth, and yet, contrary to initial impressions, a wine that develops extremely well in bottle over two decades, gaining in subtlety and refinement as it does so.

Henri Duboscq likes serving his wine alongside a tournedos Rossini, and this combination certainly brings out the best in both partners. The wine is also very well suited to game dishes in general: a ten-year-old bottle served with roast pheasant and chestnut stuffing is absolutely delicious!

BORDEAUX
A.O.C. Saint-Estèphe

- *Wine selected:*
  Château Montrose
  Deuxième Cru Classé

- *Grape varieties:*
  Cabernet-Sauvignon 65%,
  Merlot 25%,
  Cabernet-Franc 10%
- *Average vine age:*
  30 years
- *Vineyard size:*
  68 hectares
- *Soil type:*
  Heavy gravel over clay and marl
- *Production:*
  240,000 bottles

Finest Vintages:
1998, 1996, 1995, 1990, 1989, 1986

Château Montrose
33180 Saint-Estèphe
Tel. (0033) 556 59 30 12
Follow the D2 northwards from
Pauillac. Turn right directly after Cos
d'Estournel, and follow the road some
1.8 km; the private road leading to
Montrose is on the right, indicated by
a panel.
- *Owner:* Jean-Louis Charmolüe
- *General Manager:* Philippe de
  Laguarigue
- *On-site sales:* Yes
- *Visits:* By appointment
- *Price:* ★★★★

CHÂTEAU MONTROSE

Of all the Médoc *Crus Classés*, Château Montrose has one of the finest vineyard sites. The vines are a mere stone's throw from the river, and the stable riverside micro-climate enables the owner to harvest his earlier-ripening grapes several days in advance of his peers. It is thus less at the mercy of October rains, and can produce top-quality wine with great regularity. This estate fully deserves its *Deuxième Cru* classification.

An area of scrub transformed into vineyard

The land originally formed part of the giant Calon estate, owned at the end of the seventeenth century by the powerful de Ségur family. In 1778 Calon was bought by Etienne Théodore Dumoulin, and then in 1812 passed down into the hands of his like-named son.

The young Dumoulin had spotted a part of the estate, an area of scrub on a rise overlooking the Gironde, where he thought vines might grow well. After successful trial plantings, he planted some 6 hectares, and at the same time put up buildings for making the wine. Dumoulin sold Calon in 1824, but retained his new creation; he was convinced of its potential, and started buying up parcels of land with a view to creating a decently sized estate.

By 1825 this mini-estate was known as Montrose—so named, it is widely believed, because of the pink bloom of the heather that had covered the rise before the vines' arrival. By 1855 the vineyard covered 50 hectares, and the wine was duly classified *Deuxième Cru*, making it, with its similarly classed rival Château Cos d'Estournel, one of Saint-Estèphe's two top estates. On Dumoulin's death, Montrose passed to his two adopted children, who sold it a mere five years later to Mathieu Dollfus.

An impeccably maintained estate

The twenty-year Dollfus tenure was very beneficial to the estate and its workers: not only did he continue enlarging the vineyard, he also created a veritable village on the estate, and was acutely concerned by his staff's well-being. Visiting Montrose today, one is struck by the tidiness and order that are noticeable everywhere, from the compact layout of the buildings, neatly surrounded by the single vineyard parcel, to the organization and pristine conditions of the vathouse. Louis Charmolüe, who bought the estate in 1896, his son Albe and grandson Jean-Louis, the present incumbent, have taken pains to maintain Dollfus's standards. This is the sort of place where one would expect to find superlative wine. And indeed one does!

A softer and easier style

Montrose combines power, complexity, and finesse, and is a wine for long-term keeping. In the 1960s and 1970s it was often, and rightly, criticized for excessive structure: the wines were too unyielding for their own good. Since 1986 the style of the wine has been modified in order to make it rather more user-friendly, principally by reducing the proportion of Cabernet-Sauvignon in the blend.

At the estate they recommend serving the wine with a leg of tender Pauillac lamb—those lambs reared on the salty riverside grass and slaughtered at eight months old. The 1976 Montrose would be just perfect for this: a very successful vintage with an expansive bouquet, rich, ripe, and mature, and with lingering but inoffensive tannin; still with the blackcurrant flavor of Cabernet, yet made more complex by exquisite nuances of leather, cedarwood, and spice developed over the years.

BORDEAUX
A.O.C. Pauillac

- *Wine selected:*
Château Lafite-Rothschild
Premier Cru Classé

- *Grape varieties:*
Cabernet-Sauvignon 72%,
Merlot 23%, Cabernet-Franc 3%,
Petit Verdot 2%
- *Average vine age:*
35 years
- *Vineyard size:*
100 hectares
- *Soil type:*
Gravel

Finest Vintages:

1999, 1998, 1996, 1990, 1989,
1988, 1986, 1983, 1982

Château Lafite-Rothschild
33250 Pauillac
Tel. (0033) 556 73 18 18
Follow the D2 northwards out of
Pauillac. In approximately 2 km,
just before the hill leading up to Cos
d'Estournel, there appears on the left
a property fairly well hidden behind
some imposing weeping willows. You
are in front of Lafite.
- *Owner:* S.C. du Château
Lafite-Rothschild
- *Director:* Charles Chevallier
- *On-site sales:* No
- *Visits:* By appointment
(Tel. 00 33 153 89 78 00)
- *Price:* ★★★★★

CHÂTEAU LAFITE-ROTHSCHILD

Although it is pointless to try and establish a hierarchy among the *Premiers Crus*, many professionals and ordinary wine-lovers over the last two hundred years have put Château Lafite at the top of their lists, indeed the wine this century has earned the epithet Rolls-Royce of Bordeaux.

An international reputation acquired

Although it already had three hundred years of history and wine-making behind it, Lafite did not start producing fine wine until it was acquired by Alexandre de Ségur, owner of Château Latour, just before his death in 1716. His son Nicolas Alexandre added Mouton and Calon to the family holdings two years later, and earned himself the nickname Prince des Vignes. During his tenure the Lafite estate was enlarged and its wine improved, and it was at this time that it was first mentioned by enamoured foreign connoisseurs.

An exceptional family of managers

After Nicolas Alexandre's death in 1755 his spoilt and dissolute son ran up enormous debts, and Lafite had to be put on the market in 1784. There followed numerous changes of ownership and absentee landlords, and Lafite was only saved from sinking into mediocrity by the Goudal family, who occupied the post of administrato for seventy years and ran the estate as if they owned it. The estate was sold in 1868 to Baron James de Rothschild, of the branch associated with the French bank, and has remained in the hands of his descendants ever since.

The end of a difficult period

The wine went through a difficult period in the 1960s and 1970s, possibly because the administrator lived in faraway Paris, possibly also because it underwent extremely protracted aging in barrel before bottling; what is more, the bottling was carried out over a number of months, which explains the variation between bottles of this era. However, following the appointment in 1975 of the current administrator, Baron Éric de Rothschild, there has been re-thinking and much investment, notably in a new vatroom housing twenty stainless steel vats, which lies next to the existing vatroom with its thirty oak vats, and in an equally impressive circular maturation cellar, capable of holding 2,200 barrels. In 1990 a cooper was installed, enabling in-house fabrication of the 2,000 barrels required annually for maturing the wines of Lafite, Duhart-Milon, and Rieussec.

Factors of greatness

The secret of the wine's greatness must lie in several factors. The first is the quality of the land, composed of deep gravel on a bed of marl, which itself lies on limestone. Secondly, the extreme attention to detail in the vineyard, the high average age of the vines, and their low production. And thirdly, the severity of the selections when blending the *grand vin*. All in all, a recipe for finesse, delicacy, intensity of flavor, and harmony.

A mature Lafite calls for a simple dish of top-quality ingredients. The 1976 vintage, now a seigneur with a wonderfully fresh and sweet cedarwood and spice flavor, has just the room it needs to express itself when served with a simple leg of lamb braised with spring onions.

BORDEAUX
A.O.C. Pauillac

- *Wine selected:*
  Château Latour
  Premier Cru Classé

- *Grape varieties:*
  Cabernet-Sauvignon 75%,
  Merlot 20%,
  Cabernet-Franc 4%
- *Average vine age:*
  40 years
- *Vineyard size:*
  65 hectares
- *Soil type:*
  Deep gravel and clay
- *Production:*
  360,000 bottles

Finest Vintages:
1999, 1998, 1996, 1995, 1994, 1991,
1990, 1989, 1988, 1986, 1982

Château Latour
33250 Pauillac
Tel. (0033) 556 73 19 80
Proceed northwards from Saint-Julien
along the D2. Latour can be seen on
your right. Pass between the two
Pichons, then take the first road on
the right, which leads up to it.
- *Owner:* François Pinault
- *President:* Frédéric Engerer
- *On-site sales:* No
- *Visits:* By appointment
- *Price:* ★★★★★

CHÂTEAU LATOUR

Of all the Bordeaux vineyards it is possibly at Château Latour that the Cabernet-Sauvignon expresses its personality the most forcefully. In great vintages Latour is dense, austere, powerful, and impenetrable, and requires many years to open up and reveal its multidimensional complexity. Its heavy tannic structure and sheer volume of fruit then combine to give a very long-lasting wine; indeed many fine vintages of the nineteenth century are still in fine form, testimony to its legendary longevity. Latour has also deservedly gained a reputation for the quality of the wines it produces in lesser years.

The rise to greatness

The land which now constitutes Château Latour is first mentioned by Froissart in his *Chroniques*, as he describes the capture by the British-Gascon army of the Tour de Saint-Maubert, built to protect the estuary, during the Hundred Years' War. The estate was gradually turned over to viticulture. The great wine-making epoch of this grand estate starts more recently however, with its acquisition by Alexandre de Ségur in 1695.

In 1716, just before his death, de Ségur also acquired Lafite. His son Nicolas Alexandre, Marquis de Ségur, two years later bought Mouton and Calon. At this time English high society's demand for fine Bordeaux was greatly increasing, and the "Prince des Vignes" aimed at satisfying that exacting market. He improved his wines to such an extent that between 1714 and 1767 the price fetched by Latour increased fivefold. The turbulent times of the Revolution followed shortly after, yet de Ségur's descendants managed somehow to keep the property in the family, and in 1842 created the first *Société civile agricole*.

In and out of British ownership

The large majority of the *Société*'s shares remained in the family until 1962, when it was decided to sell a 53 percent shareholding to the English holding company Pearson. The British company Allied Lyons, already a 25 percent shareholder, bought Pearson's holding in 1989, and became majority shareholder. Finally Latour reverted to French ownership in 1993, when Allied Lyons sold its holding to the French businessman François Pinault.

A vineyard of the very highest quality

The vineyard, unsurprisingly, is at the root of Latour's greatness. The *grand vin* comes exclusively from a naturally drained 47-hectare parcel known as L'Enclos, perfectly situated on the first ridge inland from the Gironde, which benefits from an extremely even climate. The density of plantation of the vines —10,000 per hectare—is also an important factor, as it limits the vines' natural productivity, and thus ensures very high-quality grape juice.

An invitation to culinary invention

As might be expected, for a successful gastronomic tête-à-tête Latour requires a dish of character which can hold its own. Jacques Puisais, in *Le Goût Juste*, suggests accompanying the magnificent 1966 Latour with grilled geese hearts and a purée of haricot beans: "The setting is magical. The beans are there to calm the wine, whose fleshy and sensual side then finds common ground for discourse with the grilled geese hearts. This seigneur is not accustomed to such meetings, yet he leaves the scene enraptured, for it all went off perfectly."

BORDEAUX
A.O.C. Pauillac

• *Wine selected:*
Château Lynch-Bages
Cinquième Cru Classé

• *Grape varieties:*
Cabernet-Sauvignon 75%,
Merlot 15%, Cabernet-Franc 10%
• *Average vine age:*
35 years
• *Vineyard size:*
90 hectares
• *Soil type:*
Gravel over limestone
• *Production:*
520,000 bottles

Finest Vintages:
1998, 1996, 1995, 1990,
1989, 1986, 1985, 1982

Château Lynch-Bages
33250 Pauillac
Tel. (0033) 556 73 24 00
Take the D2 northwards towards
Pauillac. On leaving Saint-Lambert,
just south of Pauillac, take the road
that forks off to the left towards
Lynch-Bages.
• *Owners:* Cazes family
• *On-site sales:* Yes
• *Visits:* By appointment
• *Price:* ★★★/★★★★

CHÂTEAU LYNCH-BAGES

The Bages plateau, which overlooks the town of Pauillac and the Gironde, is home to several classed growths. The greatest, Lynch-Bages, has been producing wine for almost four centuries, and owes its name (as does Lynch-Moussas, further inland) to the Lynch family, who emigrated there from Ireland in 1690.

The Cazes family

Thomas Lynch became proprietor of the château at the end of the eighteenth century, and remained at the helm until 1825. Under the following owner Château Lynch, as it was then known, was classified *Cinquième Cru* in 1855. The property changed hands several times, and was bought in 1937 by Jean-Charles Cazes, a talented wine maker and owner of the fine bourgeois Château Les Ormes de Pez. Both properties were passed down to his son André in 1966, and André's son Jean-Michel in turn took them over in 1973.

An outstanding return to form

Today, whenever the thorny subject of the reclassification of the Médoc's wines is brought up, Lynch-Bages is one name all connoisseurs and professionals cite as being worthy of promotion. The wine was recognized as great—and sold for a suitable price—in the eighteenth century. Yet the modest rating it attained in the 1855 classification must mean that under Thomas Lynch's successors it suffered a definite decline in quality. Fortunately, recent years have seen an outstanding return to form.

The decade of the 1950s produced a succession of very fine wines; the 1960s and 1970s were variable, and Jean-Michel Cazes had a difficult start—two poor vintages, 1973 and 1974, the tricky 1975, then an unsuccessful modification of style—before the outstanding run of successes produced in the 1980s. Cazes installed stainless steel vats in 1980 and reverted to the traditional Lynch-Bages style, and has not looked back. The wine is now generally recognized as being of *Deuxième Cru* standard.

A rich and powerful style

Lynch-Bages is a rich, powerful, and meaty wine, thanks in great part to a high proportion of Cabernet-Sauvignon, to new oak barrels, and to minimum filtration. When young it has a distinctive ink-black color, and a sweetness, richness and power that are slightly reminiscent of the top Californian Cabernets. It ages very well, indeed the great vintages of the 1950s (1952, 1953, 1955, 1957, and 1959) are still in fine form, and it develops a fine spicy, cedary sensuality as it matures.
It is a wine which calls for a hearty red meat to set off its richness. A game pie, wild and assertive, could be just the match for a mature vintage such as the fleshy, meaty, and perfectly balanced 1981.

BORDEAUX
A.O.C. Pauillac

- *Wine selected:*
  Château Mouton-Rothschild
  Deuxième Cru Classé

- *Grape varieties:*
  Cabernet-Sauvignon 75%,
  Merlot 24%, Petit Verdot 1%
- *Average vine age:*
  35 years
- *Vineyard size:*
  75 hectares
- *Soil type:*
  Gravel
- *Production:*
  390,000 bottles

Finest Vintages:
1998, 1996, 1995, 1989,
1986, 1985, 1982

Château Mouton Rothschild
33250 Pauillac
Tel. (0033) 556 73 20 20
Follow the D2 northwards from
Pauillac. At the first junction turn left.
The road leading up to Mouton
Rothschild is about 1 km down the
road on the right.
- *Owner:* Baronne Philippine de
  Rothschild GFA
- *On-site sales:* Yes
- *Visits:* By appointment
- *Price:* ★★★★★

CHATEAU MOUTON ROTHSCHILD

If the five premiers crus classés of the Médoc and Graves had personalities, Château Mouton Rothschild would be the artist, the nonconformist, the rebel of the family. Mouton is an original, in the image of the man who gave it its identity and fame; its flamboyance (in flavor, dress and image) is in complete contrast with the sobriety of its peers, Châteaux Lafite, Latour, Margaux and Haut-Brion. Bordeaux is certainly very much the richer for having this remarkable character around.

Baron Philippe devotes himself to Mouton

Originally a small vineyard belonging to the de Ségur family, Mouton was developed into a fine estate by the de Branes, but was neglected by its subsequent owner, the banker Isaac Thuret. In 1853 the estate was purchased by Baron Nathaniel de Rothschild. With its patent excellence and command of high prices, its classification as deuxième cru—attributable probably to the neglect it suffered during Thuret's time—was widely perceived as unjust.

In 1920 Baron Henri, Nathaniel's grandson, inherited the estate, yet did not have the time to occupy himself with it. Knowing that his son Philippe felt a great attachment to the place, Henri gave him control. The 20 year-old Philippe decided to dedicate his life's work to Mouton, and tackled the job with the energy and flair that were characteristic of him.

Putting right the error of 1855

His overriding ambition was to have the error of 1855 rectified, to see Mouton promoted to premier cru. For this to be possible—for no change to the classification had ever been accorded—he had to produce exceptional wine, year in, year out. His first

decision was to bottle the entire vintage at the estate —unheard-of at the time—and thus put an end to the risk of his wine being adulterated once it had left the estate. He then imposed a draconian selection of what went into the wine, and created a second wine, Mouton Cadet, for using up what was rejected.

Wine and art

It was also necessary to promote the wine, and the Baron was nothing if not a highly gifted self-publicist. He had the brain wave of commissioning a work from a known artist every year from 1945 onwards for the label, thus associating wine and art. Among the contributors have been Cocteau, Braque, Chagall, Dali, Warhol and Bacon, and this has naturally made Mouton labels eminently collectable.

In 1973 the Baron's ambition was achieved when Jacques Chirac, then Minister of Agriculture, at last signed a decree according Mouton premier cru status. Fifteen years later he passed away, leaving Mouton in the capable hands of his daughter, Philippine.

Opulence and exoticism

In the mouth Mouton is thick and chewy, with a tight-grained texture. It has an intense blackcurrant flavor, with nuances of roasted coffee and vanilla oak. Vintages with bottle age offer up a fascinating palette of aromas: cedarwood, minerals, mint, spices, leather... This is truly great wine.
When the long-awaited day arrives and one's precious bottle has its cork drawn, it is better to keep things simple at table: a rib of prime beef, barbecued over vine-wood, will not intrude on, and yet will not be lost in, Mouton's fascinating aroma development in the glass and on the palate.

BORDEAUX
A.O.C. Pauillac

- *Wine selected:*
  Château Pichon-Longueville red
  Deuxième Cru Classé

- *Grape varieties:*
  Cabernet-Sauvignon 75%,
  Merlot 24%, Petit Verdot 1%
- *Average vine age:*
  35 years
- *Vineyard size:*
  65 hectares
- *Soil type:*
  Gravel
- *Production:*
  390,000 bottles

Finest Vintages:
1996, 1995, 1990, 1989, 1988, 1986

Château Pichon-Longueville
33250 Pauillac
Tel. (0033) 556 73 17 17
Follow the D2 northwards out of the
village of Saint-Julien-Beychevelle.
About 1.5 km past the famous Léoville
Las Cases arched vineyard gateway, the
road passes between the two Pichons.
Pichon-Longueville is on the left.
- *Owner:* AXA Millésimes
- *General Manager:*
  Jean-Michel Cazes
- *On-site sales:* Yes
- *Visits:* By appointment
- *Price:* ★★★/★★★★

CHÂTEAU PICHON-LONGUEVILLE

The decline of one of the greatest Pauillac estates, Château Pichon-Longueville, during the 1960s and 1970s was a source of sadness to lovers of fine Pauillac. Happily however this period was brought to an abrupt end in 1987, when the estate was acquired by the insurance group AXA, which has provided the huge investments necessary for it to regain its former magnificence (on the label it is called Château Longueville, au Baron de Pichon-Longueville; nowadays it is often referred to as Pichon-Baron). Pichon-Longueville is once more one of the Médoc's greatest wines, a wine made for aging, which combines power, richness, and finesse.

Separation and decline

This estate and its neighbor Pichon-Longueville Comtesse de Lalande were originally one. After 1860 the two properties' wines were made separately. The Pichon-Longueville family remained owners of the estate until 1933, then that year sold it to the Bouteiller family. In the first years, when Jean Bouteiller was in control, business prospered, for the wine had an excellent reputation and a ready market.

However, his sons were young when he died in 1961, and problems started to accumulate. The eldest son, Bertrand, took over responsibilities but lacked experience and dedicated staff, and unfortunately did not have the funds for reinvestment in the vineyard and the wine-making equipment, which was already aging. The wine as a result became undistinguished and inconsistent, and in many vintages lacked ripeness, definition, and balance. In 1986 the family received an offer from AXA for the property, and their decision to accept it heralded a new lease on life for the wine.

A long-term investment for AXA

The sum needed to buy the vineyards, château, wine-making facilities, and wine lying in stock, and to bring things up to scratch totalled 320 million francs, but Claude Bébéar, AXA's chairman, had assessed Pichon's future profitability and was convinced it was a good risk. Bébéar had known the talented Jean-Michel Cazes, owner of Lynch-Bages, since school days, and persuaded him to take on the management of the estate.

Cazes straightaway introduced manual harvesting, and new oak was bought for maturation of the wine; the vineyard received the necessary attention, and one large plot which lay neglected was planted; the superb eye-catching château, in a state of near-dilapidation, was renovated. However, the principal investment was in the construction of a new underground vatroom, a spectacular, circular building with computer-controlled stainless steel vats, incorporating reception area and tasting laboratory, which was ready for the 1991 vintage. A bottling room was also fitted out, for this had previously been done outdoors by a contractor, in the sweltering summer heat!

A great Pauillac reborn

Since the construction of the new vathouse, Pichon-Longueville has produced wines one could describe as remarkable, despite unfavorable climatic conditions. The Baron is now on a par with the Comtesse in the "super second" category, although the two are very different. It is now a serious rival to Latour, and, like the latter, would form a surprising and memorable gastronomic pairing with grilled geese hearts, served with a purée of haricot beans.

BORDEAUX
A.O.C. Pauillac

- *Wine selected:*
**Château Pichon-Longueville
Comtesse de Lalande**
Deuxième Cru Classé

- *Grape varieties:*
Cabernet-Sauvignon 45%,
Merlot 35%, Cabernet-Franc 12%,
Petit Verdot 8%
- *Average vine age:*
35 years
- *Vineyard size:*
75 hectares
- *Soil type:*
Gravel over clay, with presence of
ferruginous water
- *Production:*
400,000 bottles

Finest Vintages:
1996, 1995, 1986, 1983, 1982

**Château Pichon-Longueville
Comtesse de Lalande**
33250 Pauillac
Tel. (0033) 556 59 19 40
Follow the D2 northwards out of the
village of Saint-Julien-Beychevelle.
About 1.5 km past the famous Léoville
Las Cases arched vineyard gateway,
the road passes between the two
Pichons. Comtesse de Lalande is on
the right.
- *Owner:* May-Éliane de Lencquesaing
- *On-site sales:* Yes
- *Visits:* By appointment
- *Price:* ★★★★

Château Pichon-Longueville - Comtesse de Lalande

Sensual, seductive, silky, succulent… If one had to choose just one wine to represent all Bordeaux, for serving to someone who had never drunk claret, the best choice would surely be Château Pichon-Longueville—Comtesse de Lalande. Its instant and huge appeal, its finesse, harmony, and sheer quality, make it a wine that is thoroughly irresistible. Yet there is nothing frivolous about this wine: Pichon is a wine for laying down, which develops well over two decades in bottle.

Three centuries of superlative wine

In the second half of the seventeeth century Pierre des Mesures de Rauzan, having founded the Rauzan estate in Margaux, bought some land next to Château Latour, and planted vines. The wine rapidly gained a reputation. This new estate gained its name shortly afterwards, when he gave it to his daughter Thérèse as dowry for her marriage to Jacques de Pichon, Baron de Longueville. A half-century later the wine was rated second only to that of its neighbor, Château Latour, in the commune of Saint-Lambert.

The division of the Pichon-Longueville estate

In 1850 the estate was divided, in conformity with the Napoleonic Code. Raoul de Pichon inherited what is today Pichon-Longueville Baron, and his sister Virginie, wife of Comte Henri de Lalande, received the rest, which duly came to be known as Pichon-Longueville—Comtesse de Lalande. The two continued to be run as one for a another ten years until, on Raoul's death in 1857, his sister decided to separate her inheritance from his. Virginie, passionately interested in her vineyard, proved a very gifted manager and left her mark on the property, which has proudly retained her name.

The Lalande lineage petered out at the turn of the century, and the estate for several decades was passed down from aunts to nieces. Then in 1925 it was purchased by Édouard and Louis Miailhe, descendants of an ancient Bordeaux family of vineyard-owners and brokers. In 1978 May-Éliane de Lencquesaing, Édouard's daughter, took up her heritage, and remains its inspired and indefatigable owner to this day.

Softness, elegance and bouquet

To understand why Pichon is so sensual and seductive, one must look to the vineyard, which is composed of a topsoil of pure gravel lying on a clay subsoil, and is planted with a relatively large proportion of Merlot, the variety that gives flesh, roundness and suppleness to wine. Harvesting only at perfect ripeness, and a very rigorous selection of what goes into the *grand vin*, are but two explanations for the wine's voluptuousness and finesse. Curiously (and significantly) the estate has 11 hectares of vines actually in the Saint-Julien commune, another explanation for the wine's elegance and magnificent bouquet.

Irresistible, at two or twenty-two years of age!

Pichon is one of the rare Pauillacs that are delicious, and not mouth-puckeringly tannic, when very young. At a dozen years of age it has generally acquired a lovely bouquet, a soft, velvet texture, and a fat, rich presence on the palate, with nuances of cedarwood, cinnamon, and leather that complement the primary blackcurrant flavor. This wine is perfectly offset by roast meats, or roast pigeon, served with fresh garden vegetables.

BORDEAUX
A.O.C. Saint-Julien

- *Wine selected:*
  Château Ducru-Beaucaillou
  Deuxième Cru Classé

- *Grape varieties:*
  Cabernet-Sauvignon 65%,
  Merlot 25%, Cabernet-Franc 5%,
  Petit Verdot 5%
- *Average vine age:*
  38 years
- *Vineyard size:*
  50 hectares
- *Soil type:*
  Deep gravel
- *Production:*
  220,000 bottles

Finest Vintages:
1996, 1995, 1990, 1989,
1986, 1985, 1982

Château Ducru-Beaucaillou
33250 Saint-Julien-Beychevelle
Tel. (0033) 556 59 05 20
Follow the D2 northwards to the
village of Beychevelle. Follow the road
as it curves to the right opposite
Château Saint-Pierre and continue for
some 200 meters. The road leading up
to Ducru is on the right, indicated by a
little sign.
- *Owner:* J.-E. Borie SA
- *Managing Director:* François-Xavier
  Borie
- *On-site sales:* No
- *Visits:* By appointment
- *Price:* ★★★★

CHÂTEAU DUCRU-BEAUCAILLOU

The commune of Saint-Julien can boast no *Premier Cru* properties, yet it has several *Deuxièmes Crus* that regularly produce some of Bordeaux's finest wines, and that would be candidates for promotion were there ever a revision of the 1855 classification. One of these properties is Château Ducru-Beaucaillou.

A soil of fine pebbles

Ducru came into existence when the huge Beychevelle estate was split up at the end of the seventeenth century. Clive Coates tells us that the original name of the vineyard was Maucaillou, for the pebbles (*cailloux*) that made up the soil were unsuitable (*mauvais*) for any agricultural activity except viticulture; only when it was realized just how good a wine could be made here were they viewed in a different light, and considered fine (*beau*).

After the Revolution the estate was bought by Bertrand Ducru, who built the bulk of the present château, enlarged the vineyard, and greatly raised the wine's reputation. Ducru's daughter sold the estate in 1866 to Nathaniel Johnston, a *négociant* of Irish ancestry, and it was his manager who, quite by accident, came up with a remedy for mildew, a scourge which was then sweeping the vineyards hard on the heels of the phylloxera aphid.

he invention of Bordeaux mixture

Fed up with the depredations of thieves stealing fruit from the vineyard, the manager had painted the vines nearest the road with a ghastly-looking blue-green copper sulphate solution he had concocted. It was noticed that these vines did not suffer from the mildew attack, and so experiments were carried out to find out why. In such a way the properties of the solution were discovered, and Bordeaux mixture, still widely used today, was born.

Francis Borie puts the estate back on its feet

The first years of this century were hard: the slump, and the disappearance of his sizeable American market as a result of Prohibition, obliged Johnston to sell in 1928. His successor fared no better, and thirteen years later Ducru, in a rather run-down state, was acquired by Francis Borie. An ambitious program of replanting, rebuilding, and refurbishment was immediately put into action, and by the time of Borie's death in 1953, the wine had regained its previous stature. He was succeeded by his son, the late Jean-Eugène, whose own son François-Xavier now runs the estate.

The quintessential Saint-Julien

Many claret lovers regard Saint-Julien as the quintessential claret, and Ducru as the quintessential Saint-Julien: fragrant, elegant, and refined. The vineyard, lying principally on the first gravel ridge parallel to the river and composed of particularly large *beaux cailloux* in great depth, is ideal for production of this type of wine. The best vintages of Ducru generally take a dozen years to show their real quality, complexity, and finesse, and go on to live long and distinguished lives.

Ducru's exquisite finesse and balance are best served at table by fine fare, such as red meat, poultry, or winged game, treated simply. The exquisite 1966 vintage, now fully ready, all softness and velvet on the palate and with nuances of cedarwood and spice, digs deep into its reserves of eloquence in the presence of roast pigeon, served with a selection of spring vegetables.

BORDEAUX
A.O.C. Saint-Julien

- *Wine selected:*
  Château Gruaud-Larose
  Deuxième Cru Classé

- *Grape varieties:*
  Cabernet-Sauvignon 57%,
  Merlot 30%, Cabernet-Franc 7%,
  Petit Verdot 4%, Malbec 2%
- *Average vine age:*
  30 years
- *Vineyard size:*
  84 hectares
- *Soil type:*
  Gravel and sand over calcareous
  marl
- *Production:*
  450,000 bottles

Finest Vintages:
1998, 1996, 1995, 1989, 1988,
1986, 1985, 1983, 1982

Château Gruaud-Larose
33250 Saint-Julien-Beychevelle
Tel. (0033) 556 73 15 21
Follow the D2 northwards until the
village of Beychevelle, and continue
straight on into the village instead of
following the bend to the right. Go
through the village and take the Saint-
Laurent road. Gruaud-Larose is just
outside the village on the left.
- *Owner:* Groupe Bernard Taillan
- *General Manager:* Jean Merlaut
- *On-site sales:* No
- *Visits:* By appointment
- *Price:* ★★★/★★★★

CHATEAU GRUAUD-LAROSE

Château Gruaud-Larose has for all its 250-odd years of documented history produced excellent, firm Saint-Julien wine. It is a huge estate, and its production finds its way to all corners of the globe where there are claret lovers. Rarely are they anything less than thoroughly satisfied, for it largely merits its *Deuxième Cru* status.

King of Wines, Wine of Kings

The first known owners, the Gruaud brothers, a priest and a magistrate, added a number of plots to the vines they already had, and created an estate of 116 hectares. The magistrate died in 1778, and the estate passed to his son-in-law, who had some time before bought out the priest.

This new owner, Monsieur de Larose, Lieutenant-Governor of the Jurisdiction of Guyenne, frequented high society, and did not hesitate to promote his wine to anyone who would listen, or taste it. It was rapidly being served at official functions, indeed even at court, and Larose dreamt up a catchy slogan for it: "Le Roi des Vins, Le Vin des Rois" (The King of Wines, The Wine of Kings) is proclaimed on the label to this day. He died in 1795, and his heirs, unable to come to an agreement over their valuable heritage, were in the end obliged to sell it off just to pay for the legal expenses occasioned by their squabbling.

An unstable nineteenth century

There followed a complicated period of seventy-two years of multi-ownerships, buy-outs, and hand-downs, which culminated in 1867 in the division of the estate into two parts: Gruaud-Larose-Sarget, owned by Baron Sarget, and Gruaud-Larose-Bethmann, the property of three Bethmann children. This latter part subsequently become known as Gruaud-Larose-Faure.

In 1917 the Sarget part was offered for sale, and acquired by Désiré Cordier; however, he had to wait until 1934 before he could acquire the Faure part, and reunite the two. Exactly fifty years later the conglomerate La Hénin gained a controlling interest in Domaines Cordier. That company was subsequently absorbed by the Compagnie de Suez, which in 1993 sold Gruaud-Larose to the French telecoms giant, Alcatel-Alsthom. Finally it was acquired in 1997 by Groupe Bernard Taillan.

Dense and structured for a long life

The Gruaud-Larose vineyard today occupies 84 hectares of prime land at the south end of the Saint-Julien commune, composed of gravel and sand on a calcareous marl base. The wine is fairly solid and dense for a Saint-Julien, and never particularly good to drink young; it is only after a dozen or so years that it softens up, that its many attributes harmonize on the nose and in the mouth—but even at that age it is a mere adolescent! Great vintages can live a long time, as anyone who has tasted the magnificent 1929 and 1928 will testify.

Gruaud-Larose's great richness, flesh, and velvety texture make it a wine for the table. The renowned French chef Alain Senderens applied his talents to concocting the perfect dish for the great 1982 vintage, a wine redolent of undergrowth and game flavors, with finesse, structure, and great length. He came up with stewed knuckle of veal, served with carrot fondue and stuffed calf's foot. "The dish brings out all the qualities in the wine, which in its turn adds an extra dimension to the meat!" reported *La Revue du vin de France* of this magical combination.

BORDEAUX
A.O.C. Saint-Julien

- *Wine selected:*
  Châteaux Léoville-Barton and Langoa-Barton
  Deuxième Cru Classé (Léoville)
  Troisième Cru Classé (Langoa)

- *Grape varieties:*
  Cabernet-Sauvignon 72%,
  Merlot 20%, Cabernet-Franc 8%
- *Average vine age:*
  28 years
- *Vineyard size:*
  47 hectares (Léoville),
  16 hectares (Langoa)
- *Soil type:*
  Gravel over clay subsoil
- *Production:*
  240,000 bottles (Léoville),
  85,000 bottles (Langoa)

Finest Vintages (Léoville):
2000, 1996, 1995, 1990, 1989,
1988, 1986, 1985, 1982

**Châteaux Léoville-Barton and
Langoa-Barton**
33250 Saint-Julien-Beychevelle
Tel. (0033) 556 59 06 05
Proceed northwards from the village
of Beychevelle on the D2. The Barton
properties are halfway between
Beychevelle and Saint-Julien. The
beautiful château on the left is
Château Langoa, the Barton family
home, and it is here that the two
wines are made.
- *Owner:* Anthony Barton
- *General Manager:* Michel Raoult
- *On-site sales:* No
- *Visits:* By appointment
- *Price:* ★★★

CHÂTEAUX LÉOVILLE-BARTON AND LANGOA-BARTON

The destinies of two of Saint-Julien's finest estates are inextricably linked. Château Léoville-Barton and its neighbor Château Langoa-Barton have both belonged to the Barton family since the 1820s, and have shared wine-making facilities since that time.

A great Irish Bordeaux dynasty

The Bartons came from Ireland. Hugh, grandson of the first Barton émigré Tom. In 1821 purchased Langoa, an estate with its origins in the beginning of the eigteenth century. Five years later he purchased one quarter of the vast Léoville estate, which was founded in 1638 and split into four after the Revolution. The two estates flourished during the next thirty years, but Hugh died in 1854 and did not live to see them listed as *Deuxième* and *Troisième Cru* in 1855. Over the following seventy years they passed down three generations, until in 1927 becoming the responsibility of Ronald Barton.

However, events soon complicated things: the fall of France thirteen years later obliged him to flee and fight the enemy from abroad. The estates were looked after by Daniel Guestier, his friend and partner in the family *négociant* firm Barton et Guestier, until Ronald's return. The post war period was not a very happy one, involving as it did static revenues, spiraling costs and the dreadful frosts of 1956, which destroyed a large part of the vines. In 1983 Ronald handed over the properties to his nephew Anthony. He passed away three years later, and Anthony has been at the helm ever since.

Subtle differences of *terroir*

The Léoville vineyard, when Hugh Barton bought it, did not come with a château or any wine buildings, and to this day the family has resided at and made both wines at Château Langoa.

The Barton vines grow in medium-sized gravel over a calcareous clay subsoil, a combination which explains the mixture of finesse and body in the wines. The two estates use exactly the same proportions of the different grape varieties, and viticultural and vinification practices are identical. As may be imagined, the wines resemble each other enormously, yet the subtle differences in the two *terroirs* result in Langoa being perhaps easier to approach in its youth and a little lighter-bodied than its sturdier brother.

Quality and reliability at a very reasonable price

Both wines age extremely well, and the great vintages of the 1950s are testimony to this quality. Unfortunately, there was a slight fall in quality in the 1970s, but since 1983, thanks to Anthony's enthusiasm and a number of slight modifications to the wine making, a string of fine vintages have been produced which have put both properties back amongst Saint-Julien's finest. Fortunately for all lovers of these wines, they continue to be available at extremely reasonable prices, indeed they are regularly two of Bordeaux's best buys.

The Barton wines make a fine choice for special meals. For a spring luncheon one could partner Langoa 1975 with quails, cooked with grapes and singed with cognac; on a cold winter's day something more consequent is called for. Go on, let yourself be tempted. Fetch up a Léoville 1955 and serve it with haunch of venison!

BORDEAUX
A.O.C. Saint-Julien

- *Wine selected:*
  Château Léoville-Las Cases
  Deuxième Cru Classé

- *Grape varieties:*
  Cabernet-Sauvignon 65%,
  Merlot 19%, Cabernet-Franc 13%,
  Petit Verdot 3%
- *Average vine age:*
  30 years
- *Vineyard size:*
  97 hectares
- *Soil type:*
  Deep gravel

Finest Vintages:
2001, 2000, 1999, 1998, 1996, 1995,
1990, 1989, 1988, 1986, 1985, 1982

Château Léoville-Las Cases
33250 Saint-Julien-Beychevelle
Tel. (0033) 556 73 25 26
Follow the D2 northwards out of the
village of Beychevelle. Léoville Las
Cases is the first château on the right
as you enter Saint-Julien.
- *Owner:* SC du Château Léoville-Las
  Cases
- *Director:* Jean-Hubert Delon
- *On-site sales:* No
- *Visits:* By appointment
- *Price:* ★★★★

CHÂTEAU LÉOVILLE-LAS CASES

At the northern edge of the commune of Saint-Julien lies one of the Médoc's largest, greatest and oldest properties, Château Léoville-Las Cases. This property enjoys a global reputation, for it produces benchmark claret of *Premier Cru* quality year after year, with admirable consistency.

The division of the original Léoville estate

The great Léoville estate, originally called Mont-Moytié, was created in 1638. By the 1750s, when it was in the hands of Blaise Alexandre de Gascq, Lord of Léoville, it was already producing the best wine in Saint-Julien, and fetching prices second only to those of Châteaux Lafite, Latour, Margaux, and Haut-Brion.

At the time of the Revolution the estate was owned by four of de Gascq's heirs: the Marquis de Las Cases-Beauvoir, his brother and two sisters. The Marquis fled abroad, and the State was set on confiscating the whole property. However, the brother and sisters split it in four, and managed to persuade the revolutionaries that the Marquis' part alone should be sequestered and sold off. This quarter was to become Léoville-Barton.

In 1840 the remainder was split in two, and the larger part, owned by Pierre-Jean, the new Marquis de Las Cases, became Château Léoville-Las Cases.

The directors progressively buy up the estate

Since 1900 the estate has been run by Théophile Skawinski and his descendants. This family has gradually bought up shares over the years, with the result that they now own the entire estate. Michel Delon, Skawinsky's great-grandson, held the post of administrator from 1976 until his death in 2000; he has been succeeded by his son Jean-Hubert, who had shared responsibilities with him since 1994.

A two-wine estate

The bulk of the Léoville-Las Cases vines are perfectly situated on the first gravel ridge inland from the Gironde, on the commune's northern boundary with Pauillac, and next to those of Château Latour. This explains the character of the wine, which is as much Pauillac as Saint-Julien, a wine of firmness and power as much as fragrance and elegance. Yet the soil alone does not create a wine like this, it also requires a perfectionist wine maker, driven by a burning desire to produce the finest wine possible every year. Las Cases and the exquisite Clos du Marquis (a second wine of a quality far exceeding the norm for that category) bear witness to the devotion to their art of the Delon Family.

Richness, finesse, and elegance

Las Cases is a wine which requires a good number of years to soften up in bottle before becoming ready to drink, but when it eventually does, it is one of the very finest and richest Médocs, a textbook example of what can be done with gravel, Cabernet fruit, and oak. Since 1996 its elegance has become more accentuated however, and it seems more approachable in its youth, although its potential longevity does not seem to have changed. The Clos du Marquis is more typically Saint-Julien, and comes round more quickly than its elder brother. Once the long waiting years are over, Las Cases is excellent with simply prepared red meat, such as rib of beef, grilled over dead vine wood, or a choice porterhouse steak.

BORDEAUX
A.O.C. Saint-Julien

- *Wine selected:*
  Château Léoville-Poyferré
  Deuxième Cru Classé

- *Grape varieties:*
  Cabernet-Sauvignon 65%,
  Merlot 25%, Petit Verdot 8%,
  Cabernet-Franc 2%
- *Average vine age:*
  25 years
- *Vineyard size:*
  80 hectares
- *Soil type:*
  Deep gravel and sand
- *Production:*
  450,000 bottles

Finest Vintages:
1996, 1990, 1989, 1986,
1985, 1983, 1982

Château Léoville-Poyferré
33250 Saint-Julien-Beychevelle
Tel. (0033) 556 59 08 30
Follow the D2 northwards out of
the village of Beychevelle. The
intermingled buildings of Las Cases
and Poyferré are the first as one
enters Saint-Julien. The Léoville
Poyferré offices are on the left.
- *Owner:* G.F.A. des Domaines de
  Saint-Julien
- *General Manager:* Didier Cuvelier
- *On-site sales:* Yes
- *Visits:* By appointment
- *Price:* ★★/★★★

CHÂTEAU LÉOVILLE-POYFERRÉ

Château Léoville-Poyferré produced some of Bordeaux's greatest wines in the inter-war years. However, devotees of the wines of Saint-Julien observed with frustration its increasing mediocrity during the 1960s and 1970s, for the Poyferré land is regarded as of the very highest quality by many in Bordeaux. Happily the last fifty years have seen a dramatic reversal of fortunes. This estate is once more making a wine largely worthy of its *Deuxième Cru* ranking.

Frequent changes of ownership

Poyferré was originally part of the vast Léoville estate, which was split up at the time of the Revolution. One quarter had been sold to the Barton family, and two-thirds of the remainder were owned by Pierre-Jean, Marquis de Las Cases. The remaining third passed to Jeanne d'Abbadie. Jeanne gave the estate to one of her daughters, who shortly afterwards sold it to her sister, the Baronne de Poyferré. However, the estate was not to remain in the Poyferré family for long, for the Baronne's son was ruined by imprudent investments in the Russian railways, and in 1866 had to sell his inheritance. Poyferré was bought by the owner of Château Cantenac-Brown, a *négociant* named Armand Lalande. He left it to his daughter in 1894, and this lady sold it in 1920 to its present owners, the Cuvelier family.

Didier Cuvelier takes on a challenge

The Cuveliers, already owners of Châteaux Le Crock and Camensac, entrusted the management of Poyferré to the Delon family, owners of Château Phélan-Ségur and related to the Delons of Léoville-Las Cases. The first decades of the Cuvelier/Delon arrangement went well and produced some classic wines; however, as time went by there was no regular investment in the property, and Roger Delon, the manager in the 1960s, was getting on in years. This started to show in the wines.

In the summer of 1978 the Cuvelier family gathered to discuss matters, and Didier Cuvelier, thirty years of age and an accountant by training, offered his services. He was profoundly inspired by the challenge, and managed to persuade the rest of the family that a full program of investments was necessary to lick the wine back into shape, and that this would eventually be financially rewarding. He was given the go-ahead to get on with the job.

Richer and more harmonious in style

On the advice of the famous enologist Émile Peynaud, Cuvelier straightaway put into action a program of soil analysis and treatment, plot by plot. He was appalled to find that 30 hectares of land—prime Saint-Julien vineyard, no less—were not even planted. This was a godsend, for it gave him the chance to modify the style of the wine. There followed the rebuilding and re-equipping of the vatroom, the construction of a new barrel cellar, the introduction of a policy of rigorous grape selection, the use of a more suitable amount of new oak barrels for the wine's aging.

The improvement was plain to see with the 1982 and 1983 vintages, and has steadily continued as the vines have grown older. Poyferré now has fragrance and harmony, richness and ripeness; gone are the astringency and coarseness of the 1970s. It is now a lovely wine, a classic Saint-Julien of elegance and breeding, which finds its perfect match in loin of lamb, served on a bed of celery and truffles..

BORDEAUX
A.O.C. Moulis-en-Médoc

- *Wine selected:*
  Château Poujeaux
  Cru Bourgeois

- *Grape varieties:*
  Cabernet-Sauvignon 50%,
  Merlot 40%, Cabernet-Franc 5%,
  Petit Verdot 5%
- *Average vine age:*
  25 years
- *Vineyard size:*
  52 hectares
- *Soil type:*
  Gravel
- *Production:*
  300,000 bottles

Finest Vintages:
1998, 1996, 1995, 1990,
1989, 1988, 1986, 1982

Château Poujeaux
33480 Moulis-en-Médoc
Tel. (0033) 556 58 02 96
Follow the D2 northwards through and
out of Arcins. At the next crossroads,
about 2 km later, turn left onto the D5
and follow the road for about 2.5 km,
crossing the railroad tracks.
Poujeaux's *chais* are in the cream-
colored building on the left.
- *Owner:* Jean Theil S.A.
- *On-site sales:* Yes
- *Visits:* By appointment
- *Price:* ★★

CHÂTEAU POUJEAUX

For full-flavored wine with finesse, style, and aging potential, and a reasonable sales price to go with it, one could hardly do better than Château Poujeaux. But that is no news to its clientele, who buy up more or less the entire crop as futures (*en primeur*). An expression of faith which only inspires the Theil brothers to push themselves to new limits in their quest for perfection.

A sixteenth-century estate divided into three

Poujeaux's origins go back at least as far as 1544, when there existed a great estate known as La Salle de Poujeaux. Vines were first planted there on a large scale probably in the mid-eighteenth century, possibly by the Marquis de Brassier de Budot. De Brassier sold the estate to his sister, perhaps to finance the construction of the château at Beychevelle, which he also owned, and she in turn sold it in 1806 to André Castaing. It passed down several generations of Castaings, but in 1880 was split into three parts to resolve an inheritance problem. As a result there existed thereafter a Poujeaux-Philippe Castaing, a Poujeaux-Élisabeth Castaing, and a Poujeaux-Jeanne Castaing.

The Theils reunite the estates

On the death of Philippe Castaing in 1920, his part was acquired by François Theil, who sold his Léognan property Le Pape to finance the acquisition. Unfortunately, Theil did not live to see his dream of reuniting the three parts come to fruition. It was his son Jean who eventually brought that about, but he had to wait until 1957 to do so. He passed away in 1981, and two of his seven children, François and Philippe, have run Poujeaux ever since.

A winning team

They run it with great love and skill, to such a point that they have no difficulty in rapidly selling off each new vintage, and the wine is widely acclaimed as being of *Cru Classé* quality. Poujeaux was classified *Cru Grand Bourgeois exceptionnel* in 1966, and has brilliantly proved its reputation by twice winning the *Coupe des Crus Bourgeois*, in 1991 and 1995, as well as being runner-up once and semi-finalist twice gainst over one hundred other contenders, in just twelve years since the *Coupe* was inaugurated in 1985.

Rich, fleshy, and succulent

Poujeaux is a full-favored wine with a structure for aging, and needs at least a half-dozen years to develop before it really starts to show its qualities. That fact can be attributed in large part to its six-week maceration period and to frequent *remontages* (pumping up and spraying of the wine over the cap of skins), which enable the extraction of a great deal of tannin, color pigments and aromatic elements. In good vintages it is aged in 50 percent new oak, and the wine is never filtered.

All this might give the impression of a rather daunting wine, but it is actually very fleshy and succulent, thanks to harvesting at nothing less than full ripeness, and a severe selection of the raw material and subsequently of the barrels.

It is a wine which is rich and self-confident enough to get on well with many types of red meat and game: a Poujeaux 1979 served alongside a *filet de bœuf en croûte de poivres*—beef coated in coarse-ground black, green, and white pepper—would be just the thing for a Sunday lunch!

BORDEAUX
A.O.C. Margaux

• *Wine selected:*
  Château Margaux
  Premier Cru Classé

• *Grape varieties:*
  Cabernet-Sauvignon 75%,
  Merlot 20%, Cabernet-Franc/Petit
  Verdot 5%.
• *Average vine age:*
  35 years
• *Vineyard size:*
  78 hectares
• *Soil type:*
  Gravel, clay, and limestone
• *Production:*
  390,000 bottles

Finest Vintages:

1998, 1996, 1995, 1990, 1989,
1988, 1986, 1985, 1983, 1982

Château Margaux
33460 Margaux
Tel. (0033) 557 88 83 83
Follow the Route des Vins (D2)
northwards until you arrive at the
village of Margaux. Take the very first
turn on the right as you enter the
village (opposite Durfort-Vivens), and
proceed several hundred meters until
you are obliged to turn left. There, in
front of you, is Château Margaux.
• *Owner:* S.C.A. Château Margaux
• *Director:* Paul Pontallier
• *On-site sales:* No
• *Visits:* By appointment
• *Price:* ★★★★★

CHÂTEAU MARGAUX

One of the most evocative of all Bordeaux's wine names, a synonym for fragrance, elegance, and refinement, is that of Margaux. These qualities may be appreciated in most of the commune's wines, but are hallmarks above all of the wine produced at Château Margaux itself, which probably produces the very quintessence of fine, rich, and aromatic Médoc.

The dream of Fernand Ginestet

In 1921, some seven hundred years after the first mention of wine making on the site, the estate of Château Margaux was purchased by a consortium of businessmen, and the *Société vinicole de Château Margaux* came into being. One member of the consortium, Fernand Ginestet, who was head of the large Ginestet *négociant* firm and owned Château Cos d'Estournel and Clos Fourtet, had his mind set on personally acquiring the property. He gradually bought up the other members' shares, but it was his son Pierre who finally brought his father's dream to fruition in 1949.

The Ginestets proceeded to invest heavily in the property. However, after a string of marvelous vintages in the 1950s, quality sank in the 1960s, probably as a result of financial problems. Then came the oil crisis and the 1973–1975 collapse of the Bordeaux wine market. The Ginestet empire was hit hard. They were obliged to sell in 1977.

A reversal of fortunes

Château Margaux found its saviour in André Mentzelopoulos, majority shareholder of the Parisian wine-retailing chain Nicolas. He poured in large sums of money to drain and replant the vineyard, re-equip the vathouse and construct a new underground *chai* for aging the wine. The reversal of fortunes was instantaneous: from the 1978 vintage Château Margaux once again became one of the greatest of Bordeaux's wines. Mentzelopoulos died in 1980, not living to see the fruit of his investment and labor, but his widow Laura and daughter Corinne decided to carry on, and to this day every vintage has in its context been a dazzling success.

The quintessence of harmony and breeding

Paradoxically, Margaux is a wine of both power and delicacy, opulence and finesse, body and fragrance. On the nose the taster often detects aromas of violets, blackcurrants and blackberries, tinted by a certain subtle spiciness and, when young, unmistakable oak vanilla flavors. In the mouth the wine is perfectly balanced, impossibly harmonious, genuinely aristocratic. What is more, behind this wave of instantly seductive aromas lie fine ripe tannin and tingling acidity; this really is a wine that repays at least a dozen years' cellaring. After fifteen years the great 1983 is coming into its own, a profound and complex wine of great intensity and exemplary definition—but of course it is still a mere adolescent.

Since a great wine calls for a great dish, it would be an excellent idea to serve this Margaux 1983, decanted thirty minutes in advance, with a tournedos Rossini. Such combinations are not easily forgotten!

BORDEAUX
A.O.C. Margaux

- *Wine selected:*
  Château Palmer
  Troisième Cru Classé

- *Grape varieties:*
  Cabernet-Sauvignon 50%,
  Merlot 45%, Cabernet-Franc 1%,
  Petit Verdot 4%
- *Average vine age:*
  30 years
- *Vineyard size:*
  50 hectares
- *Soil type:*
  Deep Garonne gravel
- *Production:*
  265,000 bottles

Finest Vintages:
1999, 1998, 1989, 1983

Château Palmer
33460 Cantenac
Tel. (0033) 557 88 72 72
Follow the D2 northwards out of the
village of Cantenac. Proceed through
the hamlet of Issan. Château Palmer is
on your right as you leave Issan.
- *Owner:* S.C.I. Château Palmer
- *Director:* Bertrand Bouteiller
- *On-site sales:* No
- *Visits:* By appointment
- *Price:* ★★★/★★★★

CHÂTEAU PALMER

There is one estate in the Margaux appellation which produces wine that is never far behind Château Margaux itself in quality terms, a rival sufficiently serious to keep the *Premier Cru* from complacency. That estate is the *Troisième Cru* Château Palmer, and, if proof were needed of just how well it can perform, there are a good number of vintages, such as 1961, 1966, 1970, 1983, or 1989, to provide the necessary demonstration.

A chance meeting

Château de Gasq, as it was then called, was mentioned as a property in its own right in the 1760s, but it was not until the arrival of General Charles Palmer that it started producing wine much above the ordinary. Palmer at the time was thirty-seven, and at the height of a successful military career. As the story goes, he was traveling in 1814 from Lyons to Paris, a three-day journey, when he made the acquaintance of Marie Brunet de Ferrière, widow of Blaise de Gasq. This lady told him she was on her way to Paris to sell her late husband's estate —a very fine property, second to none bar Lafite, she said—in order to divide up the inheritance equitably, as the law required, between the entire family. He was touched by her story, and by the time they had arrived in Paris, he had bought the estate.

Ambition, naïvety and tragedy

Over the next fifteen years Palmer lavished vast sums on it, and increased its size by buying up many parcels of land. He appointed a certain Mr. Gray as his agent in Bordeaux, who was by all accounts a charming man but a complete rogue. Palmer naturally set about promoting his wine in London high society, and the Prince Regent gave a dinner to put the wine to the test. It was much appreciated by all, until it was compared with the Prince Regent's own wine, which was strengthened with Hermitage. This wine naturally made the Palmer seem rather anemic, and the Prince Regent advised him to try planting different vines and put more stuffing into it.

Palmer unfortunately listened to him, returned to Bordeaux and ripped out all his vines. He tried all sorts of misguided experiments, and fell further and further into debt, while all the while being fleeced by Mr. Gray. Progressively, bits of land had to be sold off, then in 1844 the remainder of the estate was sold to his main creditor, the Caisse hypothécaire (State Mortgage bank), in Paris. Today Palmer is co-owned by several families. The vineyard now counts 45 hectares, most of which are on a plateau just south of Château Margaux's vines, where the soil is of deep Garonne gravel.

Finesse, balance, and impeccable breeding

Palmer is essentially a wine of finesse and delicacy, of fragrance and subtlety. It is never very full-bodied, indeed can seem positively lean in its youth, but always has perfect balance. With age it often becomes fleshier, softer, and more generous. Above all, it is a wine of unmistakable breeding.
It is shown to its best advantage alongside simply prepared fare: the fine 1978, with hints of spice and tobacco, now has just the self-assurance to engage in dialogue with a rib of beef *bordelaise*, a roast turkey with chestnut stuffing, or with *côtelettes d'agneau* Champvallon—lamb chops cooked in a terrine with onions, garlic, and potatoes.

BORDEAUX
A.O.C. Margaux

- *Wine selected:*
  Château Rauzan-Ségla
  Deuxième Cru Classé

- *Grape varieties:*
  Cabernet-Sauvignon 54%,
  Merlot 41%, Petit Verdot 4%,
  Cabernet-Franc 1%
- *Average vine age:*
  25 years
- *Vineyard size:*
  51 hectares
- *Soil type:*
  Gravel and clay
- *Production:*
  100,000 bottles

Finest Vintages:
1998, 1996, 1995, 1990,
1988, 1986, 1983

Château Rauzan-Ségla
33460 Margaux
Tel. (0033) 557 88 82 10
Follow the D2 northwards from
Cantenac. Take the road to the left at
the entry of the hamlet of Issan. Turn
down the first road on the right, a few
hundred meters further on. Rauzan-
Ségla is on the left.
- *Owner:* Château Rauzan-Ségla SA
- *Managing Director:* John Kolasa
- *On-site sales:* No
- *Visits:* By appointment
  (Tel. 00 33 557 88 82 14)
- *Price:* ★★★

CHÂTEAU RAUZAN-SÉGLA

The famous *Deuxième Cru* Château Rauzan-Ségla is, arguably, second only to Château Margaux in the Margaux appellation's hierarchy. Like many others it has had its ups and downs over the course of its existence, but is today putting its fine vineyard of deep gravel soil to good use, producing raw material of the highest standard and making wine of splendid refinement and harmony.

The price tag of a *Premier Cru*

In 1661, a large estate was established by the rich merchant Pierre des Mesures de Rauzan, who, as was customary, gave it his name. He and his descendants worked hard to establish its reputation, with success it would seem, as the wine was referred to as one of the finest Médocs in 1790 by Thomas Jefferson. At the time of the classification of the Gironde's wines in 1855 Rauzan-Ségla was listed as a *Deuxième Cru*, in second place behind Mouton, for it was regularly producing wine of exceptional quality, and continued to do so for the remainder of the nineteenth century. This was the zenith of its fortunes and reputation, indeed its prices frequently equalled those of the *Premiers Crus*. At some stage and for some unknown reason it was renamed Rausan, with an *s*.

A long recovery

In 1903 it was bought by Frédéric Cruse, who set about replanting the vineyard, which had been hard hit by the scourge of phylloxera, as well as renovating the wine buildings and having the existing château built. The Cruse family were to own the estate until 1957, after which it changed hands several times over a short period, which did the wine no good. The 1980s, under the ownership of the English companies John Holt & Co. and then Brent Walker, saw the wine progressively return to form, attaining the *Deuxième Cru* standard it had lacked in the previous years. Finally, in 1994, Rausan-Ségla was sold to its current owners, the Wertheimer family, owners of Chanel.

Thenew proprietors got a program of investments under way in order to bring their acquisition up to the very highest level, which included the draining and replanting of the vineyard, the construction of new cellars and the renovation of other buildings. Other investments in quality are made every year, notably the severe limitation of the crop every year and the selectivity exercised in the choice of the raw material for the *grand vin*; a second wine, Ségla, has been introduced, thus limiting the financial implications of such selectivity. The new determination was also signalled by a change of label for the wine and a return to the original spelling of Rauzan.

The epitome of fine Margaux

At last Rauzan-Ségla is once more showing its exquisite true colors: it is by nature medium-bodied, elegant, and refined, with raspberries and violets on the nose, and the vanilla aroma of new oak filling out the background. It is subtly but undeniably structured for a couple of decades' life, perfectly balanced, stylish, and classy. In short, it epitomizes all that is best about Margaux wines.

It calls for simple fare at table—something such as roast pigeon, with a pan-fried selection of wild mushrooms—so that its finesse and elegance may be appreciated to the full.

BORDEAUX
A.O.C. Haut-Médoc

- *Wine selected:*
  Château Sociando-Mallet

- *Grape varieties:*
  Cabernet-Sauvignon 55%,
  Merlot 43%, Cabernet-Franc 2%
- *Average vine age:*
  25 years
- *Vineyard size:*
  58 hectares
- *Soil type:*
  Gravel over limestone and clay
- *Production:*
  350,000 bottles

Finest Vintages:
1996, 1990, 1986, 1982

Château Sociando-Mallet
33180 Saint-Seurin-de-Cadourne
Tel. (0033) 556 73 38 80
Follow the D2 to Saint-Seurin-de-
Cadourne. Take the road out of the
east end of the village, leading in the
direction of the river. This leads to
Sociando-Mallet.
- *Owner:* Jean Gautreau
- *On-site sales:* Yes
- *Visits:* By appointment
- *Price:* ★★

CHÂTEAU SOCIANDO-MALLET

It was apparently the splendid view of the Gironde which incited Jean Gautreau to buy the estate of Sociando-Mallet in 1969. However, Gautreau, who had absolutely no experience of making wine, was soon thoroughly involved in his vineyard. He is a perfectionist, he learnt fast, and very quickly the wine started to show real distinction. Sociando-Mallet is today much in demand, for it is one of the élite of the Médoc *Crus Bourgeois* estates, that handful which regularly produce wine of *Cru Classé* standard.

The noble lands of Sieur Sociando

There was an estate of *nobles terres* in the parish of Saint-Seurin-de-Cadourne in the 1630s, which was known by the name of its owner, a Sieur Sociando. However, who first planted vines here, and when, is not documented. At the height of the Terror, in 1793, the Revolutionary forces arrived and took away the proprietor of that time, a famous Bordeaux lawyer named Guillaume de Brochon. The estate was confiscated and eventually sold off to a Monsieur Lamothe. In the middle of the following century it was acquired by the widow Mallet, who added her name to the existing one, as was customary. This lady remained proprietor for two decades, and then Sociando underwent five more changes of ownership in the century following her tenure.

A new lease of life

When Jean Gautreau arrived, the estate was in shambles. There were a mere 5 hectares under vine. Two of them contained pre-phylloxera vines, and these Gautreau refused to uproot until 1978, when they were producing between them a niggardly 10 hectoliters! For a man who swears by old vines, the prospect of completely replanting must have been daunting. There are today 58 hectares in production, and Gautreau continues to enlarge the vineyard by purchases, as and when suitable land comes up for sale. The vathouse had to be renovated, and new oak barrels purchased in order to make the type of wine he envisaged. Finally the château itself, a modest country house which was in a dire state, had to be completely refurbished.

Sociando soars ever higher

In the first years of the 1970s Gautreau produced little wine, for he had only the few old vines at his disposal—yet these wines, made during some climatically awful years, were excellent. The 1973, still in fine form, is a testament to his talent. Then followed a period when production increased as the young vines came on tap. Finally, from about 1982, everything started to fall into place, and he could benefit from a succession of great vintages to produce some wines which attracted much publicity and a rapidly growing clientele. In 1989 Sociando-Mallet was victor of the hotly disputed annual *Coupe des Crus Bourgeois*. This, in a way, was confirmation of his arrival.

Black as ink, and made for keeping

Sociando-Mallet is made for extended cellaring. Its color when young is always ink-black and it is without fail rich, concentrated, structured, and impeccably balanced. It is the perfect wine for red meat, such as a succulent leg of lamb, or a tournedos *forestière*. Sociando-Mallet is one of the most worthy candidates for promotion to *Cru Classé*. It is definitely a wine to discover!

BORDEAUX
A.O.C. Saint-Émilion Grand Cru

- *Wine selected:*
  Château Angélus
  Premier Grand Cru Classé B

- *Grape varieties:*
  Merlot 50%, Cabernet-Franc 47%,
  Cabernet-Sauvignon 3%
- *Average vine age:*
  35 years
- *Vineyard size:*
  23.4 hectares
- *Soil type:*
  Siliceous clay and limestone
- *Production:*
  110,000 bottles

Finest Vintages:
2000, 1998, 1996, 1995, 1990, 1989

Château Angélus
33330 Saint-Émilion
Tel. (0033) 557 24 71 39
Leave Saint-Émilion by the west road,
towards the cemetery. Pass through
the village of Saint-Martin-de-Mazerat
and continue down the road for another
500 meters. Angélus is on the left.
- *Owners:* De Bouard de Laforest
  family
- *On-site sales:* Yes
- *Visits:* By appointment
- *Price:* ★★★★

CHÂTEAU ANGÉLUS

One of the most spectacular improvements in performance to have been seen recently in any Saint-Émilion wine must be that of Château Angélus, in the hamlet of Mazerat. From the beginning of the 1980s, a complete reappraisal of the way things were done has given the wine a new identity, much appreciated around the world. This improvement has rocketed its standing and value, and was rewarded with promotion in the Saint-Émilion hierarchy in 1996. Angélus is an excellent illustration of how great terrain is not in itself sufficient for producing great wine, but needs a dedicated and perspicacious wine maker to make best use of its gifts.

Where all the church bells may be heard...

In 1909 Maurice de Bouard de Laforest inherited an estate of 13 hectares called Domaine de Mazerat from his aunt. Maurice was, it seems, a veritable dynamo, and with his irrepressible energy found markets for his wine in many countries. He bought a neighboring parcel of 3 hectares from the Gurchy family in 1924, and when two of his sons took over the property after the Second World War, they combined the two and baptized the whole Angélus—because, as the story goes, it was the one place in the area where the bells of the chapel of Mazerat and the churches of Saint-Martin and Saint-Émilion could all be heard ringing the Angelus —and gave it the label it sports today. Other parcels of land have been added to the estate since. The author of the estate's renaissance has been Hubert, son of Maurice's son Jacques, who has been at the helm since 1985, in tandem in recent years with his cousin Jean-Bernard Grenié.

The rise and rise of Angélus

The dramatic turn around came in a number of stages. The pre-1980s Angélus had always been fruity and rich, but was also usually rather rustic, lacking class. Hubert, a newly qualified enologist, started using a proportion of new oak for maturing the wine, which until then had seen nothing other than concrete at any stage of its career. Over the course of the 1980s the old fermentation vats were replaced with temperature-controlled stainless-steel ones; since their installation the fruit has been fermented at a rather high 82–90°F (28-32°C), and maceration is protracted. Since 1992 the wine has subsequently been transferred to oak barrels for its second, malo-lactic fermentation—a risky and costly business that was at the time practically unheard of in Bordeaux, only viable for limited-scale production. After aging in oak, which in good years is all new, it is bottled without filtration.

Concentration, power, and richness

Improving the raw material is a constant obsession: a green harvest in July reduces the number of bunches on each vine, to improve the quality of the remainder; the harvest is minutely examined on arrival at the reception area, in order to retain only perfect grapes; and a second wine has been introduced for marketing any wine not considered of top quality (which also includes old-vine wine from excellent but unclassified parcels). Unfortunately the modern Château Angélus is prohibitively expensive, but it is undeniably a very good wine, redolent of toasted oak, coffee, and black fruit, rich and assertive.

At table it needs a flavorful dish to balance its power —something with *foie gras* and truffles, for example, such as the sumptuous *contre-filet* Prince Albert—a fillet of beef stuffed with *foie gras* and truffles, and decorated with strips of whole truffle.

BORDEAUX
A.O.C. Saint-Émilion Grand Cru

- *Wine selected:*
  Château Ausone
  Premier Grand Cru Classé A

- *Grape varieties:*
  Merlot 60%, Cabernet-Franc 40%
- *Average vine age:*
  40 years
- *Vineyard size:*
  7 hectares
- *Soil type:*
  Clay over limestone
- *Production:*
  24 000 bottles

Finest Vintages:
1999, 1998, 1997, 1996, 1995, 1990,
1989, 1988, 1986, 1983, 1982

Château Ausone
33330 Saint-Émilion
Tel. (0033) 557 24 70 26
Leave Saint-Émilion by the bottom of
the town, taking the D122 towards
Libourne. After only a few meters
there is a small road leading off to the
right. Follow this for some 300 meters.
Ausone is on the left.
- *Owners:* Mme Micheline Vauthier,
  Mlle Catherine Vauthier & Alain
  Vauthier
- *On-site sales:* No
- *Visits:* By appointment
- *Price:* ★★★★★

CHÂTEAU AUSONE

There is a pretty little château, surrounded by a small vineyard, which sits on the slopes of Saint-Émilion's hill under the town's medieval walls. For the beauty of the site and for a taste of the wine, this estate is worth going out of one's way to visit. This is Château Ausone, and here one of France's greatest and rarest wines is made.

Mademoiselle Challon's inheritance

The estate is named after the Roman poet Ausonius, who reputedly had a property in the area. In 1808 it passed from the Cantenat family to the Laffargues, and was later inherited by Mademoiselle Challon, niece of one Monsieur Laffargue, who then married Édouard Dubois. The vineyard prospered under their ownership, and Édouard purchased the neighboring Château Belair in 1916. The estate was duly passed down to their son Jean and daughter Cécile, and is today in the hands of the latter's descendants, the Vauthiers. Ausone has been run since 1974 by Alain Vauthier, aided until recently by Pascal Delbeck.

Like many a historic Bordeaux estate, Ausone has had its ups and downs. The post-war period saw many a poor, thin vintage, but that ceased when Vauthier took over. Since the 1975 vintage Ausone has once again been one of Bordeaux's greatest wines.

A claret estate of Burgundian dimensions

At Ausone things are done very much in a traditional, handcrafted way. The steep 7-hectare vineyard, facing east and southeast and partly terraced, is worked manually. Its orientation protects it from the cold northerly and southwesterly winds and the grapes ripen easily in the well-drained limestone clay topsoil and permeable limestone subsoil. The wine from the venerable forty-year-old vines is made in Ausone's vast, cool, and humid cellars, quarried out of the soft limestone. Fermentation proceeds in small wooden 60-hectoliter vats, and is followed by up to a month's maceration before transfer into new oak barrels for maturation. At no point is the wine filtered.

Great vintages never die

Ausone is deceptively light-colored and unyielding when young, and is a wine made for long aging; it frequently requires fifteen or twenty years before its bouquet blossoms and its assertive tannin softens up. When mature it has a splendid complex flavor of Mocha coffee, spices, minerals, and oak, and a firm texture. Great vintages are almost eternal. Serena Sutcliffe, the well-known English wine taster, reported in *Decanter Magazine* on a tasting of vintages back to 1831 which left all present spellbound. Of the 1831 she wrote: "A wonderful vintage, served at Madame Dubois-Challon's wedding! Now a warm, treacly brown, with an utterly warm Saint-Émilion nose—amazing to have appellation characteristics in a wine of this age… Pretty marvellous wine."

What should the fortunate Ausone-sipper eat with his wine? Were he to have chosen a bottle of the majestic, opulent, spicy, and mineral 1976 (still a tannic adolescent nevertheless), he could do far worse than choose the firm, tasty meat of a game bird such as woodcock, not hung—it should not be so strongly-flavored as to interfere with the complexity of the wine's flavor—served in its gravy and accompanied by a simple potato gratin.

BORDEAUX
A.O.C. Saint-Émilion Grand Cru

- *Wine selected:*
  Château Beau-Séjour Bécot
  Premier Grand Cru Classé B

- *Grape varieties:*
  Merlot 70%, Cabernet-Franc 24%,
  Cabernet-Sauvignon 6%
- *Average vine age:*
  35 years
- *Vineyard size:*
  16.5 hectares
- *Soil type:*
  Limestone and clay over
  calcareous rock
- *Production:*
  70,000 bottles

Finest Vintages:
1998, 1995, 1990

Château Beau-Séjour Bécot
33330 Saint-Émilion
Tel. (0033) 557 74 46 87
Leave Saint-Émilion by the road
leading towards the hamlet of Saint-
Martin. Take the right fork just before
arriving there; this leads up to Beau-
Séjour Bécot.
- *Owners:* Gérard & Dominique Bécot
- *On-site sales:* Yes
- *Visits:* By appointment
- *Price:* ★★★

Château Beau-Séjour Bécot

The wide variety of soils around the town of Saint-Émilion, combined with individual wine-making techniques, make for a significant diversity of styles in its top wines. Château Beau-Séjour Bécot is one of the most soft, perfumed, and heavily oaked of all of these.

A doctor who cared not for his wine

The property was originally one half of a great and venerable estate called Beauséjour, which was split in 1869. In 1924 the Ducarpe family sold it to Dr. Jean Fagouet. Beauséjour-Fagouet, as it was known, was a mediocre wine, for the doctor was not interested in it, and it is rather surprising that it was classified *Premier Grand Cru Classé* in the 1954 classification. In 1969 the doctor sold the estate to Michel Bécot, owner of the nearby Château La Carte.

Michel Bécot fulfils his ambition

Bécot had ambitions for his new acquisition and rapidly launched a complete program of investments, for the existing equipment was too archaic for producing the sort of wine he envisaged. He laid a new drainage system in the vineyard; he knocked down the existing vathouse and had a new one built, containing stainless steel vats equipped with temperature control; he had the underground cellar enlarged with a view to accommodating a large number of barrels, for new oak featured prominently in his plans; and, wishing to make his property accessible to clients and visitors, he also had roomy facilities built for welcoming them and holding tastings of his wine. The efforts and investment paid off, and the reception area now regularly hums with the sound of groups appreciatively sampling the wine.

Demotion and reinstatement

The estate was demoted to *Grand Cru Classé* status in the revision of 1985, because Bécot decided to incorporate both his Château La Carte and another neighboring property, Château Les Trois Moulins, acquired in 1979, into Beau-Séjour Bécot. These two estates were simple *Grands Crus*, and the authorities decided that their inclusion into a *Premier Grand Cru Classé* wine was unacceptable. Opinions were divided about the justice of this, for the newly incorporated land was of similar quality and make-up to that of the Bécot vineyard. As it happened, the demotion had a positive effect, and in the following years the wine greatly improved. The selection of the raw material, and then of the vats which form the *grand vin*, became that much stricter, and the wine's richness and complexity was increased by fuller use of new oak barrels.

Bécot retired in 1985, and it was his sons Gérard and Dominique, at the helm since then, who had the satisfaction of seeing their efforts rewarded in 1996 with Beau-Séjour Bécot's reinstatement as a *Premier Grand Cru Classé*.

Opulence and voluptuousness

Beau-Séjour Bécot is one of the most opulent Saint-Émilions, generally fully mature after a dozen years, at which stage its plump, voluptuous body, giving off a beautiful perfume of soft black fruit, oak, and cinnamon, is irresistible—a textbook example of richness, balance and harmony. This wine calls for a rich yet subtle game dish—roast woodcock in a cream sauce, for example.

BORDEAUX
A.O.C. Saint-Émilion Grand Cru

- *Wine selected:*
  Château Belair
  Premier Grand Cru Classé B

- *Grape varieties:*
  Merlot 80%, Cabernet-Franc 20%
- *Average vine age:*
  40 years
- *Vineyard size:*
  12.5 hectares
- *Soil type:*
  Limestone and clay over
  calcareous rock
- *Production:*
  50,000 bottles

Finest Vintages:

1999, 1998, 1996, 1995, 1994, 1993,
1990, 1989, 1985, 1983, 1982

Château Belair

33330 Saint-Émilion
Tel. (0033) 557 24 70 94
Leave Saint-Émilion by the bottom of
the town, taking the D122 towards
Libourne. After only a few meters
there is a small road leading off to the
right. Follow this for some 300 meters.
Château Belair is on the left.
- *Owner:* Mme J. Dubois-Challon
- *Manager:* Pascal Delbeck
- *On-site sales:* Yes
- *Visits:* By appointment
- *Price:* ★★

CHÂTEAU BELAIR

Directly beneath the town walls on the southern side of Saint-Émilion lies the historic estate of Château Belair. Not only is it the oldest of the region's properties, but it was up until the end of the last century the most prestigious. Although the area now counts a good number of estates producing wine at least on a par with Belair's, it remains one of Saint-Émilion's finest.

The great "cru de Canolle"

The estate's history goes back to the Middle Ages, when it was part of the lands of Robert de Knolles, Grand Sénéchal and governor of Guyenne during the English occupation of the region. Although the English were ejected following their defeat at the Battle of Castillon, some of Knolles' descendants remained in the area, and their name (the k in those days being pronounced) eventually evolved into Canolle. Their Saint-Émilion property produced wine at least as early as the 1750s, and it was known as "cru de Canolle". This, we are told by Clive Coates M.W. in his *Grands Vins: The Finest Châteaux of Bordeaux and Their Wines*, sold for three times the price of other Saint-Émilions in the years before the Revolution, and was subjected to experiments at château—bottling as early as 1802.

The competition stiffens

Numerous nineteenth century authorities attest that Belair was the leading wine of the Saint-Émilion *côtes* throughout the last century. However its vineyard was hard-hit by phylloxera, and the emergence at the same time of other properties, and the gradual recognition of the quality of *graves* Saint-Émilions such as Château Cheval Blanc, removed Belair from the limelight somewhat towards the turn of the century. The estate was bought in 1916 by Edouard Dubois-Challon, and is today owned by his widowed daughter-in-law, Madame Jean Dubois-Challon.

A young manager and a return to form

Château Belair went through an indifferent patch from the 1960s until the mid-1970s, but the arrival in 1978 of the young Pascal Delbeck signaled a return to form. Two-thirds of Belair's vines lie on the plateau at the top of the escarpment, while the remaining third march down towards the La Gaffelière vineyard. With their produce Delbeck makes a wine which is middle-weight, soft and aromatic, rich and elegant, and markedly less structured and powerful than Châteaux Canon and Magdelaine, other estates which also have their vines on the plateau and on the slope. It reaches maturity after a decade, but can last another decade at its peak before starting to tire.

Its softness and elegance make it a very suitable wine for serving with quails, roasted en *caissettes*, *aux choux* or *aux raisins*, or braised with vegetables.

BORDEAUX
A.O.C. Saint-Émilion Grand Cru

- *Wine selected:*
  Château Canon-La Gaffelière
  Grand Cru Classé

- *Grape varieties:*
  Merlot 55%, Cabernet-Franc 40%,
  Cabernet-Sauvignon 5%
- *Average vine age:*
  40 years
- *Vineyard size:*
  19.5 hectares
- *Soil type:*
  Limestone and clay, sand
- *Production:*
  95,000 bottles

Finest Vintages:
1998, 1997, 1996, 1995,
1990, 1989, 1988

Château Canon-La Gaffelière
33330 Saint-Émilion
Tel. (0033) 557 24 71 33
Leave Saint-Émilion by the bottom
of the town, taking the D122 towards
Libourne. Canon-la-Gaffelière is on
the right after about 1 km, just after
the railroad tracks.
- *Owner:* Comtes de Neipperg
- *On-site sales:* Yes
- *Visits:* By appointment
- *Price:* ★★★/★★★★

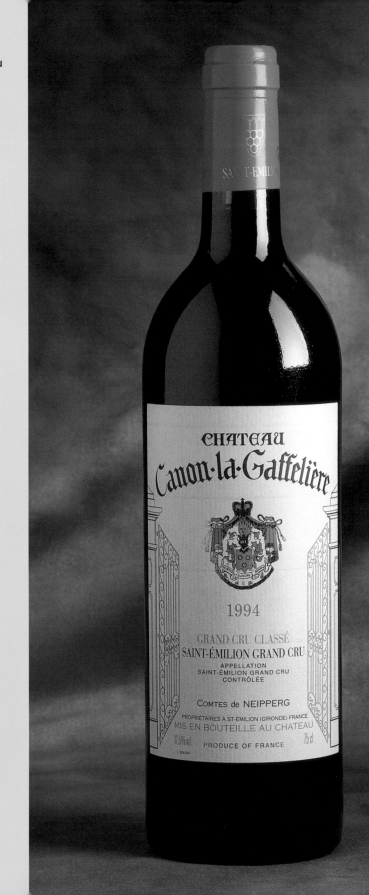

CHÂTEAU CANON-LA GAFFELIÈRE

For many years Château Canon-la-Gaffelière produced uninspired, dull, and weak wines, and had a justly indifferent reputation. Then a new man took charge, a twenty-seven-year-old with a deep belief in the estate, since whose arrival the wine has undergone a complete metamorphosis. It is now a serious rival to the top Saint-Émilions, and continues to make progress with every new vintage.

A German wine dynasty invests in Bordeaux

The property was originally known as La Gaffelière-Boitard, after the Boitard family who owned it from the eighteenth to the end of the ninteenth centuries. Towards the end of this period one of the Boitard daughters married a doctor called Peyraud, who took on the management of the estate and did a lot towards improving the wine and its reputation. It remained in the Peyraud family until 1953, when the Peyraud heirs sold it to the mayor of Saint-Émilion, Pierre Meyrat. Like many another property it is probable that Canon-la-Gaffelière suffered as a result of the economic depression of the inter war years, and Meyrat was unable to reverse its decline. Following his death, his widow put the estate up for sale. In 1971 it was purchased by Count Joseph-Hubert von Neipperg, whose renowned family of farmers, viticulturists, and soldiers have made wine in Germany since the thirteenth century.

The young Count takes up the challenge

By that time the château was a ruin, the wine-making buildings in dire need of renovation and re-equipment, and the wine's reputation non-existent. The Count offered the task to his son Stephan, who eagerly accepted and in 1984 took over the management of the estate. After a year of observation and preparation of his plan of attack, he got to work.

First it was necessary to improve the drainage of the vineyard, which lies on the slope and at the foot of the Saint-Émilion escarpment, and revive its potassium-saturated soil with natural treatments. Viticulture was adapted from the start favoring strict limitation of the yields. Harvesting by hand, followed by selection in the field and in the reception area became *de rigueur*. A second wine was introduced in 1986. The vathouse had to be renovated and equipped with temperature-controlled stainless steel vats, and the quantity of new oak barrels was increased from 10 percent to 60 percent—and is now increased to up to 90 percent in great years. Finally an underground cellar with space for one million bottles was constructed. And of course the dilapidated château had to be renovated.

A warm, rich, plummy wine

All these measures have resulted in a wine which is unrecognizable compared with the vintages of the 1960s and 1970s. Canon-la-Gaffelière is invariably very deeply colored, with a warm, rich, plummy flavor which in certain vintages (such as 1988) is dominated by an exotic spiciness, suggestive of cinnamon in particular. When young it is also gently oak-flavored. The wine is finely balanced and has a big tannic structure, which is less noticeable in great years than in average ones. These modern Canon-la-Gaffelières may be expected to benefit from a sojourn of between six and fifteen years in the cellar, depending on the vintage.

When served at table they cry out for red meat or game as accompaniment; a fillet of beef *en brioche* would be an excellent choice for the succulent 1985, a medium-weight wine which is now just about ready.

BORDEAUX
A.O.C. Saint-Émilion Grand Cru

- *Wine selected:*
  Château Cheval Blanc
  Premier Grand Cru Classé A

- *Grape varieties:*
  Cabernet-Franc 57%, Merlot 41%,
  Cabernet-Sauvignon 1%, Malbec 1%
- *Average vine age:*
  33 years
- *Vineyard size:*
  36 hectares
- *Soil type:*
  Gravel and sand over hard
  iron-rich clay
- *Production:*
  120,000 bottles

Finest Vintages:

1999, 1998, 1995, 1994, 1990,
1989, 1986, 1985, 1982

Château Cheval Blanc
33330 Saint-Émilion
Tel. (0033) 557 55 55 55
- *Owner:* S.C. du Château Cheval Blanc
- *General Manager:* Pierre Lurton
- *On-site sales:* No
- *Visits:* No
- *Price:* ★★★★★

CHÂTEAU CHEVAL BLANC

Until December 1998 Château Cheval Blanc was one of very few top Bordeaux properties to have remained in the same family since its creation. This continuity must have accounted at least in part for the wine's continued excellence: there has never been a significant dropping-off in quality, ever since Cheval Blanc was recognized in Jean Laussac Fourcaud's time as being the finest of the *graves* Saint-Émilions. Certain turn-of-the-century vintages, the 1893, 1899, and 1900, and the more recent 1921, 1947, and 1982 are regularly cited as wines of anthology. This is without doubt one of the greatest of Bordeaux's wines.

The dowry of Henriette Ducasse

Some 160 years ago it was part of the huge Figeac estate, Saint-Émilion's only equivalent to the great Médoc estates. Cheval Blanc came into being in two stages, when Figeac's owners sold off 15 hectares of land in 1832 and then a further 15 hectares five years later to the Ducasse family, owners of the neighboring Château L'Évangile. In 1854 Mademoiselle Henriette Ducasse married one Jean Laussac Fourcaud, and brought him the estate as dowry.

By 1868 Fourcaud had increased the landholding to 40 hectares. After his death in 1893, Albert, one of his eight children, took over responsibilities, and bought out his brothers and sisters. He inverted his name to Fourcaud-Laussac and sired five children, to whom he bequeathed the estate in the form of shares in the *Société civile du Cheval Blanc*.

His descendants owned all the shares until 1998, when they were sold to two businessmen, the Frenchman Bernard Arnault and the Belgian Albert Frère. Yet continuity there still is, and quality should not be affected, for General Manager Pierre Lurton remains at the helm and his team remains unchanged.

An original mix of grape varieties

When Saint-Émilion's wines were classified in 1954, Cheval Blanc was given the supreme ranking of *Premier Grand Cru Classé* A. It lies on the Saint-Émilion plateau on the border with Pomerol, with the fine Pomerol estates of L'Évangile and La Conseillante as neighbors, and this terrain consists of gravel, clay, sand and in some places limestone, on the region's hard iron-rich clay subsoil, the *crasse de fer*. Cheval Blanc lies on the finest gravel soil, and this—allied to an original blend of Cabernet-Franc and Merlot grapes—gives birth to a unique wine of sensuality, finesse, and body, as much Pomerol as Saint-Émilion in character.

Richness, opulence, and great depth of flavor

It does not have the obvious tannic structure of the great Médoc wines, and is approachable young; however, its great richness, opulence, sheer depth of flavor—imparted in part by aging in new oak barrels—and subtle tannin and acidity give it the wherewithal to improve over many decades. Tasting notes of mature vintages frequently include such epithets as sweet, voluptuous, cedary, spicy, roasted, coffee and so on.

A personality as exotic as this naturally requires a very special companion at table. Georges Lepré, the eminent French sommelier, suggests serving the magnificent and barely mature Cheval Blanc 1966 with a *contre-filet* Prince Albert—a fillet of beef stuffed with *foie gras* and truffles, and decorated with strips of whole truffle. A gastronomic experience no one could forget in a hurry!

BORDEAUX
A.O.C. Saint-Émilion Grand Cru

• *Wine selected:*
Château Figeac
Premier Grand Cru Classé B

• *Grape varieties:*
Cabernet-Franc 35%, Cabernet-
Sauvignon 35%, Merlot 30%
• *Average vine age:*
40 years
• *Vineyard size:*
40 hectares
• *Soil type:*
Gravel
• *Production:*
150,000 bottles

Finest Vintages:

1999, 1998, 1996, 1995,
1994, 1990, 1989, 1982

Château Figeac
33330 Saint-Émilion
Tel. (0033) 557 24 72 26
Leave Saint-Émilion by the north-
west, on the D243. The road leading
up to Figeac is on the right, 4 km
further along.
• *Owner:* Thierry Manoncourt
• *Director:* Éric d'Aramon
• *On-site sales:* No
• *Visits:* By appointment
• *Price:* ★★★/★★★★

CHÂTEAU FIGEAC

On the Pomerol boundary, north west of the town of Saint-Émilion, lies one of the region's finest estates, Château Figeac. As Saint-Émilions go, Figeac, along with its neighbor Château Cheval Blanc, are a category apart, for they lie on deep gravel ridges similar to those of the Médoc; this geological differentiation makes them very dissimilar characters to Saint-Émilion's eleven other *Premiers Grands Crus Classés*, which lie on the limestone and clay land which surrounds the town. Figeac is a wine of great elegance, harmony and breeding; it is one of the Gironde's finest ambassadors.

A vast estate founded in the second century

In days gone by the Figeac estate was far larger than it is now, occupying a vast 500-hectare tract of land stretching from the town of Saint-Émilion to the outskirts of Libourne. Its origins go back to the second century, when, it is thought, a family called Figeacus lived in a villa on the site of the present château. In the Middle Ages the estate belonged to the Lescours family, then passed into the de Cazes family, and subsequently to the de Carles, a family of businessmen, bankers, *négociants* and vineyard owners.

It was the widow of the Comte de Carle who at the beginning of the nineteenth century was obliged to start selling off parcels of what was then a 200-hectare estate in order to support her extravagant lifestyle. This dismemberment spawned a good number of properties that include Figeac in their name. In the 1830s a prime 30-hectare parcel known as Cheval Blanc was sold off to Monsieur Ducasse, who made use of the wine's great reputation by continuing to sell the produce of his new acquisition as Vin de Figeac until 1853, when he rechristened it Cheval Blanc. In 1838 the de Carles sold the remainder of the diminished Figeac, and it then changed hands seven times in the following half-century. In 1892, once more up for sale, it was bought by André Villepigue, who left it to his daughter, Madame Antoine Manoncourt. This lady's son, Thierry, became director in 1947, and inherited the estate in 1981. He is now assisted by his daughter Laure and son-in-law Comte Éric d'Aramon.

An important role for the Cabernet-Sauvignon

When Thierry Manoncourt took over, the estate's reputation was rather faded —the inevitable result of so many changes of ownership and absent landlords. However, he tackled the job of putting it back on its pedestal with energy and determination, and the results were soon felt.

An agricultural engineer by training, Manoncourt has engaged in much viticultural and vinification research and innovation on the estate, much to the benefit of Bordeaux's wine makers as a whole. Figeac has a unique blend of grapes, which includes 35 percent Cabernet-Sauvignon, a far higher proportion than is usual in Saint-Émilion yet well-suited to its special gravel soil. This, combined with careful viticulture, low yields, severe selection, and painstaking vinification give Figeac its special character and sheer class.

It is rich and quite tannic when young, then soft, silky and profound when older; a wine which beguiles by its elegance, harmony, and pedigree. A wine to accompany top-quality meats, served with gravy rather than a rich sauce: filet steak, for example, or turkey with a truffle stuffing. What a delight!

BORDEAUX
A.O.C. Saint-Émilion Grand Cru

- *Wine selected:*
  Château Le Tertre Rôtebœuf
  Grand Cru

- *Grape varieties:*
  Merlot 80%, Cabernet-Franc 20%
- *Average vine age:*
  40 years
- *Vineyard size:*
  5.6 hectares
- *Soil type:*
  Clay and limestone
- *Production:*
  25,000 bottles

Finest Vintages:
1998, 1996, 1995, 1990, 1989, 1988

Château Le Tertre Roteboeuf
33330 Saint-Émilion
Fax: (0033) 557 24 70 57
Leave Saint-Émilion by the bottom
of the town, taking the D122 towards
Libourne. Take the first road on the
left, the D245, towards Saint-Laurent-
des-Combes. Proceed past Châteaux
Pavie, Larcis-Ducasse and Bellefont-
Belcier, then take the first turn on
the left. Tertre Rôtebœuf is at the
top of the slope on the left.
- *Owners:* François & Émilie Mitjavile
- *On-site sales:* No
- *Visits:* By appointment
- *Price:* ★★★★

CHÂTEAU LE TERTRE-RÔTEBOEUF

This is the story of a modest little property in Saint-Émilion, which came into the hands of an inspired man and started producing top-quality wine. In little more than a dozen years it was hauled from the anonymous ranks of the Saint-Émilion petits châteaux and firmly established among the top players of the region. The inspired man is François Mitjavile, and the property is Château Tertre-Rôteboeuf.

A yearning for the country life

Vines have been planted on the slope which Le Tertre-Roteboeuf occupies since Gallo-Roman times. The château, rebuilt after a fire around 1730, is a typical example of the *maison noble* of the seventeenth and eighteenth centuries.

François and his wife Émilie worked in Paris, but quietly harbored a yearning for the country life. Émilie's father had owned a small vineyard called Le Tertre, which had been rented out since his death in 1961, and the Mitjaviles decided to take the plunge, reclaim Émilie's inheritance, and make wine for a living. After two years' training at Château Figeac, François took the property over.

Putting the estate back in order

The realization of his dreams took time, for the property did not contain any wine-making equipment. First of all he concentrated on bringing the vineyard up to scratch—a matter principally of long hours and physical energy. Then he borrowed from all possible sources to invest in wine-making equipment and oak barrels. By dint of delaying harvesting until the grapes were almost over-ripe, restricting the yields, rigorously picking through the raw material in order to use only what was perfect, and vinifying in such a way as to produce the fleshy, rich, and structured *vin de garde* he imagined in his head, he managed to produce a wine of a quality way above those of many of his peers.

A lucky break brings the first orders

However, that was only the first step; it remained to get people interested in it, for Saint-Émilion is not short of good wine. This took time, but finally his lucky break came when a well-known consumer magazine picked out Le Tertre-Rôteboeuf as winner in a blind tasting of 1982s. François started receiving orders, and could at last afford to invest in new oak barrels, essential for the type of wine at which he was aiming, and raise his prices sufficiently to make the whole business viable. Since this turning-point, which came with the 1985 vintage, the wine has gained in richness, elegance, and finesse. Current vintages continue to improve as François refines his techniques. This is a wine to look out for!

In a gastronomic context Le Tertre-Roteboeuf partners *foie gras* very well, and red meats in sauce. Let us take that idea a little further: a fillet of prime beef, *foie gras*, truffles, and ruby port, are the ingredients of that majestic dish, tournedos Rossini. What better partner for this magnificently fleshy wine?

BORDEAUX
A.O.C. Pomerol

- *Wine selected:*
  Château La Conseillante

- *Grape varieties:*
  Merlot 65%, Cabernet-Franc 30%,
  Malbec 5%
- *Average vine age:*
  40 years
- *Vineyard size:*
  12 hectares
- *Soil type:*
  Sandy gravel over hard iron-rich clay
- *Production:*
  75,000 bottles

Finest Vintages:
1999, 1998, 1995, 1990,
1989, 1985, 1982

Château La Conseillante
33500 Pomerol
Tel. (0033) 557 51 15 32
Head east out of Catusseau. At
the fork take the right-hand road,
leading to Montagne-Saint-Émilion.
La Conseillante is less than 1 km
down the road, on the left.
- *Owner:* SC Héritiers Nicolas
- *On-site sales:* No
- *Visits:* By appointment
- *Price:* ★★★★

Château La Conseillante

Lying right on the Pomerol commune boundary with Saint-Émilion, and surrounded by L'Évangile, Vieux Château Certan, Petit-Village and Cheval Blanc, lies Château La Conseillante. This estate can lay claim with some justification to producing one of Bordeaux's most elegant and refined wines.

A pioneering lady wine maker

The estate came into being in the mid-eighteenth century, one of the first of the properties on the Pomerol plateau that we know today. Its creator was a lady named Catherine Conseillant, who started accumulating parcels of land from about 1735 and letting them out on a share-cropping basis. Finally she decided to cultivate them herself, and from 1756 saw fit to name the resulting wine after herself—and La Conseillante it has remained to this day.

From the outset it was one of the area's finest wines, and it has maintained this reputation over all the intervening years. We do not know what happened to Madame Conseillant, but by the 1840s the estate was briefly in the hands of the Leperche-Princeteau family, then in 1871 it was acquired by Louis Nicolas. It has remained in the Nicolas family to this day.

Hand-crafted in the finest tradition

The wine is made in the traditional way, spending a long period macerating on its skins before being matured for twenty to twenty-four months in oak barrels, which are renewed in their entirety every year. It is not filtered, and all movement of the wine is by gravity, never by pump.

La Conseillante's greatest qualities—its elegance and its refinement—can surely be put down to the gravel-laden clay and the sand of its soil. What marks it out is its silky texture, beautifully rich fruit, concentration, complexity, and exquisite harmony.

Harmony and finesse

As with nearly all Pomerols, it is delicious in its youth, but this harmony enables it to age very well in bottle. Its flavor is generally reminiscent of blackcurrants or plums, violets, spice, and sometimes chocolate.

Naturally, a lady of such finesse should not be overwhelmed by overly flavored meats and rich sauces: La Conseillante would be far more happy engaged in a tête-à-tête with a roast woodcock.

BORDEAUX
A.O.C. Pomerol

- *Wine selected:*
  Château L'Église-Clinet

- *Grape varieties:*
  Merlot 85%, Cabernet-Franc 15%
- *Average vine age:*
  45 years
- *Vineyard size:*
  5 hectares
- *Soil type:*
  Gravel and clay over hard iron-rich clay
- *Production:*
  20,000 bottles

Finest Vintages:
1999, 1998, 1996, 1990,
1989, 1986, 1985, 1982

Château L'Église-Clinet
33500 Pomerol
Tel. (0033) 557 25 99 00
On arriving at Catusseau from the
west, turn left opposite Château
Nenin, and continue as far as the
Pomerol school. L'Église-Clinet is
opposite it, near the main entry to
the cemetery.
- *Owner:* Denis Durantou
- *On-site sales:* No
- *Visits:* By appointment
- *Price:* ★★★★/★★★★★

CHÂTEAU L'ÉGLISE-CLINET

Some of Pomerol's brightest stars—Trotanoy, Lafleur, and Certan de May come to mind—are wines that are rarely seen on sale, let alone tasted, simply because the tiny production is snapped up as soon as it is marketed. There is no depth of stock, as provided by most Médoc estates, which will continue to supply the requirements of the world's professional buyers for a number of years. Another case in point is the excellent Château L'Église-Clinet. Therefore, lovers of fine Pomerol, do not hesitate when you have a chance of acquiring a bottle of this wine, for it may not be available tomorrow!

The creation of a new estate

Clos L'Église-Clinet, as it was christened, was created in 1882 from parts of Clos L'Église and Château Clinet by their owner, Monsieur Mauléon-Rouchut. It is a small vineyard, which lies around the church of Saint-Jean in the heart of Pomerol's plateau, and it has remained in the hands of his descendants to this day: Mauléon-Rouchut's daughter married Jean Rabier, and they had a daughter named Germaine who married a Durantou. It is this couple's grandson, Denis Durantou, who has run the estate since 1983.

Farmed out for forty years

In the forty years prior to Denis Durantou's takeover the vines were tended and the wine made by Pierre Lasserre, the owner of Clos René, an estate on Pomerol's western edge, as Durantou's father was not a vigneron. Lasserre maintained the estate's reputation with many a fine vintage of dense, rich, and structured wine, made by traditional methods: little temperature control during fermentation, maceration on a proportion of the stalks, and a good two years' maturation in old wood. When Lasserre eventually retired, Durantou, newly graduated from Bordeaux University and harboring ambitions for the wine, took over.

Durantou puts theory into practice

Priority was put on reducing the yield—already moderate, for the vines are very old—and rigorous selection of what went into the vats. In 1986 he introduced a second wine, which on average accounts for one-third of the production—a praiseworthy decision, given the size of the estate. He renovated the vats, installed temperature-control equipment, and now destems entirely before vatting. He uses one-third new oak every year, and has reduced to fifteen–eighteen months the time the wine is aged in it.

Elegance and charm accentuated

The wine as a result has gained in freshness and aromatic definition, and now is plumper than before, with more elegance and charm. It has a flavor reminiscent of a mixture of plums, morello cherries, and sometimes blackberries, with burnt oak nuances. It is approachable when young, but really needs eight to ten years' keeping to reveal all its qualities; the best vintages last for twenty years or more. When at last the cork is drawn, the Durantous recommend serving the wine with stewed guinea fowl, or roast veal garnished with morels.

BORDEAUX
A.O.C. Pomerol

- *Wine selected:*
  Château L'Évangile

- *Grape varieties:*
  Merlot 78%, Cabernet-Franc 22%
- *Average vine age:*
  40 years
- *Vineyard size:*
  14 hectares
- *Soil type:*
  Siliceous gravel and clay over iron-
  oxide subsoil
- *Production:*
  60,000 bottles

Finest Vintages:
1999, 1998, 1990, 1989, 1985, 1982

Château L'Évangile
33500 Pomerol
Tel. (0033) 557 51 15 30
Head east out of Catusseau. At the
fork, take the right-hand road towards
Montagne-Saint-Émilion. L'Évangile is
after La Conseillante, on the left.
- *Owner*: S.C. Château L'Évangile
- *On-site sales:* No
- *Visits:* By appointment
- *Price:* ★★★★/★★★★★

CHÂTEAU L'ÉVANGILE

Château L'Évangile has always produced fine wine, and a glance at the map shows why: this estate lies on the Pomerol plateau, surrounded by the likes of La Conseillante, Vieux Château Certan, Pétrus, and La Fleur-Pétrus, and has a similar microclimate and soil. In 1990 the Domaines Barons de Rothschild (of Lafite) bought 70 percent of the equity. With the financial stability afforded by the Rothschilds, the long-term quality of L'Évangile is now guaranteed.

One of the first Pomerol wine estates

L'Evangile was the creation of the Leglise family, who were part of the small group of people which included the Arnauds (Pétrus), Catherine Conseillant (La Conseillante), and M. Giraud (Trotanoy), who established the nucleus of the Pomerol vineyard in the mid-eighteenth century. At that time the estate was known as Fazilleau. Why Fazilleau became L'Évangile (The Gospel) we do not know—the author of this change, proprietor in the first half of the nineteenth century, was the lawyer Izambert. The estate was subsequently bought by Paul Chaperon in 1862, and it has remained with his heirs, the Ducasse family, ever since.

Paul Chaperon's legacy

It seems to have been Chaperon who raised the wine to the standing it enjoys today. He died at the turn of the century, yet his widow ably continued his work. She left the estate to her daughter Louise, who in her turn bequeathed it to one of her three sons, Paul Ducasse. After Ducasse's death his widow continued to run the estate until 1956, the year of the terrible frosts. This lady's nephew Louis Ducasse took over that year, and he had the huge task of putting the estate back on its feet. He died in 1982, and L'Évangile has been run by his widow since then.

Soils and grape varieties

Interestingly, geologists have identified a vein of soil which originates in the Pétrus vineyard, and traverses those of L'Évangile and Cheval Blanc before petering out at Figeac. L'Évangile's vineyard is made up of 50 percent clay, 30 percent siliceous gravel and 20 percent pure gravel, and lies over the iron-rich subsoil specific to this part of the region. It is planted with 78 percent Merlot and 22 percent Cabernet Franc, and the wines to which it gives birth have particular breeding and elegance.

L'Évangile has its own particular vinification procedure, in which the solids are kept immersed permanently in the liquid, and which also features protracted vatting of variable duration according to the vintage; the wine is subsequently matured in oak for eighteen to twenty-two months.

A mass of opulent fruit

In the mouth the structure is submerged under a great mass of opulent fruit, with blackcurrant and plum flavors, licorice, and spice. This is Pomerol at its most lush.

At table L'Évangile partners *foie gras* very well, and red meat in sauce. Let us combine the two. A fillet of prime beef, *foie gras*, truffles and ruby port are the ingredients of that majestic dish, tournedos Rossini. A fine partner for this sensual wine.

BORDEAUX
A.O.C. Pomerol

- *Wine selected:*
  Château Gazin

- *Grape varieties:*
  Merlot 90%, Cabernet-Franc 3%,
  Cabernet-Sauvignon 7%
- *Average vine age:*
  35 years
- *Vineyard size:*
  24 hectares
- *Soil type:*
  Clayey gravel over hard iron-rich clay
- *Production:*
  80,000 bottles

Finest Vintages:
1998, 1996, 1995, 1994,
1990, 1989, 1988

Château Gazin
33500 Pomerol
Tel. (0033) 557 51 07 05
Internet: www.gazin.com
Head east out of Catusseau and follow
the D121 north-east. After about 1 km
a road forks off to the right towards
Gazin—the estate is well signposted.
- *Owner*: GFA Château Gazin
- *On-site sales:* No
- *Visits:* By appointment
- *Price:* ★★★

CHÂTEAU GAZIN

Situated a stone's throw to the east of Pétrus in the heart of Pomerol's finest land, Château Gazin is an estate with a long history, which has this century had its share of ups and downs. Nowadays it is firmly in the ascendant, and producing very fine, characterful Pomerol.

A prize-winning 19th-century wine

The name of Gazin is first mentioned in 1741, as a village of 22 tax-paying vignerons. However Gazin's modern history really starts a century later, when the Bayonne family arrives, and the village gradually mutates into a wine estate. The Bayonnes were succeeded by David Fabre, who apprised the Bordeaux *négociants* of its existence, and in 1874 the wine was qualified as "amongst Pomerol's first growths" in the professionals' 'bible', the Féret. During the brief tenure of Fabre's successor, the wine won a prize at the Exposition universelle in Paris in 1878, and then again in Antwerp in 1885. That same year the estate was sold to Léon Quenedey, under whom it won more prizes in Barcelona and Brussels in 1888, and Paris in 1889.

A hard time for wine-makers

However, hard-hit by the phylloxera epidemic and then the collapse of the wine market at the turn of the century, the unfortunate Quenedey was obliged to sell up in 1917. The purchaser was Louis Soualle, great-grandfather of the present owners, who also purchased Château La Dominique in Saint-Émilion at the same time. He was succeeded by his son-in-law Édouard de Bailliencourt dit Courcol.

Yet things were not prospering. In the hard post-war period La Dominique was sorely neglected. Then the savage frosts of February 1956 took their toll, necessitating a large replanting program. Édouard died in 1969, and three of his four heirs no longer had the stomach to continue; Étienne was the only one who wished to do so.

Étienne de Bailliencourt fights on

The only way he could buy up his sister's and nephews' shares and keep the Gazin estate together was by selling off La Dominique (by then almost a ruin), and by selling 4.5 hectares of Gazin vineyard to his neighbor Pétrus. Things were rock bottom. The estate struggled on, helped by its popularity and wide distribution, but the tender-aged vines produced mediocre wine. Now, however, they have at last reached a respectable age, and Étienne's sons Nicolas and Christophe, who have progressively taken over since 1987, have introduced important modifications to working practices. Things have improved at Gazin.

Rich, intensely fruity and powerful

In style Château Gazin is rich, intensely fruity and powerful; in flavor black fruit and plum when young, and progressively more cigar-box, spice, leather, undergrowth and truffles when mature—the latter imparted, it is generally thought, by the *crasse de fer*. The rusticity the wine used to have has disappeared, replaced since the end of the 1980s by finesse. It is now a very fine wine.

When serving Gazin at table, the age and character of the wine will dictate the dish most suitable. A young, fruity, 'modern' Gazin will be perfect with a simple joint of beef cooked *à la ficelle*; however a mature Gazin with the rustic element of days gone by needs a good savory country dish, such as saddle of hare with cabbage and rosemary stuffing.

BORDEAUX
A.O.C. Pomerol

- *Wine selected:*
  Château Lafleur

- *Grape varieties:*
  Merlot 50%, Cabernet-Franc 50%
- *Average vine age:*
  Over 30 years
- *Vineyard size:*
  4.5 hectares
- *Soil type:*
  Clay and gravel with sand over
  hard iron-rich clay
- *Production:*
  15,000 bottles

Finest Vintages:
1998, 1995, 1990, 1989,
1988, 1982, 1981

Château Lafleur
33240 Mouillac
Tel. (0033) 557 84 44 03
- *Owner:* Mlle Marie Robin
- *Managers:* Jacques & Sylvie
  Guinaudeau
- *On-site sales:* No
- *Visits:* No
- *Price:* ★★★★★

CHÂTEAU LAFLEUR

The greatest authorities on Pomerol's wines are in general agreement: if there is any wine that comes near attaining the sublime qualities of Pétrus, it is Château Lafleur. This vineyard is little known, for it is one of the tiniest of the region, but it has for many years produced magnificent wine, enjoyed by the privileged and wealthy few who are in the know.

"Qualité passe quantité"

Like most of today's Pomerol estates, Lafleur's history does not go far back. Its origins are in the adjoining Le Gay estate. Towards the 1870s the Widow Greloud, owner of Le Gay, handed down her property to her son Henri. Henri decided to separate the finest plots from the rest and make of them a new entity called Lafleur. The new wine rapidly gained an excellent reputation and was by the end of the century generally reckoned third best after Pétrus and Vieux Château Certan. The two estates were then handed down to Greloud's son Charles, who shortly afterwards sold them to his brother-in-law André Robin.

Robin was apparently fond of the dictum *Qualité passe quantité* (Quality above quantity), and this was duly put into practice throughout his tenure at the two estates. The properties were passed down to his two daughters, Thérèse and Marie Robin, in 1946. Neither of these two ladies married, and after her sister passed away in 1984, Marie Robin handed over the running of Lafleur to her cousins Jacques and Sylvie Guinaudeau, who are in charge today.

A glorious wine made in a barn

Lafleur's château, like many in Pomerol, is in fact a *maison de vigneron*, and the wine is made and matured in a building more akin to a barn than the average vathouse and cellar. More than one observer has expressed incredulity that such a glorious wine could have been made in such cluttered and unsanitary conditions, sharing space with poultry, rabbits, and the like. Since the Guinaudeaus' arrival things have been tidied up, and the wine's roommates been expelled; no doubt, in view of the wine's value today, it was decided that too much was at stake to take the risks of yesteryear, which did lead to the occasional flawed vintage.

To safeguard a reputation

Harvesting, naturally, is by hand, and the pickers pass several times through the vines in order to pick only grapes that are perfectly ripe. The fruit is also closely examined on a conveyor belt before pressing. Commendably, given the size of the crop and the financial sacrifice, the Guinaudeaus introduced a second wine which accounts for about one-fifth of the production every year. Indeed in 1987 they declassified the entire crop in order to safeguard Lafleur's reputation.

Voluptuous, sensual and exotically perfumed

Epithets most frequently used to describe Lafleur include powerful, concentrated, voluptuous, of great breeding. This wine is very much in the Pétrus mould, and this fact must be attributed to the similarity of soils. It is a sensual, exotically perfumed wine with a tannic structure such as to guarantee it a lifespan of two or three decades, if not more.

Any wine lover lucky enough to have a bottle of Lafleur in the cellar may serve it, when it is eventually mature, with truffled capon encased in a coarse-salt pastry and roasted. Such feasts can be relived in the memory for many years!

BORDEAUX
A.O.C. Pomerol

- *Wine selected:*
  Pétrus

- *Grape varieties:*
  Merlot 95%, Cabernet-Franc 5%
- *Average vine age:*
  40 years
- *Vineyard size:*
  11.5 hectares
- *Soil type:*
  Clay on gravel, over hard
  iron-rich clay
- *Production:*
  36,000 bottles

Finest Vintages:

1998, 1995, 1990, 1989,
1988, 1985, 1982

Pétrus
1 Rue Pétrus-Arnaud
33500 Pomerol
Tel. (0033) 557 51 17 96
- *Owner*: S.C. du Château Pétrus
- *General Manager:* Christian Moueix
- *On-site sales:* No
- *Visits:* No
- *Price:* ★★★★★

PÉTRUS

The tiny 800-hectare Pomerol region produces one of Bordeaux's most mythical wines, sought out by connoisseurs, speculators, and collectors alike: Pétrus. Its 11.5 hectares produce a meager three thousand cases of one of the world's most opulent and concentrated red wines.

The Arnauds nurture their estate

The first recorded proprietors of Pétrus were the Arnaud family, who owned the estate from the 1830s until after the First World War. By the end of their tenure it was recognized as the top Pomerol, and the prices fetched by its better vintages were the equivalent of those of the Médoc *Deuxièmes Crus Classés*. The Arnauds created the *Société civile du Château Pétrus*, and from 1925 its shares were progressively bought up by Madame Edmonde Loubat, the owner of several minor properties in the region, who finally became sole proprietor in 1945.

Madame Loubat creates a myth

It was this lady who, passionately believing in Pétrus's potential and value, in between 1945 and 1961 hauled it onto the pedestal it now occupies. In 1947 she appointed the young Libourne *négociant* Jean-Pierre Moueix as sole agent, thus starting the Pétrus-Moueix partnership which lasts to this day. Before her death in 1961 the childless Madame Loubat left her shares to her niece Madame Lily Lacoste and her nephew M. Lignac. In 1964 Moueix bought Lignac's shares and took over the direction of the estate; it is his son Christian who is now in charge.

Perfectionist viticulture in unique soil

The Pétrus land is unique: a topsoil of blue-tinged clay and a subsoil of gravel, the whole lying on Pomerol's iron-rich *crasse de fer*. The choice of grape varieties, and the extreme attention to detail, count for much also. 95 percent of the vineyard is planted with Merlot, and 5 percent with Cabernet-Franc, yet the latter is often not included in the *grand vin* for want of maturity; Pétrus is thus frequently a 100 percent Merlot wine. The average age of the vines is forty years, where thirty or thirty-five is the norm.

The estate goes to extreme lengths to safeguard the quality of its fruit: in 1987, to counter the effect of rain at harvest-time, a helicopter was hired to hover over the vines and dry them with its down-wash; in 1992 plastic sheets were used to cover the ground and prevent the incessant rains from infiltrating the soil; and at Pétrus harvesters only pick in the afternoon, so that any dew on the fruit will have evaporated.

Polish, flesh, and opulent fruit

The wine itself is extremely concentrated, thanks to the age of the vines and to their limited production. The overwhelming impression is one of polished texture, of fleshy, opulent fruit, with, when mature, spices, chocolate, Mocha coffee, and truffles... perfectly balanced, of course, and with exceptional length. Pétrus generally reaches maturity after about fifty years, but can last for up to fifty!

What should one serve on the once-in-a-lifetime occasion? One dish this great wine particularly appreciates is roast pheasant *à la périgourdine*. A sumptuous encounter, not to be easily forgotten!

BORDEAUX
A.O.C. Pomerol

• *Wine selected:*
Le Pin

• *Grape varieties:*
  Merlot 92%, Cabernet-Franc 8%
• *Average vine age:*
  30 years
• *Vineyard size:*
  2 hectares
• *Soil type:*
  Clay, gravel and sand over hard
  iron-rich clay
• *Production:*
  6,000 bottles

Finest Vintages:
1998, 1996, 1990, 1989, 1985, 1982

Le Pin
Les Grands Champs
33500 Pomerol
Tel. (0033) 557 51 33 99
Head east out of Catusseau. At the fork,
take the left-hand (D121) road. 500
meters further, stop at Vieux Château
Certan and present yourself there.
• *Owner*: SCA du Château du Pin
• *General Manager:* Jacques Thienpont
• *On-site sales:* No
• *Visits:* By appointment
• *Price:* ★★★★★

LE PIN

The last two decades of the twentieth century saw the emergence of several fine, if tiny, new estates in the Saint-Émilion and Pomerol regions. The thoroughly untraditional, flamboyant style of these "garage" wines left no one indifferent, and their rarity and the hype surrounding them have generally had the effect of pushing their prices into orbit very quickly. Perhaps the greatest example of this phenomenon is Le Pin.

The Thienponts set themselves a challenge

In the middle of the 1970s no one had heard of Le Pin. The one-hectare vineyard belonged to a Madame Loubie, who since 1967 had rented it to a grower who produced a wine named Le Pin, à Lalande. When she died in 1979 the vineyard was bought by Marcel and Gérard Thienpont, of the large Belgian family which owns Vieux Château Certan, Château Labégorce-Zédé, and other estates. Six years later the Thienponts had the chance of buying another hectare. Instead of incorporating this land into their neighboring Vieux Château Certan, as most would have done, they decided to create a new wine, with the declared aim of proving the worth of this then underestimated piece of land.

Particularly poor soil for a great wine

The Le Pin vines are situated on the edge of the Pomerol plateau, surrounded by Vieux Château Certan, Trotanoy, Petit Village, and La Violette.

The soil is composed of gravel and clay and a little sand, and lies on Pomerol's *crasse de fer*, the hard iron-rich base. It is particularly poor—and thus all the more ideal for making great wine—because for a long time before Madame Loubie's death it had not been fertilized.

The wine, like Pétrus, is to all intents and purposes made entirely with Merlot, although there is a small quantity of old Cabernet-Franc in the blend. The yield is kept to a very low average of 30 hectoliters per hectare. The must is fermented and the wine macerated in stainless-steel vats, then transferred to new oak barrels for its malo-lactic fermentation and subsequent eighteen to twenty-four months of maturation. Le Pin is rarely filtered.

The perfect expression of Merlot

What then does this trail blazer taste like? As might be expected in a wine made entirely of Merlot, from low yields and aged in new oak, the principal impressions given by Le Pin are of lushness, opulence, and richness; of softness and sensual flesh, covering a fine tannic structure; of perfect balance and great length. It is indeed a very fine wine.

It is so easy to sip on its own, and yet a wine of this caliber really benefits from the presence of a well-chosen partner at table: truffled capon, encased in coarse-salt pastry and roasted, is a fine match, providing Le Pin with an attentive ear, encourageing it to open up and regale those present with the brilliance of its repartee.

BORDEAUX
A.O.C. Pomerol

- *Wine selected:*
  Vieux Château Certan

- *Grape varieties:*
  Merlot 60%, Cabernet-Franc 30%,
  Cabernet-Sauvignon 10%
- *Average vine age:*
  35 years
- *Vineyard size:*
  13.5 hectares
- *Soil type:*
  Gravel and sand over hard
  iron-rich clay
- *Production:*
  55,000 bottles

Finest Vintages:
1998, 1995, 1993, 1990, 1989, 1988,
1985, 1982

Vieux Château Certan
33500 Pomerol
Tel. (0033) 557 51 17 33
Head east out of Catusseau. At the
fork, take the left-hand (D121) road.
500 meters further on, Vieux Château
Certan is on the right.
- *Owner:* SC du Vieux Château Certan
- *General Manager:* Alexandre
  Thienpont
- *On-site sales:* No
- *Visits:* By appointment
- *Price:* ★★★

VIEUX CHÂTEAU CERTAN

Pomerol's reputation owes a lot to Vieux Château Certan, which during the whole of the nineteenth and the first half of the twentieth centuries was probably the region's greatest estate. It is still one of the handful of great names which form today's Pomerol aristocracy. This is an exquisite wine, and is all the more interesting for having a flavor quite unlike that of its peers.

A Scottish family in Pomerol

The Certan estate has been dedicated exclusively to viticulture since before the French Revolution. At that time it was owned by the Demay family, of Scottish origin, and covered 16 hectares.

In 1858 the estate was split when the Demays sold the bulk of it to Charles de Bousquet, keeping for themselves the small part since known as Certan de May. De Bousquet started to reconstruct the château—one of the rare ones in the area which is actually more than a farmhouse—but ran out of funds before his schemes were completed; the result is a somewhat unbalanced edifice with two towers of differing heights and materials, but which is nonetheless elegant.

The Thienponts acquire the property

Certan was acquired by its present proprietors, the Belgian Thienpont family, in 1924. Georges, the patriarch, had bought Troplong Mondot three years previously, yet he remained in Belgium at the helm of his wine business and supervised his Bordeaux properties from afar. The youngest of his many children, Léon, arrived in Bordeaux in 1949 and took on responsibility for the estate in 1965. He maintained and increased its reputation until his death in 1985. Since then Certan's fate has been in the hands of Léon's son Alexandre—and his hands have turned out to be very sure indeed.

An enclave of gravel and Cabernets

Vieux Château Certan is situated right in the heart of Pomerol's plateau, surrounded by other prestigious estates such as Pétrus, Certan de May, L'Évangile, La Conseillante, and Petit-Village. Its soil is composed of gravel and clay with a little sand, and lies over the plateau's iron-rich clay subsoil, the *crasse de fer*. Despite its geographic proximity the wine differs somewhat from those of its neighbors because of this relatively important gravel content, which gives elegance at the expense of power. And since gravel is the ideal soil for the Cabernets, these varieties are present in greater proportions in the vineyard than is usual on Pomerol's plateau.

A pure, elegant Pomerol in the Médoc style

The result is a wine of somewhat Médoc character: less opulent and with more structure, less oak-influenced and with purer fruit, more elegant and, arguably, of greater finesse. The flavor itself, unsurprisingly in view of the proportion of Cabernet, tends more towards blackcurrant, with hints of mint, than stone-fruit.

This wine makes a wonderful partner for winged game: roast pheasant with chestnut stuffing is an appreciative dining companion, sufficiently well-mannered to afford the Certan the space it needs to demonstrate the depth and finesse of its poetry. Vieux Château Certan is without any doubt one of Pomerol's greatest wines.

BORDEAUX
A.O.C. Pessac-Léognan

• *Wine selected:*
Domaine de Chevalier white
Cru Classé

• *Grape varieties:*
Sauvignon 70%, Sémillon 30%
• *Average vine age:*
30 years
• *Vineyard size:*
4 hectares
• *Soil type:*
Black sand over clayey gravel
• *Production:*
15,000 bottles

Finest Vintages:
2000, 1999, 1996, 1992,
1990, 1985, 1983

Domaine de Chevalier
102 Chemin de Mignoy
33850 Léognan
Tel. (0033) 556 64 16 16
Internet:www.domainedechevalier.com
From the centre of Léognan take the
road towards Cestas. Go past the
church and take the second left turn
about some 500 m further on (Château
Haut Bergey marks the spot). Chevalier
is on the right shortly thereafter.
• *Owner:* : SC du Domaine de
Chevalier
• *Managing-Director:* Olivier Bernard
• *On-site sales:* No
• *Visits:* By appointment
• *Price:* ★★★★

DOMAINE DE CHEVALIER

South of Léognan there is a handsome, modern property surrounded by woods, which has never had the pretension (unlike a good number of less significant addresses) to ennoble itself with the title Château. There is a lack of ceremony here, and a charming young proprietor who puts his visitors at ease. Yet, once they sample his wines, they realize they are face to face with grandeur, for both the red and the white Chevalier are unmistakably great wines.

A vanishing vineyard reappears

It was a man called Chibaley who carved out the estate and planted the vineyard, at some time before 1763. Gradually the name became corrupted to Chevalier. The wine gained a reputation, and then, for some unknown reason, the vines were uprooted and replaced by pines. Fortunately a Bordeaux *négociant* called Jean Ricard, who owned the Léognan estate of Malartic-Lagravière, had not forgotten the great wine produced in this clearing in the woods. In 1865 he purchased the property and replanted it with vines. On his death Ricard left Chevalier to his son-in-law, Gabriel Beaumartin, who re-established the wine among the best produced in the Graves. In 1942 the estate was inherited by his son-in-law, coincidentally also named Jean Ricard, who in turn handed over the reins in 1948 to his son Claude.

Claude Ricard leaves his mark

Previously a concert pianist, Claude had studied wine making under the renowned Professor Peynaud at Bordeaux University, and thanks to his unstinting work the wines were classified *Grand Cru* in 1959, and the estate's reputation abroad acquired. One of his priorities was to perfect the white Chevalier wine, and he introduced the Sauternes practice of harvesting by successive passages through the vineyard, in order to pick only the grapes which had reached perfect ripeness. The wine attained a reputation as one of France's greatest, a worthy stable-mate to its exquisite red.

In 1983, as a result of inheritance problems, Claude Ricard and his brothers and sisters had to sell the property. The purchaser was the Lucien Bernard distillery family. The young Olivier Bernard was offered the chance of running the estate, and Claude stayed on as manager, helping him acquire a deep understanding of its nature. Since then Olivier and his team have worked hard, reviewing every aspect of the business: the winery has been rebuilt and re-equipped, the vineyard is today fully planted at a density of 10,000 vines per hectare (6,500 is the norm), the frost problem specific to this vineyard in the woods has been addressed by partial clearing of trees. No stone has been left unturned in the quest for quality.

Limited production and exacting standards

The Domaine's white wine is much sought-after by connoisseurs. Oliver Bernard has limited its vineyard to 4 hectares, the most he can process while maintaining the wine's splendid quality. Fermented in oak, it is full-bodied and richly flavored, fat and succulent, but with a certain austerity not found in its peers. It needs time to develop—a good decade at least—and is rich and intense on the palate, with impeccable balance. Essentially honeyed, it takes on nut flavors with time, and can resemble a dry Sauternes. At table, this grandee appreciates the company of lobster, grilled on a spit.

BORDEAUX
A.O.C. Pessac-Léognan

- *Wine selected:*
  Château de Fieuzal

- *Grape varieties:*
  Sauvignon 50%, Sémillon 50%
- *Average vine age:*
  30 years
- *Vineyard size:*
  10 hectares
- *Soil type:*
  Deep gravel
- *Production:*
  35,000 bottles

Finest Vintages:
2000, 1999, 1996, 1995

Château de Fieuzal
124 Avenue de Mont-de-Marsan
33850 Léognan
Tel. (0033) 556 64 77 86
Leave Léognan by the Saucats road.
Fieuzal is approximately 1.5 km down
on the right.
- *Owner:* : S.A. du Château de Fieuzal
- *Chairman & Managing Director:*
  Gérard Gribelin
- *General Manager:* Jean-Luc Marchive
- *On-site sales:* Yes
- *Visits:* By appointment
- *Price:* ★★★

CHÂTEAU DE FIEUZAL

Besides producing a fine red, which earned it its inclusion in the original 1953 classification of the Graves wines, Château de Fieuzal is one of the region's foremost names in white wine production. Fieuzal was not classified for that, because its tiny production made it ineligible. Happily, today the estate is making commercial quantities of it.

Dereliction and renaissance

In 1892 Alfred de Griffon sold Fieuzal, a sixteenth-century property named after its previous owners, to Abel Ricard, a member of the family which already had interests in Domaine de Chevalier and Malartic-Lagravière. The wine of that era must have been good, for one of his customers was Pope Leo XIII. However the estate then went through the same problems as many of its fellows during the Great War I and the depression that followed it, and gradually fell into a state of dereliction. Ricard died during the Second World War, and his daughter Odette and her Swedish husband Eric Bocké subsequently took it over.

The birth of a white wine

One of the first tasks they undertook was the replanting of the vineyard, and as well as black-grape vines they decided to plant a few rows of white. The estate was gradually hauled back to its previous standard, and in 1953 the owners' pains were duly rewarded with the classification of the red wine. Odette Bocké died in 1974, and her husband sold the estate shortly afterwards to Georges Nègrevergne.

Nègrevergne's son-in-law Gérard Gribelin was given the task of running the estate, and it is his dynamism, perfectionism, and ambition that have lifted Fieuzal to its present, previously unknown, heights. The new prosperity resulting from its increasing reputation and sales has enabled Gribelin to enlarge the vineyard and invest in new wine-making equipment—and the wines have obviously benefited still further. In 1994 Nègrevergne's heirs sold the château to the *Banque Populaire*; Gérard Gribelin nevertheless continues to run the estate.

Complex wines for laying down

The red is definitely a wine for aging; it is quite full-bodied, rich, and structured for a Léognan wine, and with time develops finesse and a fine complexity of flavors. However, it is the white wine that has really made wine lovers sit up in the last decade. In 1984 Gribelin started vinifying it in oak barrels, and, after fermentation, leaving it on its lees, which are regularly stirred up, for roughly a year. These two changes of practice have given the wine a great increase in flavor, complexity, and fatness, and the wherewithal for improvement in bottle over a dozen or so years.

Citrus flavors and an opulent texture

When young the wine is redolent of citrus fruit and peaches, well balanced with oak flavors and fine acidity. As it develops in bottle, it frequently acquires a honeyed, nutty aspect to complement the fruit, while the oak becomes more discreet and the texture more fat, even opulent.

This wine gets on famously with many fish or white meats in sauce, and with goat's cheeses; however, any hedonist wishing to push his or her gastronomic horizons a little further should open the white Fieuzal 1985 and serve it with a pike, barded with bacon, roasted, and served with lentils!

BORDEAUX
A.O.C. Pessac-Léognan

- *Wine selected:*
  Château Haut-Bailly
  Cru Classé

- *Grape varieties:*
  Cabernet-Sauvignon 65%,
  Merlot 25%, Cabernet-Franc 10%
- *Average vine age:*
  30 years
- *Vineyard size:*
  29 hectares
- *Soil type:*
  Gravel and sand over alios
- *Production:*
  120,000 bottles

Finest Vintages:
1999, 1998, 1996, 1990,
1989, 1988, 1983

Château Haut-Bailly
33850 Léognan
Tel. (0033) 556 64 75 11
Follow the RN113 from Bordeaux to
Cadaujac. On arriving at Cadaujac turn
right onto the Léognan road. Go past
Carbonnieux, turn right onto the
D651E3, then pass before La Louvière
before arriving at Haut-Bailly,
approximately 4 km from Cadaujac.
- *Owner:* : Bob Wilmers
- *Director:* Jean Sanders
- *On-site sales:* Yes
- *Visits:* By appointment
- *Price:* ★★★

CHÂTEAU HAUT-BAILLY

There are a certain number of Bordeaux wines which can be safely recommended to even the most exacting wine lover, whatever vintage is at hand. Château Haut-Bailly is one such wine. It is superb, whatever the quality of the year; thoroughly satisfying, and demonstrating admirably the special soft, smoky, cedary character which makes many Léognan wines so irresistible.

Cognac in the barrels, and ungrafted vines

It was Alcide Bellot des Minières who from 1872 established Haut-Bailly at the forefront of Graves' finest, and towards the end of the century it was regularly selling at the prices of top Médoc *Deuxièmes Crus*. Apparently the wine was helped somewhat by a practice which would be frowned on today: the owner had the habit of cleaning out his barrels with small quantities of cognac, and "forgetting" to empty them before filling them with wine!

Des Minières was a noted opponent of the practice of grafting vines onto American rootstock, the method reluctantly adopted by everyone as the only way of defeating the phylloxera aphid which ravaged vineyards everywhere from the 1860s onwards. Some 25 percent of the Haut-Bailly vineyard is still made up of very old "French" vines.

Daniel Sanders stops the rot

Des Minières died in 1906, and the property subsequently passed through many pairs of hands. It gradually fell into neglect. At the time of the first classification of the Graves wines in 1953 there remained a mere 9 hectares planted, and the château and wine buildings were in dire need of renovation.

In 1955 the estate was purchased by Daniel Sanders, a Bordeaux wine merchant of Belgian origin. Sanders gradually reconstituted the vineyard and regained for the wine its excellent reputation by dint of painstaking traditional wine making. He died in 1980 and was succeeded with great flair by his son Jean, who remains in charge today despite the sale of the estate in 1998 to the American Bob Wilmers.

Traditional wine-making for exemplary fruit

Of course, wines of this quality are only born in well-sited vineyards. The Haut-Bailly vineyard, consisting of one single parcel, is on the highest ground of the Léognan commune, and benefits from natural drainage. The soil is composed of gravel rich in sandstone, on a base of hard sandstone rock.

After harvesting, the grapes undergo a rigorous quality control before being vinified in the traditional manner, following which the vats are also subjected to a rigorous scrutiny to decide what will or will not be bottled as *grand vin*. The wine is subsequently matured for eighteen months in oak, of which some 50 percent is renewed for richer vintages.

A seductive, warm, and smoky flavor

The end result manages to combine richness and finesse, structure and softness—indeed it has so much appeal that many tasters assume that Merlot is its principal grape variety. Haut-Bailly has a seductive, warm, smoky, black fruit flavor, which often develops roast coffee and cedary nuances with age.

Jean Sanders is against recommending any gastronomic combinations involving his wine, since, as he rightly points out, factors such as the weather, the people around the table, their mood, and the cook's talent can make or break any recommended combination.

BORDEAUX
A.O.C. Pessac-Léognan

- *Wine selected:*
  Château Haut-Brion
  Premier Cru Classé

- *Grape varieties:*
  Cabernet-Sauvignon 45%, Merlot 37%
- *Average vine age:*
  36 years
- *Vineyard size:*
  43 hectares
- *Soil type:*
  Gravel over sandy clay subsoil
- *Production:*
  225,000 bottles

Finest Vintages:

1998, 1996, 1995, 1990, 1989,
1988, 1986, 1985, 1982

Château Haut-Brion

133, avenue Jean-Jaurès
33600 Pessac
Tel. (0033) 556 00 29 30
Leave the centre of Bordeaux by the
rue de Pessac. Cross the boulevard
and follow the Cours du Maréchal-
Galliéni (N250); the entrance to Haut-
Brion is about 1.8 km further along, on
the right. If coming from out of town,
leave the Rocade by exit no. 13
(Alouette Pessac Centre). Head
towards the centre of town, either by
Avenue Pasteur and Avenue Jean-
Jaurès, or by the route indicated
"Pessac Centre", then "Les Échoppes",
which takes one down Rue de Madran,
Rue du Docteur-Nancel and Avenue
Jean-Jaurès. Haut-Brion is about 1 km
from the Rocade, on the left.
- *Owner:* Domaine Clarence Dillon S.A.
- *Assistant Managing Director:*
  Jean-Bernard Delmas
- *On-site sales:* No
- *Visits:* By appointment
- *Price:* ★★★★★

CHÂTEAU HAUT-BRION

In 1855 just one estate from outside the Médoc was included in the classification of the Gironde's red wines, but the sheer quality of that wine made it out of the question to exclude it. Château Haut-Brion was ranked *Premier Cru*, and today it goes on proving with outstanding regularity the worthiness of its rank.

An international reputation from early on

The great Haut-Brion estate was created in 1533 by Jean de Pontac. From the outset the de Pontacs had ambitions for their wine, steadily improving it and enlarging the vineyard. Arnaud III de Pontac put into practice new vinification techniques such as topping up the wine in barrels and racking, with the aim of giving his wine aging potential. The wine started trickling out onto export markets, notably England, where "New French Claret" was coming into fashion. It was the first Bordeaux wine to be explicitly referred to by name there, when the diarist Samuel Pepys mentioned having tasted "Ho-Bryan" in the Royal Oak Tavern in London.

The estate remained in the De Pontac family until 1801, when it passed into the hands of Napoleon's Foreign Minister, de Talleyrand. The wine, as a result, was served at numerous grand functions, and its prestige increased accordingly. Then in 1836 the estate was acquired by a banker, Joseph Larrieu, and remained in his family until 1923. The Larrieus were passionately committed to their wine, but by 1922 there were so many members of the family with a stake in the property that this created insurmountable problems. Haut-Brion had to be sold.

The estate passes into American ownership

Its purchaser was one of New York's greatest financiers, Clarence Dillon. Legend has it that Dillon set off in his limousine one freezing and foggy day to purchase Château Cheval Blanc, also for sale at the time. However the thirty-five-kilometer drive in the fog was not practicable, and, passing Haut-Brion, he decided that that estate would be equally acceptable. It is his granddaughter Joan, Duchesse de Mouchy, who is today at the helm, as President of the Domaine Clarence Dillon S.A. Haut-Brion is fortunate in being run by Jean-Bernard Delmas, one of France's foremost experts in viticulture and ampelogy; his mastery of vine-clone selection in Haut-Brion's fine deep gravel soil has ensured that the wine continues to be one of Bordeaux's top wines.

The hallmarks of a great wine

Silkiness, breeding, and concentration of flavor are its hallmarks. In its youth it often seems more lightweight than the great Médocs, but this impression is deceptive; Haut-Brion improves with aging over long periods just as much as its peers. The exquisite 1953 is perfect now: silky and regal, with nuances of game, black truffles, leather, and spice. Its finesse is underlined by simple, top-quality fare, such as a fillet of beef, with a pan-fried assortment of wild mushrooms and a potato gratin. The estate also produces minute quantities of one of France's greatest dry white wines, fermented and aged in oak barrels.

BORDEAUX
A.O.C. Pessac-Léognan

- *Wine selected:*
  Château Laville-Haut-Brion
  Cru Classé

- *Grape varieties:*
  Sémillon 70%, Sauvignon 27%,
  Muscadelle 3%
- *Average vine age:*
  51 years
- *Vineyard size:*
  3.7 hectares
- *Soil type:*
  Gravel over sandy clay
- *Production:*
  13,000 bottles

Finest Vintages:
1997, 1996, 1994, 1990, 1989, 1985

Château Laville-Haut-Brion
33602 Pessac cedex
Tel. (0033) 556 00 29 30
See Château Haut-Brion. Laville Haut-
Brion is opposite, on the other side of
the road.
- *Owner:* : Domaine Clarence Dillon S.A.
- *Assistant Managing Director:*
  Jean-Bernard Delmas
- *On-site sales:* No
- *Visits:* By appointment
- *Price:* ★★★/★★★★

CHÂTEAU LAVILLE-HAUT-BRION

Unfortunately for wine lovers, Château Laville Haut-Brion is not easy to come by, for its vineyard is minute, and demand for the wine greatly exceeds supply. However, this is one of France's greatest dry white wines, and as such, rare though it is, any lover of rich complex whites that improve with keeping should at least once in his life make the effort to find a bottle of it.

Frédéric Woltner plants his white vineyard

Laville Haut-Brion is a young wine. The parcel that constitutes today's vineyard was originally a demarcated part of Château La Tour Haut-Brion, a red-wine vineyard, and was farmed in the seventeen th century by Arnaud de Laville. After the Revolution the plot kept his name. It passed through the hands of Pierre David Bouscasse, then Léopold Bibonne, and at some stage was reincorporated into the vineyard of La Tour Haut-Brion.

When Frédéric Woltner started making the La Tour wine in 1920, he noticed that a part of the vineyard, this same de Laville plot on the southern side, did not have the same soil; the gravel was less deep than elsewhere, and had a higher clay content, making it less well-adapted to red-wine production. In 1923 he pulled out the Cabernet and Merlot vines and substituted them with Sémillon and Sauvignon, the noble varieties that produce the great white Graves and Sauternes wines, and in 1928 produced the first vintage of white wine.

Steel gives way to oak

As with his red wines, the white rapidly became a textbook example of what could be produced with great land and an inspired wine maker. At first Woltner made it in the same revolutionary glass-lined steel vats he introduced at La Mission; under Jean-Bernard Delmas' aegis it is now fermented and aged in new oak barrels, which give it the richness and structure for prolonged improvement in bottle.

A fascinating range of flavors

As with all serious Graves and Sauternes, the full use of oak (adapted to the quality of the vintage) adds its valuable contribution, not only by allowing the maturing wine to breathe but also by adding to its palette of flavors. In young vintages the oak flavors are very noticeable, but with time these blend with the other aromas to give a fat, luscious wine with honeyed and sometimes spicy nuances. When very old, Laville develops nutty, toffee, even caramel flavors and sometimes resembles a dry Sauternes.

Unusual gastronomic possibilities

A wine with such a complex personality is a wine for the table. Only the most appreciative of wine-loving friends should be invited. At this memorable feast, one's best mature bottle of Laville should be brought up from the cellar, to be served with lobsters grilled on a spit, barded pike roasted and served with lentils, or oysters cooked au gratin. The guests will not forget that evening in a hurry!

BORDEAUX
A.O.C. Pessac-Léognan

- *Wine selected:*
  Château La Mission-Haut-Brion
  Cru Classé

- *Grape varieties:*
  Cabernet-Sauvignon 48%,
  Merlot 45%, Cabernet-Franc 7%
- *Average vine age:*
  21 years
- *Vineyard size:*
  20.9 hectares
- *Soil type:*
  Gravel over sandy clay
- *Production:*
  108 000 bottles

Finest Vintages:
1998, 1996, 1990, 1989, 1988, 1982

Château La Mission-Haut-Brion
33602 Pessac cedex
Tel. (0033) 556 00 29 30
See Château Haut-Brion. La Mission-
Haut-Brion is its neighbor.
- *Owner:* : Domaine Clarence Dillon S.A.
- *Assistant Managing Director:*
  Jean-Bernard Delmas
- *On-site sales:* No
- *Visits:* By appointment
- *Price:* ★★★/★★★★

Château La Mission-Haut-Brion

The origins of the estate of La Mission-Haut-Brion are uncertain: was it at one time part of the Pontac family's Château Haut-Brion? What we do know of its history as an independent property goes back some three hundred years. But it has only been during this century, thanks to inspired and talented owners, that it has been a model of consistency and greatness. La Mission is today one of Bordeaux's finest wines.

A succession of proprietors

The first documented owners of the estate were the Lestonnac family. Olive de Lestonnac in 1664 bequeathed her vineyard to the Congregation of Priests of the Mission, a missionary order also known as the Lazarists. The missionaries enlarged the vineyard and built a chapel there, which still stands today. On the consecration of the chapel in 1698 the estate and its wine became known by the name of La Mission-Haut-Brion. The Revolution brought an end to the missionaries' tenure. The State sequestered the property and sold it off to Martial-Victor Vaillant, and it subsequently changed hands five times before the start of what one could term its modern era, when in 1919 it was acquired by the Woltners.

An inspired and talented wine-making family

Frédéric Woltner was an inspired wine maker with a burning and continual desire to improve his wine. When he bought the property, it was in a fairly run-down state. He re-equipped the vathouse with glass-lined steel fermentation vats, unheard-of at the time, to give him greater control of the temperature of the fermenting must. Stainless steel vats with automatic thermoregulation are now, of course, commonplace in almost all top Bordeaux properties.

Frédéric's son Henri took over on his death in 1933, and continued the Woltner quest for perfection; his obsession was with fermenting at a relatively cool temperature, in order to retain many of the volatile aromatic elements and increase the wine's complexity. Henri Woltner died in 1974, and control of the property passed to the Dewavrin branch of the family.

In 1983, as a result of family differences, it was decided to sell La Mission. The buyer was Domaine Clarence Dillon, the owner of the vineyard across the road, Haut-Brion.

Surrounded by the Bordeaux suburbs

La Mission and its stablemates La Tour, Laville and Haut-Brion itself are hemmed in by urban sprawl, and it is estimated that the vineyards are one degree warmer as a result— which is, of course, a boon for ripening grapes. The vines lie on a rise of some twenty-five meters, in very deep gravel lying on a subsoil of sand and clay; the drainage here is excellent.

To power and flavor comes elegance

When tasting La Mission alongside its *Premier Cru* brother, the difference between the two personalities is striking: La Mission is powerful and full-flavored, while Haut-Brion is softer, more elegant and more refined. In the Woltner days, La Mission was supremely concentrated, fat and voluptuous, yet with a formidable tannic structure making it a wine which required long keeping. Under the Haut-Brion team it seems to have gained in silkiness, elegance, and harmony—yet it still retains its manly concentration, and fascinating aromatic complexity. This is a wine to open with very special friends, on a chilly October evening, and to serve with jugged hare.

BORDEAUX
A.O.C. Pessac-Léognan

- *Wine selected:*
  Château Pape Clément
  Cru Classé

- *Grape varieties:*
  Cabernet-Sauvignon 60%, Merlot
  40%
- *Average vine age:*
  40 years
- *Vineyard size:*
  30 hectares
- *Soil type:*
  Gravel with clay and sand over
  limestone
- *Production:*
  80,000 bottles

Finest Vintages:

2000, 1999, 1996, 1990, 1989, 1988,
1986

Château Pape Clément
216 Avenue du Docteur-Nancel-Pénard
33600 Pessac
Tel. (0033) 557 26 38 38
Internet: www.pape-clement.com
Leave the centre of Bordeaux by the
Rue de Pessac. Cross the boulevard
and follow the Cours du Maréchal-
Galliéni (N250), then the Rue du
Docteur-Nancel-Pénard; the entrance
to Pape Clément is on the left.
- *Owner*s: Léo Montagne
  & Bernard Magrez
- *Director:* Eric Larramona
- *On-site sales:* No
- *Visits:* With 48 hours' notice
- *Price:* ★★★

CHÂTEAU PAPE CLÉMENT

The very oldest of today's Bordeaux wine-producing estates, Château Pape Clément, having made wine for some 630 years, very nearly ceased to exist in the 1930s—as a result of a brief owner's lack of interest, and a hailstorm. Fortunately, a saviour was waiting in the wings, and Pape Clément is now alive and well, a venerable seven hundred-year-old which fully deserves its place in wine lovers' cellars.

The wine of the Pope and Archbishops

The estate's first known owner, Bertrand de Goth, Archbishop of Bordeaux from 1299, was in 1306 elected Pope, and chose the name Clément V. He installed the papacy at Avignon, and left his Pessac estate to the archbishopric of Bordeaux, in whose hands it remained until it was confiscated at the time of the Revolution. Throughout their tenure the wine was known as Vigne du Pape-Clément, and was reserved by the ecclesiastics for their own use.

A poet comes to the rescue

After the Revolution the property had a succession of owners, of whom a Monsieur J. B. Clerc seems to have been the most inspired, bringing its standards and reputation in the 1860s to a high level. Unfortunately, the estate's owner during the inter war years was not of the same stamp, and let it run down to such an extent that production almost ceased. Its death knell was almost sounded by a savage hailstorm in 1937, which destroyed most of the remaining vines. At that time the concrete and tarmac of new Bordeaux suburbs were marching inexorably in the direction of Pessac, and the vineyard was hungrily eyed by property developers. Pape Clément was rescued at the last moment by the poet Paul Montagne, who purchased it in 1939 and put in place a program of replanting in the vineyard and renovation of the wine-making facilities and château.

Pape Clément's renaissance, somewhat retarded by the war, was heralded by its magnificent 1953 vintage, and the following twenty years produced many fine wines. There was a slip in quality during the decade following the 1975 vintage, attributed by many to lack of investment, which was smartly reversed as soon as the investment was forthcoming. In 2001, the quest for quality led to the installation of oak fermentation vats, the use of gravity every step of the way from the vineyard to the barrel, and the destalking, grape by grape, of the entire crop by hand. Montagne's descendants, aided by the talented estate-director Eric Larramona, today maintain the wine's quality and reputation with brio.

Smoky, roasted, and mineral flavors

The vineyard, made up of two parcels, is composed of gravel on a limestone base. In character the wine is fragrant, soft, and elegant, with concentrated black fruit flavors on the palate and smoky, roasted, and mineral nuances. Despite its softness, it is a wine with a significant tannic and acid structure which ages well over several decades.

It shows well alongside many meats, and could be served with feathered game, for instance, or a succulent and tender morsel of braised veal. Indeed younger, tannic vintages even hold their own well against creamy cheeses.

Pape-Clément is known as a red-wine estate, yet it has for a long time produced small quantities of a very fine barrel-fermented white, which is improved by bottle age.

BORDEAUX
A.O.C. Pessac-Léognan

- *Wine selected:*
Château Smith-Haut-Lafitte

- *Grape varieties:*
  Sauvignon Blanc 95%,
  Sauvignon Gris 5%
- *Average vine age:*
  35 years
- *Vineyard size:*
  10 hectares
- *Soil type:*
  Deep gravel
- *Production:*
  35,000 bottles

Finest Vintages:
1999, 1998, 1997, 1995

Château Smith-Haut-Lafitte
33650 Martillac
Tel. (0033) 557 83 11 22
From Bordeaux's Rocade take the Toulouse-Langon highway, and turn off at the first exit (direction Martillac-Montesquieu). At the roundabout turn right (RN 113), follow the road briefly, then turn left 50 meters after the Esso garage, into the Chemin de la Morelle. Follow this road for 1 km, then turn right at the crossroads and follow the signs to Smith-Haut-Lafitte.

- *Owners:* Daniel and Florence Cathiard
- *On-site sales:* Yes
- *Visits:* By appointment
- *Price:* ★★★

CHÂTEAU SMITH-HAUT-LAFITTE

One of the most complete turnarounds of an established but under-performing Bordeaux wine estate in recent times has been that of Château Smith-Haut-Lafitte, in the northern Graves. Smith's renaissance dates from its purchase in 1990 by Daniel and Florence Cathiard, both of whom, after highly successful business careers, sought a new challenge, which they found in the gravel of Martillac.

A long viticultural history

As far back as 1365, the gravel plateau on which Smith lies (*fitte* is a word from the Middle Ages meaning "mound") was put to viticulture, first by the du Boscq family, who remained there until 1549, and then by the Verdier family. In 1720 the Verdiers sold the estate to a Scotsman called George Smith, who exported large quantities of his newly named wine to England on his own ships. In 1856 the mayor of Bordeaux, Sadi Duffour-Dubergier, bought the estate. By the end of the century it consisted of 68 hectares of red wine and 5 of white wine vineyards, and the wines fetched the price of a Médoc *Quatrième* or *Cinquième cru*.

The Duffour-Dubergier tenure came to an end in 1902, with the sale of Smith to a German *Handelsgesellschaft* (commercial company). That same year the *négociant* firm Eschenauer entered into an exclusive contract for the production of the wine. At the onset of World War I, the estate, being enemy property, was sequestered by the government, and was eventually sold off after the war to the French Treasurer-General in Indochina.

Long and gradual decline

Eschenauer continued to produce and market the wine, and took advantage of the chance to buy the property in 1958. A program of costly investments was put under way, but it would seem that Eschenauer's ambitions were not compatible with the firm's means, for the wine from this period on went through a period of decline. The estate was eventually put up for sale, and was purchased by its present owners in 1990.

The Cathiards take on a challenge

Daniel and Florence Cathiard were new to the world of wine. To the relief of many, they intended from the start to have a hands on approach, and applied themselves to learning about wine making. They invested heavily in new equipment, and one of their first acts was to get rid of the mechanical harvester. By dint of rigor and ecology in the vineyard, restriction of the yields, severe selection of the grapes harvested, and meticulous vinification, the wines made great strides—particularly the white, which was rapidly lauded by the world's experts.

Two wines back on key

Until the 1993 vintage the red wine could have been criticized for being too lean and somewhat one-dimensional—but not since! With the succeeding vintages it has gained in body and complexity, while retaining its habitual silky texture and perfect balance. The white wine positively explodes with flavor. Exotic fruit rub shoulders with minerals, grass, and toasted wood, all coated in a magnificent fleshy opulence, and kept alert by perfect acidity. This wine makes an excellent *apéritif*, and also gets along well with fish and white meat in sauce, and shellfish; Florence Cathiard also recommends serving it with lightly spiced oriental dishes.

BORDEAUX
A.O.C. Sauternes

- *Wine selected:*
  Château de Fargues

- *Grape varieties:*
  Sémillon 80%, Sauvignon 20%
- *Average vine age:*
  35 years
- *Vineyard size:*
  15 hectares
- *Soil type:*
  Gravel over clay and gravel
- *Production:*
  12,000 bottles

Finest Vintages:
1995, 1990, 1989, 1988, 1986, 1983

Château de Fargues
33210 Fargues-de-Langon
Tel. (0033) 557 98 04 20
Once in the village of Fargues (take the
D125 if driving from Preignac), look out
for the imposing ruins of the old
château. The estate entry, opposite the
village school, is heralded by a long
alley of umbrella-pines.
- *Owners:* Lur-Saluces family
- *General Manager:* François Amirault
- *On-site sales:* Yes
- *Visits:* By appointment
- *Price:* ★★★★

CHÂTEAU DE FARGUES

There are several Sauternes wines which for one reason or another were not classified in 1855, yet which command prices and have reputations equal or superior to those of the *Premiers Crus*. One of these is the rare and exquisite Château de Fargues.

One owner since 1472

Fargues belongs to the owner of Château d'Yquem, the Comte Alexandre de Lur-Saluces, and is made by the same exacting methods. What more need one say? The property has been in his family since 1472, when Izabelle de Monferrand, heiress to the Château de Fargues, married Pierre de Lur. In 1586 their descendant, on wedding the daughter of the Marquis de Saluces, changed his name to Lur-Saluces.

The birth of a sweet wine

Fargues is a large polycultural estate, and red wine was part of its production for a long time. It was only in the 1930s that Bertrand de Lur-Saluces, the present incumbent's uncle, decided to give up the production of red and dedicate his best plots to the white *liquoreux* variety, and the first bottling of Fargues Sauternes was in 1943. The wine therefore has no classification. From the outset the owner's intention was to produce as great a wine as the *terroir* made possible, with the same quest for perfect quality, at whatever financial sacrifice, as at Yquem.

Exacting viticulture and vinification

The two wines are made with identical proportions of Sémillon and Sauvignon grapes, identical vineyard treatments and identical harvesting procedures, involving picking by repeated passages in order to gather only sufficiently "nobly" rotten grapes; the only slight difference is that Fargues is made in barrels already used once at Yquem, not in new wood as at Yquem. However there is a similarly long period of maturation—more than 3 years—before bottling, and it goes without saying that the wine is never filtered.

Nectar which can be mistaken for Yquem

Tasting it on its own, it is easy to mistake Fargues for Yquem. It is only on comparing the two that one tastes the difference. What sets Yquem apart is its phenomenal depth and complexity, and its sublime richness. But then, we are comparing Fargues with a unique, unrivaled wine! Considering that Fargues costs less than half the price of its stablemate, it is great value; it is just a shame that so little of it is produced.

When finally one manages to procure a bottle of this nectar, it deserves to be sipped on its own initially, for the sheer hedonistic pleasure. It could then be served with a *foie gras* of duck *en terrine*, followed by cold jellied chicken served with selected vegetables and truffles *en feuilleté*. Then a brief tête-à-tête with some good Roquefort, and finally, to round off this memorable encounter, a little light-hearted dallying with an unsugared fruit tart.

BORDEAUX
A.O.C. Sauternes

- *Wine selected:*
  Château Gilette

- *Grape varieties:*
  Sémillon 90%, Sauvignon 8%,
  Muscadelle 2%
- *Average vine age:*
  50 years
- *Vineyard size:*
  4.5 hectares
- *Soil type:*
  Sandy gravel over limestone
- *Production:*
  6,000 bottles

Finest Vintages:
1979, 1978, 1976, 1975, 1970,
1967 (Cuvée "Crème de tête")

Château Gilette
33210 Preignac
Tel. (0033) 556 76 28 44
Château Gilette's office and cellars are
behind Preignac's church, in a recently-
renovated building with blue doors.
- *Owners:* Christian Médeville
- *On-site sales:* Yes
- *Visits:* By appointment
- *Price:* ★★★★

CHÂTEAU GILETTE

Diners in a number of the most prestigious restaurants in Europe, running their eyes down the wine list, will come across a Sauternes which they may well not have heard of: Château Gilette. It will be listed beside the best *Premier Cru* wines, although it is not itself classified. They will then notice that the vintages proposed are mature classics, obtainable with difficulty today. And therein lies the secret of this wine's originality and greatness.

A highly original maturation process

Gilette's originality lies in its *élevage*, or maturation, prior to bottling. Up until that stage it is made like all other top Sauternes, by waiting for the hoped-for appearance of the fungus *Botrytis cinerea*, by picking bunches or individual grapes as they become sufficiently shriveled by the fungus, and then by vinifying slowly at a fairly low temperature.

It is at this point that Christian Médeville, Gilette's owner and maker, departs from normal practice. Instead of maturing the wine in oak casks, he uses large tanks, and he leaves his wine in these not for around two years, but for over fifteen! The first year is spent in stainless steel, after which the wine is transferred to sealed cement tanks for its lengthy sojourn before being bottled. And finally, as if he could not bear to part with his treasures, Médeville, known as the Antiquary of Sauternes, then matures them for some four years in bottle before letting his eager clients carry them off.

As a result of this extended aging, Gilette is at least twenty years old when it comes onto the market, long after most of its peers of the same year have been consumed. And it is a remarkable twenty-year-old which juxtaposes exuberant youthful freshness and rich, mature Sauternes aromas.

A procedure born of hard times

The difficult interwar years gave birth to this procedure. Gilette, owned by the Médeville family since 1822, is a tiny property—it was not classified in 1855 because no one had heard of it—and when Christian Médeville's father René inherited it in the 1930s, it was so unprofitable that the purchase of new oak barrels was out of the question. Rather than subject it to old barrels or sell it off in bulk, he preferred to hold on to the wine, and had concrete tanks built for the purpose. He had unwittingly hit on an innovative idea, and was no doubt amazed on eventually tasting the results.

Different qualities depending on the year

The greatest vintages give birth to a *crème de tête* wine, while in merely good vintages Médeville produces a Gilette *doux*; some years there are both, while in poor years there is neither, the wine being sold off in bulk.

This marvelous wine merits a little culinary daring: one should try serving it with a stew of capons stuffed with *foie gras*, or with *langoustes thermidor*, for an experience which guests will remember for long afterwards. And the meal can be brought to an end sipping Gilette alongside a plum tart or a pear and pine seed pudding.

BORDEAUX
A.O.C. Sauternes

- *Wine selected:*
  Château Lafaurie-Peyraguey
  Premier Cru Classé

- *Grape varieties:*
  Sémillon 90%, Sauvignon 5%,
  Muscadelle 5%
- *Average vine age:*
  30 years
- *Vineyard size:*
  41 hectares
- *Soil type:*
  Pyrenean gravel
- *Production:*
  56,000 bottles

Finest Vintages:

1999, 1998, 1997, 1996, 1995,
1990, 1989, 1988, 1986, 1983

Château Lafaurie-Peyraguey
33210 Bommes
Tel. (0033) 556 76 60 54
From Preignac take the D8 southwards
towards Villandraut. After about 5 km
turn right at the D116 crossroads.
Continue for 1.5 km, then turn left
onto the D125. Lafaurie-Peyraguey
is on the right shortly thereafter.
- *On-site sales:* No
- *Visits:* By appointment
  (Tel. 05 56 95 53 00)
- *Price:* ★★

CHÂTEAU LAFAURIE-PEYRAGUEY

On a site just to the west of Château d'Yquem, in the walls of a fortified castle dating from the thirteenth century, lies one of Sauternes' finest estates: Château Lafaurie-Peyraguey. Exactly when vines were first planted here we cannot be sure. The first recorded wine maker was Baron de Pichard, owner of Château Lafite and the Barsac estate Château Coutet.

A succession of proprietors

The estate was confiscated at the time of the Revolution, following the flight into exile of the Baron, and sold to a Monsieur Lafaurie, a highly esteemed wine maker. It was he who first gained the wine its reputation; when he purchased Lafaurie-Peyraguey, the wine was reckoned to be of *Deuxième Cru* standard, yet by the time of the 1855 classification of the Sauternes wines he had raised it to such a level that it was rated third best of all the wines of the region, and duly awarded *Premier Cru* status.

Lafaurie died soon afterwards, and the estate passed to his wife's new husband, and then to Count Duchâtel, the owner of Château Lagrange. By 1875 the Count and his wife had both died, and, in order to resolve inheritance problems, their children put the property up for sale. In the end it was sold in two parts, and the Clos Haut-Peyraguey came into being. The reduced Lafaurie-Peyraguey was acquired by two men, Monsieur Farinel and Grédy, who in 1913 also acquired a neighboring estate, Château Barrail-Peyraguey, and incorporated it into the *Premier Cru*. However they let the quality of the wine slip somewhat.

Finally, in 1917 Lafaurie-Peyraguey was bought by the Bordeaux *négociant* Désiré Cordier. It remained in the hands of the family company, Domaines Cordier, until 1986.

Wine making in the finest Sauternes tradition

The vineyard consists of three separate plots, all of Pyrenean gravel, and the bulk of it is planted with the Sémillon grape, so beloved of the *Botrytis cinerea* fungus. As one would expect of a *Premier Cru* property, the harvest takes place over a good number of weeks, with pickers passing several times through the vines in order to gather only the fruit with noble rot. Since 1977 the wine has been made in oak barrels, fermented slowly at a low temperature; it is then matured for twenty-four to thirty months, one-third in new oak, before bottling. Throughout the Cordier ownership, Lafaurie-Peyraguey always maintained a certain level of quality; however, recent years have seen it shine remarkably brightly. A new manager and wine maker, Michel Laporte, was appointed in 1983. Aided by the talented Cordier enologist Georges Pauli, he gave the wine greater complexity, depth and *Botrytis* flavor. Today son Yannick Laporte is carrying on his retired father's good work.

Remarkable finesse and freshness

Lafaurie-Peyraguey is firmly established among Sauternes' leading estates, purveying its own particular style—one of finesse rather than power, crisp raciness rather than rich opulence ; it is as much Barsac as Bommes or Sauternes in character.

This relative delicacy makes it a wine to serve with the gentler sort of dessert, for example, pears cooked in puff-pastry, or peach sabayone with Sauternes. It should be served well chilled, at about 43°F (6°C), and the diners' pleasure will only be increased by the hot-cold contrast.

BORDEAUX
A.O.C. Sauternes

- *Wine selected:*
  Château Raymond-Lafon

- *Grape varieties:*
  Sémillon 80%, Sauvignon 20%
- *Average vine age:*
  35 years
- *Vineyard size:*
  18 hectares
- *Soil type:*
  Gravel and clay
- *Production:*
  24,000 bottles

Finest Vintages:

1999, 1998, 1997, 1996, 1990,
1989, 1988, 1986, 1983

Château Raymond-Lafon
33210 Sauternes
Tel. (0033) 556 63 21 02
Follow the D8 from Preignac in the
direction of Sauternes. At the hamlet
of Arrançon turn right, pass through
Boutoc and take the first left. The
entrance to Raymond-Lafon is
approximately 800 m further,
on the left.
- *Owners:* Meslier family
- *General Manager:* Marie-Françoise
Meslier
- *On-site sales:* Yes
- *Visits:* By appointment
- *Price:* ★★★

CHÂTEAU RAYMOND-LAFON

In the vicinity of Châteaux d'Yquem and Lafaurie-Peyraguey lies a smallish estate called Raymond-Lafon. This is the source of a magnificent Sauternes of at least *Premier Cru* standard.

Too young for classification

This property was created by Raymond Lafon in 1850. By the time of the classification, five years later, it had hardly started producing wine, and was thus not concerned. After passing down one generation of Lafons, the estate was inherited by Louis Pontallier at the turn of the century. It was already renowned for its wine. In 1953 the Pontalliers sold it to a doctor called Bourdier, who in turn sold it to the Mesliers in 1972.

The Yquem wine maker's own wine

Pierre Meslier was manager and wine maker at Château d'Yquem, and set about making his own wine with the same perfectionist attention to detail as that demanded by his employer. At the same time he went about buying up parcels of land around the estate as they came up for sale, for the vineyard only covered 3.5 hectares at the time of the purchase. In 1989 he retired and handed the estate down to his three children.

Waiting for noble rot

There are now 18 hectares under vine, planted with Sémillon and Sauvignon in the traditional ratio of 80:20. The most rigorous viticultural and vinification techniques are practiced at Raymond-Lafon, starting with respect for the soil and severe pruning to reduce the vines' yield. As elsewhere, when the morning mists caused by the nearby Ciron stream have combined with the afternoon heat, the *Botrytis cinerea* fungus will hopefully appear. It will then "nobly" rot the grapes by reducing the water in their juice, by adding sugars such as glycerine, by increasing the acidity, and finally by giving the juice a special spicy flavor.

As the fungus does not appear evenly throughout the vineyard, a number of pickings are carried out in order to gather just the sufficiently rotten grapes. At Raymond-Lafon as many as eleven passages may be necessary in difficult years, which have been known to extend the harvest into December. Picking must take place in dry conditions, and there is naturally an enormous risk of gray rot if the weather breaks before the harvest is finished.

Severe selection and luxury aging

Fermentation is followed by up to three years' maturation. The wood is of the finest tight-grained quality, coming from 180- to 250-year-old trees. Finally, as on all the most quality-driven properties, a severe selection of the vats takes place before bottling, which invariably entails declassifying some 20 percent of the wine; sometimes, as in 1985, it is as much as 65 percent! All this leaves at most some two thousand cases of Raymond-Lafon per year for the eighteen countries where it is sold.

It is highly adaptable at table, accompanying *foie gras*, chicken, and other white meats, fruit tarts, and blue cheeses extremely well. The Mesliers recommend serving it with a Roquefort *soufflé*.

BORDEAUX
A.O.C. Sauternes

• *Wine selected:*
Château Rieussec
Premier Cru Classé

• *Grape varieties:*
Sémillon 90%, Sauvignon 7%,
Muscadelle 3%
• *Average vine age:*
34 years
• *Vineyard size:*
75 hectares
• *Soil type:*
Gravel over clay

Finest Vintages:
1999, 1998, 1997, 1990,
1989, 1988, 1986, 1983

Château Rieussec
33210 Fargues
Tel. (0033) 556 62 20 71
Leave Preignac by the Villandraut road
(D8). After about 6 km take the
Langon road on the left. Rieussec is
about 800 meters further, on the left;
it is well sign-posted.
• *Owners:* Château Rieussec S.A.
• *Director:* Charles Chevallier
• *On-site sales:* No
• *Visits:* By appointment
(Tel. 01 53 89 78 00)
• *Price:* ★★★

CHÂTEAU RIEUSSEC

Just east of Château d'Yquem, looking down on the surrounding vineyards from its elevated site, lies Château Rieussec, one of Sauternes' top properties. Rieussec has with impressive consistency always been among the top wines of the area, but since being purchased by the Rothschilds it has climbed to even greater heights.

Great regularity despite numerous owners

In the eighteenth century the property belonged to the Carmelite friars of nearby Langon. It was sequestrated during the Revolution and sold off to Monsieur Mareilhac, owner at the time of Château La Louvière, in Léognan. Rieussec's ensuing history, from the time of the Revolution up until today, has been peppered with changes of ownership, making the general consistency of its wine through all that time nothing if not surprising. After Monsieur Mareilhac sold it in 1846, it had eight owners before being acquired by Albert Vuillier in 1971.

Vuillier was passionately involved in his estate, but bought it at the wrong time, just before a run of years which were highly unfavorable for Sauternes production. As a result of the ensuing lack of profits he could not fully capitalize on the good years at the end of the 1970s. He started looking for a partner with money to invest. In 1984 the Rothschilds, owners of Châteaux Lafite and Duhart-Milon, bought a controling interest. Funds were at last available for pushing Rieussec to the limits of its potential.

The Rothschilds invest in quality

A number of significant refinements in policy were rapidly adopted: the number of times pickers pass through the vineyard was increased, in order to harvest only perfectly "nobly" rotten grapes; the quantity of new oak barrels ordered from Lafite's cooper for the wine's maturation was greatly increased; and a more severe selection of the vats was made, with the result that more wine was bottled under the second label of the estate. More recently, experimentation has been carried out over the last few years into extended barrel-aging of the better vintages, and into barrel fermentation. And in 1987 a cryo-extraction chamber was installed. Cryo-extraction technology is designed to separate water and grape juice by chilling the must to just under $32°F$ ($0°C$). At this temperature the water freezes and the ice can be extracted, while the sweet must, with a freezing-point of around $23°F$ ($-5°C$), remains liquid.

The power and richness of the Sémillon

Château Rieussec is now probably second only to Yquem in sheer richness, weight, and power, partly no doubt a result of the decision to cease using the Sauvignon juice in the wine. This now goes into R, the estate's dry white wine. As may be expected, Rieussec is a wine with a great life-expectancy, assuming that owners of bottles manage to resist opening them before time!

It is an undemanding wine at table, matching dishes incorporating Roquefort cheese, *foie gras*, and other powerful flavors perfectly. If served at the end of the meal it is excellent with unsugared fruit tarts, and is one of the rare wines that can hold its own against chocolate dishes.

103

BORDEAUX
A.O.C. Sauternes

- *Wine selected:*
  Château d'Yquem
  Premier Cru Classé - Supérieur

- *Grape varieties:*
  Sémillon 80%, Sauvignon 20%
- *Average vine age:*
  30 years
- *Vineyard size:*
  102 hectares
- *Soil type:*
  Mosaic of gravel, clay and sand
- *Production:*
  100,000 bottles

Finest Vintages:
1995, 1990, 1989, 1988, 1986, 1983

Château d'Yquem
33210 Sauternes
Tel. (0033) 557 98 07 07
Follow the D8 from Preignac in the
direction of Sauternes. Traverse the
hamlet of Arrançon, 5 km from
Preignac; approximately 1.5 km later
the road leading to Yquem forks off
to the right.
- *Owner:* L.V.M.H.
- *Director:* Comte A. de Lur-Saluces
- *On-site sales:* No
- *Visits:* By appointment, small groups
- *Price:* ★★★★★

SAUTERNES-APPELLATION CONTRÔLÉE

Château d'Yquem

Lur-Saluces

·· 1945 ··

MIS EN BOUTEILLE AU CHÂTEAU

CHÂTEAU D'YQUEM

With a *Premier Cru Supérieur* classification all of its own, a mystique fueled by a long tradition of perfectionist wine making, and a price way beyond that of the other top Sauternes, Château d'Yquem is a wine many wine lovers dream of tasting, if only once in their lifetime.

Four centuries of continuity

Continuity of ownership has been just one factor responsible for Yquem's enduring reputation: after being owned by the Sauvage family for two hundred years, it passed by marriage into the hands of the Lur-Saluces family in 1785; the family then remained outright owner until 1999, when a majority holding was acquired by the luxury-goods groups L.V.M.H. Even now Comte A. de Lur-Saluces remains in charge on the estate however, and continues to preside over Château d'Yquem's reputation.

The vineyard's microclimate is another: it is situated on a rise in the land, and is perfectly drained by nearly 100 kilometers of drains laid by Comte A. de Lur-Saluces's great-grandfather.

A single glass per vine

The visitor to Yquem will be told that it takes a whole vine to produce a single glass of Yquem; this is easy to believe in view of the many steps taken in the constant pursuit of quality. Harvesters pass through the vineyard at the very least four (and certain years up to a dozen) times to pick individual grapes which have attained the right degree of "noble" rot. After fermentation the wine is aged for over three years in new oak barrels, then before bottling a selection of the best barrels is undertaken, which can entail, as in 1978, the rejection of 80 percent of the wine! Indeed in certain years such as 1972, 1974, and 1992 Comte de Lur-Saluces has not hesitated to declassify the entire crop, judging it unworthy of bearing the name of Yquem.

Such draconian measures reflect the family's philosophy of aiming at producing a wine second to none, of perfect quality, whatever the financial sacrifice. Such measures explain the wine's high price, and justify it.

A wine of legendary longevity

Thanks to its extraordinary richness, alcohol level, and high acidity, great vintages can last a century or more, developing a magnificent deep tawny hue and spicy, caramel, and sometimes slightly oxidized flavors. Certain vintages, which have benefited from perfect storage conditions, may even exceed this lifespan: Michael Broadbent, the renowned expert who has been dubbed the Memory of Wine, in 1988 tasted the 1825 vintage, and wrote in *Decanter* magazine: "Alive and bright. Beautiful scent, incredible fragrance. Blossomed further and after an hour had a fantastic ethereal fruit salad with pineapple bouquet. Still sweet, fullish body. Tasted of fresh figs. Concentrated. Fabulous acidity and aftertaste."

The ideal partner for many dishes

Yquem's richness and acidity, its hallmarks, make it the ideal partner for many dishes. Suggestions put forward at the château include *foie gras*, fish in white sauce, roast chicken, and other white meats, Roquefort cheese, and unsugared fresh fruit tarts.

BORDEAUX
A.O.C. Barsac

- *Wine selected:*
  Château Climens
  Premier Cru Classé

- *Grape varieties:*
  Sémillon
- *Average vine age:*
  35 years
- *Vineyard size:*
  29 hectares
- *Soil type:*
  Red sand and gravel over limestone
  subsoil
- *Production:*
  45,000 bottles

Finest Vintages:
2001, 1997, 1990, 1989, 1988, 1986

Château Climens
33720 Barsac
Tel. (0033) 556 27 15 33
On arriving at Barsac from Bordeaux,
turn right at the Château Nairac
corner. Turn left about 600 m further
(just past the railroad tracks), then
turn right after the second level
crossing. Climens is on the right,
about 3 km further on.
- *Owners:* Bérénice Lurton
- *On-site sales:* Yes
- *Visits:* By appointment
- *Price:* ★★★

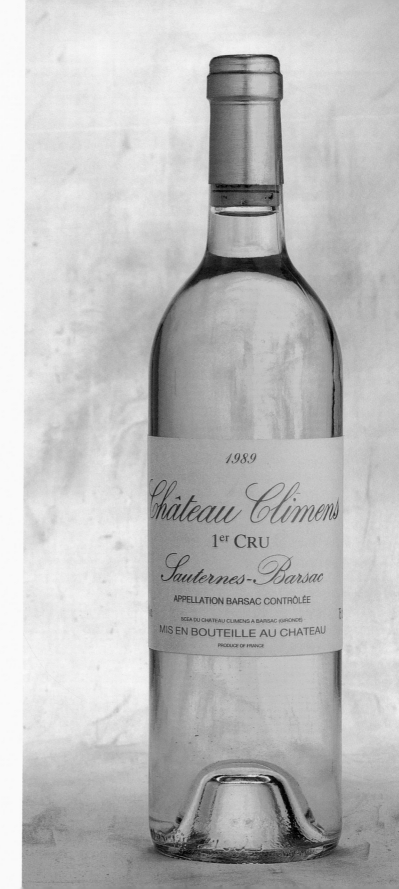

CHÂTEAU CLIMENS

The commune of Barsac, in the northernmost part of the Sauternes region, contains two properties classified *Premier Cru* in 1855, one of which is Château Climens. Climens has its own style, a blend of the characteristics of both Barsac and Sauternes. This is one of France's greatest sweet wines, and inspires particular passion among its devotees.

A succession of dedicated owners

In 1547 Guirault Roborel, King's Prosecutor at Barsac, acquired some plots of land in a place named Climens (the origins of the name are unknown) and planted vines there. The estate thrived, and remained in the hands of his descendants until 1800, before passing briefly through the hands of one Jean Binaud and then being acquired by a Bordeaux *négociant* named Éloi Lacoste, who also owned Château Pexiotto—a *Deuxième Cru* that has since been integrated into Château Rabaud-Promis. In Lacoste's hands the wine attained new heights, and his efforts were duly rewarded in 1855.

The two estates were acquired in 1871 by Alfred Ribet, who not long afterwards had the misfortune to see them succumb to the ravages of the phylloxera aphid. In 1885 he decided to sell, and found a buyer for Climens in the owner of the nearby *Deuxième Cru* Château Doisy-Dubroca, Henri Gounouilhou. The Gounouilhou family earned Climens the reputation it enjoys today, and produced many great vintages which are still marvelous. They owned the two properties until 1971, when they sold them to Lucien Lurton. Since 1992 Bérénice Lurton has run the estate.

Sémillon grapes and stringent selections

Unusually, Climens is made exclusively from Sémillon. The vineyard, one well-drained plot of 30 hectares of red sand and gravel lying over a limestone base, is worked traditionally. At harvest time it is visited a number of times by the pickers in order to gather only those grapes with just the required degree of "noble" rot. The grapes are then sifted through in the trailer for an additional quality control prior to arrival at the vathouse, where they are pressed.

The must is then vinified lot by lot in oak barrels, of which between one-and two-thirds are new, before selection of the best barrels for the *grand vin*, and blending. The selection is draconian, and in certain years the Lurtons decide not to make a *grand vin*. Such was the case in 1984, 1987, 1992, and 1993. The wine is then left to mature for two years before bottling.

Power and delicacy

Climens is a unique wine, in that it combines the best of Sauternes with the best of Barsac. It has the power, richness, and fat of the former and the elegance, delicacy, and raciness of the latter. This results in very long-living wines which retain startling freshness and fragrance in their venerable old age. The renowned English wine-taster Michael Broadbent, wrote of the 1929: "My last note dates from 1983, yet I relive that moment again and again with continued pleasure." Climens is a gastronome's delight, an inspired partner for *foie gras*, sweetbread, chicken curry, or pears in puff-pastry.

BORDEAUX
A.O.C. Barsac

- *Wine selected:*
  Château Coutet
  Premier Cru Classé

- *Grape varieties:*
  Sémillon 75%, Sauvignon 23%,
  Muscadelle 2%
- *Average vine age:*
  30 years
- *Vineyard size:*
  38.5 hectares
- *Soil type:*
  Limestone silt, clay, gravel and sand
  over limestone
- *Production:*
  60,000 bottles

Finest Vintages:
1997, 1996, 1990, 1989, 1988, 1981

Château Coutet
33720 Barsac
Tel. (0033) 556 27 15 46
Leave Barsac by the N113 in the
direction of Langon. After about 1 km,
when you have passed the football
stadium, take the turn right to Budos.
Coutet is on your left about 1 km after
the railway bridge.
- *Owners:* S.C. de Château Coutet
- *On-site sales:* Yes
- *Visits:* By appointment
- *Price:* ★★★/★★★★

CHÂTEAU COUTET

The sweet wines of the Sauternes region come from five communes, which all have, to a greater or lesser degree, their own style. Those of Barsac are perhaps the least luscious, but have finer acidity and crispness, and greater delicacy than the wines of the other four communes. Barsac boasts two châteaux classified *Premier Cru* in 1855, one of which, Château Coutet, is probably the quintessence of this type of wine.

A great and historic estate

Coutet, like many other estates in the region, has military rather than viticultural origins, which date back to the thirteenth century, and did not start producing wine until fully three centuries later. Just before the Revolution it belonged to the wealthy and powerful owner of Château Lafite, Baron de Pichard, who sold it in 1788 to Gabriel de Filhot, owner of the château of the same name. In the 1820s it passed by marriage into the Lur-Saluces family, owners of Château d'Yquem, and it remained in their impressive patrimony until 1922. Coutet then changed hands again several times in rapid succession. One of its owners, Henri-Louis Guy, was a manufacturer of hydraulic presses, and these were naturally installed on the premises, and are still in use today.

The creation of the Cuvée Madame

The following owners, the Rolland-Guys, created a rare wine, Cuvée Madame, for which the estate is justly famous. Dreamt up by Edmond Rolland to honour his wife, this wine is only made in great years, and little is put onto the market. Nearly all of the tiny production is reserved for special functions, birthdays and so on. It is made from carefully selected grapes, picked at absolute ripeness and a perfect state of "noble" rot, which have a potential 22–24 percent of alcohol. Generally about 100 cases are made, and this wine is reckoned by many to reach the quality level of Yquem.

The current owners, Marcel Baly and his two sons, acquired the property in 1977 and decided to continue production of Cuvée Madame, since when it has been made in 1981, 1986, 1988, and 1989.

Refined, delicate, and long-lasting

Château Coutet is made in the traditional Sauternes manner. The vineyard, one large parcel of heterogeneous soils which surrounds the château, is subjected to a number of visits by harvesters in order to gather only grapes with the required degree of "noble" rot. Sometimes this necessitates waiting until late autumn before finishing, with all the risks that that entails. The wine is fermented in oak, half of the barrels being renewed annually, then left to mature for some eighteen months before bottling.

What is imprisoned in the glass is a very refined, flowery, and delicate wine with good crisp acidity. This is a wine which keeps for decades; what is more, even in old age Coutet for some reason never maderizes, but retains its freshness.

Once at table, it is highly versatile. A mature vintage—let us say the exquisite honeyed and peachy 1971—could be enjoyed with a main course of pigeons, roasted and served with a sauce made of Barsac and Muscat grapes; or, more traditionally, with a red fruit gratin, to bring the meal to a memorable end.

BURGUNDY
A.O.C. Chablis

- *Wine selected:*
  Chablis Valmur
  Grand Cru

- *Grape variety:*
  Chardonnay
- *Average vine age:*
  30 years
- *Vineyard size:*
  0.75 hectares
- *Soil type:*
  Kimmeridge clay
- *Production:*
  4,500 bottles

Finest Vintages:

2000, 1999, 1996, 1995, 1992,
1990, 1986, 1985, 1983

Domaine François Raveneau
9 Rue de Chichée
89800 Chablis
Tel. (0033) 386 42 17 46
On arriving at Barsac from Bordeaux,
turn right at the Château Nairac
corner. Turn left some 600 meters
further on (just past the railway line),
then turn right after the second level
crossing. Climens is on the right,
about 3 km further on.
- *Owners:* Raveneau family
- *On-site sales:* No
- *Visits:* No
- *Price:* ★★

DOMAINE FRANÇOIS RAVENEAU

Small in size it may be, but Domaine François Raveneau makes quintessential Chablis of world-wide renown. Its wines are delicious young, yet more than any others they repay long keeping, developing magnificently complex flavors over the years. So limited is supply compared with demand that Raveneau wines are difficult to come by, yet anyone wanting to discover authentic Chablis should make the effort to find and taste a bottle. He or she will be anything but disappointed.

Careful traditional craftsmanship

François Raveneau founded the estate with vines from both his parents' families, and his sons Jean-Marie and Bernard have succeeded him with great talent. There are no particular innovations or sleights of hand to explain the quality of their wines, simply the basic priorities with which all good vignerons are in agreement : good healthy grapes and minimal intervention but maximum surveillance during fermentation. The vineyards are cared for by *lutte raisonnée* : following biological pratices as much as is possible, yet without rejecting artificial treatments when faced with the possibility of losing a crop due to adverse natural conditions.

Yields are actively kept down by acting at the onset of vegetation : pruning short and debudding, never by lopping off bunches in July, and normal, not excessive, grape ripeness is sought. The alcohol/acidity balance is all-important, and to this end Jean-Marie Raveneau would prefer to harvest a little early, rather than have over-ripe fruit; for him chaptalization is infinitely preferable to acidification.

Perfectly-defined terroir characteristics

Grapes are fermented at 76°F (22°C), mostly in vat but 10 percent in barrel, and the wines then undergo their malolactic fermentations. They are left in vat long enough to clarify themselves, then are transferred to barrel for aging, which lasts roughly one year. That way little deposit forms in the barrel, and the wines can usually be bottled without filtration.

What sets Raveneau-Chablis apart from nearly all others is the purity and intensity of the fruit and the perfect definition of *terroir* (oil and climate) characteristics. When young La Forest is generally fresh, elegant, and floral, Butteaux more ample and mineral, and Montée de Tonnerre leaner, tauter, and flinty; Blanchots is more reserved, manly, and structured and Les Clos somehow combining the latter's robustness with enormous refinement and elegance. After bottling these wines can be very dumb for a while, yet as they age they take on a whole range of tertiary aromas encompassing honey, mushrooms, seaweed, moss, fern, and various minerals.

Chablis-Valmur

Valmur has the power and dimension of the true *Grand Cru*, with a splendid mineral flavor with an unmistakable iodine side to it, and behind all that, hints of the vegetal. This great Chablis throws up images of a plate of seafood, served on a bed of seaweed, and indeed the two are highly complementary at the table. A mature Raveneau-Valmur makes a magnificent partner for grilled lobster, and also lends itself to fish or white meat dishes in cream sauce.

BURGUNDY
A.O.C. Chablis 1ᵉʳ cru

- *Wine selected:*
  Chablis Vosgros
  Premier Cru

- *Grape variety:*
  Chardonnay
- *Average vine age:*
  20 years
- *Vineyard size:*
  0.58 hectares
- *Soil type:*
  Kimmeridge clay
- *Production:*
  4,000 bottles

Finest Vintages:
1999, 1997, 1995, 1992

Domaine Jean-Paul Droin
14 bis Rue Jean-Jaurès
89800 Chablis
Tel. (0033) 386 42 16 78
Internet: www.jeanpaul-droin.fr
From the centre of Chablis take the
Maligny direction. The estate is on the
right and is well indicated.
- *Owners:* Droin family
- *On-site sales:* 8:30-12:00 a.m., 2:00-
  5:00 p.m. (Monday, Tuesday,
  Thursday, Friday)
- *Visits:* No
- *Price:* ★

DOMAINE JEAN-PAUL DROIN

The energetic and articulate Jean-Paul Droin has a superb 49-acres (20-ha) estate spread over many of the most coveted slopes of Chablis. Droin is an unrepentant user of new oak, and is criticized by some for swamping *terroir* qualities with the wood's opulent vanilla flavors. He accepts this criticism with the answer that he and his numerous clients like their wines that way. Whether one is for or against oaked Chablis, no one would deny that Droin follows his leanings with consummate talent.

A feel for tradition and an analytical character

The Droins are probably the senior family of *viticulteurs* in Chablis, with lineage which Jean-Paul, the town archivist and a great lover of history, has traced back until 1640. He is the twelfth generation to follow the family trade, and started working in the vineyards alongside his father and grandfather at the age of fourteen, eventually assuming total responsibility when his father retired in 1982. Today he is seconded by son Benoît, who has taken charge of vinification after studying in Beaune and Dijon.

The practical and analytical Jean-Paul is not afraid to swim against the purist tide when he judges it worthwhile. Not only with regards to new oak but equally to mechanical harvesters : he would happily use them even in his *Grands Crus* if they were not planted on such steep incline, for the machines do not lead to any greater fruit oxidation than the deep harvest baskets used by previous generations, nor do they damage the vines.

Irreproachable fruit and new oak

In many other aspects he is in perfect sync with all the other top Chablis growers. Pruning short, debudding (*essoumachage* is the local term), *rognage* (trimming and thinning growth to facilitate aeration), ecological vineyard practices, even experimentation such as *confusion sexuelle* to combat the vine various enemies including *grappe de ver*—all these practices are necessary in order to obtain fruit of irreproachable quality. The crops are so exemplary that yields of up to 749 gallons/acre (70 hl./ha.) in good years are capable of producing great wines, and that fruit selection is unnecessary.

Since 1986 *Grands Crus* and certain *Premiers Crus* have been fermented in oak, a mixture of new and one-, two- and three-year-old barrels, the choice and the amount of new wood being dependent on the vintage characteristics, while the remaining wines are fermented in vats. About one month after malolactic fermentations the wines fermented in barrels are racked off their lees, and the vat-fermented wines are transferred to these barrels, to benefit from the lees. All wines in barrel are given *bâtonnage* (lees-stirring) every ten to fifteen days.

Chablis Vosgros

Which wines one prefers in Droin's range is naturally a question of one's tolerance for new oak. While the *Grand Cru* Grenouille is undoubtedly a finely-crafted wine, it could easily be mistaken for a steely Condrieu. Vaudésir and Blanchots bring the taster nearer to home, yet more recognizable are the superb Les Clos and the exceptional *Premier Cru* Vosgros, which is fermented in both vat and barrel and aged likewise for roughly a year. Concentrated, taut and expressive, it has medium weight and a perfectly-balanced blend of gun-flint, citrus-fruit, and wood flavors. This fine wine needs some eight to ten years for the mineral side to assert itself fully, and when ready is a superlative match for fish terrine, grilled or poached fish, and goat cheeses.

BURGUNDY
A.O.C. Chablis Grand Cru

- *Wine selected:*
Chablis Les Preuses
Grand Cru

- *Grape variety:*
Chardonnay
- *Average vine age:*
32 years
- *Vineyard size:*
0.96 hectare
- *Soil type:*
clay and limestone over
Kimmeridge marl
- *Production:*
6,000 bottles

Finest Vintages:
2000, 1999, 1996, 1995, 1992, 1990

Domaine Vincent Dauvissat
8 Rue Émile-Zola
89800 Chablis
Tel. : 00 33 386 42 11 58
From Place Lafayette proceed along
Rue Jules Rathier and in front of the
bend to the right. Dauvissat is some
20 meters along the right.
- *Owners:* René & Vincent Dauvissat
- *On-site sales:*
To existing clients
- *Visits:* By appointment
- *Price:* ★★

DOMAINE VINCENT DAUVISSAT

Chablis, Burgundy's northern outpost, produces white wines which have a unique and unmistakable steely, mineral character. Vineyard sites are all-important of course, and the finest wines come from the most prestigious *Grand Cru* slopes with a subsoil of Kimmeridge marl. Yet the ambition and skill of the wine maker also play an essential role, and there is a large gulf in quality between the wines of the most talented and their run-of-the-mill equivalent. Some of the very best bottles the region has to offer are the work of Vincent Dauvissat.

Observation, experimentation and reflection

The Dauvissats have been growing vines in the region since the seventeenth century, and there are now a handful of different family branches making wine. In 1931, Robert Dauvissat decided to cease selling his wine to Chablis merchants and to bottle and sell it himself. Thanks to him, and then successively his son René and his grandson Vincent, this branch has over the intervening period gained itself an international reputation for the quality of its produce.

Since 1989 the lean, smiling Vincent Dauvissat has been in charge. Vincent's wine making is brilliantly empirical; all he knows was learned in a dozen years at his father's side, for he has never set foot in a wine school. That period involved much experimentation by the father-and-son team, which laid the foundations of the young man's habit of regular reflection on what he is doing, which no doubt explains the stunning quality of his wines today.

A succession of little details

Making good wine is a succession of little details, the visitor is modestly informed. Sensitivity towards the vine, its soil and its environment, intimate knowledge of one's vineyards in order to know what is ready for harvesting, low yields of ripe and healthy grapes from vines which know no stress. Vinification also involves habitual practices but not fixed rules. A very gentle pneumatic pressing, a short period of settling, then fermentation, partly in vat and partly in barrel; one quarter of the barrels are new, but certain years this might be increased to 60 percent. A rapid start to fermentation is preferred, which sometimes necessitates seeding with a little cultured yeast, but generally the indigenous variety is preferred. Fermentation is lengthy, after which maturation over six to twelve months, or even more, takes place in old barrels and *feuillettes*, the small local barrels that contain 132 liters. Bottling is by gravity, and is preceded by a light filtration if necessary.

Chablis Les Preuses

Existing clients of Vincent Dauvissat no doubt count themselves privileged—as do those of his cousins the Raveneaus—to be able to buy a few bottles of his different *crus*, for excessive demand means that new clients can not be accepted. Les Preuses is a fine example of Dauvissat's art, a sumptuously full-bodied, full-flavored and complete wine, which in the better vintages takes twelve to fifteen years to reach perfection. Concentration, finesse, and a wonderful mineral side make this a textbook Chablis, which would be honored by the presence of a lobster, fricasseed in Chablis wine.

BURGUNDY
A.O.C. Chambertin

- *Wine selected:*
  Chambertin
  Grand Cru

- *Grape variety:*
  Pinot Noir
- *Average vine age:*
  45 years
- *Vineyard size:*
  2.15 hectares
- *Soil type:*
  Clay and limestone
- *Production:*
  6,000 bottles

Finest Vintages:
1999, 1996, 1995, 1990, 1988, 1980

Domaine Armand Rousseau
1 Rue de l'Aumônerie
21220 Gevrey-Chambertin
Tel. (0033) 380 34 30 55
Internet: www.domaine-rousseau.com
The estate is at the top of the village
on the corner of rue de l'Église and
rue de l'Aumônerie, which leads out of
the village towards the Combe de
Lavaux.
- *Owner:* Charles Rousseau
- *On-site sales:* No
- *Visits:* By appointment
- *Price:* ★★★★

DOMAINE ARMAND ROUSSEAU

Just as it has its young super stars, the Côte d'Or has a sprinkling of senior estates which have long enjoyed a reputation for producing the very finest quality, making benchmark wines against which new estates measure themselves. Domaine Armand Rousseau is one such. If there is one estate that has consistently over a half-century offered the finest available Gevrey-Chambertin, this is it.

Synonymous with the best Gevrey-Chambertin

The young Armand Rousseau was a broker in Gevrey before World War I. Following the devastation caused by the passage of the phylloxera louse, it was not rare for vineyard land to come onto the market, and he gradually started piecing together his own estate. At first he sold his wine in bulk, but, encouraged by Raymond Baudoin, founder of the *Revue du vin de France* and consultant to a number of France's finest restaurants, he started bottling his best *cuvées*, and the restaurants were eager customers. Their clients became his clients, and then soon he had an American agent. The name Rousseau was becoming synonymous with the best Gevrey-Chambertin.

Charles Rousseau suddenly found himself in charge after losing his father in a car crash in 1959. Since then he has continued to build on his father's foundations, delighting ever more wine lovers with manly, rich wines, and continuing to enlarge the estate when suitable parcels have come onto the market. Today his son Eric and daughter Corinne work by the side of this courteous, honest gentleman, yet Charles is always available with advice and encouragement to anyone in need of it, whith unfailing modesty and good humor.

Experience and feeling

Rousseau wines are made more by experience and feeling than modern enological science. On paper the basic recipe is simple: fine land, old vines, low yields, draconian sorting, and long fermentations. Vines are left in production as long as they are remotely productive, for old wines contribute great complexity and act as yield reducers. At harvest time Rousseau demands extreme selectivity from his pickers, and the ground has been known to be carpeted with discarded fruit in difficult years. Vatting itself starts with destalking some 80 percent of the fruit and a short, natural maceration until the indigenous yeast get to work on the grape sugar. Once their work is done the rich, dark liquids are transferred to barrel for maturation. Only the Chambertin and Clos de Bèze are permitted one 100 percent new oak, for in the Rousseau's view oak flavors can too easily dominate a wine. After twenty to twenty-two months' aging, the wines are lightly filtered and then bottled.

Chambertin

The Rousseau Chambertin is one of Burgundy's greatest wines, a heady, rich, and powerful beast, which has great aromatic complexity once it has matured. Black fruit, licorice, leather, cinnamon, undergrowth—every vintage has its character, and the lesser vintages are usually as interesting, if less long-lived, than the great ones. Stored in a good cellar, a top vintage can hope for a thirty-year lifespan. For a suitable dish, *coq au Chambertin* or a truffled filet of beef followed by l'Ami du Chambertin are eminently suitable.

BURGUNDY
A.O.C. Charmes-Chambertin

- *Wine selected:*
  Charmes-Chambertin
  Grand Cru

- *Grape variety:*
  Pinot Noir
- *Average vine age:*
  26 years
- *Vineyard size:*
  0.5 hectare
- *Soil type:*
  Clay and limestone
- *Production:*
  1,500 bottles

Finest Vintages:
2000, 1999, 1996, 1995

Domaine Bernard Dugat-Py
Rue de Panteligone, BP 31
21220 Gevrey-Chambertin
Tel. (0033) 380 51 82 46
Internet: www.dugat-py.com
- *Owners:* Jocelyne & Bernard Dugat-Py
- *On-site sales:* No
- *Visits:* No
- *Price:* ★★★★

DOMAINE BERNARD DUGAT-PY

Burgundy domaines come in all sizes and qualities, although large is unusual. One of the smallest of note, a domaine with no history that is making ripples due to the outstanding quality of its wines, is that of Bernard Dugat-Py. Dugat is the quintessential craftsman, unsung and largely unknown, a young man set on making the very finest examples of his appellations possible.

A young entrepreneur invests

Dugat bought his first vineyard in 1973 at the tender age of fifteen and made his first wine, a village Gevrey, two years later. Gradually over the years he has acquired other land—his father gave him some Gevrey and some Charmes-Chambertin in 1987, and he has acquired some Chambertin, Mazis-Chambertin and *Premiers Crus* since—which brings the area of his estate, still resolutely stuck inside the village boundaries, up to 7.3 hectares. Dugat works with his wife Jocelyne from a house at the top of the village, a building which sits above three cellars, the most recent a 1980s construction, the oldest formerly a twelfth-century almonry.

Interfering as little as possible

Like all of his *confrères* who are producing the best Burgundy today, Dugat treats his vineyards and vines in as respectful a manner as possible, working the soil naturally for maximum plant health and to encourage roots to penetrate deep down under the surface. His family have been vine nurserymen, and their experience no doubt helps when selecting the best plant material for the different *terroirs*. He goes

for extremely low yields, training his vines by the low-yield-producing Guyot simple, pruning short, and debudding in the spring.

Fruit is discarded in the vineyard if it is sub-standard, and thereafter wine-making is relatively uncomplicated, Dugat's principal rule of thumb being to interfere as little as possible in the process. Vatting lasts as long as necessary, and fermentations are prolonged by limited chaptalizations towards the end of the process in order to keep it going, resulting in a more substantial texture. Then wines are matured in a finely-judged proportion of new oak, for a length of time which again is adapted to the vintage: 50–100 percent new oak for fourteen to eighteen months in the case of *Grands Crus*. Until 1989 there was little domaine bottling, and Leroy and other *négociants* came and removed the wines in barrel. Today, however, demand is great and all the wines are bottled by the grower.

Charmes-Chambertin

Like his other *Grands Crus*, and indeed his whole range, Dugat's Charmes-Chambertin has to be tasted to be believed. Beautifully deep in color, its noble, rich aroma can take the taster aback, such is its purity and definition, and on the palate the impression is just as positive! It is perfectly balanced, and so ripe is the tannin, which contributes its significant structure, that one is easily tempted to drink it young. Resist, and let it grow old and wise! Then, when the moment is right, bring it up from the cellar for an uninterrupted exchange with some perkily eloquent quails, stuffed and seasoned with blackcurrants.

BURGUNDY
A.O.C. Chambertin Clos de Bèze

- *Wine selected:*
  Chambertin Clos de Bèze
  Grand Cru

- *Grape variety:*
  Pinot Noir
- *Average vine age:*
  80 years
- *Vineyard size:*
  0.98 hectares
- *Soil type:*
  Clay and limestone
- *Production:*
  3,500 bottles

Finest Vintages:
2000, 1999, 1998, 1996,
1995, 1990, 1989

Domaine Bruno Clair
5 Rue de Vieux-Collège, BP 22
21160 Marsannay-la-Côte
Tel. (0033) 380 52 28 95
From the RN74 take the road to
Marsannay. Turn right at the first
set of lights, and turn at the first
left. Domaine Clair is several
meters further, on the right.
- *Owner:* Bruno Clair
- *On-site sales:* Yes
- *Visits:* 9-12 a.m., 2-6 p.m.,
by appointment
- *Price:* ★★★★

DOMAINE BRUNO CLAIR

In 1985, the news spread like wildfire around the Côte d'Or: a sizeable part of the large and much-admired Clair-Daü estate, which had been in the throes of family strife and quarrel for a number of years, had been sold to Maison Louis Jadot, signaling the effective break up of the estate. At the time this seemed tragic, yet the demise of Clair-Daü gave rise to the foundation of Domaine Bruno Clair, which has proved itself a top-class domaine and worthy successor.

The rise of two great estates

In 1919, Joseph Clair married Marguerite Daü. Marguerite and her sister had inherited 8 hectares of vines in Marsannay, which Joseph started looking after. That same year he came up with a brilliant invention, a rosé wine made with Pinot Noir, which subsequently brought great prosperity to the village.

Over the decades Clair invested in land and built up a fine domaine, and was joined by his son Bernard in 1939. During the 1960s and 1970s Clair-Daü enjoyed its finest hour, a worthy standard-bearer for a region that was producing at the time many substandard wines. After the break-up, Bruno Clair, Bernard's son, started making wines on his own account. He took on Philippe Brun as his wine-making associate, and the pairing has proven to be inspired.

Elegant wines from a talented team

Clair's viticultural methods are basically organic, with much attention paid to the state of the soils. Above all, however, there is flexibility, and his intimate knowledge of his various parcels enables the growth of fine fruit, and harvesting at exactly the right moment.

When the grapes arrive at Marsannay they may or may not be destalked, depending on the condition of the wood, and there is a short, cold maceration before the onset of fermentation. A prolonged vatting period is preferred, for maximum extraction of structure, color, and aroma. Temperatures are allowed to climb up to 32°C, and there are regular *pigeages*. Press wine is incorporated into the free-run wine, and the wines are then matured, the Village appellations in oak *foudres* as well as barrels, and the more prestigious wines exclusively in barrel, some third of which are renewed each year. Then the wines are bottled, which may or may not be preceded by fining and filtration. There are no fixed rules, each year requires new decisions.

Chambertin Clos de Bèze

The estate farms an entire hectare of the magnificent Clos de Bèze, the doyen of Burgundy's clos, which has existed as such since 640, when the Duke of Burgundy donated it to the Abbey of Bèze. Neighbor of Le Chambertin and ranked on at least an equal footing, in Bruno Clair's hands this wine is a masterpiece of richness, power, and breeding, with a magnificently opulent and seductive character; it has the impressive structure which one would expect, but also great finesse, one of the hallmarks of Clair's wines. It needs a decade to mature, after which it perfectly accompanies a savory braised partridge.

BURGUNDY
A.O.C. Clos de Tart

- *Wine selected:*
  Clos de Tart
  Grand Cru (monopole)

- *Grape variety:*
  Pinot Noir
- *Average vine age:*
  50 years
- *Vineyard size:*
  7.53 hectares
- *Soil type:*
  Calcareous clay, marl
- *Production:*
  25,000 bottles

Finest Vintages:
2000, 1999, 1998, 1997, 1996,
1995, 1990, 1989, 1988, 1985

Domaine du Clos de Tart
21220 Morey-Saint-Denis
Tel. (0033) 380 34 30 91
When arriving in Morey-Saint-Denis
head for the church. The Domaine du
Clos de Tart is across from it at the top
of the hill.
- *Owners:* Mommessin family
- *Manager:* Sylvain Pitiot
- *On-site sales:* Yes
- *Visits:* By appointment
- *Price:* ★★★★

DOMAINE DU CLOS DE TART

At the southern end of the Morey-Saint-Denis vineyards lies the walled Clos de Tart, one of Burgundy's oldest. This vineyard is a monopole, having never during its long history been split up. Over the last half-century the wine has not enjoyed unanimous critical approval, for regularity has not been one of its greater qualities, yet since the 1980s progress has been evident, and the most recent vintages, the work of a new manager who has reviewed viticultural and vinification practices, are sumptuous.

The wine of the Cistercian nuns

The origins of the vineyard go back to the early twelfth century, when it was known as Climat de la Forge. In 1141 the climat was sold by the friars of Maison-Dieu de Brochon to the newly-founded Cistercian convent Notre-Dame de Tart, a dependency of the Abbey de Cîteaux. The vineyard remained in the hands of the church until the Revolution, when it was sold to Nicolas-Joseph Marey, whose family subsequently remained owners throughout the nineteenth century until selling it to the Mommessin family, owners of the large Mâcon *négociant* firm, in 1932. It is still in the Mommessins' hands today.

Old vines and low yields

Over the years the Clos de Tart has been run for its owners by a succession of managers, notably Henri Perraud, who took retirement in 1996 after twenty-seven years of loyal service. Perraud has been succeeded by wine maker and author Sylvain Pitiot, who has drawn up a program of ameliorations destined to make the wine live more fully up to its *Grand Cru* standing.

The vineyard is now managed by production *intégrée*, and the use of treatments eschewed whenever possible. Yields are kept down to around 30 hl/ha. One of the vineyard's particularities is that it is planted in rows which are horizontal to the slope. This serves the dual purpose of increasing exposure to the sun's rays and preventing the erosion of the calcareous clay soil during downpours. The *clos* contains some very elderly vines, and gradual replanting at the rate of two hectares every five years is carried out, by *sélection massale*, taking cuttings of the finest vines.

Once the fruit is harvested, it is sorted through closely, then destemmed entirely before undergoing a long pre-fermentation maceration for extraction of color, tannin, aromas, and acidity. When the fermentation is well under way the liquid is transferred into barrel to finish the process, and there it undergoes its malolactic fermentation. The wine is matured for eighteen to twenty-four months in entirely new oak, and is bottled with no filtration.

Clos de Tart

Silkiness, elegance, and refinement have always been the Clos de Tart's qualities, but the wine has often lacked the element of richness which is a prerequisite in a *Grand Cru*. Sylvain Pitiot is aiming for more concentration, for a cross between Chambertin and Musigny—which is as it should be, given the vineyard's position. Morello cherries, raspberries, sometimes violets, then with time spice, licorice, undergrowth—such is the flavor of Clos de Tart. The latest vintages are beautifully crafted and intensely flavored, and call out for good red meat: a shoulder of lamb with morels, served with a mushroom *feuilleté*, provides a fine partner for this noble wine.

BURGUNDY
A.O.C. Musigny

- *Wine selected:*
  Musigny Vieilles Vignes
  Grand Cru

- *Grape variety:*
  Pinot Noir
- *Average vine age:*
  40 years
- *Vineyard size:*
  7.2 hectares (3.7 ha of Vieilles
  Vignes)
- *Soil type:*
  Clay and limestone
- *Production:*
  10,000 bottles

Finest Vintages:

2000, 1999, 1998, 1997, 1996, 1994,
1993, 1991, 1990, 1989, 1988, 1985

Domaine Comte Georges de Vogüé
Rue Sainte-Barbe
21220 Chambolle-Musigny
Tel. (0033) 380 62 86 25
Rue Sainte-Barbe is the last on the
right before Chambolle's church.
- *Owner:* Baronne Bertrand de
  Ladoucette
- *On-site sales:* No
- *Visits:* 9-12 a.m., 2-5 p.m.
- *Price:* ★★★★

DOMAINE COMTE GEORGES DE VOGÜÉ

Silk and lace are two epithets frequently used to describe the wines of Chambolle's greatest vineyard, Le Musigny, and few of its incarnations demonstrate these qualities as well as that of the Domaine Comte Georges de Vogüé. This historic estate is a byword for top-quality Chambolle-Musigny.

From the Musignys to the Vogüés

Nineteen generations separate the first known owner of what was to become the De Vogüé estate and his descendant, the current owner! The granddaughter of Jean Moisson, a benefactor of Chambolle who endowed the village with its church, married a Dijon merchant by the name of Millières in 1528, and took as dowry some vines, among which was a plot which bore the name of its fourteenth-century owners, the Musigny family. After a half-century, the vineyards passed by marriage into the Bouhier family, of which successive generations farmed them for two centuries until 1766, when the last descendant, Catherine Bouhier, married Cerice François Melchior de Vogüé. From 1925 until his death in 1987 Comte Georges de Vogüé ran the estate, and since then his daughter, Baronne Bertrand de Ladoucette, has shouldered responsibilities.

A change of team

For most of the twentieth century the domaine has had a manager. The Roumier family held the post over three generations, until the retirement of Alain Roumier in 1986, following which the Baronne appointed a new team, with François Millet as wine maker and cellar-master, and Gérald Gaudeau as vineyard manager. Alain Roumier and Comte Georges de Vogüé between them made numerous fine vintages, such as the 1959, 1969, and 1972, yet after the latter vintage the wine became lighter and less distinguished over the ensuing years.

Millet, a consultant enologist with wide experience up and down the Côte, felt his way into the job, and the return to form was seen from the 1988 vintage onwards; since then, not a single wine has been less than remarkable. His basic philosophy, inhabitual for a trained enologist, is to take every year as it comes, and to meet every situation with a suitable solution; he is against hard-and-fast rules in wine making.

Musigny Vieilles Vignes

The sublime quality of the current team's work (Gaudeau, retired, has been replaced by Éric Bourgogne) is no doubt principally the result of strict control of yields, achieved by debudding in the spring and a "green harvest" if necessary, as well as the old age of the vines and minimal interference in the vinification process.

The Musigny Vieilles Vignes has a deceptively light color, which would certainly be deemed anemic in many other regions, yet there is nothing weak about its flavor: magnificently fragrant on the nose, it has great intensity, great class, exquisite balance, and an airy personality which is not in the least fleeting! Great vintages improve over two decades or more, and give a tasting experience one does not forget in a hurry. Musigny is a superb wine to sip on its own, and gives endless thrills as one wallows in its enthralling aromas, but is also a perfect match for delicately flavored meats such as poultry or veal served with morels.

BURGUNDY
A.O.C. Côte de Nuits

- *Wine selected:*
  Clos de Vougeot
  Grand Cru

- *Grape variety:*
  Pinot Noir
- *Average vine age:*
  60 years
- *Vineyard size:*
  0.3 hectare
- *Soil type:*
  Clay and limestone
- *Production:*
  700 bottles

Finest Vintages:
1999, 1996, 1993, 1990

Domaine Confuron-Cotétidot
10 Rue de la Fontaine
21700 Vosne-Romanée
Tel. (0033) 380 61 03 39
As one goes down the RN74, Rue de la
Fontaine is the last street on the right
before leaving Vosne-Romanée in
the direction of Nuits-Saint-Georges.
Domaine Confuron-Cotétidot is on
the left.

- *Owners:* Confuron-Cotétidot family
- *On-site sales:* Yes
- *Visits:* By appointment
- *Price:* ★★★

DOMAINE CONFURON-COTÉTIDOT

A large, unremarkable house in one of the roads leading down from Vosne's town hall to the RN74 roadway is the source of a range of wines which are anything but unremarkable. This is where Jack Confuron, one of the village's most conscientious wine makers, lives and works with his wife and two sons. His wines are slowly and carefully made, and require many years to become fully ready to drink. When they are, each one is invariably among the finest of its appellation.

Evaluation of new ideas and old traditions

The Confuron-Cotétidots have lived in Vosne and made wine since the mid-nineteenth century, passing down expertise from generation to generation and building up family traditions. Jack, the late Jean-Jacques Confuron's nephew, is very much one for carefully evaluating the pros and cons of any new idea or long-established tradition, and is not afraid to change if convinced that that is the right thing to do.

One radical and courageous decision was to call in the consultant agronomist and enologist Guy Accad. Confuron was one of the first on the Côte to do so, taking Accad's advice from 1977 to 1990, and this relationship was of great benefit to his vineyards and wines. Certain Accad recommendations are now thoroughly integrated into the domaine's ways, others have been modified somewhat, and still other discarded, but one may be sure that much thought went into the matter before the final decision was taken.

Made by hand by a family team

Having planted clones and been unsatisfied, Confuron is utterly opposed to them, and is one of the very few growers to select his own plants and do his own grafting. His vineyards contain a very large proportion of old vines, and are run ecologically, with many steps taken to reduce yields and achieve the greatest fruit quality possible.

Confuron would never be seen harvesting grapes that were not perfectly ripe, whatever risk the wait might entail. In the vatroom he does not destem them but vats whole bunches. They are cooled and sulphured, although far less than was advised by Accad, and spend several days of cold maceration before the start of fermentation. Fermentation temperatures are not allowed to rise above $88°F$ ($28°C$), and in order to attain the required extraction, three *pigeages* per day are carried out. These are serious affairs, involving Confuron and his two sons getting in up to the neck to tread, a thoroughly dangerous pasttime given all the ambient CO_2.

Little new oak is used for aging, because the wealth of stalks contributes the necessary tannin, and the wines are aged for longer than is usual, generally around two years. When they are ready, they are bottled by hand, with neither fining nor filtration.

Clos de Vougeot

For maximum extraction the Confurons vatted their Clos de Vougeot 1996 for thirty-five days, and the result is a monument of a wine: dense, powerful, and with a thick layer of rich, ripe black fruit held in a rigid tannic girdle. This is one of the very best of the numerous Clos Vougeots made every year and one of the fullest-bodied, and will need a good dozen years to soften and reveal the true extent of its complex aromatic palette. Whatever the quality of the vintage, this wine makes a good companion for a haunch of venison.

BURGUNDY
A.O.C. Gevrey-Chambertin 1ᵉʳ Cru

- *Wine selected:*
  Gevrey-Chambertin Lavaux-Saint-Jacques
  Premier Cru

- *Grape variety:*
  Pinot Noir
- *Average vine age:*
  20-70 years
- *Vineyard size:*
  11.2 hectares
- *Soil type:*
  Clay and limestone
- *Production:*
  5,600 bottles

Finest Vintages:
2001, 2000, 1999, 1998, 1997, 1996

Domaine Denis Mortet
22 Rue de l'Église
21220 Gevrey-Chambertin
Tel. (0033) 380 34 10 05
- *Owners:* Mortet family
- *On-site sales:* No
- *Visits:* No
- *Price:* ★★★

DOMAINE DENIS MORTET

Thoroughness, commitment and passion are among the forces at work in the Denis Mortet vineyards and cellar, giving birth to a supremely exciting range of wines centred around Gevrey-Chambertin. Were there a hundred and one tasks to see to, this restless perfectionist would see to them all, for he abhore the second-rate and the average. His wines eloquently bear testimony to that!

A new source of Burgundy

The name Denis Mortet has not yet graced many labels and vintages, yet the progress and the quality of what has been made to date have attracted the excited attention and plaudits of the world's specialized press. Domaine Denis Mortet has existed since his father Charles took retirement in 1991 and split his estate between his two sons. Since its *début* vintage in 1992 this small estate has grown larger with the arrival of various plots of land on leasing or share-cropping arrangements, and now covers 11.2 hectares, although unfortunately the production does not meet the strong demand.

Hand-made for greater quality

To make good wine, Mortet is convinced, as many of the numerous vineyard and vatroom jobs as possible must be carried out by hand. He is fortunate in that his average vine age is high, and by hoeing the vineyards the vines are obliged to bury their roots deeper, giving better juice; chemicals are never used. Yields are kept ruthlessly down by pruning short and debudding, and it therefore usually follows that the grapes become perfectly ripe without any undue

waiting, and are harvested with impressive degrees of potential alcohol. As a result there is little need for chaptalization, giving even greater aromatic purity.

At harvest time the picked fruit is sorted through twice, once by the harvesters and then on a conveyor belt in the winery, for great wine does not tolerate the imperfect grape. The fruit is always destalked, and receives a four to five day cold maceration before fermentation takes place. This is a longish affair, conducted by the fruit's own yeast, with three to four *pigeages* per day at its height. Once it is over, the necessary press wine is added and a long period of aging or *élevage*, commences, in barrels of the finest quality. Since 1988 the wines have been bottled unfiltered. Every wine in the range has its own characteristics and personality, and it is interesting to note that these are evident from the most recent vintage in barrel through to bottled vintages of different ages, which unfortunately is not the case at all Burgundian domaines!

Gevrey-Chambertin Lavaux-Saint-Jacques

One of Mortet's most recent acquisitions is a superb 1.2-hectare plot of Lavaux Saint-Jacques, populated with vines of up to seventy years old. This wine is a masterpiece of understated elegance and finesse, with beautifully-defined aromas, concentration, and perfect balance. Firmness and breeding characterize it, rather than the robustness and power of some of its peers, and as such it makes a perfect dining-partner for a rack of lamb, or in fact farm-raised pigeon, cooked *en cocotte à la bonne femme*.

BURGUNDY
A.O.C. Corton

- *Wine selected:*
  Corton Clos des Cortons Faiveley
  Grand Cru (monopole)

- *Grape variety:*
  Pinot Noir
- *Average vine age:*
  36 years
- *Vineyard size:*
  2.97 hectares
- *Soil type:*
  Brown calcareous clay
- *Production:*
  13,000 bottles

Finest Vintages:
1999, 1996, 1990, 1978

Domaine Faiveley
BP 9
21701 Nuits-Saint-Georges Cedex
Tel. (0033) 380 61 04 55
- *Owner:* François Faiveley
- *On-site sales:* No
- *Visits:* No
- *Price:* ★★★

DOMAINE FAIVELEY

Its 124 hectares of vineyard on the Côte d'Or and the Côte Chalonnaise make Faiveley one of the largest estates in Burgundy, yet its size in no way compromises the quality of the firm's output, which is invariably among the Côte d'Or's very best. The name Faiveley is a guarantee for authentic, well-made Burgundy with great potential for development over time.

Six generations build up the estate

Founded in 1825, the firm is today run by the youthful and cultivated François Faiveley, the sixth generation of the family to do so. Successive generations had the enlightened idea of reinvesting in real estate when times were good, creating an edifice admired (and envied, no doubt) throughout Burgundy, and François Faiveley has continued that policy. However, growth is not one of his preoccupations, in fact he would rather limit the firm's expansion in order to remain in total control of its quality processes.

The magnificent patrimony accumulated by his forebears is centered around Nuits-Saint-Georges and Gevrey-Chambertin and comprises a great number of *Grands* and *Premiers Crus*, and extends to a fine Mercurey estate built up by his father. However, Faiveley has little "ordinary" land for sourcing his generic wines, and buys some 20 percent of his raw material every year to bridge this gap. The domaine's wines are predominantly red, yet it does possess a small plot of Corton-Charlemagne, with which he makes a yardstick example, as well as Rully, Montagny from domaine vines and the classic Côte d'Or whites made from purchased grapes.

The soft and sensual aroma of Pinot

Faiveley places great store on the aromatic qualities of his wines, and this colors his wine-making technique: high-quality grapes from low yields, picked at perfect ripeness, and vinified gently, slowly, and insistently, in order to extract all their aromatic qualities and finesse.

Although different growths are naturally treated differently, the operative methods of Faiveley wine-making generally follow a pattern: picking over the grapes, drying if necessary in a wind tunnel, and total destalking; pressing with a pneumatic press, cold maceration for several days with treading, followed by a long, unhurried fermentation with indigenous yeast at a relatively low 84°F (26°C); transfer into barrels (50–60 percent new for *Grands Crus*, 23 percent for *Premiers Crus*) for sixteen to eighteen month's maturation, with racking by gravity when necessary; and then equalization (again if necessary), fining with egg-white and bottling—by hand, directly from the barrel, in the case of all the best wines.

Corton Clos des Cortons Faiveley

An enclave lying in the Le Rognet-Corton vineyard in the commune of Ladoix is the source of a particularly distinguished wine. The Corton-Clos des Cortons Faiveley is always deep-colored, rich and tasty, fleshy and concentrated, with fruity blackberry opulence in its youth, and more complex aromas of leather, licorice, and spice as it matures, with, whatever its age, perfect balance and great length. This wonderful Burgundy deserves the company of noble game—a haunch of venison will do nicely!

BURGUNDY
A.O.C. Ruchottes-Chambertin

- *Wine selected:*
  Ruchottes-Chambertin
  Grand Cru

- *Grape variety:*
  Pinot Noir
- *Average vine age:*
  45 years
- *Vineyard size:*
  0.32 hectare
- *Soil type:*
  Clay and limestone
- *Production:*
  1,250 bottles

Finest Vintages:
1999, 1997, 1996, 1995, 1993, 1990

Domaine Georges Mugneret
5 Rue des Communes
21700 Vosne-Romanée
Tel. (0033) 380 61 01 57
Domaine Georges Mugneret is on the
left as one drives along Rue des
Communes from the church to the
mairie.
- *Owners:* Jacqueline, Marie-Christine
  & Marie-Andrée Mugneret
- *On-site sales:* Yes
- *Visits:* By appointment; closed
  Wednesdays
- *Price:* ★★★

1995

RUCHOTTES-CHAMBERTIN
Grand Cru
APPELLATION RUCHOTTES-CHAMBERTIN CONTRÔLÉE

Mis en bouteille à la propriété par
DOMAINE GEORGES MUGNERET
VOSNE-ROMANÉE - FRANCE

PRODUIT DE FRANCE

DOMAINE GEORGES MUGNERET

The late Doctor Georges Mugneret was one of Vosne's most respected wine makers, the creator of wonders of perfumed refinement that were sought out by Burgundy lovers far and wide. Before his premature death in 1988 his two daughters trained at his side, and they have maintained the domaine's standards with great flair. The female touch *chez* Mugneret is sure, the wines are exquisite.

Awaiting an improvement in Burgundy's fortunes

The young Georges Mugneret combined work on his parents' Vosne estate with medical studies, and went on to practise ophthalmology at Dijon, rising to become one of the country's leading specialists. He bought the fine nineteenth-century house in Vosne at an auction in 1930, and the price paid for this and his first plots of vines reflected the hard times and generally-felt pessimism with regard to the future of the region's wine industry. It was the success of his practice which enabled him to keep the unprofitable estate afloat while awaiting an improvement in Burgundy's fortunes.

Today his daughters, Marie-Christine and Marie-Andrée, and their mother Jacqueline are in fact nominally in charge of not one but two estates: Domaine Georges Mugneret comprises vineyards bought by the doctor, while Domaine Mugneret-Gibourg was the estate founded in 1928 by his parents, André Mugneret and Jeanne Gibourg. The women would like nothing more than to unite these two under one name, yet for absurd fiscal reasons this is apparently proving likely impossible, so the two estates continue to coexist.

Two sisters exact their standards

Since 1966 certain of the estate's vineyards have been looked after by sharecroppers, and today 3.5 hectares are worked by that arrangement, the crop being shared after the harvest. The rest of the vineyards are looked after by *tâcherons*, who are paid an annual fee to cultivate specific plots. Whatever the arrangement, the Mugneret sisters liaise closely with their vineyard workers to ensure that fruit is of as fine a quality as possible; short pruning and green harvesting are regular features of the estate's viticultural calendar.

In the cellars, the sisters—who are both qualified enologues—subject the fruit to a quality check on a sorting-table, and then destem it totally before giving it a cold maceration which lasts two to four days. Fermentation follows, then the wines are matured in oak for fifteen months. Some of the barrels are renewed every year, generally 20 percent for village wines, 40 percent for the *Premiers Crus* and 70–80 percent for *Grands Crus*. The wines are neither fined nor filtered.

Ruchottes-Chambertin

The Mugnerets are one of the few to make the little-seen Ruchottes-Chambertin, from the 3.3-hectare vineyard which lies above Mazis-Chambertin near the village of Gevrey. Half of their parcel was replanted in 2000, thus reducing the already tiny production of *Grand Cru* wine for some time. Their old, low-yielding vines produce a sumptuous wine of concentrated blackcurrant and spice flavors, rich in tannin and alcohol, and of great breeding. Its great purity and finesse are witness to the wine makers' mastery of their art. This noble wine needs a good dozen years to develop its complex bouquet, and, the Mugneret ladies suggest, may be enjoyed with a filet of beef in a mushroom crust, or stewed rabbit.

BURGUNDY
A.O.C. Bonnes-Mares

- *Wine selected:*
  Bonnes-Mares
  Grand Cru

- *Grape variety:*
  Pinot Noir
- *Average vine age:*
  35 years
- *Vineyard size:*
  1.45 hectares
- *Soil type:*
  Clay and limestone
- *Production:*
  4,800 bottles

Finest Vintages:

1999, 1997, 1996, 1995, 1993,
1991, 1990, 1988, 1985, 1983

Domaine Georges Roumier
21220 Chambolle-Musigny
Tel. (0033) 380 62 86 37
- *Owners:* Roumier family
- *On-site sales:* No
- *Visits:* No
- *Price:* ★★★

DOMAINE GEORGES ROUMIER

The quiet little village of Chambolle has long been recognized for the quality of the vineyards which crowd round it, yet its wine makers have not always in recent decades delivered the mesmerizing wines of which their lands are capable. One estate which always has, yet which today is nevertheless managing to surpass its previous high standards, is that founded by Georges Roumier.

Three generations of continued quality

At the origin of the estate, as so often the case, was a marriage. In 1924 Georges Roumier, a boy from nearby Saulieu, married a local girl, Geneviève Quanquin, and soon found himself running her family's estate, which owned parcels of Les Amoureuses, Les Fuées, and Bonnes Mares. Roumier soon enlarged their production by crop sharing of a plot of Musigny. From 1945 he started bottling all the production on the estate, and from the start bottles of Roumier wines gained a fine reputation—"classics of depth and harmony," Hugh Johnson judged them. The 1950s brought considerable further enlargement when he acquired one third of another estate, which included some Clos Vougeot and Bonnes Mares, and subsequently the entire Clos de la Bussière in the commune of Morey.

It was Jean-Marie, the fourth of five sons, who eventually took over in 1961 upon his father's retirement. In 1968 he gave himself a new challenge by acquiring some Corton-Charlemagne, and ten years later managed to buy the plot of Musigny, which the family had been sharecropping since the 1920s. His own son Christophe studied enology at Dijon, and started working with him in 1982. This young man is a highly talented wine maker with an inquiring and open mind, and the new impetus he has brought to the estate has taken it from the very good to the outstanding level.

Translating *terroir* into wine

The essence of his philosophy is that Nature and *terroir* stamp grapes from different vineyards, or *climats*, with different characteristics, and that the wine maker's job is to translate these as faithfully as possible into wine. The fruit itself is merely the vehicle, and wines which are merely fruity can not be considered of great interest. To carry *terroir*'s message, vines must be old, in perfect health—the Roumier vineyards are run by *lutte raisonnée*—and must produce little fruit. After that, vinification methods must be tailored to each different *terroir*; at Domaine Roumier there are no set rules, each year requires deep reflection and suitable action.

Bonnes Mares

The Roumier parcel of Bonnes Mares, the estate's flagship (if not its most prestigious) wine is made up of different geological entities, from which Christophe Roumier makes two different wines which he later blends together. Essentially there are *terres rouges*—Bathonian clay and limestone which give power, structure, and flesh—and *terres blanches*—Bajocian marl giving finesse and complexity. However, the whole is greater than the sum of its parts: a fleshy, chewy wine of great richness and breeding. It usually needs a decade to show its true colors, and will live a long adult life thereafter. On the great day there will hopefully be some marinated game and ripe, odorous Burgundian cheeses in the vicinity.

BURGUNDY
A.O.C. Nuits-Saint-Georges
1er Cru

- *Wine selected:*
  Nuits-Saint-Georges Les Saint-Georges
  Premier Cru

- *Grape variety:*
  Pinot Noir
- *Average vine age:*
  40 years
- *Vineyard size:*
  1.08 hectares
- *Soil type:*
  Clay and limestone
- *Production:*
  5,000 bottles

Finest Vintages:
2000, 1999, 1996, 1995, 1991, 1990

Domaine Henri Gouges
7 Rue du Moulin
21700 Nuits-Saint-Georges
Tel. (0033) 380 61 04 40
Domaine Gouges is on the junction of
Rue de la Duchesse and Rue du
Moulin, opposite Quai Fleury in the
center of the town.
- *Owners:* Gouges family
- *On-site sales:* No
- *Visits:* By appointment
- *Price:* ★★

DOMAINE HENRI GOUGES

Ever since its creation in 1925 the Henri Gouges estate has produced classic Nuits-Saint-Georges wines against which others have been measured. The quality of the wines stems in part from the fact that the estate has never been afraid to innovate, and recent experimentation has given them even greater finesse and *terroir* expression. This is one of the great estates of the côte de Nuits.

The champion of Burgundy's reputation

As a young man, Henri Gouges inherited 9 hectares of vineyards from his father just after World War I, and by adding other acquisitions between 1920 and 1934 gave the estate moreorless the form it has today. With the Marquis d'Angerville and a clutch of fellow growers, he set out to bring an end to the rampant fraud of the time involving large-scale blending of Burgundy with inferior wines, and started bottling his produce himself in 1933 and selling it direct to his customers. He was a champion of low-yielding Pinot Noir clones, and this obsession with tightly-controlled yields, passed down from father to son, has contributed to the enduring quality of Gouges wines. Today his grandsons Christian and Pierre run the estate, looking after wine making and the vineyard respectively.

A solution to the soil-erosion problem

One of the perennial problems on the steeper slopes of the Côte-d'Or is soil erosion after storms, which presents the unfortunate grower with the arduous task of carrying soil back up the slope. In 1975 Pierre Gouges had the idea of planting grass between the rows of vines, and this *enherbement* has been highly successful, not only in pinning down the surface soil, but also in contributing to weed prevention, reduced humidity, and thus rot, and to fruit quality and lower yields, because it obliges vines to bury their roots deeper. Furthermore, this practice has led to greater *terroir* definition in the wines. This innovation has been responsible in large part for the outstanding quality of recent vintages.

Wine-making for long aging

In the cellars, Christian Gouges prefers to destalk the entire crop. Fermentation with indigenous yeast and then maceration last some twenty days, and take place in closed cement vats. Wines are then transferred to barrels for their malolactic fermentation, and are subsequently aged for eighteen months in oak, of which at the very most 20 percent is renewed every year—the Gouges, unlike many, place new oak low on their list of priorities. Then wines are bottled, without filtration whenever possible.

Nuits-Saint-Georges Les Saint-Georges

All the Gouges wines have definite personalities, which is a tribute to the vision of the young Henri Gouges as he went about building up his superb domaine. The greatest wine is probably Les Saint-Georges, a *Grand Cru* in all but title, which needs ten years in bottle before it should be approached. This wine has the habitual tannic sturdiness of the southern Nuits vineyards, and with age develops a magnificent, powerful bouquet of leather, spice, burnt earth, meat, or game. It calls for no-nonsense meat dishes: either marinated or roast game, or red meat, grilled or served in a red-wine sauce, to be followed by medium-flavored cheeses—these will set off a Saint-Georges to perfection.

BURGUNDY
A.O.C. Richebourg

- *Wine selected:*
  Richebourg
  Grand Cru

- *Grape varieties:*
  Pinot Noir
- *Average vine age:*
  65 years
- *Vineyard size:*
  0.31 hectare
- *Soil type:*
  Clay and limestone
- *Production:*
  1,400 bottles

Finest Vintages:
2000, 1999, 1996, 1995, 1993

Domaine Jean Grivot
6 Rue de la Croix-Rameau
21700 Vosne-Romanée
Tel. (0033) 380 61 05 95
Rue de la Croix-Rameau runs
northwards from the Place de l'Église.
Domaine Grivot is on the right.
- *Owner:* Domaine Jean Grivot
- *On-site sales:* No
- *Visits:* No
- *Price:* ★★★★

DOMAINE JEAN GRIVOT

The Grivot estate has an enviable patrimony of *Grands* and *Premiers Crus* in the communes of Vougeot, Vosne, and Nuits, and has long made quintessential examples of each appellation. Yet the family laurels are never rested on, and reflection and experimentation are continual. From the village wines through to the Clos de Vougeot and Richebourg, intensity, balance, and class sing out.

A fine estate is parcelled together

After World War I, Gaston Grivot determined to build a prestigious wine domaine, and started by selling off odd family vineyards to finance the acquisition of a large parcel of Clos Vougeot. Grivot was one of the first students of enology at Dijon university, and was one of the first to bottle and sell his production himself. His bride brought him several parcels of Nuits-Saint-Georges as dowry, then his son Jean came into more vineyards upon his marriage to a Jayer. In 1984 the estate's pride and joy, a parcel of Richebourg, was acquired.

Guy Accad is consulted

Jean Grivot's son Etienne progressively took over responsibilities from his father in the early 1980s. This thoughtful young man had the feeling that, despite old vines, low yields, and suitable fermentation methods—which were at the time enabling him to make elegant, harmonious, and balanced wines—modern vintages had none of the sheer richness, power, and structure of wines of the past. What was lacking? He happened to meet the enologist Guy Accad, and found that their ideas went in the same direction. He asked Accad to counsel him, which was to earn him much jealous and uninformed criticism.

Revitalised soils and cooler fermentations

The problem lay initially in the fruit, Accad diagnosed; the soils were dying of an excess of nitrogen, potassium, and phosphorus, a legacy of excessive fertilizing over previous decades, and the fruit simply did not attain the ripeness of bygone days. Corrective measures and an organic regime were set under way. Fermentation methods were also called into question: Accad counseled a long period of maceration at a cool temperature, as naturally happened in the cold cellars of yesteryear, with liberal use of sulphur to retard fermentation, followed by fermentation itself at low temperatures.

After five vintages Grivot and Accad parted company; since then Grivot has practiced a synthesis of all the best elements of Accad's and previous methods. As the years go by the Accad-influenced wines seem to be taking on the qualities that had been missing; Grivot's courage seems to be paying off, and the scars of all the hypocritical attacks of other wine makers during this brief period are, thankfully, slowly healing.

Richebourg

Generally recognized as occupying the third step of the podium after Romanée-Conti and La Tâche, the Richebourg vineyard produces for its fortunate dozen owners a wine of majesty, opulence, refinement, and great structure, about which it is difficult to restrain the superlatives! With age its massive fruit may acquire a host of tertiary nuances, of the leather, meat, game, and spice varieties, while its succulence is irresistible. The sumptuous Grivot Richebourg, a wine for very special occasions, appreciates the company of hare *à la royale*, or a succulent cut of Charolais beef.

BURGUNDY
A.O.C. Romanée-Saint-Vivant

- *Wine selected:*
  Romanée-Saint-Vivant
  Grand Cru

- *Grape variety:*
  Pinot Noir
- *Average vine age:*
  50 years
- *Vineyard size:*
  0.99 hectare
- *Soil type:*
  Clay and limestone
- *Production:*
  2,500 bottles

Finest Vintages:
1999, 1996, 1995, 1993

Domaine Leroy
15 Rue de la Fontaine
21700 Vosne-Romanée
Tel. (0033) 380 21 21 10
- *Owner:* Domaine Leroy
- *On-site sales:* No
- *Visits:* No
- *Price:* ★★★★★

DOMAINE LEROY

One of the highest profiles in the Burgundy wine world today is that of Lalou Bize-Leroy, a smallish, attractive, and energetic woman with a strong personality and correspondingly strong convictions. This perfectionist makes wines of extraordinary quality, by viticultural methods which are decidedly risky, and then manages to sell them at outlandishly expensive prices.

A museum of Burgundy's finest

The name Leroy has long been revered by wine lovers. In 1868 the *négociant* firm Maison Leroy was founded in Auxey-Duresses, and by the efforts of François Leroy, then Joseph, and then Henri, it came to be known as a source of quintessential Burgundies. In 1942 Henri Leroy bought a half-share in the Domaine de la Romanée-Conti, and the Leroys still share the estate with the De Villaine family today. Over the years Maison Leroy has kept back stocks of its wines, and today possesses a treasure-house of several million bottles, which has given rise to comparisons with the Louvre and the national Library. Since 1955 Henri's daughter Lalou has been at the helm, and has presided over the firm with astuteness and devotion.

In recent years, in common with other *négociants* Leroy has found it progressively more difficult to come across sufficiently good wine for sale, and in 1988 Madame Bize-Leroy bought the Vosne domaine of Charles Noëllat, and subsequently that of Philippe Rémy in Gevrey, in order to provide a sure source of fruit.

Biodynamic viticulture and traditional wine-making

Her quest for *terroir* typicity and the most perfect fruit has led Madame Bize-Leroy on a passionate crusade on the behalf of Burgundy's much abused vineyard soil, and this has led her to embrace biodynamic viticulture as a way of regenerating its microorganic life. Biodynamics involve applying thoroughly ecological methods at precise moments, which are dictated by cosmic rhythms. This at the start caused many raised eyebrows and much skepticism, and her readiness to speak out against the unecological practices of others has not endeared her to everyone on the Côte. Extremely low yields are another feature of Leroy wines, and they are situated at levels that would be commercially unviable for anyone not selling at the firm's exorbitant prices.

The Leroy vinification methods are tailored for making wines for the very long term. There is a stringent quality control of the fruit, no destemming, no *débourbage* (setting of the juice), and then *élevage* (aging) in one hundred percent new oak, followed by bottling with absolutely no filtration.

Romanée-Saint-Vivant

Every year the Leroy Romanée-Saint-Vivant is one of the very finest Burgundies, and in 1995 the domaine fashioned a stunningly beautiful wine of enormous finesse and perfume, from a pitiful yield of 13 hl/ha. With a magnificent ethereal fragrance of roses, black fruit, and spice, it is exquisitely intense on the palate, precise, refined, and infinitely long. This is a wine that can be laid down for one's children. So entrancing is it that it is a shame to break the spell with the foreign savors of any dish, yet were one to do so, hare *à la royale* could not easily be bettered.

BURGUNDY
A.O.C. Richebourg

- *Wine selected:*
  Richebourg
  Grand Cru

- *Grape variety:*
  Pinot Noir
- *Average vine age:*
  40 years
- *Vineyard size:*
  0.35 hectare
- *Soil type:*
  Clay and limestone
- *Production:*
  1,200 bottles

Finest Vintages:
2000, 1999, 1996, 1993, 1990

Domaine Méo-Camuzet
11 Rue des Grands-Crus
21700 Vosne-Romanée
Tel. (0033) 380 61 11 05
Follow rue du Château, on the left
of Vosne's church. Rue des Grands-
Crus is the second on the right.
- *On-site sales:* Very few!
- *Visits:* No
- *Price:* ★★★★★

DOMAINE MÉO-CAMUZET

One of Vosne-Romanée's greatest estates was unknown as recently as the beginning of the 1980s, for its vineyards were worked by share-croppers, and the wine with which the estate was paid was sold off in bulk. Yet since 1983 much has changed at Domaine Méo-Camuzet, to the extent that it is today one of the highest fliers of Vosne and Burgundy.

A young man devotes himself to his estate

The estate's history has little in common with that of most on the Côte d'Or. It was built up by Etienne Camuzet, who was deputy for the Côte d'Or to the national assembly from 1902–1932, and mayor of Vosne. It was Camuzet, incidentally, who bought the Château du Clos de Vougeot in 1920 and sold it to the *Confrérie des Chevaliers du Tastevin* for a symbolic sum in 1945. He died in 1946 and left the estate to his daughter, but she died childless thirteen years later, and the estate then passed to Camuzet's great-nephew Jean Méo. Not long before passing away, Camuzet had approached the young Henri Jayer to ask if he was interested in operating a number of the Camuzet vineyards on a sharecropping basis, to which Jayer agreed. Jean Méo was an eminent figure in business and politics and had neither the time nor the inclination to look after the estate, so other *vignerons* were then contracted to look after the remaining vineyards. They made the wine, and the estate sold off its share in bulk.

Jayer began bottling his wine at the beginning of the 1970s and rapidly made himself a name, before officially retiring in 1988. That same year saw the arrival of Méo's son Jean-Nicolas, who had decided to devote himself to the estate. Coincidentally, several of the other sharecropper retired shortly after, and the vineyards conveniently reverted to the domaine. Méo, seconded by Christian Faurois—who had worked at the estate alongside Jayer—and Jayer himself in an advisory capacity, formed a resolute team.

From vineyard to bottle

Camuzet had bought his vineyards wisely, and the advanced age of many of the vines today only increases the superb quality of their wines. Méo and Faurois tend their vines as naturally as possible, using natural predators to eliminate the vine's adversaries where possible. Low yields, perfect ripeness, and severe selection bring top-quality raw material to the vatroom, and vinification thereafter is largely à la Jayer: total destalking, three to five days' cold maceration, fermentation with natural yeast to temperatures of 93–95°F (34–35°C); *pigeage* as the vintage requires, little chaptalization, and some eighty months' aging in barrel. *Grands* and *Premiers Crus* are matured in exclusively new oak, and Village and even Bourgogne Rouge have the luxury of 50 percent new wood.

Richebourg

The greatest of the Méo-Camuzet wines is their Richebourg, a sublimely perfumed, opulent, and sensual wine. It is always very subtle, with complex flavor nuances of beautiful purity, and it always impresses the taster with its great breeding. Ah! Fortunate indeed are the favored clients who can reserve (and pay for!) this wine every year! This is as splendid a wine as can be found on the Côte de Nuits, an aristocrat which appreciates the company of cuisine of its standing : tournedos Rossini has the necessary class.

BURGUNDY
A.O.C. Grands Échezeaux

- *Wine selected:*
  Grands Échezeaux
  Grand Cru

- *Grape variety:*
  Pinot Noir
- *Average vine age:*
  75 years
- *Vineyard size:*
  0.5 hectare
- *Soil type:*
  Clay and limestone
- *Production:*
  2,000 bottles

Finest Vintages:
2000, 1999, 1998, 1996, 1991, 1990

Domaine René Engel
3 Place de la Mairie
21700 Vosne-Romanée
Tel. (0033) 380 61 10 54
Domaine René Engel is in front
of the mairie on the left.
- *Owner:* Philippe Engel
- *On-site sales:* No
- *Visits:* 8-12 a.m., 2-6 p.m.,
  by appointment
- *Price:* ★★★

DOMAINE RENÉ ENGEL

It may not be particularly large in size, but the René Engel estate in Vosne-Romanée produces wines which are masterful examples of their appellations: aristocratic, full-bodied, richly flavored, and with structure for great longevity. This is an estate which has made great progress in recent years. Yet its present owner, René Engel's grandson, is not about to rest on his laurels!

The heritage of a great Burgundian

René Engel was a well-known figure in postwar Burgundy. Professor of enology for thirty-five years at Dijon University, a man of letters—among other works, his *Propos sur l'art de bien boire* (Remerks on the Art of Drinking well) set out in print his philosophy. And as one of the founders of the *Confrérie des Chevaliers du Tastevin*, he was unceasing in his promotion of the Côte d'Or. He inherited a 10-hectare estate and made many a glorious vintage before officially taking retirement in 1949. His son Pierre was of the same stamp, yet prolonged illness and disheartenment began to reflect in his wines, and the estate became progressively neglected. He died in 1981, five years before his father. Pierre's son Philippe, who had studied at Beaune's *lycée viticole* (a secondary school of wine making) and gained experience at his side, took over control of the estate.

A young man asserts himself

Philippe was determined from the start to halt the decline and produce the very finest wines possible. He asserted his authority in 1982 by forceably removing his grandfather—well-meaning yet ever-present— from the cellars, and started doing things his way. Initially, there were some essential improvements to be carried out, in both the vineyard and the vatroom. There had been no replacement of dead vines, and so the many spaces had to be filled; there had also been excessive fertilization with potassium-based products, and a program of bringing the soils back to life had to be put under way. In the cellars there was much old wood to be discarded and new wood to be bought.

Philippe Engel modified a number of the domaine's wine-making techniques to bring about the improvements he envisioned: yields, although never excessive in his father's time, were reduced further, and selection of the raw material accorded greater importance; a sorting table was bought in 1990. Today there is a good deal more *pigeage* than previously, and fermentations are allowed to rise to 102°F (35°C). Use of sulphur, racking, and filtering have all been reduced to the bare minimum, and new wood is bought in the quantities needed for the wines. Engel's modifications had a rapid effect, and his wines were soon back amongst the best in the village.

Grands Echézeaux

Lying on the west side of Clos de Vougeot, the 9.13 hectares of Grands Echézeaux give what Jean-François Bazin has described as "a wine for the erudite who appreciate nuances." Certainly Philippe Engel's wine will satisfy the most discerning connoisseur, offering as it does concentrated fruit, finesse, breed, and balance, with the wherewithal in great vintages to develop a supreme aromatic complexity over twenty years. What is more, this great Burgundy, ideally suited to game of both the winged and four-legged varieties, represents astonishingly good value for money compared with some of its more sought-after *Grand Cru* neighbors.

BURGUNDY
A.O.C. Romanée-Conti

- *Wine selected:*
  Romanée-Conti
  Grand Cru (monopole)

- *Grape variety:*
  Pinot Noir
- *Average vine age:*
  50 years
- *Vineyard size:*
  1.8 hectares
- *Soil type:*
  Clay and limestone
- *Production:*
  5,000 bottles

Finest Vintages:
1999, 1996, 1990, 1985

Domaine de la Romanée-Conti
1 Rue Derrière-le-Four
21700 Vosne-Romanée
Tel. (0033) 380 61 04 57
Follow Rue du Château, on the left-
hand side of Vosne's church. Rue
Derrière-le-Four is the second on the
right. The Domaine de la Romanée-
Conti is on the left.

- *Owner:* SCI du Domaine de la
  Romanée-Conti
- *Co-managers:* Aubert de Villaine,
  Henry Frédéric Roch
- *On-site sales:* Yes, depending on
  stock availability
- *Visits:* No
- *Price:* ★★★★★

DOMAINE DE LA ROMANÉE-CONTI

Few wine lovers get the chance in their lifetime to taste the legendary Romanée-Conti, although almost all have read about it, such is the wealth of print devoted to this mythical wine. Its extraordinary quality, combined with its extreme scarcity, unfortunately make it a luxury that only the inordinately well-off can afford. Romanée-Conti is the jewel in the crown of the domaine of the same name, a crown which is also set with other gems of stunning quality.

An unrivaled portfolio of vineyards

The domaine's vineyard holdings are of the very greatest quality: six red *Grands Crus*, at the qualitative pinnacle even of that exalted category, and one white *Grand Cru*, from Burgundy's finest white-wine vineyard. Plus 1.6 hectares of Vosne *Premier Cru* and a little Bâtard-Montrachet, which are never offered for sale.

The vines in all these vineyards are cosseted in a thoroughly ecological fashion. When they need to be replaced, it is done by *sélection massale*, using grafts from fifty plants in the Romanée-Conti vineyard which are selected for their health, robustness, moderate yield, fruit quality, and perfect regularity from year to year.

In preparation for a long life

Yields are kept at an extremely low level, and only when peak ripeness is attained is fruit picked by the domaine's experienced pickers, who operate an initial quality control in the vineyard, before transportation to the pressroom.

After undergoing another inspection on a conveyor belt the fruit is lightly pressed and tipped into the fermentation vats, generally with the stems. For vinification the domaine uses both open, wooden vats and stainless steel ones. A lengthy fermentation and maceration give the wines the color, tannin, acidity, and intense fruitiness to see them through a period of up to two years maturation in new Tronçais oak and many subsequent years in bottle.

Romanée-Conti

It was Louis François de Bourbon, Prince de Conti, who created the myth surrounding Romanée-Conti. Having purchased the Romanée vineyard in 1760 at ten times the rate for the finest vineyards, he withdrew it from the market and reserved it for his own glittering social events. Reclaimed as the property of the nation during the Revolution, the vineyard passed through the hands of several proprietors before passing into the ownership of the De Villaine and Leroy families. Today, such is demand that Romanée-Conti is sold singly in mixed dozens of the domaine's wines, both to satisfy a greater number of clients and as a measure against speculation.

The fabulous quality of Romanée-Conti lies in its great aromatic complexity, which evolves over the minutes in a truly awe-inspiring manner. Depending on the vintage and its age, its ethereal bouquet suggests roses, violets, cinnamon, leather, tobacco, coffee, caramel, hot earth, game...

While this wine is rich and opulent, it has an extraordinary degree of finesse, and is in no way a blockbuster. When sufficiently knowledgeable friends have been gathered, it should be enjoyed reverently, unhurriedly, and perhaps accompanied with a roast woodcock, followed by the monastic Cîteaux cheese. An indelible souvenir is guaranteed!

BURGUNDY
A.O.C. Clos Vougeot

- *Wine selected:*
  Clos Vougeot Vieilles Vignes
  Grand Cru

- *Grape variety:*
  Pinot Noir
- *Average vine age:*
  70 years
- *Vineyard size:*
  6 hectares
- *Soil type:*
  Clay and limestone
- *Production:*
  2,400 bottles

Finest Vintages:
1999, 1998, 1996, 1995,
1990, 1988, 1985

Château de la Tour
Clos de Vougeot
21640 Vougeot
Tel. (0033) 380 62 86 13
From Vougeot's main street follow the
road up to the Château du Clos de
Vougeot. In front of the entrance turn
left. Château de la Tour is on the right
approximately 100 meters further.
- *Owners:* Labet and Déchelette
  families
- *On-site sales:* Yes
- *Visits:* 10 a.m.–7 p.m., Wed.–Mon.,
  Easter until end of November
- *Price:* ★★★★

Château de la Tour

With its 50.6 hectares and eighty-two owners, Clos Vougeot epitomizes the fragmented Burgundian vineyard. As a result of its large surface area and varying soil make-up as well as its multiplicity of proprietors, Clos Vougeot wines vary greatly in quality depending on the position in the clos of the vines and on the talent of the vigneron. The most important owner is Château de la Tour, whose vines are admirably sited and whose wine is equally admirable.

Making Clos Vougeot on site

The château is actually situated inside the clos, hugging its northern side and lying below the historic Château du Clos de Vougeot. It was constructed in the late 1880s by the Beaune *négociant* Maison Beaudet Frères, who sold it and its vines to another *négociant*, Morin Père & Fils, in 1920. Eventually the estate passed into the hands of two sisters, Madames Labet and Déchelette, daughters of Jean Morin, and from the 1975 vintage, Jacqueline Labet took an active part in the day-to-day running of the estate, then in 1986 her son François took over.

François Labet consults Guy Accad

François Labet was convinced that the estate was not performing to its full potential, and got in touch with the enologist Guy Accad to work out how to improve the wine. The work commenced in the vineyard, with soil analyses, which permitted them to keep a close eye on the vines' nutrition; rectifications have since been biological. Low yields were the next target, to attain which Labet started pruning shorter and doing some serious debudding

in the spring, thus bringing to an end the green harvests and *bleeding* in the vatroom that had been estate practice. It was considered that lower yields would give better acidities, and this meant that harvesting could be delayed for extra-ripeness, without any detrimental heaviness.

The vatroom saw a good number of modifications also. Destalking of roughly half the crop became the norm, following which a prolonged maceration at 41°F (5°C), retarding the onset of fermentation by the use of sulphur, enabled the extraction of the finest aromas, color, tannin, and acidity. When fermentation got under way it was initially maintained also at a low temperature of around 79°F (26°C), although since Accad's departure Labet has allowed it to rise a little. Finally, maturing wines were treated to rather more new wood than had been the practice, up to 50 percent in good years, followed by bottling with neither fining nor filtration.

Clos Vougeot Vieilles Vignes

In exceptional years, Labet isolates the fruit of the oldest vines to make a Vieilles Vignes wine which is truly exceptional. The 1995 vintage gave birth to one such wine. Harvested at nine hl/ha, the fruit was macerated without destalking and, after fermentation, the wine spent twenty-two months in oak barrels, of which 75 percent were new. This will be a great wine, but owners of bottles will need a lot of patience! The 1989 Vieilles Vignes was starting to express itself forcefully and with great eloquence after seven years, but more structured and classic years need more time than that. When its day has finally come, enjoy it with venison, suggests Labet, in a *grand veneur* sauce.

BURGUNDY
A.O.C. Chambertin

- *Wine selected:*
  Chambertin
  Grand Cru

- *Grape variety:*
  Pinot Noir
- *Average vine age:*
  60 years
- *Vineyard size:*
  1.9 hectares
- *Soil type:*
  Clay and limestone
- *Production:*
  5,000 bottles

Finest Vintages:
2000, 1999, 1996, 1990

Domaine Trapet Père & Fils
53, route de Beaune
21220 Gevrey-Chambertin
Tel. (0033) 380 34 30 40
E-mail:
domTRAPETCHAMBERTIN@planetb.fr
The large ochre-colored Trapet
building is on the RN74, on the right
as one heads through Gevrey
southwards.
- *Owners:* Trapet family
- *On-site sales:* Yes
- *Visits:* 9–12 a.m., 2:30–5:30 p.m.,
  by appointment
- *Price:* ★★★★

DOMAINE TRAPET PÈRE & FILS

The Trapets are an integral part of the Gevrey-Chambertin scenery, having lived there and made wine for six generations. Not only has this permanence enabled the family to build up a superb vineyard patrimony, it has also led to a great understanding of the different vineyard plots, enabling the Trapets to bring out their *terroir* characteristics with great talent. Trapet wines, particularly those made since 1990, are models of purity, finesse, and balance.

A series of fine acquisitions

Louis Trapet of Chambolle married a Gevrey girl in the middle of the nineteenth century and settled in the village. His son Arthur started buying vines on Village land in the 1870s, and bought some of the *Premier Cru* Petite-Chapelle in 1877, today blended with that of the *Premier Cru* Clos Prieur, acquired in 1893. But the serious purchases came at the turn of the century, when Pierre-Arthur Trapet bought some Latricières-Chambertin in 1904, and the Chambertin itself in 1919. Each generation has added to the family holdings, the latest acquisitions being a section of the wonderfully-named Marsannay *climat* Les Grasses Têtes in 1979 and some Le Poirier and a plot of Chardonnay shortly after.

Reducing the vines' yields

Jean, the head of the house, has retired from active wine-making duties, which have been the province of his son Jean-Louis since 1990. The Trapet vineyards are the source of wonderful fruit, for many of the vines are old, and the vineyards are planted at an impressive density of twelve thousand per hectare, which restricts their productivity.

To further keep yields at a level conducive with quality, Jean-Louis debuds in the spring and if necessary also green harvests when the grapes turn color. Viticultural practices are ecological and minimal, the principal aim being to revive the micro-organic life in the soil which suffered in the post-war decades as a result of the vogue for potassium-based fertilizers, which take many years to work their way out of the soil.

Chambertin

The finest wine produced by the Trapets is without doubt the Chambertin. This noble vineyard, which gained its name (le champ Bertin) in the thirteenth century when it was a field (*champ*) lying alongside the Clos de Bèze and belonged to a certain Bertin, today mesmerizes wine lovers the world over with its complex, manly character.

The Trapet Chambertin is made with the habitual devotion, starting with a double selection process to eliminate any imperfect fruit, once by harvesters in the vineyard and again on arrival at the vathouse. The perfection of the fruit imparts enormous intensity and depth of flavor to the wine—which acquires a fleshy, opulent feel and a tannic structure guaranteeing longevity—through long, gentle fermentation. Elegance, aromatic purity, and class, these are the first words the Trapet Chambertin utters, and if he takes a moment the enchanted wine lover soons discovers the depth, complexity, and irresistible persuasiveness of this seigneur. A noble dish is called for: truffled filet of beef, or perhaps jugged partridge, followed, naturally, by that especially delicious *époisses*, *l'Ami du Chambertin* cheese.

BURGUNDY
A.O.C. Corton-Charlemagne

- *Wine selected:*
  Corton-Charlemagne
  Grand Cru

- *Grape variety:*
  Chardonnay
- *Average vine age:*
  40 years
- *Vineyard size:*
  9.5 hectares
- *Soil type:*
  Clay and limestone
- *Production:*
  48,000 bottles

Finest Vintages:
All recent vintages

Domaine Bonneau du Martray
21420 Pernand-Vergelesses
Tel. (0033) 380 215 064
Proceed to the Pernand church.
Continue along for 50 m up the Rue de
Frétille. The domaine is on the right.
- *Owner:* Le Bault de la Morinière
- *On-site sales:* Yes
- *Visits:* No
- *Price:* ★★★

Domaine Bonneau du Martray

The Pernand estate of Bonneau du Martray has two wines, a red and a white, which originate in neighboring parcels on the Corton hill, north-east of Beaune. It is principally the white wine, the Corton-Charlemagne, which has given the domaine its long-held world-wide reputation, and with reason, for this is a very fine example of its kind.

Stains on the Emperor's beard

The land around Aloxe and Pernand is generally more suited to the production of red wine than white, and a legend explains the origin of the white wine: the Emperor Charlemagne, a man of great stature and great appetite, owned a vineyard on the Corton hill which supplied him with his favorite tipple. As the years went by his beard turned progressively whiter, and the copious draughts of red wine left stains which grew ever more visible. His wife Liutgarde felt the stains detracted from his dignity, and tried to persuade him to drink white wine, so in order to accommodate her and at the same time continue imbibing his Corton, Charlemagne had some of the vineyard replanted with white-grape vines.

A historic clos

Whatever the real origin of the white-wine vineyard, the eighteenth-century historian Abbé Courtépée was of the opinion that the clos which Charlemagne donated to the collegiate church of Saulieu in 775 was that which much later belonged to M. Bonneau-Véry, the founder of Domaine Bonneau du Martray. It is situated at the top of the hillside, where the clay soil has noticeably more limestone and is much better suited to the Chardonnay vines.

The estate prospered and was handed down from generation to generation until 1969. René Bonneau du Martray, having no direct heirs, left the domaine to his niece, Comtesse Le Bault de la Morinière, and her son Jean-Charles runs it today.

Fermentation in tank and barrel

To make the Corton-Charlemagne, only pristine fruit, sorted for quality, will suffice. It is crushed gently in two membrane presses and the must is left to settle for a short while before transfer by gravity into carefully-chosen oak barrels. The alcoholic fermentation then takes place, slowly, at a controlled temperature. The lees are stirred occasionally to keep them in suspension and thereby increase the wine's aromatic qualities, and the malolactic fermentation eventually takes place. When all activity is over and the wine has had enough wood contact, it is transferred into tank again for equalization and then bottled.

Corton-Charlemagne

Bonneau du Martray's Corton-Charlemagne is one of the steeliest, for its vines face west rather than east, as is the case of the great majority of its peers, and receive more sunlight during the day. When young, it is somewhat reserved, and really requires ten years to reach its best. The citrus fruit, floral, or peach aromas of its youth (every vintage has a different personality) tend to develop into honeysuckle, hazelnut, and cinnamon flavors, while all through its life, vigor, power, and great length characterize it. Grilled lobster is a great friend, and it also gets on well with Bresse chicken *demi-deuil*.

BURGUNDY
A.O.C. Corton-Les-Bressandes

- *Wine selected:*
  Corton Bressandes
  Grand Cru

- *Grape variety:*
  Pinot noir
- *Average vine age:*
  30 years
- *Vineyard size:*
  1.71 hectares
- *Soil type:*
  Clay and limestone
- *Production:*
  3,000 bottles

Finest Vintages:
1999, 1996, 1995, 1993, 1990

Domaine Chandon de Briailles
1 Rue Sœur-Goby
21420 Savigny-lès-Beaune
Tel. (0033) 380 21 52 31
Indications to the domaine are given
at the entrance to the village.
- *Owners:* M. & Mme A.C. de Nicolay
- *On-site sales:* Yes
- *Visits:* By appointment. Closed on
  Sundays
- *Price:* ★★★

Domaine Chandon de Briailles

The simple, classical elegance of the eighteenth-century country house of Domaine Chandon de Briailles, and the neat formality of the garden which Le Nôtre laid out behind it, deepens the sense of anticipation as the visitor arrives to visit the estate and taste the wines. And indeed the elegance, refinement, and breeding are echoed in the domaine's *crus*, a fine range that is perfectly worthy of the elegant *monument historique* in which their creators reside.

Mother and daughter take charge of the estate

Domaine Chandon de Briailles had a great reputation in the post-war period, when it furnished some of the capital's top restaurants and was already exporting its wine. On the death of its owner, the Countess whose name it bore, it was bequeathed to her grandson Count Aymard-Claude de Nicolay. Unfortunately the Count worked in Paris, where he owns a real-estate business, and his wife Nadine was busy raising their young family; the estate inevitably started suffering through lack of close attention.

By the beginning of the 1980s however, with the children growing up, Nadine had time on her hands and needed to occupy herself constructively with something. Despite having the barest knowledge of how wine was made, she decided to settle in Savigny and put an end to the decline of the family estate. Her third daughter Claude also felt the call, and enrolled at Dijon University to study viticulture and vinification. Having gained her diploma, she spent a year seeing how things are done in Oregon and New Zealand, and then joined her mother in the adventure. The team was completed by a new, young, shaven-headed régisseur named Jean-Claude Bouveret, known to one and all as Kojak.

A re-examination of methods

Numerous have been the changes of practice and the refinements in technique, as the new team have re-examined methods in the light of modern enological knowledge and today's awareness of the errors of the past. Viticulture has become more ecological to protect soils and improve vine health and grape ripeness. Low yields are a priority, naturally enough, and surplus buds are removed once the shoots are out, if necessary, a green harvest is performed at the moment the fruit turns color.

The fruit is sorted through on a conveyor belt up on arrival in the vatroom, and fermentations are tailored to the *terroirs* and the production of elegant rather than robust, structured wines: maceration at 59°F (15°C) for five days, fermentations not exceeding 90°F (32°) with two remontages and two *pigeages* per day, and maturation in second-hand barrels bought from Domaine Méo-Camuzet.

Corton Les Bressandes

By far the Nicolays' largest *Grand Cru* holding, and arguably their best, is the Corton-Bressandes, which produces a very powerful wine of superb depth and complexity, that takes time to open up. When it does so, its magnificent bouquet of violets, truffle, and undergrowth is perfectly bewitching. It merits several minutes' appreciation, before it makes room on the taster's palate for a haunch of young wild boar.

BURGUNDY
A.O.C. Meursault 1er Cru

- *Wine selected:*
  Meursault Perrières
  Premier Cru

- *Grape variety:*
  Chardonnay
- *Average vine age:*
  45 years
- *Vineyard size:*
  0.52 hectare
- *Soil type:*
  Clay and limestone
- *Production:*
  2,100 bottles

Finest Vintages:
1999, 1996, 1990, 1989, 1985, 1983

Domaine Coche-Dury
9 Rue Charles-Giraud
21190 Meursault
Tel. (0033) 380 21 24 12
- *Owner:* Jean-François Coche
- *On-site sales:* No
- *Visits:* No
- *Price:* ★★

DOMAINE COCHE-DURY

The efforts of a father and his son over the last three decades have given Meursault a new estate of which to be proud, an estate which nowadays has far more clients jostling to buy its wines than it needs. Domaine Coche-Dury has become sought-after by top restaurants and specialist retailers, French and foreign, and one imagines that its loyal private clients cling to their allocations like limpets, for these are magnificent wines, which are still sold at uninflated prices.

From humble beginnings to prosperity

In the beginning, grandfather Coche acquired the first plots of vineyard land after World War I, when things were depressed and the outlook was grim; Meursault was not the prestigious name that it is today. He sold off the major part of his produce in bulk, but did a little bottling himself. He left the estate to his son in 1964. Georges, Jean-François Coche's father, set about enlarging his estate by purchase and share-cropping agreements, and increased the amount of bottling. He was proud of his wines and entered them into competitions with great success, which led to their inclusion on the wine lists of the best restaurants.

Jean-François Coche took over from his father in 1972, and over the years has managed to purchase a number of the plots he was looking after as a share-cropper. Recently he has made an excursion into the neighboring village of Puligny, with the acquisition of half a hectare of Les Enseignères.

Reduced yields and liberal use of oak

The key to quality, Coche tells his visitor, is low yields. To that end he keeps half of his Chardonnay vines trained by Cordon de Royat rather than all by Guyot simple, as is more usual, although the reverse is the case for Pinot Noir. Each variety has its preferred form, which leads to smaller bunches of smaller grapes and lower yields. Debudding early in the year is naturally regarded as an essential operation.

After a gentle pressing and settling of the lees, wines—including the Aligoté—are fermented in barrel; for the best wines half of the oak is new, for lesser wines proportionately less is new. They are given regular *bâtonnage*, and are racked twice before eventual bottling by hand directly off their finings after twenty months, without filtration.

Meursault Perrières

As well as several Village climats, Coche has two *Premiers Crus*. Les Perrières, lying above Charmes at the Puligny end of Meursault, is the Meursault *climat* that is generally reckoned to approach *Grand Cru* quality the most frequently, giving a wine of great liveliness and precision, with a steely, mineral character, and little of the overblown heaviness of certain other *climats*. Obviously, the man who makes the wine also makes a lot of difference, and the Coche-Dury Perrières combines this *terroir* personality with the polish and refinement of its maker's style, providing a wine of wonderful concentration, aromatic complexity, and harmony. This wine goes very well with lobster *à la crème*.

BURGUNDY
A.O.C. Pommard Premier Cru

• *Wine selected:*
Pommard Clos des Epeneaux
Premier Cru (monopole)

• *Grape variety:*
Pinot Noir
• *Average vine age:*
65 years
• *Vineyard size:*
5.2 hectares
• *Soil type:*
Clay and limestone
• *Production:*
20,000 bottles

Finest Vintages:

1999, 1996, 1993, 1991,
1990, 1988, 1985

Domaine Comte Armand
Place de l'Église
21630 Pommard
Tel. (0033) 380 24 70 50
The domaine is on the left of the
church. Peering into the courtyard one
can see a carved sign reading "Clos
des Épeneaux".
• *Owners:* Comtes Armand family
• *Manager:* Benjamin Leroux
• *On-site sales:* No
• *Visits:* By appointment
• *Price:* ★★

DOMAINE COMTE ARMAND

There are a fair number of Epenots wines, both Grands and Petits, made by one or other of Pommard's different estates. However, Epeneaux, the old French spelling of the same word, denotes one particular wine, the flagship wine of Domaine Comte Armand. Clos des Épeneaux is one of the finest and longest-living red wines of the entire côte de Beaune.

Nicolas Marey creates the Clos

Domaine Comte Armand is unusual for a Burgundian estate, for until recently it made only this one wine, which, equally unusual, comes from a vast monopol vineyard. What is more, the vineyard has belonged to the same family since it was pieced together shortly after the Revolution.

It was Nicolas Marey who, following the carving up of the estates of the dispossessed church and nobility, progressively bought up parcels of the Grands and Petits Epenots vineyards. He surrounded his new vineyard with a wall and started using the old French version of the name to differentiate his wine from those of his neighbors. Marey's daughter Clothilde married Jean-François Armand, and the *clos* thus passed into the Armand patrimony. Today, four generations on, it is owned by Comte Gabriel Armand.

Biodynamics and thoughtful winemaking

The Armands have traditionally worked far from Burgundy, and the estate has been run by a *régisseur* for most of the last century. In 1984 Comte Armand appointed a twenty-two-year-old Canadian named Pascal Marchand to look after things, an appointment which proved inspired, for Marchand was responsible for greatly increasing the wine's quality. After some fifteen years the Canadian was tempted away from the estate by another challenge,

and the owner hired another young man, Benjamin Leroux, who has maintained the momentum and proved himself a worthy successor.

Leroux does not come from a wine-making family, it was a passion for wine which drove him to look for work in the milieu; and more precisely, it was a passion for Pinot Noir that brought him to Burgundy. Studies at Beaune and Dijon were followed by work experience with Drouhin in Oregon, at the Medoc's Château Cos d'Estournel, in New Zealand, and finally with the Beaune firm Louis Jadot. Leroux then understudied Marchand, with whom he shared the same working philosophy, and took over in 1999. His predecessor had introduced a biodynamic regime onto part of the estate in 1988, and Leroux extended this to cover all the vineyard parcels. Every year he separates the fruit from vines of different ages and makes four Epeneaux wines. The finely-adapted aging of each and the subsequent blending just before bottling lends great intensity and balance to the final wine. The most noticeable change to the wine in recent vintages, he feels, comes from the vineyard: as the vines have become progressively healthier through biodynamics, the wine has become progressively smoother.

Pommard Clos des Epeneaux

The efforts of its two young managers have given the Clos des Épeneaux breeding and elegance which it lacked before, and have tamed the often-brutal Pommard structure to contribute greater finesse. This is still textbook Pommard, but with more refinement than most. Young, it has a mass of black-fruit richness, regimented by a corset of ripe tannin and acidity, a combination which destines it for a long and happy life. When its youthful ardor has been calmed, it makes a fine match for a crusty cheek of beef and potato pie.

BURGUNDY
A.O.C. Montrachet

- *Wine selected:*
  Montrachet
  Grand Cru

- *Grape variety:*
  Chardonnay
- *Average vine age:*
  55 years
- *Vineyard size:*
  0.31 hectare
- *Soil type:*
  Clay and limestone
- *Production:*
  900 bottles

Finest Vintages:
1999, 1997, 1992, 1990,
1989, 1986, 1982

Domaine des Comtes Lafon
Clos de la Barre
21190 Meursault
Tel. (0033) 380 21 22 17
- *Owners:* Comtes Lafon
- *On-site sales:* No
- *Visits:* No
- *Price:* ★★★★★

DOMAINE DES COMTES LAFON

There is one Meursault estate which towers above its peers, making wines that are sought out by connoisseurs the world over. Domaine des Comtes Lafon is the source of wines of supreme richness, purity, and character, achieved thanks to excellent vineyard holdings, solid family traditions and the talent and devotion of their wine maker.

Jules Lafon founds the estate

The estate came into being when Jules Lafon, a lawyer and finance controller in Dijon, married a Meursault girl, Marie Boch, in 1894. Marie had inherited a good number of vineyard plots, and the wealthy Lafon, a *bon vivant* and connoisseur, added others to their estate and swapped the lesser of hers for better-quality land. He died in 1940, leaving two sons, Pierre and Henri.

Pierre died four years after his father, and Henri, who cared not a jot for the estate, decided to sell up; however, he had failed to consult René, Pierre's son, who resisted the sale. René took on the estate, and despite the difficulties of working in Paris and financial constraints imposed on him by Henri through the courts, he managed to keep it operational, making the wine with the help of a faithful on-site employee and by selling it off in bulk. From 1961 he started bottling all on the wine estate.

Letting the wine make itself

Today's René's son Dominique is in charge, and this widely-traveled and open-minded young man has proved himself one of Burgundy's greatest and most consistent wine makers. Although the estate made its name by its white wines, Dominique Lafon has taken pride in increasing the reputation of the red wines—the estate has large parcels in three of Volnay's finest *Premiers Crus*—which he has done with great success.

The greatness of Lafon wines may be attributed first to their vineyards. Thanks to a viticultural regime which is as organic as possible, its healthy soils give healthy vines, that are pruned short and debudded at the start of the season to reduce the yield and give top-quality grapes, which are picked late for maximum aromatic concentration. Little in the way of vinification has changed over the last century, the essential action being to intervene as little as possible and let the wine make itself. Long aging in the Lafon cellars, reputed the coldest in Burgundy, then precedes bottling with careful fining and no filtration.

Montrachet

With one third of a hectare of the precious stony russet soil of Le Montrachet, bought by his great-grandfather at auction in 1918, Dominique Lafon makes a tiny amount of one of the world's greatest white wines. Deep though it is, its fine golden yellow color does not really prepare one for the intensely concentrated, fat, and opulent mouthful of flavor, stunning in the extent of its dimensions, which has formidable length once swallowed. This Montrachet should not be broached before ten years of age, and deserves nothing less than a lobster, grilled on a spit, for company—an unforgettable, once in a lifetime experience!

BURGUNDY
A.O.C. Bâtard-Montrachet

- *Wine selected:*
  Bâtard-Montrachet
  Grand Cru

- *Grape variety:*
  Chardonnay
- *Average vine age:*
  30 years
- *Vineyard size:*
  0.6 hectare
- *Soil type:*
  Clay and limestone
- *Production:*
  3,500 bottles

Finest Vintages:
2000, 1999, 1996, 1992, 1990, 1989,
1986, 1985, 1983, 1982

Domaine Étienne Sauzet
11 Rue de Poiseul
21190 Puligny-Montrachet
Tel. (0033) 380 21 32 10
- *Manager:* Gérard Boudot
- *On-site sales:* No
- *Visits:* No
- *Price:* ★★★

DOMAINE ÉTIENNE SAUZET

Gérard Boudot shows a remarkable talent for making wine and a perfect understanding of the various *terroirs* in his charge and of what great white Burgundy is all about. With every new vintage, he fashions beautiful examples of some of the greatest appellations, which are snapped up by a long list of Michelin-starred restaurateurs and loyal French clients. This is a very fine estate.

Love and a change of vocation

Gérard Boudot did not come from a wine-making family. This son of Le Creusot, west of the côte chalonnaise, was set on working in the forestry and lakes department, yet he failed the necessary exams and had to reset his sights. He enrolled in a course at Beaune's secondary school for wine making. He met Sauzet's granddaughter Jeanine after one of his rugby matches in Beaune; they duly fell in love and married, and when the moment came in 1974 for one of the grandchildren to take charge of the estate, his wife's brothers not being interested, the job fell to him.

A *négociant* activity replaces lost vineyards

Over the years Boudot had his work cut out getting the vineyards into shape, for they had suffered years of potassium-based fertilizer excesses. Patiently he applied small doses of magnesium to neutralize the potassium and had unending analyses carried out; after a decade the soils were living and breathing again. On the positive side, the experience gave him an intimate knowledge of all his charges!

In 1989 Jeanine's mother officially handed down the estate equitably to her children, and her son Jean-Marc decided unexpectedly to withdraw his portion. The Boudots thus suddenly found themselves with an estate reduced by a third. The logical answer, which is what they did the next year, was to form a *négociant* company and buy raw material to make up for the shortfall, which was possible thanks to Boudot's relationships with a good number of conscientious growers.

Limited yields and peak ripeness

His wine making holds no revolutionary secrets. Severe debudding is carried out in spring to limit yields, and harvesting is delayed until peak ripeness, which is tricky, for the slightest overripeness and accompanying acidity deficiency are undesirable. Fermentation takes place at around 8°F (20°C) in barrel, and there is then a long settling period, so that maturation will take place only on very fine lees, for maximum finesse. Wines are roused with ever-diminishing regularity until the first racking, after a year, and prior to bottling two months later they are transferred to vat for unification and fining, which lasts up to three weeks.

Bâtard-Montrachet

Demonstrating Boudot's painstaking thoroughness, the Bâtard-Montrachet, vinified in an equal proportion of new and used barrels for fifteen months, is a superbly-fashioned wine of great power and dimension. Despite being concentrated, intense and virile, it is unusually elegant, which is a hallmark of Gérard Boudot's wines, and remarkably long. It needs cellaring for at least eight years, and at table may be served, suggests Jeanine, with creamy Bresse chicken and morels, or grilled lobster.

BURGUNDY
A.O.C. Montrachet

- *Wine selected:*
  Montrachet
  Grand Cru

- *Grape variety:*
  Chardonnay
- *Average vine age:*
  35 years
- *Vineyard size:*
  0.58 hectare
- *Soil type:*
  Clay and limestone
- *Production:*
  2,280 bottles

Finest Vintages:
1999, 1996, 1995

Domaine Jacques Prieur
6 Rue des Santenots
21190 Meursault
Tel. (0033) 380 21 23 85
The Prieur estate lies at the bottom
of the Lafons' Clos de la Barre. Take
the main turn from the N74 towards
Meursault, turn right at the junction
and follow the road for 100 m. Rue
des Santenots is on the right.
- *Owner:* SCI du Domaine Jacques
  Prieur
- *Directors:* Martin Prieur & Bertrand
  Devillard
- *On-site sales:* Yes
- *Visits:* By appointment
- *Price:* ★★★★★

DOMAINE JACQUES PRIEUR

Few estates on the Côte d'Or can be as richly endowed in great vineyards as Domaine Jacques Prieur, in Meursault, which has holdings in or farms parcels of nine *Grands Crus* and twelve *Premiers Crus*, stretching from Chambertin Clos de Bèze all the way down to Le Montrachet. To the regret of connoisseurs everywhere the estate went through a prolonged period of mediocrity in the 1970s and 1980s, but it has arisen determinedly from this in recent years. Today Domaine Jacques Prieur produces wines of magnificent quality.

A great domaine fulfils its potential

The prime movers behind the recent renaissance have been Jacques Prieur's grandson's Martin and Bertrand Devillard, who represents the consortium headed by the Côte Châlonnaise *négociant* firm Antonin Rodet, which since 1988 has owned half of the domaine. Aided by the Rodet enologist Nadine Gublin, they have introduced many a change, and the improvement in quality has been radical. Reducing yields was one of the first priorities, along with improving vine health and going for greater fruit ripeness, and these aims have been brought about by shorter pruning, debudding, and green harvesting if necessary, by reviewing the way vines are trained in order to increase insolation and aeration, and by working the vineyard in as ecological a way as is possible.

At harvest time fruit is now transported in receptacles containing thirty kilograms in order to minimize the risk of damage (this is particularly important for an estate with vineyards so far from base) and a conveyor belt has been acquired for picking through the fruit on arrival. Black grapes are destemmed partially or totally and given some five days' cold maceration without crushing, before fermenting in open wooden vats. For color and tannin extraction they are given three serious *pigeages* a day, then are transferred by gravity to cask for aging. There is none of the former reluctance to invest in new oak, the new team give wines all that they need. Finally, if necessary, there is a light filtration, then unification and bottling.

Montrachet

Domaine Prieur is one of seventeen owners of the 8-hectare Montrachet vineyard, a strip of priceless, russet clay that gives what is undoubtedly the greatest, most complex, and most costly dry white wine in the world. Its cosseted fruit is pressed very, very gently in a pneumatic Bücher, and the juice is left to settle at a low temperature in stainless steel overnight before transfer by gravity into new oak casks, in which it ferments at around 72°F (22°C). The wine is stirred once a week until the alcoholic and malolactic fermentations are complete, and is then left untroubled for nineteen months, before a light filtration and bottling.

The result is a powerhouse of opulent, concentrated refinement of utter hedonism, the flavor waves of which are given edge by perfectly calculated acidity, ending with a phenomenal finish. Yet mere words are completely insufficient to describe something that so transcends the palate's usual fare. This great wine is best sipped among friends, reverently, on its own, in order to appreciate its total perfection.

BURGUNDY
A.O.C. Pommard 1ᵉʳ cru

- *Wine selected:*
  Pommard Les Rugiens
  Premier Cru

- *Grape varieties:*
  Pinot Noir
- *Average vine age:*
  80 years
- *Vineyard size:*
  0.15 hectares
- *Soil type:*
  Clay and limestone
- *Production:*
  540 bottles

Finest Vintages:
1999, 1996, 1990

Domaine Jean-Marc Boillot
La Pommardière
21630 Pommard
Tel. (0033) 380 22 71 29
- *Owner:* Jean-Marc Boillot
- *On-site sales:* No
- *Visits:* No
- *Price:* ★★

DOMAINE JEAN-MARC BOILLOT

R are is the wine maker who is as good at making red as white, or vice versa, yet Jean-Marc Boillot is one such talented individual. At his fine house, La Pommardière, on the outskirts of Pommard, he vinifies a range comprising no less than twenty different wines, equally balanced between red and white, that are deliciously full of flavor and aroma, and of which some are capable of attaining great age.

An inheritance gives birth to a new domaine

Boillot's skills were learned working with his grandfather Étienne Sauzet, and gained further experience from 1984 as the original manager and wine maker at the new Olivier Leflaive Frères *négociant* firm. In 1990 his mother, Sauzet's only child, passed down the Sauzet estate to her three children, and Boillot decided to break away with his share and set up on his own, for which no doubt the Leflaive experience proved very useful. Starting off with his inheritance of four Puligny *Premiers Crus* and some Puligny village land, he has added to these a fine selection, principally of red-wine vineyards centred around Volnay and Pommard.

The quest for maximum aroma

Surprisingly, Boillot makes all of his whites by a more-or-less unvarying formula, from Bourgogne blanc through to *Premiers Crus*, and the same goes for his reds. White grapes are pressed, and the musts cooled, chaptalized and fermented using cultured yeast, following which the wines are aged in wood with *bâtonnage* for one year. Black grapes are destalked and then macerated for four to five days at a cool temperature, and then warmed up for fermentation to start. For red wines, cultured yeast are preferred, because they give more reliable results in the eternal quest for maximum aroma. The fermentations take place in closed vats, again to preserve aroma, the lids coming off only to carry out *pigeage* and chaptalization. After three weeks' vatting the wines are run off into barrels, and spend up to eighteen months maturing before bottling. Wines across the board receive 20-25% new oak every year, with the exception of the Pommard Rugiens, for which half of the barrel is renewed annually.

Boillot is one of the rare wine makers to sing the praises of the unfashionable practice of filtering wines, and is contemptuous of the many who, he alleges, claim not to filter but do so clandestinely. Carried out carefully, he asserts, filtration enhances a wine's aromatic purity. On the evidence, how can one disagree?

Pommard Les Rugiens

The russet-colored clay and limestone soil of Les Rugiens (the name is thought to come from the soil's color) gives birth to a wine which epitomizes the virile, rich and structured Pommard character. The venerable eighty-year-old Boillot vines thrive there, yet in their old age give niggardly yields (27 hl/ha in 1996), which of course have the advantage of contributing great intensity of flavor. This wine has great concentration, richness, and structure, and a magnificent long and pure finish. Drink it with pigeon or game, says Jean-Marc Boillot, but first leave it in the cellar for many a year, and let it find its voice.

BURGUNDY
A.O.C. Musigny

- *Wine selected:*
  Musigny
  Grand Cru

- *Grape variety:*
  Pinot Noir
- *Average vine age:*
  25 years
- *Vineyard size:*
  0.7 hectare
- *Soil type:*
  Clay and limestone
- *Production:*
  2,500 bottles

Finest Vintages:
1999, 1998, 1996, 1995, 1993,
1990, 1989, 1988, 1985

Maison Joseph Drouhin
7 Rue d'Enfer–BP 29
21201 Beaune Cedex
Tel. (0033) 380 24 68 88
Internet: www.drouhin.com
Visitors to Drouhin should present
themselves at the cellar entrance in
Place Général Leclerc, in front of the
Notre Dame church.
- *Owner:* Robert Drouhin
- *On-site sales:* No
- *Visits:* By appointment
- *Price:* ★★★★

MAISON JOSEPH DROUHIN

The *négociant* house Joseph Drouhin has for long been a purveyor and champion of authentic Burgundy, unafraid of periodically reviewing its methods and innovating in the quest for self-improvement. This is a house which continues to provide the finest quality available, in a style which encapsulates fragrance, elegance, and balance—a style eminently suited to Pinot Noir and Chardonnay.

A century of growth and diversification

The house has existed since 1880, when Joseph Drouhin bought up a merchant business in Beaune and gave it his name. His son Maurice gave the firm its twentieth-century vocation by deciding to specialize in the wines of Burgundy and to invest in vineyards. After the World War II the house made concerted efforts on the export market and laid the foundations of its international reputation. Robert Drouhin succeeded Maurice in 1957 and, foreseeing the increasing demand for fine Burgundy, continued the policy of vineyard acquisitions, from 1960 expanding northwards into the Côte de Nuits, then in 1968 north west to take in a Chablis estate. Finally in 1988 the expansion culminated in the creation of Domaine Drouhin in Willamette Valley, Oregon. Drouhin's daughter Véronique is in charge of this American estate, and the wines are very promising.

Experimentation in the vineyard

Following the general trend among the more conscientious and thoughtful growers in Burgundy, the house has recently become aware of shortcomings in its viticultural practices in relation to vineyard soils and environments, and Philippe Drouhin, in charge of all the firm's vineyards since 1988, has adopted practices far more friendly to these and to the vine. They have included reintroducing hoeing to eliminate weeds instead of spraying, using organic compost, using biological products to defend the vine against certain illnesses, grassing the steeper vineyards, using bacteria and natural predators to combat cryptogamic illnesses and insect enemies of the vine. Since 1996 the firm has been trying out biodynamics, which involve administering the biological methods in accordance with the planetary calendar.

All this experimentation is driven by Drouhin's persistent quest for finer fruit, which will enable them to make even finer wines.

Musigny

Some prefer the Drouhin whites, and it is easy to see why, for they are wines of dazzling purity, definition, and finesse. The reds also are exemplary in their respective appellations, perhaps the finest being the Musigny. That great *terroir* certainly lends itself to the Drouhin style. The ethereal and bewitching fragrance, and the silky, delicate yet intense palate provide a stunningly eloquent reflection of the famous *climat*. A wine of such seduction that is difficult to resist drinking in its youth, yet the wine lover who manages to resist the temptation for a dozen years is very amply compensated! Stuffed turkey or roast leg of lamb will have sufficient respect to allow this diva to sing out to her heart's content, to the absolute rapture of all present.

BURGUNDY
A.O.C. Chevalier-Montrachet

- *Wine selected:*
  Chevalier-Montrachet
  Grand Cru

- *Grape variety:*
  Chardonnay
- *Average vine age:*
  27 years
- *Vineyard size:*
  2 hectares
- *Soil type:*
  Clay and limestone
- *Production:*
  8,000 bottles

Finest Vintages:
1999, 1996, 1995, 1992

Domaine Leflaive
Place des Marronniers
21190 Puligny-Montrachet
Tel. (0033) 380 21 30 13
- *Owner:* Leflaive family
- *Manager:* Anne-Claude Leflaive
- *On-site sales:* No
- *Visits:* No
- *Price:* ★★★★★

DOMAINE LEFLAIVE

For connoisseurs around the world the name Puligny-Montrachet is inseparable from that of Leflaive, and images of the Domaine's label, its heavy yellow lead capsule and the rich, opulent, and heady nectar in the bottle get the saliva flowing and the memory casting back to the last blissful occasion. This, in many peoples' book, is the greatest white wine estate in the world.

An implacable belief in the future

Domaine Leflaive as we know it was the creation of Joseph Leflaive, descendant of a vineyard-owning family that can trace its lineage back to 1580. Having inherited 2 hectares of vines in 1905 and believing implacably in Burgundy's future, which was at the time going through the dreadful post-phylloxera period when much land was up for sale, Leflaive set about buying up plots, and by 1925 had accumulated a fine estate of some 25 hectares of vineyards.

From the earliest days the wine was by all accounts excellent, and over the century many a great wine has been made and the great reputation forged. Joseph was succeeded by his sons Jo and Vincent, the *régisseur* François Virot by his son Jean, and in 1973 a *Société civile d'exploitation* was founded to accommodate the co-ownership of the numerous descendants. In 1990 the cousins Anne-Claude and Olivier Leflaive were named comanagers of the Domaine, and Pierre Morey, a highly respected Meursault grower, was employed as a replacement for the retired Jean Virot.

A change to biodynamic viticulture

Top estates, more than any others, are not allowed to rest on their laurels, and the present generation is doing anything but that. Uneasy about the increasing immunity of vines to vineyard treatments and the slow asphyxiation of the soil, Anne-Claude had the courage to envisage a radical change in viticultural practice, and initiated parallel tests of biological and biodynamic methods of culture on certain plots, in the hope of reviving the microorganic life in the soil and enabling the plants to develop their own system of resistance to disease. Eyebrows were raised, and there were no doubt mutterings about youthful irresponsibility with some of Burgundy's greatest vineyards. However since late 1997, after seeing enough improvement to vindicate their action, the estate has gone ahead and conducted all viticultural operations according to biodynamic principles, which necessitate applying organic treatments by the planetary calendar.

Chevalier-Montrachet

Among their fabulous patrimony of *Grand* and *Premiers Crus* the Leflaives own two of the 7 hectares of the Chevalier-Montrachet *climat*, which lies above Le Montrachet itself. This magnificently perfect liquid takes a dozen years to mature, developing infinite depth of flavor, sensuality, and refinement, and combining power and elegance with rare success. Clive Coates put it perfectly: "this is a wine to drink on bended knees and with heartfelt and humble thanks." A Leflaive Chevalier-Montrachet appreciates being served with a noble crustacean, such as lobster, *à l'américaine* or simply grilled, or *langoustes thermidor*. This must be gastronomic perfection!

BURGUNDY
A.O.C. Bienvenues-Bâtard-Montrachet

- *Wine selected:*
  Bienvenues-Bâtard-Montrachet
  Grand Cru

- *Grape variety:*
  Chardonnay
- *Average vine age:*
  35 years
- *Vineyard size:*
  0.12 hectare
- *Soil type:*
  Clay and limestone
- *Production:*
  600 bottles

Finest Vintages:
2000, 1999, 1996

Domaine Louis Carillon & Fils
21190 Puligny-Montrachet
Tel. (0033) 380 21 30 34
On entering Puligny from Meursault
Domaine Carillon is on the right, well
indicated, just before the church.
- *Owner:* Carillon family
- *On-site sales:* Yes
- *Visits:* By appointment
- *Price:* ★★★★

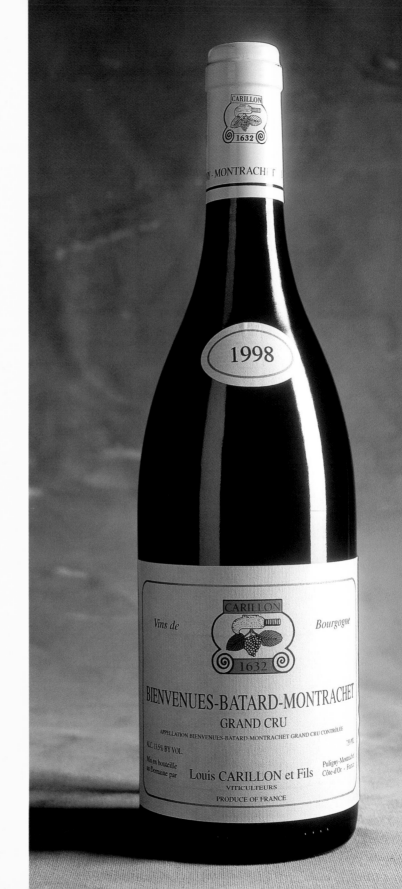

DOMAINE LOUIS CARILLON & FILS

Their stationery and labels give the date of 1632, but the Carillons have recently unearthed a document attesting to the viticultural activities of Jehan Carillon in 1520, which makes this estate the doyen of Puligny, predating even the Leflaives. Carillon wines have their own style, which might be summed up as medium-bodied, rich, and elegant, with just a hint of oakiness. They are made for the long term, and are delicious.

Time, mortality and continuity

A visit to the Carillon estate can induce a bout of reflection on time, mortality, and continuity. Here is a family that will soon be able to celebrate its half-millennium, which today comprises three generations: grandfather Robert, retired but always around and ready with advice, father Louis, head of the domaine, and sons Jacques and François, both now taking care of all the day-to-day operations. No doubt in the near future there will be younger heads peaking for the first time around the cellar door, discovering perhaps a little apprehensively the mysterious environment of the wine cellar! And here history is everywhere: the courtyards, nooks, and passages all have their story to tell, with much that has survived since the Revolution. Yet at the same time history rubs shoulders with the late twentieth-century, whose stainless steel vats and other accoutrements of the modern wine maker's art sit at ease in the cellars of a bygone age.

Indeed the Carillons seem to blend tradition with modernity in their aim for uncompromising quality. In the vineyard they are as ecological as is practical, ploughing the soil to keep weeds at bay and using treatments only when examination of vines has informed them that they are necessary. Replanting is carried out parcel by parcel, in order to have a good mixture of vine ages, and the soil is left fallow for a number of years before receiving the young vines; this sacrifice of a few years' crops, to revive the soil for the benefit of following vintages, is indicative of the Carillon spirit. Grapes are harvested by hand at peak ripeness, that is after some and before others, for the Carillons do not want over-ripe any more than underripe fruit.

When it comes to making the wines, after pressing and a short period of settling the better wines are fermented in barrel. Exotic, tropical fruit aromas are not appreciated, and therefore fermentations are carried out at around 77°F (25°C), *bâtonnage* is not done to excess, and the amount of new wood used each year is at most 20 percent for *Grand* and *Premiers Crus* and 10% for Village wines. In such a way the natural, citrus purity of the fruit and the terroir character are never swamped by artificial vinification flavors.

Bienvenues-Bâtard-Montrachet

A mere six hundred bottles are produced in an average year of the Carillons' greatest wine, Bienvenues-Bâtard-Montrachet. This seigneur combines power and delicacy, fragrance, and intensity, and—thanks to the flair of its creators—manages to avoid the heaviness and dominant oakiness of certain other versions.
It should not be broached before its sixth year, for its rich fruitiness takes time to find its voice. A masterpiece of restraint and class, it calls for the noblesse of a lobster *à l'armoricaine*.

BURGUNDY
A.O.C. Beaune 1ᵉʳ Cru

- *Wine selected:*
  Beaune Clos des Ursules
  Premier Cru (monopole)

- *Grape variety:*
  Pinot Noir
- *Average vine age:*
  35 years
- *Vineyard size:*
  2.2 hectares
- *Soil type:*
  Clay and limestone
- *Production:*
  15,000 bottles

Finest Vintages:
1997, 1996, 1993, 1990, 1989, 1985

Maison Louis Jadot
21 Rue Eugène-Spuller
21200 Beaune
Tel. (0033) 380 22 10 57
Enter the old town by way of Rue de
Lorraine, and take the first left, Rue
Emmanuel. Turn left, then right, cross
Place Morimont and proceed along
the one-way Rue Spuller. Jadot is on
the right.
- *Owner:* Kopf family
- *Chairman & Managing Director:*
  Pierre-Henry Gagey
- *On-site sales:* Yes
- *Visits:* By appointment
- *Price:* ★★★

MAISON LOUIS JADOT

Wearing the twin caps of merchant and grower with equal ease and distinction, the Beaune firm Louis Jadot makes some 130 wines, the quality of which shines out every year. Fortunately for the world's thirsty Burgundy-lovers Jadot has many grower-suppliers and access to large quantities of grapes, and large quantities of the various wines are thus shipped off around the world. That quantity should rhyme with quality is here an undeniable and welcome paradox!

Merchant and grower

Louis Jadot founded his firm in 1859, and from the very start invested profits in vineyard land. As the *négociant* business grew, therefore, so the estate expanded. After his death his son Louis-Baptiste continued reinvesting profits in real estate. Louis-Baptiste's son Louis-Auguste spent much time developing sales in export markets, and in 1954 employed the young André Gagey to help him cope with the ever-growing business.

Gagey was to play a greater role in the firm's future than Louis-Auguste could have suspected, for after the latter's death and the premature death of his son Louis-Alain in 1968 Gagey was better equipped than anyone to run the firm, and was duly appointed to the top job. Since then he, and since his retirement his son Pierre-Henry, have directed the firm with rock-steady assurance, and prepared it for the uncertain future in the only way possible for a *négociant*, by continuing to invest in land. Today the firm manages four estates: Domaine Louis Jadot (comprising the former Domaines Clair-Daü and Champy), Domaine Héritiers Louis Jadot, Domaine Duc de Magenta, and Domaine André Gagey. In 1985 the Jadot family parted ways with their firm, selling it to the owners of Kobrand, their American importer.

Bringing out terroir characteristics

Since 1970, the responsibility for wine making has been held by Jacques Lardière, who with every new vintage demonstrates once more his talent for bringing out the *terroir* characteristics of each wine —no small feat with such a long list of wines, where it would be so easy for a house style to speak louder than all these individual voices.

Lardière is a traditionalist, one of the non-interventionist school who prefer to let nature rather than man make the wine. Long vattings, lasting sometimes more than thirty days, and no tampering with fermentation temperatures, which have been known to rise to 104°F (40°C) without any ill effect, these give his wines the body and aromatic depth, and, of course, the *terroir* personality, which Burgundy lovers so appreciate.

Beaune Clos des Ursules

The Jadots' very first vineyard holding, Clos des Ursules, is an enclave in the Vignes Franches vineyard which was the property of the Ursuline Convent in Beaune in the seventeenth century. This wine's characteristics are a relative lightness—the soil in the *clos* is very stony at the top end, and this sector has a slightly lower clay content than that of the more full-bodied *Premiers Crus* nearer Savigny— with great purity, elegance, and perfume, and enough structure to make it a wine for laying down for a dozen years in a good vintage. In the succulence of full maturity it makes a fine match for roast guineafowl, and is a fine bottle indeed.

BURGUNDY
A.O.C. Corton-Charlemagne

- *Wine selected:*
  Corton-Charlemagne
  Grand Cru

- *Grape variety:*
  Pinot Noir
- *Average vine age:*
  35 years
- *Vineyard size:*
  9.65 hectares
- *Soil type:*
  Clay and limestone
- *Production:*
  45,000 bottles

Finest Vintages:
2000, 1996, 1992, 1990

Maison Louis Latour
18 Rue des Tonneliers
21204 Beaune
Tel. (0033) 380 24 81 00
Internet: www.louislatour.com
- *Owner:* Louis Latour
- *On-site sales:* No
- *Visits:* No
- *Price:* ★★★

MAISON LOUIS LATOUR

For some four centuries the Latour family have been active in the vineyards of the Côte de Beaune, during which time they have contributed much to the advancement of Burgundy's wines and renown. Today Maison Louis Latour encompasses both its principal activity as *négociant* and also Domaine Latour—owner of a fabulous vineyard portfolio—and produces an extended and fine range of wines which now even includes a Chardonnay wine from the Ardèche region and a Pinot made in the Var.

A long lineage in the service of Burgundy

The Latour family lineage has been traced back as far as Emiliand Latour, a winemaker–vine grower in the seventeenth century. The last seven generations have named Louis, which has led to the quasi-regal use of numbers for identification.

The family and Burgundy as a whole owes a lot to the astute Louis Latour III. He was convinced that the only real solution to the phylloxera crisis which was ravaging France was to graft French plants onto American rootstock. He had built up the family's vineyard holdings around Aloxe and then in 1890 bought the Corton-Grancey estate at what must have been a very low price in those desperate times. He proceeded to replant 17 hectares of vineyards by grafting, and encouraged his fellow growers to observe and do likewise. He also uprooted the Aligoté and Pinot Noir that occupied some of the prime limestone soils of the Corton hill and replanted them in 1891 with Chardonnay, thus effectively creating the *Grand Cru* Corton-Charlemagne.

Traditional and controversial wine-making

White-wine production, carried out at a fine, modern vatting centre in Beaune, is traditional at Latour, and produces wines of very high quality. Musts are put into tanks to start off their fermentation, and then all but the humblest wines are transferred to barrel to continue it. The firm employs a cooper, who uses nothing but top-quality french Allier oak, air-dried at Aloxe, and the whites spend a year maturing in his barrels, with two rackings, before bottling.

Red wines are entirely destalked and then fermented without previous cold maceration. Fermentation, with regular human *pigeage*, lasts a mere ten days, after which the wines are transferred to barrel to mature. The rapidity of the whole process gives wines whose structure and concentration have never been the strong points, which has earned the firm a fair amount of criticism.

Corton-Charlemagne

Domaine Latour has an extraordinary holding of no less than 9.65 hectares of Corton-Charlemagne, enabling them to make some forty-five thousand bottles of this great wine per year. And great it is, one of the best, initially with typical Charlemagne austerity yet over the years softening up, displaying its richness and power, and at the same time great elegance and style. It is a wine which improves over fifteen to twenty years in great vintages, at the end of which time it makes an admirable partner for *foie gras* and braised chicken with tarragon.

BURGUNDY
A.O.C. Volnay 1er cru

- *Wine selected:*
  Volnay Clos des Ducs
  Premier Cru (monopole)

- *Grape variety:*
  Pinot Noir
- *Average vine age:*
  30 years
- *Vineyard size:*
  2.4 hectares
- *Soil type:*
  Clay and limestone
- *Production:*
  10,000 bottles

Finest Vintages:
2000, 1999, 1998, 1996, 1990, 1989

Domaine Marquis d'Angerville
21190 Volnay
Tel. (0033) 380 21 61 75
Pass on the right of the church up Rue Derrière-l'Église, then turn right at the intersection. The estate is several meters further, on the right.
- *Owner:* Marquis Jacques d'Angerville
- *On-site sales:* By appointment
- *Visits:* By appointment
- *Price:* ★★★

DOMAINE MARQUIS D'ANGERVILLE

Angerville is one of the great names of Burgundy. Prominent after the World War I in speaking out against the fraudulent practices which were rife in the *négociants'* cellars, and, matching words with actions, one of the first to promote authenticity by bottling and selling directly all of the crop, Angerville is a name that has long been synonymous with top-quality Volnay. Indeed Marquis d'Angerville wines have been amongst Burgundy's finest for just about the entire twentieth century.

A number of prime vineyard acquisitions

The Marquis d'Angerville estate was founded by the Baron du Mesnil, *sous-préfet* of Autun, in 1804. Around a fine country house that he had built on a prominent position on the northern side of Volnay, as it was then known, he added a number of prime vineyard acquisitions to form a very fine ensemble. His great-grandson Jacques, Marquis d'Angerville, came into the estate in 1906, shortly after the phylloxera louse had wreaked its ravages, and set about the task of replanting on a large scale. He did this by taking cuttings from his healthiest vines, an experience which later led him and his son to develop their own strain of Pinot fin, which has borne the family name ever since. Clones have never found their way into the Angerville vineyards, and the vines are allowed to grow to a venerable age before being individually replaced. Angerville's son, also named Jacques, made his first vintage in 1945, and inherited the estate on the death of his father in 1952. He is today helped by his son-in-law Renaud de Villette.

Unashamedly conservative wine making

Like his father, the present Marquis is thoroughly conservative in his wine-making practices, believing that it is best to leave well enough alone. Yields are kept well in hand by acting at the start of the growing cycle, and once harvested the fruit is entirely destalked when it arrives at the vatroom. Fermentation thereafter is allowed to proceed much as it wishes, rising as high as 95°F (35°C), and is followed by eight to ten days' maceration, with *remontages* but no *pigeages*. New barrels are not held in particularly high esteem on the estate, the highest proportion used being 35%, for the top wines, and even then the wines are transferred to older wood once the malolactic fermentations are over. When maturation is complete the wines are fined and lightly filtered before bottling, which takes place fifteen to eighteen months after the harvest.

Volnay Clos des Ducs

The wine for which the Angervilles are perhaps best known is their Clos des Ducs, a fine *monopole* vineyard lying on the north side of the family residence, which was once part of the estate of the Dukes of Burgundy. This wine is somewhat firmer than the Taillepieds, Cailleret, and Champans, more Pommard than Volnay in style, yet has a remarkably harmonious and fragrant personality, enhanced by great volume and richness. Like all the D'Angerville wines the Clos des Ducs proves that Volnays can age with as much grace as many a Côte de Nuits, and can make a fine match for refined dishes such as filet of beef *en brioche*.

BURGUNDY
A.O.C. Chassagne-Montrachet
1ᵉʳ Cru

- *Wine selected:*
  Chassagne-Montrachet
  Les Chaumées
  Premier Cru

- *Grape variety:*
  Chardonnay
- *Average vine age:*
  30 years
- *Vineyard size:*
  1.5 hectares
- *Soil type:*
  Clay and limestone
- *Production:*
  10,000 bottles

Finest Vintages:

1999, 1998, 1996, 1995, 1992,
1990, 1989, 1986, 1985

Domaine Michel Colin-Deléger & Fils

3 Impasse des Crêts
21190 Chassagne-Montrachet
Tel. (0033) 380 21 32 72
- *Owners:* M. et Mme Colin-Deléger
- *On-site sales:* No
- *Visits:* No
- *Price:* ★★

DOMAINE MICHEL COLIN-DELÉGER & FILS

Every year some eight thousand cases of white Burgundy of Village level and better leave the Chassagne estate of Michel Colin-Deléger & Fils to seduce the palates of the world's wine lovers. Among their number may be found no less than six different *Premiers Crus* from the village and two more from neighboring Puligny, one of which is the rare and exquisite Les Demoiselles. There is also one majestic *Grand Cru*, Chevalier-Montrachet. These wines are fine ambassadors for the region, and a delight for anyone who is interested in tasting terroir rather than grape.

The convolutions of a Burgundy wine estate

The Colins have been in the village since 1878, and with time the original estate has become three. Michel Colin learned his trade working from 1964–1975 alongside his father, and has built up his business considerably since 1975. He is now helped by his sons Philippe and Bruno.

While some of the vineyards were inherited from his father and others came from his wife's family, a good number are either leased or share cropped, and some wines are made from both owned and leased or share-cropped fruit in the same vineyard; on the other hand the top wine, Chevalier-Montrachet, is made from grapes bought from his wife's uncle. Such are the convolutions of a Burgundy wine estate!

Unceasing attention to detail

The Colins set out to make aromatic, pure wine which contains the different *terroirs'* signatures; elegant and fruity, nothing too heavy or overblown. Their method of making wine is unexceptional, it is just the unceasing attention to detail which makes the difference between these and less distinguished offerings from the village. Firstly the quality of the raw material is checked twice, in the vineyard and on arrival at base. Then the fruit is pressed gently but insistently in a pneumatic press, which leaves only the finest of lees, eliminating the need for *débourbage*. Fermentation of the smaller quantities takes place in barrel, while the larger quantities are initially put into stainless-steel vats with temperature control. Colin renews one fifth of his stock of barrels each year, and the wines spend ten to twelve months maturing on their lees with weekly *bâtonnage* up until the malolactic fermentation. Bottling is carried out in the September following the vintage.

Chassagne-Montrachet Les Chaumées

As might be hoped, while they share the language of the Chardonnay grape, Colin's six *Premiers Crus* all have different accents. The four on the Puligny side of the village have greater finesse than the Maltroie and Morgeot, which are more robust and spicy. Les Chaumées is perhaps the most elegant: a beautiful, refined and flowery wine of great balance and breeding, which benefits from six to eight years in bottle to round it out. Apart from making a wonderful *apéritif* wine, this complements starters as diverse as baked eggs in a creamy, curry sauce, fresh-fish dishes such as salmon served *en croûte*, and indeed numerous white-meat dishes.

BURGUNDY
A.O.C. Volnay 1ᵉʳ Cru

- *Wine selected:*
  Volnay Clos des Chênes
  Premier Cru

- *Grape variety:*
  Pinot Noir
- *Average vine age:*
  45 years
- *Vineyard size:*
  0.9 hectare
- *Soil type:*
  Clay and limestone
- *Production:*
  3,500 bottles

Finest Vintages:
1999, 1996, 1993, 1990

Domaine Michel Lafarge
21190 Volnay
Tel. (0033) 380 21 61 61
From behind the church head along
Rue de la Combe. Domaine Lafarge is
approximately 100 meters along on
the left.
- *Owners:* Lafarge family
- *On-site sales:* Yes
- *Visits:* By appointment
- *Price:* ★★

DOMAINE MICHEL LAFARGE

The quiet little village of Volnay, tightly hemmed in by its surrounding vineyards, is home to some ninety-five growers, and the general standard of their output is high. There are a handful of exceptional producers, however, who manage to produce yardstick wines year in, year out, in which the exquisite finesse and delicacy of Volnay's terroir sings out. Domaine Michel Lafarge is one of them.

Father and son perpetuate a tradition

The Lafarge family is an integral part of the village fabric, having been very active in Volnay's affairs during the last century: Michel Lafarge, his father and grandfather were all mayor of the village. Yet their involvement in wine goes much further back than that, for it was their ancestors who gradually started buying plots of land and taking their destinies into their own hands. A section of the Clos des Chênes was bought in the late nineteenth century, and the Clos du Château des Ducs soon after. Michel Lafarge bought some Beaune Grèves in 1954 and his eldest son Frédéric has added his stone to the edifice with some Pommard Pézerolles and some Volnay Caillerets, as well as more Village land. Continuity, and the handing-on of received and acquired expertise, is all-important to the family. Michel learned his trade working with his father, and Frédéric, having studied enology and gained experience in other wine regions, has been working alongside him for the last twenty years. Yet this is not just a simple case of teaching the next generation how to do it; here they operate on teamwork, two minds each contributing their own ideas and working together to make the best use of what nature brings them each year. As at all great estates, every year sees a review of what has been done in the past, and with what degree of success, the better to use what the new vintage brings.

Bringing out terroir characteristics

For the Lafarges their responsibility is to cultivate their vines in such a way as to bring out the finest characteristics of each *climat*; the typical characteristics of the vineyard from which it came, they feel that they have failed in their mission. As a result this is a fine domain to get to know if one wishes to learn the essential differences in character between the wines of Volnay, Pommard, and Beaune —the finesse, fragrance, and delicacy of the first; the power and structure of the second; and the flesh, robustness, and spice of the third.

Volnay Clos des Chênes

The 15-hectare *climat* Clos des Chênes lies at the southern end of Volnay at some three hundred meters altitude, and enjoys a perfect south and southeast orientation. Here the Lafarge vines, of a high average age of forty-five years, produce a wine of wonderful purity and finesse. It is deceptively easy to drink when young, for the tannic structure is invariably hidden in the seductive and ample flesh of the wine, yet the Clos des Chênes is made for keeping, and the best vintages need a good dozen years to open up fully. Even the difficult years, such as 1994, wines the Lafarges reflect with great talent the quality of the *terroir*, and, when ready, express themselves with great eloquence. If there is a fattened and truffled bird on the table, so much the better!

BURGUNDY
A.O.C. Volnay 1er Cru

- *Wine selected:*
Volnay les Taillepieds
Premier Cru

- *Average vine age:*
28 years
- *Grape variety:*
Pinot Noir
- *Vineyard size:*
0.78 hectares
- *Soil type:*
Clay and limestone
- *Production:*
3,500 bottles

Finest Vintages:
1999, 1998, 1996, 1993, 1990, 1989

Domaine de Montille
Rue du Pied-de-la-Vallée
21190 Volnay
Tel. (0033) 380 21 62 67
From behind the church head along
Rue de la Combe. Domaine de
Montille is on the right just past Rue
Derrière-la-Cave.
- *Owner:* Hubert de Montille
- *On-site sales:* Yes
- *Visits:* No
- *Price:* ★★★

DOMAINE DE MONTILLE

The wines of Volnay do not have a reputation for great longevity, that is more the bailiwick of its neighbor Pommard. Yet the Volnays produced by the De Montille estate belie this reputation and require long cellaring before they show themselves in their finest light. Needless to say, the same goes for the estate's Pommards. Whichever one chooses, de Montille wines are among the very finest of their kind.

Responsibility from a tender age

Hubert de Montille was thrown into the deep end after his father died while he was young, he made his first vintage in 1947 at the age of seventeen, then took on entire responsibility for the estate four years later. However, times being hard and the estate covering a mere 2.5 hectares, the young man trained as a lawyer. Thereafter, until his recent retirement, his entire professional life was devoted to his practice in Dijon, with extended presence on site only during the vintage season. De Montille's son Étienne has been progressively shouldering responsibilities since 1988, and his two daughters Isabelle and Alix despite having their own careers are also on hand when help is needed.

Pure fruit and long life expectancy

De Montille wines favor finesse, relative lightness of body, rich fruit, and good structure. One year the young De Montille miscalculated the amount of chaptalization necessary for one of them, and the wine, with merely 11.5 percent of alcohol, turned out far better than the others of the vintage. Therein lay a lesson which he did not miss, and minimal chaptalization has been one of his rules ever since, and delicacy one of his wines' trademarks.

His aim has always been to produce wines in which the pure Pinot Noir flavor dominates, and vinifications are adapted to this end. The manually harvested fruit is partially destalked and then fermented in wooden vats at a fairly high temperature, with lots of *pigeage*. De Montille is not convinced of the worth of cold pre-fermentation maceration for his wines. After the fermentation is finished, however, there follows a two-week maceration of the wine, which is then run off into wooden casks. New oak is considered to mask the true Pinot character, and he is thus heartily disdainful of it; even the greatest vintages are matured for the most part in used casks. Aging lasts in all some twenty-two months, during which it has long been the custom to rouse the lees in the barrel from time to time, then, when ready, the wines are bottled with fining but without filtration.

Volnay Les Taillepieds

The three named Volnay *Premiers Crus* are among the finest examples produced by anyone in Burgundy. Each has its own character, but all have the unmistakable De Montille elegance and refinement, beautiful balance and sumptuous perfume. Taillepieds is perhaps the most elegant of the three, irresistible when young yet needing two decades to reveal the stunning complexity of tertiary aromas that it develops after sufficient time in bottle. This is a remarkably fine bottle, well suited to white meats such as roast turkey with chestnut stuffing.

BURGUNDY
A.O.C. Montrachet

- *Wine selected:*
Montrachet
Grand Cru

- *Grape variety:*
Chardonnay
- *Average vine age:*
30 years
- *Vineyard size:*
0.9 hectare
- *Soil type:*
Clay and limestone
- *Production:*
1,200 bottles

Finest Vintages:
2000, 1998, 1992, 1990, 1985

Olivier Leflaive Frères S.A.
Place du Monument
21190 Puligny-Montrachet
Tel. (0033) 380 21 37 65
The firm is at number 3, next to the
village grocer and baker.
- *Owner:* Olivier Leflaive
- *On-site sales:* Yes
- *Visits:* By appointment
- *Price:* ★★★★★

OLIVIER LEFLAIVE FRÈRES

As at many of Burgundy's top estates, excessive demand has for many years been a problem at Domaine Leflaive, and a source of frustration for would-be clients. The situation led one of the younger generation of Leflaives to create a *négociant* business in 1984, in order to satisfy what would otherwise simply have been lost custom. Olivier Leflaive Frères is now well established and making commercial quantities of very fine wines.

As it would have been done at the Domaine

From the start Leflaive's idea was to buy grapes or must, but never fermented wine, and treat the raw material in exactly the way he would have treated it had it been grown on the family estate. Sourcing high-quality Puligny grapes is of course not that easy, yet Olivier Leflaive was in the fortunate position of having contacts and good relations with many a grower in the white-wine villages of the Côte de Beaune, thanks to his family's long history and important role in the region.

He took on the talented Jean-Marc Boillot as *régisseur* and wine maker, and together the two of them got down to making the wines. The business started thriving, then in 1991 Boillot left in order to manage an inheritance, and Franck Grux, who had previously been with Jean-Marc Roulot, took his place. Unsurprisingly, given that he was brought up seeing things from the grower's point of view, Leflaive has started buying vineyard plots, and Olivier Leflaive Frères is now a Domaine as well as a Maison.

Traditional wine making and respect for terroir

Wine making is carried out in the most traditional manner and with all due respect for *terroir* characteristics. After a gentle pneumatic pressing and a day's settling, musts are fermented in oak barrels, some 20-25% of which are new, depending on the quality of the vintage. The oak comes from the french Allier forests and is given a light toasting, making it thoroughly suitable for long periods of aging, interspersed with lots of *bâtonnage*. The wines' development is monitored by regular tasting, and the first racking takes place at one moment or another after some twelve to fifteen months, following which the various barrels are unified in vat. Several weeks later the wines are fined, and thereafter bottled, sometimes with, sometimes without a light filtration.

Montrachet

The most impossible task for any *négociant* is finding a source of the supremely desirable Montrachet, yet Olivier Leflaive has one, enabling him in 1996 to make four barrels, giving one thousand two hundred bottles. This is a very great bottle of wine, concentrated, rich, and powerful, fat on the tongue yet with a high level of acidity to keep its opulence in check; still rigid and unformed after two years, it really needs at least another ten to soften up and develop all its inherent complexity. In *jambon persillé* it will find a soul mate who speaks with the same accent, yet when mature it will demand more refined company; sweetbread, or a noble crustacean, will be eminently suitable.

BURGUNDY
A.O.C. Meursault 1er Cru

- *Wine selected:*
Meursault Les Perrières
Premier Cru

- *Grape variety:*
Chardonnay
- *Average vine age:*
30 years
- *Vineyard size:*
0.52 hectare
- *Soil type:*
Limestone
- *Production:*
2,500 bottles

Finest Vintages:
1999, 1996, 1995, 1992,
1990, 1989, 1985

Domaine Pierre Morey
9 Rue Comte-Lafon
21190 Meursault
Tel. (0033) 380 21 21 03
- *Owner:* Pierre Morey
- *On-site sales:* No
- *Visits:* No
- *Price:* ★★

DOMAINE PIERRE MOREY

Given the number of wines he makes these days, it is not easy to see how Pierre Morey manages to dedicate sufficient time to each one, yet he does. Be they from his own estate, from his *négociant* business, or those of Domaine Leflaive, his touch is sure, and the wines are masterpieces of their respective appellations.

An ultimatum to look after the estate

Morey's family is distantly related to the many Moreys in Chassagne, for during the terror which followed the french Revolution in 1793, an ancestor named Alexis Morey met a local girl, married her, and settled in the village. He built up a small viticultural property, but over the years and the changes of generation it was subdivided several times until the pieces were too small to support a family.

Morey's father, Auguste Morey-Genelot, duly inherited his share in 1930, but seeing no future in wine making he left to become a traveling salesman. After a couple of years, Auguste's father, an invalid veteran of the World War I who was getting on in years, gave him an ultimatum to come back and look after the estate or he would sell it. Auguste came back. Although he did not have enough faith in the future to buy land, he took on 4 hectares of prestigious appellations—Meursault Perrières, Genevrières, and Charmes, and 35 ares of Le Montrachet—on a share-cropping basis for the Lafon family, and later on some Bâtard-Montrachet and Pommard Épenots.

Compensation for lost vineyards

Pierre Morey started working with his father at the age of eighteen, and total responsibility passed to him on his father's retirement six years later, in 1972. After some fifteen years he saw all the magnificent Lafon holdings reclaimed by Dominique Lafon as the contracts expired, leaving a dearth of quality appellations in his cellar. To compensate for these losses, in 1990 he set up a *négociant* business named Morey-Blanc, enabling him to buy grapes or must and make wine, and has since found sources of Genevrières, Charmes, and Montrachet itself, as well as Bouchères, Les Narvaux, and Saint-Aubin Les Combes.

Morey's talent and devotion to his work was rewarded in 1988 with an invitation to understudy Jean Virot as wine maker at Domaine Leflaive with a view to succeeding Virot on his retirement, and Morey was duly offered and took up that post in 1990. Critics have noted a clear improvement in quality at the domaine in the 1990s.

Meursault Les Perrières

In 1987 Morey managed to buy a half-hectare parcel of Les Perrières which he had operated as share cropper since 1973, since which time some two thousand five hundred bottles of a wonderfully concentrated, mineral-flavored wine have epitomised his style of wine-making and graced his cellar every vintage for a short time before being snapped up by eager clients. It is to be hoped that they all have cellars and patience, for perhaps more than any other of his wines this individual needs time to develop. Some eight to ten years at least, but preferably two decades or more are required for it to express itself to the fullest due to its excellent acidity and balance. It makes a fine partner at the table for sea-perch *en croûte*.

BURGUNDY
A.O.C. Bienvenues-Bâtard-Montrachet

- *Wine selected:*
  Bienvenues-Bâtard-Montrachet
  Grand Cru

- *Grape variety:*
  Chardonnay
- *Average vine age:*
  50 years
- *Vineyard size:*
  0.5 hectare
- *Soil type:*
  Clay and limestone
- *Production:*
  2,500 bottles

Finest Vintages:
1999, 1996, 1995, 1992, 1990

Domaine Ramonet
4 Place des Noyers
21190 Chassagne-Montrachet
Tel. (0033) 380 21 30 88
- *Owners:* Ramonet family
- *On-site sales:* No
- *Visits:* No
- *Price:* ★★★★

DOMAINE RAMONET

Anyone wanting to taste the very best in white Burgundy, to see where the limits lie in what can be done by fermenting Chardonnay juice, should just open up a bottle of Ramonet. This is one of the Côte d'Or's two or three legendary estates, and for good reason.

From humble origins to international acclaim

Ramonet's story could be said to start with the marriage of Pierre Ramonet, a young vineyard worker of humble origins, and Lucie Prudhon, whose father was a director of culture. Pierre, born in 1906, had left school at the age of eight to help his father, a manuel laborer, and he and Lucie undoubtedly knew the meaning of hard work and saving. With their savings they bought a parcel of the Chassagne Premier Cru Ruchottes in the 1930s, and his 1934 vintage was imported into the United States, newly emerged from Prohibition, making it one of the first Burgundy estates to be exported and, rapidly, to gain an international reputation. Over the years Pierre displayed an uncommon genius for fashioning magisterial wines, and the Ramonets invested in vineyard land when there were savings available, in 1955 buying their parcels of Bâtard- and Bienvenues-Bâtard-Montrachet, and, in 1978, 25 ares of Le Montrachet itself.

Pierre and Lucie had a son, André, who in turn had two boys, Noël and Jean-Claude. Throughout his life André had precarious health, and never entirely took over from his father. The two together made their last vintage in 1983, after which the young brothers took over. Since then these two have upheld the family name with consummate talent, going about the numerous tasks that occupy a wine maker

with unerring instinct, for it is empiricism, not enology diplomas, that makes the wines at Ramonet.

White wines for the long term

The whites are made for long term aging, which in the case of Ramonet means several decades, while the reds, which should on no account be ignored, are ready after six years or so. Old vines receive great respect (any vine under eighteen years old is considered young) and low yields are the cornerstone of quality.

The white wines are fermented with their gross lees, initially in tank and subsequently in barrel, with no real temperature control, and then remain in barrels until the first racking becomes essential. All this solid matter obviates the need for anything but the occasional *bâtonnage*, and then when the aging, generally in 35 percent new wood with a light toasting, has run its course, the wines are given a light fining and filtration, and are then bottled.

Bienvenue Bâtard-Montrachet

While the domaine's range of *Premiers Crus* is of breathtaking quality, the three Grands Crus mark a distinct climb into a higher orbit. The Montrachet is usually the finest of the three, but there is never a great deal to separate them. The Bâtard is invariably firmer and more austere than the Bienvenues, which, Noël states, is a question of using different wood. The Bienvenues is a majestic display of opulent seduction, a triumph of extraordinary dimensions and complexity, with an unbelievably long finish. Parsleyed frogs' legs or a *chaud-froid* of chicken with tarragon are suitable dining companions for this great wine.

BURGUNDY
A.O.C. Savigny-lès-Beaune
1er cru

- *Wine selected:*
  Savigny-lès-Beaune
  Aux Vergelesses
  Premier Cru

- *Grape variety:*
  Pinot Noir
- *Average vine age:*
  50 years
- *Vineyard size:*
  3 hectares
- *Soil type:*
  Clay and limestone
- *Production:*
  14,000 bottles

Finest Vintages:
2000, 1999, 1998, 1996, 1990

Domaine Simon Bize & Fils
12 Rue du Chanoine-Donin
21420 Savigny-lès-Beaune
Tel. (0033) 380 21 50 57
When arriving in Savigny from
Beaune, pass the entrance to the
château, cross the square and
continue. Take the first street on the
left. Domaine Bize is 100 meters along
on the right.
- *Owner:* Domaine Bize & Family
- *On-site sales:* Yes
- *Visits:* 8–12 a.m., 2–6 p.m.
- *Price:* ★★

DOMAINE SIMON BIZE & FILS

Little is predictable at the large Savigny estate of Simon Bize apart from the quality of the wines, which can itself be attributed to the very lack of the systematic coupled with and the readiness to try out new ideas. Adapting themselves to the vine's demands every season, the Bize family makes a fine list of Savigny-lès-Beaunes, interspersed with a few other appellations, in which the character of each vineyard shines through.

A healthy disrespect for wine schools

Three generations of Bizes, all named Simon, made wines in the village before responsibility for the estate settled on the shoulders of Patrick Bize in 1988. Patrick learned his trade at his father's side and received invaluable advice on all sides of the business from such luminaries as Henri Jayer, Aubert de Villaine and the Marquis d'Angerville, which has stood him in good stead ever since. He has a healthy disrespect for wine schools and the inflexible theory that they cram into the heads of their students.

Bringing out the best of each vintage

While the Bize philosophy embraces respect for the soil, the estate does not sit firmly in any particular camp as regards viticultural regime; Patrick Bize knows his plots and treats each according to the needs presented by the vintage. Old vines and low yields are the principal quality factors of the wines —25–40 hl/ha is the aim for the red wines—and harvesting never takes place until peak ripeness has been attained.

Once the fruit has arrived at the vatroom all the grapes from young vines (less than twenty years of age!) are destalked, while the adults are vatted whole. Fermentation, carried out by indigenous yeast, takes place in open wooden vats and starts in its own good time, without preliminary cold maceration. Temperatures are not allowed to rise beyond 91°F (33°C), and three *pigeages* per day enable sufficient extraction of aroma, color and tannin. In all, vatting can last up to twenty-one days. Then it is tasting, and not laboratory analysis, that tells Bize when to run off the wine into barrel. The pulp is not used at this estate, the wines consisting exclusively of free-run wine.

The first racking takes place after some eight to ten months, when the malolactic fermentations have finished, and during this period the *Premiers Crus* will have been lodged in 50–100 percent new oak, depending on the vintage. Generally the wines are unified before being fined and filtered—tasting again decides whether these operations will take place or not—and subsequently bottled.

Savigny-lès-Beaune Aux Vergelesses

Of the five *Premiers Crus* made by Bize, the southeast-facing Aux Vergelesses, on the eastern side of the village at the Pernand-Vergelesses extremity, produces probably the most distinguished wine, which combines structure, finesse, and elegance, and invariably has great complexity and intensity as a result of the advanced average age of its vines and, needless to say, low yields. This, it could be argued, is Savigny's finest wine, which takes a dozen years to reveal all its character. When it does, it is enhanced by the accompaniment of partridge *à la mode bourguignonne*.

RHÔNE VALLEY
A.O.C. Côte-Rôtie

- *Wine selected:*
  Côte-Rôtie Les Grandes Places

- *Grape variety:*
  Syrah
- *Average vine age:*
  65 years
- *Vineyard size:*
  0.7 hectare
- *Soil type:*
  Schist
- *Production:*
  2,000 bottles

Finest Vintages:
1999, 1995, 1991, 1990, 1989, 1988

Domaine Clusel-Roch
15 Route du Lacat—Vérenay
69420 Ampuis
Tel. (0033) 474 56 15 95
If heading north on the RN86 from
Ampuis, once in the hamlet of Verenay
take the Route du Lacat on the left.
Domaine Clusel-Roch is signposted,
about 300 m down the road.
- *Owners:* Gilbert Clusel
  & Brigitte Roch
- *On-site sales:* Mon.–Sat.,
  by appointment
- *Visits:* By appointment
- *Price:* ★★★★

DOMAINE CLUSEL-ROCH

Ampuis might be the historic heartland of Côte Rôtie production, yet there are growers making excellent wines on the outlying slopes north and south of the town. One such is Domaine Clusel-Roch, based at Vérenay. From promising beginnings the work of Gilbert Clusel and his wife Brigitte Roch has regularly improved, gaining them an ever-increasing reputation. Today their Côte Rôties are among the finest.

Reverting to traditional practices

René Clusel had one hectare of vines in Les Grandes Places, which he had bottled since 1969, and also grew apricots and vegetables. When his son Gilbert joined him in 1980 after studying wine making at Beaune, it was decided to enlarge their vineyard holdings, as Côte Rôtie was enjoying increasing popularity and demand. René retired in 1986, and Gilbert's wife Brigitte started working with him soon after.

The couple now own or rent 3.5 hectares of vines, of which 50 ares lie on the coteau de Chéry in Condrieu, making them 1,500 bottles a year of magnificent white wine, the remainder being in Côte Rôtie. There they work 1.5 hectares in La Vaillère and 80 ares in Le Champon with which they produce their "classic" Côte Rôtie, and 70 ares of old vines in Les Grandes Places, which since 1988 they have kept apart in the best years and made as a special *cuvée*.

Like many up-and-coming growers in the Rhône Valley, Clusel and Roch have reverted to traditional vineyard practices: there is no mechanization—the 45° angle of the slopes itself dictates manual labor anyway—and from 1993 they progressively started working the soil by hand. Five years later the whole estate was worked that way, and today spray treatments are only used as a last resort against fungal outbreaks such as mildew and oidium. Even then, the treatments are based on sulphur and Bordeaux mixture.

Vinification "à l'ancienne"

The Côte-Rôties are made very much in the ancestral fashion, by fermentation on their stalks by their own yeast in concrete vats for some fifteen days. For extraction of color, tannin, and aroma there is lots of pigeage in the first days of vatting, and the liquid is subsequently pumped up and sprayed over the floating cap of solids (*remontage*) regularly to increase this. After the alcoholic fermentation the free-run wine is run off and the solid matter pressed by means of an old vertical wooden press. This press wine is then reincorporated after the free-run has undergone its malolactic fermentation, and the wine is then matured in oak barrels for two years before bottling, unfined and unfiltered.

Côte Rôtie Les Grandes Places

What sets the domaine's top *cuvée* apart from the regular one is the greater age of the vines, the absence of any Viognier in the blend (there is some 4 percent in the regular wine, which softens up the Syrah somewhat) and the higher proportion (50 percent) of new oak in which the wine is reared. These factors all contribute to shaping a wine which is more powerful and structured and therefore less approachable in its youth; a wine which is destined for greater things, over a longer time scale. When after eight to ten years it is approaching maturity, one may envision serving Les Grandes Places with a haunch of venison.

RHÔNE VALLEY
A.O.C. Côte-Rôtie

- *Wine selected:*
  Côte-Rôtie La Turque

- *Grape varieties:*
  Syrah 93%, Viognier 7%
- *Average vine age:*
  20 years
- *Vineyard size:*
  0.9 hectare
- *Soil type:*
  Siliceous limestone with iron oxide
- *Production:*
  4,000 bottles

Finest Vintages:
1999, 1996, 1995, 1991,
1990, 1989, 1988, 1985

Maison E. Guigal
Route Nationale
69420 Ampuis
Tel. (0033) 474 56 10 22
The Guigal offices and cellars lie on
the main road at the southern end of
Ampuis.
- *Owner:* E. Guigal S.A.
- *Chairman & Managing Director:*
  Marcel Guigal
- *On-site sales:* Yes
- *Visits:* By appointment
- *Price:* ★★★/★★★★

MAISON E. GUIGAL

Some 40 percent of all Côte Rôtie is made by the Guigal family of Ampuis. Through the exceptional quality of their wines they have been responsible for putting the appellation on the map for numerous wine lovers around the world, creating a demand which has brought a degree of prosperity to all its growers and resulted in much-improved general standards. Maison Guigal is today a large and thriving business, where quantity and quality manage to go hand in hand.

A young man makes good

The firm was founded in 1946 when Étienne Guigal, who as a young man had started off as a cellar hand and worked his way up at the famous Ampuis firm Vidal-Fleury, left to set up his own business. For fifteen years things prospered, then in 1961 he was suddenly struck blind, and his seventeen-year-old son Marcel was summoned to help out. Blessed with an innate feeling for making wine, rigorous, methodical, and perfectionist, and having a flair for public relations which many a company boss would envy, by the end of the 1970s Marcel Guigal's wines were being praised by critics and connoisseurs far and wide.

Grower and *négociant*

Over the years the Guigals have painstakingly acquired prime parcels of land. The jewels in the crown are their three Côte Rôtie crus, La Mouline, La Landonne, and La Turque, for which there is much too little supply to meet the ferocious demand. In 1994 a prestige Condrieu named La Doriane was inaugurated, and the following year, the year Guigal's son Philippe first participated in the wine making, the Côte Rôtie Château d'Ampuis was launched.

Besides these, the products of Guigal's own 12 hectares, the firm produces a range of northern- and southern-Rhône wines from grapes bought from over seventy growers. The range encompasses all the important appellations, and all the wines are of very good if not excellent quality.

Top-quality fruit and protracted vinification, the quality of Guigal wines derives from faultless raw material and perfectionism in the vatroom and cellars. Guigal vineyards are worked organically, the vines' production is ruthlessly limited, and the grapes are harvested at optimum ripeness, and these same criteria are demanded of the firm's supplying growers. Arriving fruit undergoes rigorous examination before admission to the vatroom, where it is carefully vinified in the most suitable manner, taking into account its origin and the quality of the vintage.

The top red wines are aged in nothing but new oak barrels—a fact which initially earned much criticism—and this treatment lasts no less than forty-two months. Yet the wines are so rich that after several years in bottle the oak influence is barely detectable. During this time they are racked no more than six times, and eventually bottled unfined and unfiltered. After such protracted treatment, their longevity is no surprise.

Côte Rôtie La Turque

Lying in between the two côtes, La Turque has both the virility typical of the Côte-Brune and the feminine subtlety of the Côte-Blonde. Very dark, rich, spicy, and complex, with a red-fruit character when young, its intensity on the nose and palate is breathtaking, and its potential is underlined by an exceptionally long and complex finish. A haunch of venison is called for here!

RHÔNE VALLEY
A.O.C. Côte-Rôtie

- *Wine selected:*
  Côte-Rôtie

- *Grape variety:*
  Syrah
- *Average vine age:*
  20 years
- *Vineyard size:*
  7 hectares
- *Soil type:*
  Schist
- *Production:*
  30,000 bottles

Finest Vintages:
1999, 1997, 1991, 1989

Domaine Jamet
Le Vallin
69420 Ampuis
Tel. (0033) 474 56 12 57
Follow the RN86 north from the
Ampuis church for approximately
200 m and take the road on the left.
The Jamet estate is 4 km from
Ampuis, and is signposted.
- *Owners:* Jean-Paul & Jean-Luc Jamet
- *On-site sales:* Yes
- *Visits:* By appointment
- *Price:* ★★

DOMAINE JAMET

U p in the hills away from Ampuis and the busy RN86 the Jamet brothers craft their single wine, a Côte Rôtie, with all the devotion and attention to detail of the master wine maker, and each new vintage demonstrates just how high are the standards they set themselves. Jean-Paul and Jean-Luc Jamet can be counted without any hesitation among the élite of the young generation of Côte Rôtie growers.

From difficult times to prosperity

The estate was founded by Joseph Jamet in the early 1950s. Economic circumstances at the time were difficult for wine makers, and for a long while he grew apricots, peaches, and nectarines on his plateau land, for Côte Rôtie sold too cheaply. Gradually little parcels were added to the initial 35 ares, and as the appellation started to enjoy a revival he found an outlet for his produce with the major *négociants* Jaboulet, Chapoutier, and Delas. He did not start bottling until 1976, but his wines were soon recognized for their quality.

Having trained his sons he handed over responsibilities to them in the mid-1980s and retired. Since then, by dint of hard work and talent, some notable vintages have been notched up— 1988, 1989, 1991, and 1995 are all remarkable, and the lesser years are generally excellent within their context—and the family holdings have been further expanded. Today they cover 7 hectares, and are spread fairly widely, principally on the Côte Brune.

Every step is aimed at eventual perfection

The viticultural cycle always starts with severe pruning, and this is followed later on by a careful debudding operation, for yield reduction is naturally at the core of vineyard policy. Leaf-stripping is a handy measure to improve aeration and ripening, and if yields are still higher than required a green harvest around the end of July is necessary.

The brothers always hold on until the grapes are as ripe as possible before beginning the harvest, and then proceed with the wine making in their own fashion. They never destem the fruit, but lightly crush it and then ferment it in stainless steel by the action of the fruit's own yeast. Daily *remontages* help to extract the color, tannin and aroma, and temperature control preserves the wine's purity and finesse. The period of fermentation and maceration lasts some eighteen to twenty days, at the end of which the wine, stiffened by the addition of the press-wine, is run into *foudres* and casks for its malolactic fermentation and subsequent *élevage*. One fifth of the casks are renewed each year. Finally the wine is bottled without filtration.

Côte Rôtie

In style the Jamet Côte Rôtie is medium-bodied, well balanced, and harmonious. Its fruit is always very pure, ripe, and well-defined, its structure never excessive nor aggressive, and it is always remarkably elegant. These qualities enable it to develop well in bottle over a good fifteen to twenty years in the better vintages, and it is guaranteed to delight the taster with its sumptuous bouquet of bilberry, licorice, and spice, which often has a smoky aspect and takes on nuances of truffle, leather, and wood as it ages. Rabbit fricassee or filet of beef *en brioche* make very suitable table companions for this great wine.

RHÔNE VALLEY
A.O.C. Côte-Rôtie

• *Wine selected:*
Côte-Rôtie Les Grandes Places

• *Grape variety:*
Syrah
• *Average vine age:*
15–80 years
• *Vineyard size:*
1.3 hectares
• *Soil type:*
Mica-schist
• *Production:*
5,000 bottles

Finest Vintages:
1999, 1995, 1991

Domaine Jean-Michel Gerin
19 Rue de Montmain
Vérenay
69420 Ampuis
Tel. (0033) 474 56 16 56
If heading north on the RN86 from
Ampuis, once in the hamlet of Vérenay
take the Route du Lacat on the left.
Rue de Montmain is 100 m down
on the left.
• *Owner:* Jean-Michel Gerin
• *On-site sales:* 9–12 a.m., 2–6 p.m.
• *Visits:* No
• *Price:* ★★★

DOMAINE JEAN-MICHEL GERIN

In a short period of time Jean-Michel Gerin has forcefully inscribed his credentials alongside those of the other star producers of Côte Rôtie and Condrieu, with wines eminently capable of satisfying the most exacting enophiles. Gerin is a man who has seen tradition at work, compared it with some of the more modern options, and made up his own mind. His wines are well worth seeking out.

A young man goes it alone

Gerin's family is well-known in the area, for his father Alfred was local senator and mayor of Ampuis, and the instigator of a planting program in the 1960s which gave birth to the Domaine de Bonserine. Gerin Junior started out on his own in 1983. Today his estate comprises 1.3 hectares of Les Grandes Places, a half-hectare of La Landonne and 5.5 hectares in the northern part of the Côte Rôtie appellation, as well as 2 hectares of Viognier at Condrieu, on the coteau de la Loye. All of these parcels are on slopes.

Being of the same outlook as many other thinking growers of his generation, his vineyards are cultivated with the greatest respect for soil, vine, and environment, for only by respecting the soil can the terroir express itself. To protect the soil's micro-organic life vineyard maintenance tasks such as weeding are therefore carried out manually, and no synthetic insecticides or fertilizers are used.

Selection and rejection

Perfect ripeness being considered essential for quality wine, Gerin never rushes to harvest, and when his pickers start work they not only cut off the bunches but also examine them and reject all that is not fit for vinification. The fruit is placed in shallow crates of a capacity of 25 kilograms in order to avoid any of it getting crushed, and is then rushed off to the cellars.

Since his early days Gerin has taken the advice of the enologist Jean-Luc Colombo for the wine making. Grapes are entirely destalked and then receive twenty-five to thirty days' *cuvaison* in stainless-steel vats with narrow tops, with lots of *pigeage* to extract as much color, tannin, and aroma as possible. To that end also temperatures in the vat are allowed to rise higher than many others would countenance. In years of rain dilution a *saignée* is carried out to increase the ratio of solid matter to liquid, for greater concentration.

After fermentation comes *élevage*. Here Gerin is revealed in his true modernist colors, for there is not a *foudre* nor a *demi-muid* in sight in his cellars. His Condrieu is fermented and reared in 228-liter barrel and his two Côte Rôties also make close acquaintance with small oak for their *élevage*. He opts for barrels with a heavy "toast".

Côte Rôtie Les Grandes Places

Gerin's single-parcel Les Grandes Places is reared in nothing but new oak for two years, and is a remarkably elegant, balanced, and harmonious example of Côte Rôtie. Soft on the palate, rich, and refined, its subtlety of structure makes it very different to that of Clusel-Roch, for example. That this bottle gives tasters pleasure and incites them to conviviality, that is Gerin's hope; at table it has the necessary manners to look a *Chateaubriand maître d'hôtel* in the eye.

RHÔNE VALLEY
A.O.C. Condrieu

- *Wine selected:*
  Condrieu Coteau de Chéry

- *Grape variety:*
  Viognier
- *Average vine age:*
  45 years
- *Vineyard size:*
  3 hectares
- *Soil type:*
  Granite
- *Production:*
  8,000 bottles

Finest Vintages:
2000, 1998, 1996, 1995, 1991

Domaine André Perret
Verlieu
42410 Chavanay
Tel. (0033) 474 87 24 74
Perret's establishment lies on the
RN86, 200 m past the church as
one heads up to Condrieu.
- *Owner:* André Perret
- *On-site sales:* Yes
- *Visits:* By appointment
- *Price:* ★★

DOMAINE ANDRÉ PERRET

Condrieu's unique and highly prized wines are made exclusively with the Viognier grape, on terraces of granitic soil looking down on the Rhône. There are few really good producers of Condrieu, for Viognier is notoriously difficult to grow, yet the most talented handful maintain standards with zeal, passion, and devotion. One of the foremost is the young André Perret, who produces wines that invariably display the quintessential qualities that make this wine so sought-after.

Different soils for different wines

Perret took over from his father in 1982, and has enlarged the estate from the 0.5 hectare that was exploited at the time—in those days fruit was the mainstay of the family business—to 10 hectares. No less than 4 of these lie in the Condrieu appellation, while the remainder produce red and white Saint-Joseph and red Côtes-du-Rhône.

Perret produces his Condrieus from two vineyards which have different soils, and thus give wines which have distinctly different characters. The Coteau de Chéry, lying over a bend in the Rhône between Condrieu and Vérin, has a layer of arzelle, a powdery soil of granite, mica, and schist; this is one of Condrieu's finest slopes, and this soil is reckoned by many to give body and power to its wines. A few kilometers further south, looking down on Chavanay, lies Clos Chanson, whose soil has a higher clay content, and gives a wine that is perhaps less demanding of the taster, yet is redolent of the exquisite floral aromas which characterize Viognier wines.

Limited yields and barrel fermentation

There are many essentials which can not be ignored if one is to produce quality fruit with this variety. Yields must be kept very low and fruit must be allowed to ripen fully before harvesting; Perret is never reluctant to prune, and the high average age of his vines also works against large yields, and makes for really top-quality juice. Insecticides are not used, manure is organic, and all viticultural operations are based on *lutte raisonnée*.

Coteau de Chéry and Clos Chanson are both fermented and matured exclusively in barrels, while the third, young-vine Condrieu knows stainless steel as well as wood. Malolactic fermentations are systematically encouraged, taking place in barrel for the two main wines, and the Burgundian technique of stirring up the lees is used to increase flavor and texture. After twelve months the wines are ready for bottling.

Condrieu Coteau de Chéry

Starting out—as do many Condrieus—a fine yellow gold color, the Coteau de Chéry is more marked initially by its terroir than the wines of most other slopes, and requires three to five years for the varietal characteristics to come into their own, by which time (atypically for a white wine) the color will have lightened up somewhat. At a half-dozen years of age André Perret's Coteau de Chéry brilliantly combines power, richness, and fascinating aromatic complexity, with a delicious and original bouquet of herbs and violets. At that age, suggests Perret, it is the perfect partner for shrimps' tail *gratin*.

RHÔNE VALLEY
A.O.C. Condrieu

- *Wine selected:*
  Condrieu Deponcins

- *Grape variety:*
  Viognier
- *Average vine age:*
  10 years
- *Vineyard size:*
  1 hectare
- *Soil type:*
  Decomposed granite and mica
- *Production:*
  4,500 bottles

Finest Vintages:
2000, 1999, 1997

Domaine François Villard
Montjoux
42410 Saint-Michel-sur-Rhône
Tel. (0033) 474 56 83 60
Drive up to and through Saint-Michel
and continue for 200 m. A large new
building just after the fork in the road
houses Domaine François Villard.
- *Owner:* François Villard
- *On-site sales:* Yes
- *Visits:* By appointment
- *Price:* ★★

DOMAINE FRANÇOIS VILLARD

No line-up of good Condrieu would be complete without one or two of François Villard's wines, about which it is easy to be too liberal with the superlatives. Powerful, intensely aromatic, and impeccably balanced, they show just how magnificent the Viognier grape is, and how at home it is in the decomposed granite and mica-schist of Condrieu's terraces. And they show just what a gulf there is between Condrieu and wines made elsewhere from the Viognier.

A change of job

Villard's rise to prominence has been as remarkable as it has been meteoric, since he does not come from a wine-making background. The young man was a hospital cook until giving up that job at the start of 1988 to make wine. Knowing nothing more about the subject than the average wine-loving man in the street he signed up to do a *sommellerie* course in Tain-l'Hermitage, and followed that with a viticulture course at the Macon-Davayé *lycée agricole* (secondary school for wine making).

He started off with one hectare of land, planting it in 1989, and in the intervening years has progressively added to his portfolio, which in spring 1999 covered 7 hectares. Since each new acquisition has had to be planted, the age of his vines is still very low. Yet that in no way compromises the richness and complexity of his wines!

Noble rot and late harvest

Low yields for the red wines, and over-ripeness for the whites, these are the cornerstones of Villard's wine making. In the vineyards all is as natural as possible, with organic soil-enriching and manual weeding; however he is considering leaving the grass to grow on his terraced vineyards in order to anchor the topsoil, the better to protect it from being washed down the slope during rainy spells.

Every year Villard hopes that his Viognier will be attacked by *Botrytis*, which does happen often, but even failing the fungus's appearance the fruit is left on the vine for long enough to develop very concentrated, sweet juice, which explains the intense, powerful aroma of his Condrieus. If only some of the other, early-picking growers would follow his example! He makes four different wines from three different sites, fermenting them in cask at a low temperature and then aging them in cask for the best part of a year, with weekly *bâtonnage* for the first eight months. They are not racked during the year, in order to preserve their fragrance.

Condrieu Coteaux de Poncins

Villard's ten-year-old vines on the splendid Poncins slopes, lying opposite Château-Grillet, give birth to a wine of sublime intensity and fragrance, with an overt peach, dried-apricot, and vanilla character, which is equally remarkable for the juxtaposition of its thick, opulent flesh, significant alcohol, and impeccable acidity; here is a Condrieu which, unlike most, might acquire some interesting characteristics over a decade or so in the cellar. In its youth it has sufficient flavor to look some *foie gras de canard* in the eye, and enough breeding to charm a dish of scallops in *crème d'artichauts*.

RHÔNE VALLEY
A.O.C. Condrieu

- *Wine selected:*
Condrieu Coteau de Vernon

- *Grape variety:*
Viognier
- *Average vine age:*
60 years
- *Vineyard size:*
1.5 hectares
- *Soil type:*
Granite
- *Production:*
5,000 bottles

Finest Vintages:
2000, 1998, 1997, 1995,
1991, 1990, 1989

Domaine Georges Vernay
1 Route Nationale
69420 Condrieu
Tel. (0033) 447 56 81 81
Internet: www.georges-vernay.fr
Domaine Vernay is situated at the
northern end of Condrieu, on the N86.
There is a car park for visitors.
- *Owner:* Domaine Georges Vernay
- *On-site sales:* By appointment
- *Visits:* No
- *Price:* ★★★

DOMAINE GEORGES VERNAY

Since setting up on his own in 1953 with 1.5 hectares of vines, Georges Vernay has become a repository of all there is to know of the fickle Viognier grape, and has forged himself a reputation second to none for his intensely perfumed Condrieu wines. They are quintessential examples of their appellation, eloquently proving that Condrieu is one of the great dry white wines of the world.

On the verge of extinction

Wine lovers owe Vernay a debt of gratitude not just for the quality of his wines but for Condrieu's very existence, for it was he who championed it when, unprofitable and unfashionable, the vineyard risked disappearing in the 1960s. By 1965 this historic wine region had been reduced to a pitiful 8 hectares. Gradually, thanks to several obstinate growers and above all Georges Vernay and his consistently excellent production, international interest slowly picked up, which had the effect of renewing confidence locally in the future. The terraces, abandoned or occupied by other fruit or vegetables, started to be reclaimed by the vine.

Vernay is now officially retired, and the domaine's wines are made by his daughter Christine, who learned her trade following her father around from an early age, and his son Luc, who divides his time between the estate and his microlite school. However the patriarch is always around, ready to help his children and indeed other growers with generous advice and encouragement.

The terraces of hell

The estate has been gradually enlarged whenever suitable land has come up for sale, to the point where it covers 16 hectares today, and produces red Syrah wines from Côte Rôtie and Saint-Joseph as well as Viognier wines. Vernay has always produced two Condrieus, a generic and the Coteau de Vernon, however in response to a problem of excessive demand for the latter he introduced the evocatively named Les Chaillées de l'Enfer (the terraces of hell) in 1992, which lies between the other two in terms of quality, being a selection of fruit from the best slopes. How then do the Vernays make such beautifully aromatic wines? Very dense plantation, old vines, and low yields—18 hectoliters per hectare is not unheard-of in the case of the Coteau de Vernon— are the inescapable requisites in the vineyard. Fruit is harvested as late as possible for maximum aroma, even at the expense of acidity, and vinified at a cool 57–64°F (14–18°C) in stainless steel and *foudre*, or cask in the case of the Chaillées and the Vernon. Malolactic fermentations are generally encouraged.

Condrieu Coteau de Vernon

The Vernays' top Condrieu is aged in oak barrels, one-fifth of which are renewed each year, for twelve to eighteen months, with periodic stirring of the lees to increase aromatic intensity. It could well be the quintessential expression of the Viognier grape: its intense flavor of apricot, peach, and violets is absolutely irresistible, and it is fat and succulent on the palate, with just the right acidity for balance. It is delicious on its own, yet the Vernays recommend drinking it with lobster, *langoustine* or *foie gras*. Sublime!

RHÔNE VALLEY
A.O.C. Condrieu

- *Wine selected:*
  Condrieu Ayguets

- *Grape variety:*
  Viognier
- *Average vine age:*
  30 years
- *Vineyard size:*
  2 hectares
- *Soil type:*
  Granite and sand
- *Production:*
  4,000 bottles

Finest Vintages:
2000, 1997

Domaine Yves Cuilleron
Verlieu
42410 Chavanay
Tel. (0033) 474 87 02 37
Yves Cuilleron's cellars lie next to the
Verlieu church
- *Owner:* Yves Cuilleron
- *On-site sales:* Yes
- *Visits:* 9–12 a.m., 2–6 p.m.
- *Price:* ★★

DOMAINE YVES CUILLERON

Among the young generation of Condrieu wine makers one particularly bright star has emerged, making wines of stunning purity, harmony, and breeding. Yves Cuilleron is without doubt a master wine maker, a young man who knows what he is aiming at and nurtures his vines, vats, and casks in such a way as to get it.

A young man takes on a challenge

The estate was previously exploited by Antoine Cuilleron, his uncle. There being no direct heir available to take over, an important question mark hung over its future, until the young nephew Yves Cuilleron persuaded the family to let him take on the challenge. After graduating at Mâcon's enology school and gaining experience for a year at the Courbis estate, he started work in 1986.

Once he was in the driving seat, Cuilleron set about increasing the 4-hectare estate to give himself a variety and spread of vineyards on a level with his ambitions; today it covers 24 hectares, producing not only Condrieu but also Côte Rôtie as well as red and white Saint-Joseph.

Far transcending general standards

Method and attention to detail are the linchpins of Cuilleron's work, and the young man is fired by a strong will to surpass himself year after year. The Condrieus are magnificently perfumed, with exemplary definition and great balance—not the easiest thing with the fickle Viognier, which is low in acidity and high in alcohol. The same goes for the white Saint-Josephs, which far transcend the standards generally achieved, and are stunningly rich and intense, indeed probably the finest expressions of pure Marsanne around today. Of his reds, the Saint-Joseph particularly is remarkably deep and rich for an appellation which is often the source of rather simple wines, given the potential of the magnificent Syrah.

The renaissance of a Roman vineyard

Not content with what he has already achieved, Yves Cuilleron and fellow growers Pierre Gaillard and François Villard have replanted the abandoned slopes of Seyssuel, north of Vienne, which were first cultivated by the Romans and made highly reputed wine, praised by Pliny the Elder and many others over the centuries, until their devastation by the phylloxera bug. In view of their exceptional *terroir* and the talent of the three young men, the wines of the Domaine des Vins de Vienne will no doubt become highly prized as their vines grow older.

Condrieu Ayguets

Another, more recent, tradition preserved by Cuilleron and one or two others is that of late-harvested Condrieu. When conditions are right some of his fruit is affected by *pourriture noble*, the famous "noble rot" of Sauternes, and equally if the weather does not break fruit may sometimes be left on the vine until very late in the year, becoming progressively more shriveled and concentrated. By visiting the vineyard half-a-dozen or more times to harvest grapes in these two conditions, Cuilleron makes a massive, sublimely unctuous, rich, and perfumed wine which almost defies description, so unusual and so masterful it is. Any rare bottle found on sale should be snapped up and reserved for a very special occasion, to be sipped on its own or, as favored by its maker, drunk with chocolate cake.

RHÔNE VALLEY
A.O.C. Hermitage

- *Wine selected:*
  Hermitage Les Bessards

- *Grape variety:*
  Syrah
- *Average vine age:*
  60 years
- *Vineyard size:*
  6 hectares
- *Soil type:*
  Decomposed granite
- *Production:*
  5,000 bottles

Finest Vintages:
1999, 1998, 1997, 1996, 1991

Maison Delas Frères
Z.A. de l'Olivet
07300 Saint-Jean-de-Muzols
Tel. (0033) 475 08 60 30
From Tournon follow the RN86 north
towards Saint-Jean-de-Muzols.
Maison Delas is very well signposted
from the main road.
- *Owner:* S.A. Champagnes Deutz
- *On-site sales:* Yes
- *Visits:* 9:30–12:00 a.m., 2:30–6:30 p.m.
- *Price:* ★★★★

MAISON DELAS FRÈRES

Delas Frères is one of largest of the northern Rhône *négociant* houses, yet it maintains a low profile on the world wine stage, despite producing several exceptional wines from the most prestigious northern Rhône appellations. Its greatest strength lies in its Hermitages, homegrown wines of great individuality with all the complexity and depth one could wish for.

The original Rhône Valley vineyard

The vast majority of its production, which encompasses all the Rhône appellations, comes from grapes and must which it buys in. Its choicest land in its own portfolio is that which lies on the Hermitage hill.

This awe-inspiring lump of granite, dominating the towns of Tain and, across the river, Tournon, is reckoned by historians to have been the original Rhône Valley vineyard, dating at least from Roman times, or in the view of locals from as far back even as 600 B.C. Eight hectares of the Delas land are planted with Syrah, for red wine, and are situated mainly in the *climat* Les Bessards, as well as in l'Hermite and Le Sabot. The remaining two are planted with the white grapes Marsanne and Roussanne, principally in l'Hermite.

Geological nuances play their role

Despite being composed predominantly of granite, the hill's different parcels each have their own geological nuances, which duly shape the character of their produce. Lying on the southwest slope of the hill, steep to the point of ruling out any mechanization, Les Bessards, with its loose soil of gore (decomposed granite) produces some of the most structured and powerful of the hill's wines. Blended with the produce of the other *climats*, it can be refined, given more elegance, suppleness, aroma, and so forth. In 1990 Delas inaugurated a single-vineyard Les Bessards wine, which the firm only makes in the finest years; on a regular basis its best fruit makes up the excellent Marquise de la Tourette wine.

Hermitage Les Bessards

For the *prestige cuvée* the oldest Bessards vines, yielding a niggardly 15–20 hectoliters per hectare, are vinified in small open concrete vats with a prolonged maceration with *pigeage* and *remontages*, so as to fully extract the *terroir* character. The finished wine is then aged in cask for sixteen to eighteen months, during which it is racked regularly. A very dark purple to the eye, a young Bessards is powerful, dense, and massively structured, with peppery aromas of blackcurrant and blackberry, and a suggestion of toasted oak. The nobility of the wine is stunning, and one can only try to imagine how it will enthral the taster after twenty years' keeping or more. Jacques Puisais might have been thinking of this wine when he wrote in *Le Goût Juste*: "It needs its freedom. It will revel in an escapade with a hare *à la dauphinoise*, lightly creamed, or an ascent at the side of a leg of *chamois grand veneur*. It will dominate the scene, serenely, and on the way back down will toy with a few wild mushrooms *au gratin*."

RHÔNE VALLEY
A.O.C. Hermitage

- *Wine selected:*
  Hermitage red

- *Grape variety:*
  Syrah
- *Average vine age:*
  45 years
- *Vineyard size:*
  10 hectares
- *Soil type:*
  Granite, loess, pudding-stone, clay
  and limestone
- *Production:*
  30,000 bottles

Finest Vintages:
2000, 1999, 1998, 1995, 1990

Domaine Jean-Louis Chave
37 Avenue de Saint-Joseph
07300 Mauves
Tel. (0033) 475 08 24 63
- *Owners:* Gérard & Jean-Louis Chave
- *On-site sales:* No
- *Visits:* No
- *Price:* ★★★★

DOMAINE JEAN-LOUIS CHAVE

Very few wine makers, not only in the Rhône Valley but all over France and further afield, are held in such high esteem as Gérard Chave, whose red and white Hermitage are masterpieces of complexity, elegance, and harmony. These great wines take time to develop their personalities and blossom, yet with the passing of the years they reward the patient wine lover with a nectar which has no equivalent. Indeed both red and white have exceptional longevity—a half-century for a good vintage, left in a good cellar, is perfectly possible!

Five hundred years of direct succession

Having looked after his own vines since the tender age of seventeen, Chave already had a wealth of practical experience when he succeeded his father Jean-Louis eighteen years later, in 1970. Yet wine making no doubt runs in the blood of this family, for the Chaves celebrated a remarkable five hundred years of direct, uninterrupted succession in 1981. And the line is not about to peter out, for Gérard's son, named after grandfather Jean-Louis, has been thoroughly trained by his father and today plays an ever more important role in the family business.

Perfectionism and unrivaled intuition

The Chaves own no less than 15 hectares on the Hermitage hill, which are spread over nine different *climats* and therein lies one factor explaining the quality of their wines. Yet to that one must add the even more important perfectionism of their makers, who with rare intelligence do nothing by routine. Having given their vines the best possible conditions for bearing excellent fruit—yields are kept well down,

manual vineyard labor is preferred to herbicide, compost to artificial fertilizer, and fruit is never harvested before peak ripeness—they take each year's crop on its merits, vinify it accordingly, parcel by parcel, and age the different wines separately. Chave has tried new wood for aging, and is not for it. Instead he prefers to use second-hand Burgundian *pièces*, with just the odd new cask being admitted to the cellar to replace those due for retirement.

Only when the *élevage* of the different wines is complete are they blended. In a demonstration of unrivaled intuition the Chaves look for affinity and complementarity between the wines of the different parcels, to make a harmonious whole which reflects the character of the vintage. All the wine is therefore not necessarily used every year, and that which is surplus to requirements is simply sold off in bulk to the *négoce*.

Hermitage

Nothing is sadder than the sight of very young bottles of Chave Hermitage being opened and consumed, as so often happens in France's top restaurants, for these are wines which give little pleasure when young, yet undergo a veritable metamorphosis if left alone for twelve to twenty-five years. The red Hermitage, densely colored and with an earthy blackcurrant nose when young, gradually takes on a fascinating range of aromas of the smoked, roasted variety, with hints of tar, leather, cigar-box, prune, and spice, which call for something special at table. Gérard Chave, a renowned gourmet, would no doubt approve of a saddle of hare.

RHÔNE VALLEY
A.O.C. Hermitage

- *Wine selected:*
  Hermitage Chante-Alouette

- *Grape variety:*
  Marsanne
- *Average vine age:*
  40 years
- *Vineyard size:*
  45 hectares
- *Soil type:*
  Loess and alluvial limestone
- *Production:*
  20,000 bottles

Finest Vintages:
2000, 1999, 1998, 1992, 1990, 1989

Maison M. Chapoutier
18 avenue Dr. Paul-Durand
BP38
26601 Tain-l'Hermitage
Tel. (0033) 475 08 28 65
Internet: www.chapoutier.com
Maison Chapoutier is 50 m from
the Tain railway station.
- *On-site sales:* Yes. Telephone
  for opening hours
- *Visits:* By appointment
- *Price:* ★★★

MAISON M. CHAPOUTIER

Chapoutier, founded in 1808, is one of the most venerable names in the northern Rhône, a firm which has produced numerous great wines over the course of its long and illustrious existence. Yet following a change of generation the 1990s have seen it making what are perhaps more exciting wines than ever before—wines which are earning the praises of international experts and wine lovers everywhere.

A change of style

This new lease on life is the result of a total re-evaluation of viticultural and vinification practices by Michel Chapoutier. If the truth be known, the firm seemed to get in a rut in the 1970s and 1980s, continuing to produce the heavy, oxidized wines which had been popular in earlier times, whereas growers all around were focusing on terroir definition and vintage characteristics.

The major problems, as Michel Chapoutier saw it, lay in the raw material, overproduced and thus giving wines of little identity, and the *élevage*, which took place in old chestnut barrels and lasted until sales necessitated bottling, which often resulted in excessive oxidation.

Adoption of biodynamic viticultural methods

The quest for better raw material led Chapoutier to embrace biodynamic viticultural methods, which are the most effective way of promoting the living, healthy soil essential to the health of vines and thus to the production of fine grapes. Weedkiller, pesticides, and synthetic fertilizer have therefore been banished from the vineyards. Yields are rigorously controlled by severe pruning and the presence of old vines.

The firm buys large quantities of grapes as a supplement to the fruit of the 300 hectares it cultivates itself, in order to be able to provide a complete range of Rhône wines. To improve the quality of the bought-in grapes, Chapoutier now pays its growers by the size of their vineyard rather than the quantity they produce—relieving them of a difficult dilemma—and encourages them to work along biodynamic lines.

Wine making techniques brought up to date

Vinification is seen as merely the conclusion of the viticultural year. Nevertheless, here also there has been much change: use of indigenous yeast, not cooling excessively, aging whites on their lees with *bâtonnage*, vatting periods for the reds of up to six weeks with *pigeage* and *remontage*, and new oak for aging, with bottling as soon as tasting indicates that it is time. Perfect grapes and perfectionist wine making is the simple recipe which has changed everything. Even the labels, in an original and admirable initiative, are now printed in Braille.

Hermitage Chante-Alouette

Selecting a single wine is difficult, so excellent are they all at their own levels. Take the magnificent white Hermitage from the *lieu-dit* Chante-Alouette: it transcends the usual dimensions of its kind, rewarding the taster with a thick, fleshy texture and concentrated, toasted flavor, with complex spicy and fruity highlights. Its firmness, good acidity, and long finish promise a long, rewarding life, at the end of which it would want to find itself at table with a deserving companion: scallops cooked in saffron will get it talking!

215

RHÔNE VALLEY
A.O.C. Hermitage

- *Wine selected:*
  Hermitage Le Gréal

- *Grape variety:*
  Syrah
- *Average vine age:*
  50 years
- *Vineyard size:*
  1.2 hectares
- *Soil type:*
  Limestone
- *Production:*
  4,500 bottles

Finest Vintages:
2001, 2000, 1999, 1998, 1995,
1991, 1990, 1989, 1988, 1983

Domaine Marc Sorrel
128 bis Avenue Jean-Jaurès
26600 Tain-l'Hermitage
Tel. (0033) 475 07 10 07
From the church of Tain head towards
the RN7 and turn right. The cellars
are situated about 200 m down on
the right.
- *Owner:* Marc Sorrel
- *On-site sales:* Yes
- *Visits:* By appointment
- *Price:* ★★★

DOMAINE MARC SORREL

Besides the large *négociant* firms who own the lion's share of the Hermitage hill, there exist a few small growers who have plots here and there, making in some cases wine of remarkable quality, albeit in quantities so small that the wines are usually difficult to track down. Marc Sorrel is one such, a young man who makes both red and white Hermitage with equal, consummate talent.

A change of career

Marc Sorrel's father Henri, from a family present in Tain-l'Hermitage since at least the beginning of the twentieth century, was the Tain *notaire*, and until the 1970s the fruit produced on his 3.4-hectare holding was sold to the *négoce*. Then halfway through that decade Henri Sorrel started making and bottling wine himself, producing in 1978 and 1979 two extremely successful vintages.

However he was suffering declining health, and his son Marc, who had embarked on his own professional career, returned in 1982 at Henri's request to help him with the estate. Marc applied himself to learning the business without losing any time. Two years later, after Henri had passed away, he found himself irrevocably cast in the role of *vigneron*.

Mastery of the two colors

Sorrel inherited 2 hectares of Henri's vines, the remainder going to his brothers, and has since acquired further land on the Hermitage hill and in Crozes-Hermitage, as well as renting a half-hectare parcel of fifty-year-old Marsanne at Larnage, which all in all has doubled to 4 hectares the land at his disposal. With that he produces three red and three white wines.

His two white Hermitages are fermented at some 64°F (18°C) in Burgundy barrels which have already been used a good half-dozen times; the essential differences between the two wines come from the age of the vines and the length of aging prior to bottling. These are splendid examples of white Hermitage, which if really necessary may be enjoyed in their first few years, but should ideally be allowed to traverse their subsequent dumb period and then be consumed at ten to fifteen years of age. Sorrel's white Crozes-Hermitage is also praiseworthy.

The red Hermitages, both the Classique and the Le Gréal, are never (or rarely) destalked, and are fermented in a mixture of stainless steel and open wooden vats for eighteen to twenty days, then left to mature for sixteen to twenty months before bottling unfined and unfiltered. There are generally three bottlings over a six-month period.

Hermitage Le Gréal

Do not look for Le Gréal on a map of the Hermitage hill, for it is the name Sorrel has given to his blend of 1 hectare of old Le Méal vines and 20 ares of younger Les Greffieux plants. These two adjacent *lieux-dits* are composed respectively of limestone with stones and sandy clay and limestone, which goes a long way to explaining the nature of the Sorrel Le Gréal: rich and savory on the palate, medium bodied, and exquisitely aromatic. Licorice, blackcurrant, and spice are generally the dominant aromas and it is unusually elegant. This Hermitage ranks among the greatest, and is naturally a wine which amply repays long cellaring, at the end of which it is ready to take its place at table opposite a duck and *foie gras* pie.

RHÔNE VALLEY
A.O.C. Hermitage

- *Wine selected:*
  Hermitage La Chapelle

- *Grape variety:*
  Syrah
- *Average vine age:*
  30-70 years
- *Vineyard size:*
  20 hectares
- *Soil type:*
  Granite, limestone and quartzite
- *Production:*
  90,000 bottles

Finest Vintages:

2000, 1999, 1998, 1997, 1996, 1995,
1994, 1991, 1990, 1989, 1988, 1985,
1983, 1982

Maison Paul Jaboulet Aîné
Les Jalets
Route Nationale 7
La Roche-de-Glun
26600 Tain l'Hermitage
Tel. (0033) 475 84 68 93
The Jaboulet building lies on the
RN7 a few kilometers south of Tain,
on the right as one drives south.
- *Owners:* Jaboulet family
- *Chairman:* Michel Jaboulet
- *On-site sales:* Yes
- *Visits:* Yes
- *Price:* ★★★★

MAISON PAUL JABOULET AÎNÉ

Which Rhône-wine admirer has not heard of Hermitage La Chapelle? Perhaps more than any other it has been this wine, a quintessential expression of the Syrah grown in an ideal location, which has opened the eyes of the world's wine lovers to the delights of Rhône wines in recent years, and which has inspired many a grower, French or foreign, to buy some cuttings of Syrah (or Shiraz) and try to emulate them!

A family business of worldwide renown

Despite its size, Paul Jaboulet Aîné has always been a family-run affair. Founded by Antoine Jaboulet in 1834, it was developed by his twin sons Paul and Henri and thereafter passed down Paul's side of the family. Today the third and fourth generations, Michel, Jacques, Philippe, Odile, Frédéric, Nicolas, and Laurent look after the numerous tasks that occupy any firm which exports a large product range to seventy countries. The year 1997 was sadly marked by the untimely death of Jacques' brother Gérard, who had been the urbane, globe-trotting, public face of the firm.

The comprehensive Rhône range

As Rhône wines have gained in popularity, the Jaboulet range has been widened, and now includes just about all the major appellations of both the north and the southern parts of the Rhône Valley. However the popularity and growing demand is a two-edged sword, for growers are more reluctant to sell their best vats, preferring to bottle and sell them themselves; it can therefore be a problem for Jacques Jaboulet, in charge of purchasing and wine making, to source material of sufficient quality. The finest wines undoubtedly come from the northern section, from

Jaboulet's own Hermitage, Crozes-Hermitage, and Cornas vineyards, where rigorous viticulture and low yields guarantee a regular supply of top-quality raw material. The Domaine de Thalabert, the superb 1996 acquisition Domaine Raymond Roure, the 1993 Cornas acquisition Domaine de Saint-Pierre, and the firm's 5 hectares of white vines spread over the Hermitage hill which make the Chevalier de Stérimberg, all provide a worthy escort to the firm's principal wine.

Hermitage La Chapelle

The name La Chapelle refers not to a vineyard plot but to the tiny Saint-Christophe chapel near the top of the Hermitage hill, erected, as the legend would have it, by the knight Gaspard de Stérimberg in 1235. Wounded while on crusade, the returning knight fell in love with this spot and spent the rest of his days leading the life of a hermit there.

Besides owning the chapel since 1919, Jaboulet hasa magnificent 20-hectare holding spread over the various *climats* of Hermitage, and La Chapelle comes from their vines in the exceptional Bessards and Méal plots. Granite is associated with limestone and quartzite, and old Syrah vines. La Chapelle needs a dozen years to digest its tannic structure and start revealing its extraordinary richness and complexity, and thereafter develops sumptuous aromas of leather, truffle, and undergrowth, so compelling that its remarkable harmony and finesse is often overlooked. The greatest vintages of this wine can live for a half-century! Decanted well before the service, a mature La Chapelle served alongside a haunch of venison or a saddle of hare provides a memorable experience.

RHÔNE VALLEY
A.O.C. Hermitage

- *Wine selected:*
  Hermitage

- *Grape variety:*
  Syrah
- *Average vine age:*
  Very old!
- *Soil type:*
  Granite
- *Production:*
  4,000 bottles

Finest Vintages:
1999, 1998, 1996, 1995

Maison Tardieu-Laurent
Chemin de la Marquette
84360 Lauris
Tel. (0033) 490 08 32 07
The Jaboulet building lies on the
RN7 a few kilometers south of Tain,
on the right as one drives south.
- *Owners:* Michel Tardieu &
  Dominique Laurent
- *On-site sales:* No
- *Visits:* By appointment
- *Price:* ★★★

MAISON TARDIEU-LAURENT

A small *négociant* firm was set up in 1994 with the aim of buying wines in the best *crus* of the Rhône valley, north and south, and producing the purest, most natural and authentic examples possible of each wine. Tardieu-Laurent's success has been rapid and total, and such are the sensitivity and perfectionism which drive it, one can harbor few doubts about the firm's future pre-eminence in the Rhône wine world.

A meeting leads to a partnership

The firm was set up by Michel Tardieu, a civil servant and dedicated enophile, after a meeting with the highly talented *éleveur* of Burgundies, Dominique Laurent. As Thierry Gontier recounts it in *Le Rouge et le Blanc*, Tardieu, who out of hours was responsible for the wine list of the great Lourmarin restaurant La Fenière, was presenting Laurent's wines with the man himself, and the two got on so famously that the idea of a partnership was born.

It did not take much time to turn the idea into reality. Cold cellars—a rarity in that hot part of France—were not easy to find, but eventually Tardieu was able to rent the old vaulted chapel under the Château de Lourmarin, equip it with enough barrels for his needs and go out in search of suitable wines.

Non-interventionist wine making

The partners' aim was to treat the finest appellations of the Rhône valley in much the same manner as had made Laurent's reputation in Burgundy. First of all *vignerons* are persuaded to part with choice lots of their finest old-vine wines, those they do not really wish to sell. After blending them, Tardieu's and Laurent's role is then to transform the wines by slow cosseting in wood, the aim being to give them both a gentle yet thorough airing through the wood's pores and a deep oaking—contrary to imparting the oaky make-up which disfigures so many wines. The preparation of the oak, from two hundred-year-old Allier trees, is naturally of primary importance: new oak barrels are bought not with their inside surfaces burnt, for the *éleveurs* do not want any toasted flavors, but cooked, in order to eliminate the wood's natural flavors, which are not wanted either.

The partners' philosophy might be described as non-interventionist, for the wines are left to themselves to feed off their lees wherever possible, with a minimum of racking, for that usually involves a dose of SO_2 on each occasion, not to mention much disturbance for the wine. When it is eventually necessary to separate the wine from its lees, the operation is done by gravity, never pumping. Wines are finally bottled after two years, all by hand, with neither fining nor filtration.

Hermitage

Tardieu and Laurent source their Hermitage components in the cellars of several producers with land in the *climats* of Le Méal, Les Rocoules, Beaumes, Les Diognières, Les Greffieux and l'Hermite, giving their end-product great complexity indeed. Very dark in color, it is a supremely elegant and harmonious example of its kind, demonstrating just why Hermitage has enjoyed such a long reputation for its *grands vins*. This eminent ambassador particularly enjoys the company of woodcock *ragoût*.

RHÔNE VALLEY
A.O.C. Crozes-Hermitage

- *Wine selected:*
  Crozes-Hermitage La Guiraude

- *Grape variety:*
  Syrah
- *Average vine age:*
  25 years
- *Vineyard size:*
  17 hectares
- *Soil type:*
  Alluvial
- *Production:*
  15,000 bottles

Finest Vintages:
1999, 1998, 1996, 1990, 1989

Domaine Alain Graillot
Les Chênes Verts
26600 Pont-de-l'Isère
Tel. (0033) 475 84 67 52
- *Owner:* Alain Graillot
- *On-site sales:* No
- *Visits:* No
- *Price:* ★★

DOMAINE ALAIN GRAILLOT

The appellation Crozes-Hermitage, which for long years lived off the reputation of Hermitage and was used to market numerous wines of dubious provenance, is now the source of some excellent bottles thanks to a new generation of wine makers. The turning-point came around 1985, and its instigator was probably Alain Graillot. Proving that it is possible to produce good wine without any family wine-making tradition or experience if one really wants to, in a mere handful of years Graillot has become one of the appellation's leading growers.

A change of vocation

A job as an international sales representative with a Parisian agricultural products firm left Graillot unsatisfied. Having made up his mind that a change was in order and that he wanted to make wine—and Syrah wine at that—this fourty-year-old son of Vienne arrived a mere few weeks before the 1985 harvest, and set about making his first wine with rented vines during leave from his job, with no practical experience. The result was more than promising, and several years later he and his wife had acquired their estate near La Roche-de-Glun, a few kilometers south of Tain-l'Hermitage. Taking the advice of growers such as Marcel Guigal, Gérard Jaboulet, and Gérard Chave from whom he used to buy bottles but a few years before, Graillot was rapidly making some of the finest Crozes around.

Excellent soil for red wine

The land he chose is at the root of his wines' quality. Lying principally in the Les Chassis locality east of La Roche-de-Glun, where the soil is composed of several meters of stones, his land is eminently suitable for making quality red wine. The estate's viticultural policy is built around careful cultivation of the vineyard with respect for the soil and its microorganic life, which means very little use of artificial treatments, soil enriching by organic substances, and no *désherbage*—the grass is left to grow, which obliges the vines to bury their roots deeper, making them less vulnerable to climatic surprises and giving greater *terroir* expression. Graillot aims for moderate yields of perfectly ripe, but not over-ripe, fruit, and his pickers, as might be expected, work by hand, discarding any imperfect fruit as they go along.

The uncrushed grapes are given a long vatting period in concrete and are then reared mainly in Burgundian *pièces*, which have already held several wines. The lack of overt, new-oak flavor sets his wines apart from those of most of his fellow growers.

Crozes-Hermitage La Guiraude

The better vintages are the occasion for Graillot to produce his La Guiraude, a selection of the casks which seem to him to have perfect balance and harmony. Such is its quality that the word has got around, and the wine is unfortunately rapidly sold out. Good as the standard *cuvée* is, La Guiraude is significantly richer and more complex, with a thick, juicy, morello-cherry flavor that gains nuances of tar, herbs, and licorice with bottle age. This really is an exceptional bottle of wine for a modest appellation, and is well worth its price—if one can find stocks! Rib of beef, grilled over a barbecue, enhances its qualities to no end.

RHÔNE VALLEY
A.O.C. Crozes-Hermitage

- *Wine selected:*
  Crozes-Hermitage
  Tête de Cuvée

- *Grape variety:*
  Syrah
- *Average vine age:*
  25 years
- *Vineyard size:*
  5 hectares
- *Soil type:*
  Sandy silt
- *Production:*
  12,000 bottles

Finest Vintages:
1999, 1996, 1995

Domaine Bernard Chave
La Burge
26600 Mercurol
Tel. (0033) 475 07 42 11
From Tain-l'Hermitage take the D532
towards Romans. The Chave estate is
on the road on the left leading to
Mercurol just after the highway.
- *Owner:* Bernard Chave
- *On-site sales:* Yes
- *Visits:* By appointment
- *Price:* ★

DOMAINE BERNARD CHAVE

Lovers of good Crozes-Hermitage would do well to discover the Bernard Chave estate, for it is the source of beautifully made, soft, fruity wines of some complexity. The Chaves are at the forefront of the new generation of Crozes-Hermitage growers who have raised general standards so much.

A new estate comes into being

Domaine Bernard Chave was set up in 1970 when Bernard, an independent spirit who was employed on the land, took the step and realized his lifetime dream of starting up his own wine exploitation. As is common in this region so well suited to agriculture in general, vines are not the only crop produced on the estate, for the family also cultivate apricots and peaches. Today Bernard looks after the family fruit business, and his son Yann, summoned from a banking career in Paris to help out, makes the wine. From small beginnings the estate has gradually been enlarged over the years, and now covers 13.5 hectares in Crozes-Hermitage, of which 12 are planted with Syrah for the red wine, while the remainder, 70 percent Marsanne and 30 percent Roussanne, contribute fruit for the white. The family also own 1.5 hectares of Hermitage, enabling them to produce five thousand bottles of that majestic wine.

Respect for the vineyard environment

Vineyard practices amount to what is known as *lutte raisonnée*—respect for the vineyard environment and the soil and its microorganic life—and there are therefore no routine treatments or spraying. All weeding is by plowing, all soil-enriching organic.

Only when there is real danger of fungal attack will the Chaves resort to artificial protective products.

Yields are kept well inside the permitted limits, by severe pruning and systematic green harvesting. The Chaves pride themselves on picking their fruit only when it is perfectly ripe, particularly so in the case of the white wine, for which they require an ample, *gras* character. The two white varieties, Marsanne and Roussanne, are vinified together in stainless steel at 68–72°F (20–22°C) and always undergo their malolactic fermentations, giving a softer acidity consistent with the type of wine required. They are then aged for a whole year, mainly in vat but also with one-tenth in cask. As for the reds, all the Syrah grapes are destalked nowadays, although this was not always the case. Both the Hermitage and the Crozes wines are made in the same way using fermentation in cement vats with regular *pigeage*, with only the length of vatting differing: one week longer for the Hermitage than the Crozes' two weeks. Both are matured in demi-muid for twelve months before bottling.

Crozes-Hermitage Tête de Cuvée

A small vineyard at Pont-de-l'Isère of plants reproduced by *sélection massale* is the source of the *Tête de Cuvée*. Made for the first time in 1997 exclusively from the free-run wine of their small grapes, it is capable of improving in bottle over five to six years. Supple in the mouth, rich, and deeply fruity with an intriguing chocolate aspect, it can nevertheless give pleasure from Day One, for its ripe, tannic structure is well enfolded in fleshy matter. This is an excellent Crozes-Hermitage; it merely demands a roast pheasant to set it off to perfection.

RHÔNE VALLEY
A.O.C. Crozes-Hermitage

- *Wine selected:*
  Crozes-Hermitage Clos des Grives

- *Grape variety:*
  Syrah
- *Average vine age:*
  45 years
- *Vineyard size:*
  4.5 hectares
- *Soil type:*
  Alluvial with quartzite stones
- *Production:*
  18,000 bottles

Finest Vintages:
2001, 1999, 1995, 1990

Domaine Combier
Route Nationale 7
26600 Pont-de-l'Isère
Tel. (0033) 475 84 61 56
Domaine Combier lies on the RN7
between Pont-de-l'Isère and Tain.
- *Owners:* Combier family
- *On-site sales:* Yes
- *Visits:* By appointment
- *Price:* ★★

DOMAINE COMBIER

Fruit lovers in the Pont-de-l'Isère region have long known the name Combier, for many years the source of fine cherries, apricots, peaches and apples. Now it is the turn of wine lovers. The word is getting around fast, as people discover the splendid wines of great purity, succulence, and character made by Laurent Combier.

Fired with a desire to make wine

As has happened at other estates, the arrival of a new generation has signaled an end to the deliveries of grapes to the cooperative. And here, the co-operative's loss is every Crozes-Hermitage lover's gain! After training in Orange and working in Burgundy, Provence, and Châteauneuf-du-Pape, Laurent Combier took over from his parents in 1990, fired with the desire to make wine himself. And not just any old wine! To go about the task, he had a new vatroom and cellars built, designed to make the best use of gravity for movement of fruit and liquid, and equipped it with the necessary stainless-steel hardware, with temperature-control facilities.

A pioneer of biological agriculture

Combier was fortunate in inheriting a splendid vineyard, not only from a geographical point of view but also from that of the health of the soils and plants. Nine-tenths of the vines lie in vicinity of Châssis, on alluvial soil with quartzite stones, which is reckoned the source of the finest red Crozes-Hermitage; the remainder, lying north of Tain-l'Hermitage in lighter soil, give excellent white wines. As far back as 1970 Combier's father Maurice recognized the importance to agricultural crops of a healthy, living soil, and embraced the methods of biological agriculture, both for his vines and his other fruit.

Different styles for different occasions

Today Domaine Combier has 20 hectares of fruit orchards and 14 hectares of vineyard. Two *cuvées* of red wine are made, the standard Domaine wine and Clos des Grives, and the same is the case for the white wine. The Domaine wines are a conscious attempt to produce typical Crozes-Hermitage in a light, easy-drinking style which is good young, while the Clos des Grives wines are altogether more serious —a selection of the fruit of old vines, from lower yields, the red enjoys longer vatting and rearing in oak casks, while the white is fermented and reared in cask with weekly *bâtonnage*. Any wine which is judged of insufficient quality, which can be anything up to 10 percent of the production, is sold off in bulk.

Crozes-Hermitage Clos des Grives

When making his red wines Laurent Combier prefers to destem his fruit in its entirety and then compensate for that with a longer *cuvaison*, a choice which endows the Clos des Grives with a rich, succulent, and fleshy presence on the palate and ripe red-fruit aromas of great intensity. The tannic structure remains discreetly hidden beneath the surface, and when young the wine bears the imprint of its *élevage* in 40 percent new and 60 percent recent oak, yet the whole has breeding and harmony from Day One. Most red meats partner the Clos des Grives very well—tournedos *forestière* in particular—as do veal's liver and kidneys.

RHÔNE VALLEY
A.O.C. Saint-Joseph

- *Wine selected:*
  Saint-Joseph Le Berceau

- *Grape variety:*
  Syrah
- *Average vine age:*
  50 years
- *Vineyard size:*
  1 hectare
- *Soil type:*
  Granite
- *Production:*
  1,800 bottles

Finest Vintages:
2000, 1999, 1998, 1996,
1995, 1991, 1990

Domaine Bernard Gripa
5 Avenue Ozier
07300 Mauves
Tel. (0033) 475 08 14 96
Bernard Gripa's establishment lies on
the main street in the center of the
village of Mauves.
- *Owner:* Bernard Gripa
- *On-site sales:* 8–12 a.m., 2–7 p.m.,
  Mon. –Sat.
- *Visits:* By appointment
- *Price:* ★★

DOMAINE BERNARD GRIPA

Stretching down the right bank of the Rhône all the way from Condrieu, which appellation it overlaps, to Valence, Saint-Joseph wines come in both the light and fruity variety for quaffing young, and the serious structured variety needing bottle age, and are made to very different degrees of quality. The best have traditionally come from the original area encompassing the communes Vion, Lemps, Saint-Jean-de-Muzols, Tournon, Mauves and Glun, and it is in Mauves that one finds the very talented Bernard Gripa.

Extension and reduction of the vineyard area

Saint-Joseph's delimited vineyard area has undergone several radical changes over the years. In 1956, when the appellation was created, it covered just 97 hectares of mainly terraced vineyards in the original heartland, and the general level was high, according to those who remember the wines of that period. However, in 1969 the area permitted for viticulture was increased to an astonishing 7,000 hectares, encompassing much flat, fertile land incompatible with quality wine. Since the extension many mediocre wines have tarnished Saint-Joseph's name, obliging the authorities to review matters again. In 1992 they therefore reduced the area to 3,004, of which 795 were declared by their owners as producing a crop in 1995. Syrah is the red-wine grape, to which may be blended 10 percent of either the Marsanne or Roussanne white grapes; these two, together or singly, are responsible for all white Saint-Joseph.

The cradle of the appellation

Bernard Gripa is the fourth generation of his family to make wine, having taken over from his father in 1964. At the time other fruit and cereals constituted the bulk of the family production, and even today the grape is not alone on the terraces. Gripa's vineyards are situated in Mauves and Tournon, and he also has one hectare of Saint-Péray, from which he produces a remarkably fresh and elegant example of that wine.

He produces two red and two white Saint-Joseph wines, a standard blend and a *cuvée* named Le Berceau (the cradle), which John Livingstone-Learmonth, in *The Wines of the Rhône*, tells us refers to the Tournon *lieu-dit* Saint-Joseph, the cradle of the appellation, where the fruit is grown. Gripa's red-wine methods are thoroughly traditional: grapes are left on their stalks, and the bunches are tipped uncrushed into the open wooden vats, where they macerate and ferment for some two to three weeks with daily treading to extract color, tannin, and fruit, before spending a year in cask prior to bottling. White wines are fermented and aged in barrel, roughly one quarter of which are new.

Saint-Joseph Le Berceau

Gripa's red Le Berceau is a very distinguished wine, very deep purple in color and pungent on the nose, with a deep, spicy, black-fruit flavor, soft and concentrated on the palate and with a structure enabling it to benefit from seven to eight years' development. This excellent Saint-Joseph goes very well with a leg of lamb, or stuffed veal's breast.

RHÔNE VALLEY
A.O.C. Saint-Joseph

- *Wine selected:*
  **Saint-Joseph Le Paradis
  Saint-Pierre**

- *Grape variety:*
  Marsanne
- *Average vine age:*
  40 years
- *Vineyard size:*
  0.8 hectare
- *Soil type:*
  Clay and limestone
- *Production:*
  3,000 bottles

Finest Vintages:

2001, 2000, 1999, 1998, 1995, 1991,
1990, 1989, 1985, 1983

Domaine Pierre Coursodon
3 Place du Marché
07300 Mauves
Tel. (0033) 475 08 18 29
Place du Marché is at the center of
Mauves.
- *Owner:* Pierre Coursodon
- *On-site sales:* Yes
- *Visits:* By appointment
- *Price:* ★★

DOMAINE PIERRE COURSODON

One of the best-known names in Saint-Joseph is Coursodon. Four generations of this Mauves family have dedicated themselves to the vine and wine, and since 2000 Jérôme, of the fifth generation, has been sharing responsibilities with his father. The Coursodons fashion a range of red and white Saint-Josephs which are generally acknowledged today as being of excellent quality.

To obtain fruit of the finest quality

Since Pierre Coursodon took over from his father Gustave in 1982 he has considerably increased the size of the estate, to meet growing demand, clearing and replanting a number of sites which had lain abandoned since Gustave's father's time, and now has at his disposal 14 hectares. The vineyards are on the slopes above Mauves and Tournon, and the steepness and openness to the elements make cultivation of the ten-odd parcels hard work indeed, for all operations must be carried out by hand.

The vines, red and white, are impressively old—the two prestige red wines, L'Olivaie and Le Paradis Saint-Pierre, are the product of octogenarian plants —and are planted densely. Old age reduces yields, and density of plantation, while also acting as a brake on production, obliging the plants to bury their roots deeply to obtain the mineral salts, oligo-elements, and water they need. These two factors go some way to explaining the wines' quality.

A green harvest is carried out in the vineyards, again to reduce yields, and when it arrives at the reception area the crop is picked through on a sorting table to ensure that nothing but fruit of the finest quality and condition finds its way into the vats. Thereafter its treatment will differ greatly, depending on its color.

Reds and whites of equal distinction

The black grapes are mostly destemmed, then macerated and fermented in open wooden vats for some eighteen days. Several *pigeages* are carried out per day, in order to extract as much color, aroma, and tannin as possible, for the Coursodons have always aimed to make wines of both finesse and power, with aging potential. The resulting wines are aged for twelve to fifteen months in large barrels and tuns, then bottled without filtration. These, particularly Le Paradis Saint-Pierre and L'Olivaie, are magnificent, full-bodied and flavorsome characters which benefit from six to eight years in the cellar.

Unlike some, Pierre Coursodon's whites are at least as accomplished as his reds. The juice of his Marsanne grapes is gently extracted by pneumatic pressing, and left to settle overnight. The standard white is then fermented in vat, but fruit destined to make the white Le Paradis Saint-Pierre is fermented in barrel at 64°F (18°C), and also undergoes its malolactic fermentation there. It then spends a year enriching itself on its lees with weekly *bâtonnage*, before being bottled.

Saint-Joseph Le Paradis Saint-Pierre

Barrel fermentation gives Le Paradis Saint-Pierre fatness and depth that make it that much more serious than the basic Saint-Joseph white, excellent though that is, and destined to a different vocation. With its pure and intense floral aromas and underlining oaky thickness, this is a wine to bring joy to the gourmet's heart, particularly when associated with such delicacies as morels in puff pastry.

RHÔNE VALLEY
A.O.C. Saint-Joseph

- *Wine selected:*
  **Saint-Joseph Clos
  de la Cuminaille**

- *Grape variety:*
  Syrah
- *Average vine age:*
  18 years
- *Vineyard size:*
  6 hectares
- *Soil type:*
  Clay and limestone
- *Production:*
  30,000 bottles

Finest Vintages:
1999, 1996, 1995

Domaine Pierre Gaillard
42520 Malleval
Tel. (0033) 474 87 13 10
From Malleval take the road to
Pélussin, and after 2 km take the left
turn towards Martel. From that village
the estate is signposted.
- *Owner:* Pierre Gaillard
- *On-site sales:* By appointment
- *Visits:* By appointment
- *Price:* ★

DOMAINE PIERRE GAILLARD

A decade of experiment, analysis, and refinement has steadily brought the wines of Pierre Gaillard to their current high standard, making this a very reliable address for the lover of Saint-Joseph, Condrieu, and Côte Rôtie. Yet his vines are still young, and Gaillard is not one for sitting on his laurels; one can confidently expect great things from him in the future.

An entrepreneur studies and starts up

Like a number of start-ups of his generation in the northern Rhône Valley Pierre Gaillard did not become a vigneron on inheriting a family business but chose to set up as such, and did the necessary studies at Beaune and Montpellier. He then spent a number of years with Vidal-Fleury and subsequently Guigal, initially as *chef de culture* —it was he who planted the La Turque vineyard in 1982—and then working on the wine making itself. During that period he started buying and planting land, and by 1986 was ready to launch his own exploitation.

Excellence in both colors

All his parcels are well-sited, the Saint-Joseph vineyards sloping gently towards the east, while the Côte Rôtie and latterly acquired Condrieu face south-southeast on more precipitous slopes.

The meticulous Gaillard has demonstrated a sure touch from the start with his white wines. There are three: a Condrieu, a Saint-Joseph made entirely with Roussanne, and a Côtes-du-Rhône Viognier. Severe pruning for low yields followed by patience at harvest time give Gaillard rich, ripe fruit that he vinifies in barrel at a fairly low 64°F (18°C). Once the alcoholic and malolactic fermentations are over the wines are aged in barrel, with weekly *bâtonnage* to keep the lees in suspension and increase the richness and aromatic intensity. The oak barrels are renewed regularly at the rate of 10 percent per year for the white wines.

Gaillard's reds have taken a little while to achieve their current excellence, for their maker was convinced for a long time that destemming the grapes was an error which detracted from a wine's typicity. Recent years have seen a change of policy, however, much to the wines' benefit. The reds naturally are also treated to oak-aging, with a more important renewal rate of 20 percent per year.

Saint-Joseph Clos de la Cuminaille

Proving that the slopes above Chavanay, in the northern (extended) sector of Saint-Joseph, can make wine to rival that of the hallowed heartland around Mauves, Tournon, and Saint-Jean-de-Muzols, Pierre Gaillard makes a deeply-colored and superbly complex wine from his 6 hectares of Syrah in the Clos de la Cuminaille.

His method is to give these grapes five days' cold maceration, then ferment them rapidly over five days at a high 93–95°F (34–35°C) with triple *pigeage* daily, and round off the extraction with ten days' maceration at 86°F (30°C). The result is most impressive, a classy wine of great concentration and finely judged balance, redolent of Syrah's red fruit and spiciness with a touch of vanilla in the background. This has far greater potential for improvement over the years than most red Saint-Joseph, and partners red meats such as beef *à la ficelle* very well.

233

RHÔNE VALLEY
A.O.C. Cornas

- *Wine selected:*
  Cornas Les Vieilles Fontaines

- *Grape variety:*
  Syrah
- *Average vine age:*
  35 years
- *Vineyard size:*
  1 hectare
- *Soil type:*
  Granite
- *Production:*
  3,200 bottles maximum

Finest Vintages:
1999, 1998, 1995, 1990, 1985, 1983

Domaine Alain Voge
4 Rue de l'Équerre
07130 Cornas
Tel. (0033) 475 40 32 04
From Cornas' church turn southwards
along Grande-Rue, then take Rue du
Midi, the second on the left. From there
signs direct one to Domaine Voge.
- *Owner:* Alain Voge
- *On-site sales:* Yes
- *Visits:* 8–12 a.m., 2–6 p.m.
- *Price:* ★★★

DOMAINE ALAIN VOGE

The best wines of Cornas are avidly sought out by connoisseurs, yet on the whole the appellation is little in demand, no doubt because it still suffers from its age-old reputation for producing massive, tannic, rustic, and alcoholic brutes. This image is still merited rather too often, yet the better producers do manage to produce wines which, while always equipped for long lives, can nevertheless count fruitiness, charm, and balance among their various qualities. There is one, Alain Voge, whose wines are even described as elegant. He has long been among the village's finest growers.

A young man arrives in the village

Voge owns 8 hectares of Cornas, a holding which is positively vast in an appellation where the average is less than 3. This ex-rugby player arrived in the village in 1958 at the age of eighteen, and started bottling his production almost from the start. As time went by he bought up additional plots every so often, with the result that his vines are today scattered over a dozen sites, all in prime locations.

A good many of the vines are very old, enabling him to make three different *cuvées* of Cornas: besides the generic wine there is a Vieilles Vignes *cuvée*, produced from 4 hectares of vines aged from twenty to eighty years, and in the finest vintages a wine named Vieilles Fontaines, a selection of the best grapes from the finest plots.

Experimentation, observation, and analysis

Voge's wines have been compared by the American writer Robert Parker with the finest Hermitages. This is tribute indeed, for despite the fact that both appellations are made exclusively with the Syrah grape and on similar granite slopes, the extreme heat in Cornas's sheltered, steep vineyards often precludes finesse in the finished product—indeed Cornas in Celtic means "burnt land".

Voge sets out to make wines of intense, fresh fruitiness and relative delicacy, and for him they are unbalanced if their alcohol level exceeds 12.5 percent. Old vines are 50 percent destemmed, younger ones not at all, and he then ferments the fruit in a mix of stainless-steel and cement vats with either *pigeage* or *remontages*, or both; vatting time lasts fifteen to seventeen days. The wines are then lodged in oak barrels which have already seen three to five vintages and aged for twenty to twenty-four months in the case of the Vieilles Vignes or twenty-eight to thirty months in the case of the Vieilles Fontaines, before being bottled in one fell swoop. This method of proceeding is the result of many years of practice, observation and analysis, yet it is in no way systematic for, like all great wine makers, Voge is always tinkering and experimenting with the aim of refining even further his product.

Cornas Les Vieilles Fontaines

Thanks to the extreme severity with which he selects the raw material for his Vieilles Fontaines, it has a gorgeously fleshy, intense, sensual character, and gives pleasure young, although of course longevity is one of its natural attributes. Drink it with any roast meats, advises Voge, indeed serve a mature bottle with a roast rib of *fin-gras* beef from Mézin in Ardèche, prepared with slivers of *foie gras* and fresh truffle and served with Cornas gravy, as served at Michel Chabran's at Pont-de-l'Isère.

RHÔNE VALLEY
A.O.C. Cornas

• *Wine selected:*
Cornas

• *Grape variety:*
Syrah
• *Average vine age:*
15 and 60+ years
• *Vineyard size:*
4.5 hectares
• *Soil type:*
Granite
• *Production:*
15,000 bottles

Finest Vintages:
1999, 1996, 1995, 1990

Domaine Auguste Clape
146 Route Nationale
07130 Cornas
Tel. (0033) 475 40 33 64
Domaine Clape is on the main road
passing through the village of Cornas,
opposite Restaurant Ollier.
• *Owners:* Auguste & Pierre Clape
• *On-site sales:* No
• *Visits:* By appointment
• *Price:* ★★★

DOMAINE AUGUSTE CLAPE

The village of Cornas owes a lot to its premier vigneron and long-time mayor, Auguste Clape, for it has been he who has brought the village name to the attention of faraway critics and consumers, by the superlative quality and laudable regularity of his wines. Thanks to the Clape effect other growers now generally have no problem selling their annual production, and even if Cornas does not enjoy the prestige of Côte Rôtie and Hermitage, their landholdings have nevertheless taken on some value in recent years.

Against which others are judged

Clape is frequently compared with his Mauves counterpart Gérard Chave and Marcel Guigal of Ampuis, for he seems to have an innate feel for blending the produce of his various parcels of vines to produce a harmonious whole. This feel, bolstered by a half-century's experience, makes a single Cornas against which all others are judged and generally found wanting.

Densely planted on slope and terrace

The Clape vineyards are very well sited, mostly on steep slopes and terraces above the village. At 7,500–10,000 plants per hectare they are planted extremely densely, obliging each vine to bury its roots deeply in the search for nutrients and water, and they contain many an old vine, which give far lower yields than when young. These two factors explain the quality of Clape's raw material. On this estate the owner and his son Pierre would never dream of harvesting at anything less than perfect ripeness, and once cut they give the fruit a rigorous quality control.

A champion of traditional methods

The grapes are left on their stalks for vinification, and fermentation is conducted by the fruit's natural yeast. Fermentation and then maceration take place over some twelve days in concrete vats with two *pigeages* per day, and the wines are then transferred to *foudre* for their malolactic fermentation and subsequent aging. New wood is definitely not part of the Clapes's way of doing things.

The wines of the different parcels are not blended until just before bottling, which enables a finer appreciation of their personality. After a light fining the bottling process is carried out without filtering the wines, in several sessions over several months.

Cornas

Showing a typical, dense purple-black Cornas color in its youth, and giving off (with some reticence) classy aromas of blackcurrant, pepper, and violets, the Clape Cornas takes no prisoners: extremely rich, sweet and full-bodied, impressively structured and given edge by the right degree of acidity, it is a complete wine of great breed. It needs time to develop its bouquet and harmony: at twenty years of age the legendary 1978 was sumptuously soft, with a splendid, generous and complex bouquet of roasted meat, leather, and herb aromas, with young blackcurrant essence still present in the background. A gloriously long finish underlined the sheer quality of the wine. The Clapes recommend serving young vintages with rib of beef, mature ones with hare *à la royale*.

RHÔNE VALLEY
A.O.C. Cornas

- *Wine selected:*
  Cornas Les Ruchets

- *Grape variety:*
  Syrah
- *Average vine age:*
  70 years
- *Vineyard size:*
  1 hectare
- *Soil type:*
  Granite
- *Production:*
  3,000 bottles

Finest Vintages:
1999, 1996, 1991

Domaine Jean-Luc Colombo
La Croix des Marais
La Roche
26600 Tain-l'Hermitage
Tel. (0033) 475 84 17 10
- *Owner:* Jean-Luc Colombo
- *On-site sales:* Yes, during the week
- *Visits:* By appointment
- *Price:* ★★★

DOMAINE JEAN-LUC COLOMBO

One of the most influential figures in Rhône wine making in the last fifteen years has been the Bordeaux-trained enologue Jean-Luc Colombo, who advises many a grower on his wine making and has built up his own estate at Cornas. Colombo's wines demonstrate what he preaches; they are impeccably vinified, richly fruity, and heavily oaked wines without rough edges.

An outsider with a message

Having tasted widely in all the Rhône appellations and been convinced that many growers were in a wine-making rut Colombo set up his *Centre œnologique* in the mid-1980s. The mission he gave himself was to tighten up viticultural practices and change sloppy wine-making habits, the frequent cause of premature oxidation, dried-out fruit, farmyard smells, and so on, which often masqueraded as tradition. As an outsider with a relatively undeveloped sense of diplomacy his criticisms grated on many ears, particularly those of older growers whose ancestral methods found themselves in his sights, yet by dint of conviction and sincerity he has built up an impressive roster of clients, including some very prestigious names.

Steps towards purity and richness

Good wine can only be made with perfectly ripe grapes from healthy vines, and Colombo therefore advises an organic regime in the vineyard wherever possible. Yield limitation is essential, as is quality control of the grapes at harvest time.

The cellar practices he advocates are hardly innovatory, they are to be observed in Bordeaux châteaux and the cuveries of the Burgundian clients of another controversial enologue, Guy Accad. Cellar hygiene is all-important, for dirty conditions are a potential source of rusticity, and destemming is obligatory in order to avoid unripe, green flavors; tannin is extracted not from the stalks but by lengthy maceration, along with color, aroma, and acidity. Malolactic fermentation in barrel is advised for finer harmony between fruit and wood, and when the wine is made *élevage* takes place in new or nearly new oak, followed by bottling in one single go with neither fining nor filtration.

Colombo's counsels have made for noticeable improvements on many estates, yet he has not let his involvement stop there. He has created Rhône Vignobles, a loose association of some of his clients, the aim of which is to pool their experiences, exchange ideas and generally work as a think-tank on ways of improving the fortunes of the Rhône Valley wines.

Cornas Les Ruchets

Use of a Bordeaux bottle and modernist packaging has done nothing to endear Colombo to his fellow growers, yet this also is indicative of a desire to break out of tradition's mold. But appearances aside, it is what is in the bottle which counts: Les Ruchets, an ideally-sited parcel lying high above the village, gives a deeply colored wine with a fabulous, intense black-fruit fragrance, lushness on the palate, and a structure enveloped in ample flesh. A strong toasted flavor and hints of licorice and spice add to the complexity of the whole, which has a fine long finish. Les Ruchets, paradoxically powerful and delicate, is a magnificently complete wine, which partners jugged hare very well.

RHÔNE VALLEY
A.O.C. Cornas

- *Wine selected:*
  Cornas Reynard

- *Grape variety:*
  Syrah
- *Average vine age:*
  40 years
- *Vineyard size:*
  1.7 hectare
- *Soil type:*
  Granite
- *Production:*
  6,000 bottles

Finest Vintages:
1999, 1996, 1995, 1991

Domaine Thierry Allemand
22 Impasse des Granges
07130 Cornas
Tel. (0033) 475 81 06 50
Allemand's establishment is on the
RN86, opposite the restaurant Ollier.
- *Owner:* Thierry Allemand
- *On-site sales:* Yes
- *Visits:* By appointment
- *Price:* ★★

DOMAINE THIERRY ALLEMAND

In an age when so many school-leavers, lured by the apparently limitless earning possibilities of high-technology businesses such as computing, Internet services, mobile telephones and so on, do not even want to consider a life on the land, it is heartening to see the odd one enthusiastically embracing the noble and traditional *métier* of *vigneron*, and working hard to earn himself a reputation. Thierry Allemand is one such, a young man who appears to have chosen a career for which he has exceptional talents.

Enamoured with the grower's life

It is not as if Allemand has wine making in his blood, for his parents lived and worked in Valence. As a teenager he helped out on Robert Michel's estate, and after leaving school worked there full time, and gradually became thoroughly enamoured with the life.

Naturally enough, before long he was thinking of making his own wine, and started keeping his ears open for any land that might come up for sale. In 1981 he acquired his first plot, which he then spent his weekends planting. Since then he has gradually acquired other land, notably a fine parcel of old vines in the Reynard *climat* which belonged to Noël Verset, bringing his holding today to 3.4 hectares. However that does not keep him fully occupied, and to supplement his income he still works part-time for the Michels.

A young traditionalist

Allemand may be part of the young generation at Cornas, but he holds perfectly traditional views as to how the wine should be made. Low yields are essential for quality, and to ensure this he carries out a crop-thinning *vendange verte* at the moment the fruit turns color. Then vinifications are carried out in such a manner as to produce wines of structure, density and power, but with perhaps a greater degree of flesh, ripeness, and charm than was usual in bygone days. Allemand leaves the fruit on its stalks and treads a small amount to get the fermentation going. The liquid is then allowed to rise gradually to a high 95°F (35°C), and is all the time enriched by regular foot treading for maximum extraction of tannin, color and aroma.

Once the *cuvaison* is over the wines are transferred partly to barrel, partly to stainless steel for aging, which lasts for twelve to eighteen months. The barrels will already have held wine, for Allemand is not a believer in new oak for aging Cornas. Finally the wines are racked by gravity, if necessary fined, and bottled without being filtered.

Cornas Reynard

Of his two wines, the Reynard is the more profound and complex. It is a simple question of a better site and older vines. The wine has a true young Cornas color of very dark purple, and a sumptuous Syrah nose of blackcurrant with a touch of tar and cinnamon. Chewy and concentrated on the palate, with mouth-coating tannin and high acidity, it finishes with great length. A good vintage such as 1995 will keep for two decades without any problem. Anyone foolhardy enough to drink this in its youth should prepare a grilled rib of beef, while those who wait will find a stew of wild boar very suitable.

RHÔNE VALLEY
A.O.C. Châteauneuf-du-Pape

- *Wine selected:*
  Châteauneuf-du-Pape
  Hommage à Jacques Perrin

- *Grape Varieties:*
  Mourvèdre 60%, Grenache 20%,
  Syrah 10%, Counoise 10%
- *Average vine age:*
  55 years
- *Vineyard size:*
  70 hectares
- *Soil type:*
  Clay and limestone, quartzite
  boulders
- *Production:*
  5,000 bottles

Finest Vintages:
2000, 1999, 1998, 1995, 1994, 1990,
1989

Château de Beaucastel
Chemin de Beaucastel
84350 Courthézon
Tel. (0033) 490 70 41 00
Internet: www.beaucastel.com
Château de Beaucastel lies next to the
A7 motorway. Take the exit no. 22
marked "Orange Sud".
- *Owners:* Perrin family
- *On-site sales:* Subject to availability
- *Visits:* By appointment
- *Price:* ★★★★★

Château de Beaucastel

There is one Rhône valley estate which is perceived around the world as epitomizing the best that France has to offer. Thanks to the sheer perfection and individuality of its wines, Château de Beaucastel has steadily forged a reputation second to none over the twentieth century, and large though it is, its production is today rapidly snapped up by those wine lovers who know what is what.

The Perrins forge Beaucastel's reputation

The estate's history starts in 1549, when Noble Pierre de Beaucastel bought a property at Coudoulet. Soon his descendants had built a fine house there, where they were to live for some two centuries. Towards the end of the nineteenth century Élie Dussaud was master of Beaucastel, and it was he who witnessed the devastation of the vineyard by phylloxera. He did not replant, and in 1909 sold the estate to Pierre Tramier, who gradually did, before leaving the estate to his son-in-law Pierre Perrin. Pierre, his son Jacques, and since 1978 Jacques' sons François and Jean-Pierre Perrin—each generation of this family has contributed to the construction of Beaucastel's current pre-eminence.

A highly individual estate

The wine is individual on two counts: grape mix and vinification method. The vineyard contains all thirteen permitted varieties, yet in proportions seen nowhere else. Jacques Perrin was convinced that Mourvèdre should be the dominant grape and built his blends around it, at a time when it was distinctly unfashionable. Beaucastel is today the only red Châteauneuf-du-Pape in which the Grenache is not dominant. The top white wine, made exclusively with Roussanne, equally illustrates this independence of thought. Since Jacques Perrin's time the vines have been cultivated with utmost respect for the soil and the environment, in order to stimulate robust health and thus better-quality fruit, and today the Perrins are proud that bees, birds, cicadas, and ladybugs inhabit their vineyards.

Once the black grapes have been checked on arrival at base and then destemmed, they are subjected to a procedure conceived by Pierre Perrin and perfected by his son whereby their skins are steam-heated to 80°C and then cooled to 68°F (20°C). This enables the extraction of aroma and color from inside the skin, and also destroys certain bacteria and enzymes which cause early oxidation, and thus largely renders the use of any SO_2 unnecessary during fermentation. The net result is that fermentations are slower and longer, and the resulting wines richer and longer-living. The rest of the wine-making process is traditional, and driven by the Perrins' great perfectionism.

Châteauneuf-du-Pape hommage à Jacques Perrin

To pay homage to the farsightedness and conviction of their father, in the very finest years the Perrin brothers make a largely Mourvèdre-based special *cuvée* which is without doubt one of France's greatest red wines. Despite its thick texture, extraordinary aromatic depth and intensity, and its great structure, as with all Perrin wines the accent is on harmony and elegance. All elements combined, this makes for a very great wine. Lucky owners of this rarity could do worse than choose hare *à la royale* as supporting cast, when the great day eventually comes along!

RHÔNE VALLEY
A.O.C. Châteauneuf-du-Pape

- *Wine selected:*
  Châteauneuf-du-Pape Cuvée des Générations Gaston Philippe

- *Grape Varieties:*
  Grenache 60%, Syrah 20%, Mourvèdre 20%
- *Average vine age:*
  40 years
- *Vineyard size:*
  0.75–3 hectares
- *Soil type:*
  Clay and limestone, quartzite stones
- *Production:*
  3,000–10,000 bottles

Finest Vintages:
2001, 2000, 1999, 1998, 1995, 1990, 1989

Château de la Gardine
BP 35
84231 Châteauneuf-du-Pape
Tel. (0033) 490 83 73 20
Internet: www.gardine.com
From Châteauneuf-du-Pape take the D17 towards Roquemaure. The road leading up to La Gardine is about 1.5 km down, on the right
- *Owners:* Gaston Brunel family
- *On-site sales:* 8:30–12:00 a.m., 1-6 p.m.
- *Visits:* By appointment
- *Price:* ★★★

CHÂTEAU DE LA GARDINE

A healthy respect for tradition and a willingness to experiment go arm in arm at Château de la Gardine, where the sons of Gaston Brunel, one of Châteauneuf-du-Pape's most revered figures, craft a range of fine, flavorsome wines. The estate has always been reliable, but since the 1980s the Brunels's ambition and perfectionism have propelled it near the top of the Châteauneuf quality table.

The legacy of Gaston Brunel

La Gardine was a small 8-hectare estate when Brunel acquired it in 1943. Fiercely proud of the region and its wines, he set about enlarging it through a large planting program, giving the estate the form it has today. New wine-making facilities and underground cellars followed, enabling the vinification of the vastly increased quantities of fruit.

More importantly, he instilled in his sons Patrick and Maxime a love of their inheritance and its traditions, and ambitions for its wine. By 1965 they were seeking the advice of their fellow wine maker and friend Docteur Dufays, a renowned geological expert, to advise them on replanting, in order to attain the ideal correlation between the numerous permitted varieties they use and their land, which itself enjoys great geological diversity. That thoroughness is today paying off with great complexity in the wines.

Tradition and a willingness to experiment

The quality of their raw material has without doubt played a significant part in the great quality of recent vintages. Lower yields, increasingly organic cultivation, and the maintenance of a high average plant age all help to produce excellent grapes on which the Brunels can focus their painstaking attention.

In the vatroom there are no rules, for each vintage's fruit is assessed and vinified as befits it best: most of the fruit is usually destalked, and the various varieties are vatted together, a local tradition dating from bygone days when they grew in intermingled abandon in the vineyards. The stainless-steel vats have temperature-control devices and some contain hydraulic *pigeage* equipment, enabling extraction in a shorter time and thereby avoiding excessive dryness and astringency. The Brunels have resurrected the old Châteauneuf tradition of using casks for *élevage*—a century ago the village had six cooperages—and sensible use of oak has undeniably given their wine greater refinement than it had in the past.

Châteauneuf-du-Pape Cuvée des Générations Gaston Philippe

In years when Nature really rewards them with outstanding fruit, the Brunels release a special *cuvée* in commemoration of their father. Produced from the scanty yields of their oldest vines, from fruit cosseted and minutely checked for quality, this massive wine is aged entirely in new oak barrels. Violet-black in color, with a heady perfume of rich black fruit, spice, and vanilla, it is so rich and well-balanced that the wood influence is barely detectable after several years in bottle. Ample and smooth, it finishes with great length, a sure sign of its quality and future potential. This magnificent wine, which amply repays long keeping, has the necessary complexity to stand up to a haunch of wild boar, or jugged hare.

RHÔNE VALLEY
A.O.C. Châteauneuf-du-Pape

- *Wine selected:*
  **Châteauneuf-du-Pape
  Cuvée Chaupin**

- *Grape Variety:*
  Grenache
- *Average vine age:*
  80 years
- *Vineyard size:*
  3 hectares
- *Soil type:*
  Sandy clay
- *Production:*
  12,000 bottles

Finest Vintages:
2000, 1995, 1990

Domaine de la Janasse
27 Chemin du Moulin
84350 Courthézon
Tel. (0033) 490 70 86 29
Domaine de la Janasse lies at the
southern end of Courthézon, next to
the RN7.
- *Owners:* Aimé Sabon
- *On-site sales:* 8–12 a.m., 2–6 p.m.
- *Visits:* Yes
- *Price:* ★★★

DOMAINE DE LA JANASSE

Whether he realized it or not, when Aimé Sabon made the decision to stop taking his grapes to the cooperative in 1973 he was laying the foundations of a new star estate in the Châteauneuf-du-Pape firmament. A quarter of a century later, its wines having attained a very desirable reputation, the construction of the edifice would seem long complete to anyone but Aimé's talented son Christophe. He, however, is not a friend of routine!

Aimé Sabon goes solo

The background to this success story is anything but original: a Sabon bought some vineyard land at the turn of the century, when phylloxera was a recent memory and land for sale was plentiful and inexpensive. Vines were planted, and the land was passed down from father to son. More planting was carried out periodically, notably in 1940, and further land was bought, and all the while the harvests were taken to the local cooperative for vinification. Then came Aimé Sabon's turn at the helm in 1967.

From the start Aimé prided himself on the quality of his raw material, and made a point of restricting the yields of his vines. He brought an end to the arrangement with the cooperative and started making and bottling his own wines with the 1973 vintage, which necessitated the construction of wine-making facilities and cellar space. By the time he handed over responsibilities to his son Christophe in 1991, the family had 10 hectares of Châteauneuf-du-Pape vineyard as well as a significant holding of Côtes-du-Rhône and Vin de Pays. Having studied at Beaune, the dapper Christophe has continued to work on the estate's production with great talent, experimenting and refining methods, and using the abundant and excellent raw material to compose new and interesting cuvées following his inspiration. Nothing is static at La Janasse!

Great potential complexity

The Sabons family's 13 hectares of Châteauneuf-du-Pape lie in five different sectors, and have varied orientations and soils, providing great potential complexity. After strict quality control the black fruit is usually mostly destemmed (but the vintage is the final arbiter), and spends over three weeks in cuvaison in concrete vats, followed by some eighteen months' élevage in foudre and both new and used cask. The last operation, bottling, is carried out after a light fining but no filtration.

The majestic white Cuvée Prestige on the other hand, made principally of Roussanne supported by Clairette and white Grenache, is now made entirely in oak casks (two-thirds new) and reared for eighteen months with bâtonnage of the lees. A masterpiece to enjoy with a Bresse chicken!

Châteauneuf-du-Pape Cuvée Chaupin

The lieu-dit Chaupin, north-facing and planted with Grenache in 1912, gives a wine which is remarkable not only for its concentration and complexity (a meager yield of some 20 hectoliters per hectare and two pigeages a day see to that) but also for its finesse, harmony, and discreet alcohol; these are qualities rare in a Grenache wine, and proof of the talent of the young man at the controls. An eloquent explanation for the increasingly wide demand for his wines. Leg of lamb, seasoned with Provençal herbs, has just the finesse of repartee to merit a place at Chaupin's table.

RHÔNE VALLEY
A.O.C. Châteauneuf-du-Pape

- *Wine selected:*
  **Châteauneuf-du-Pape
  Cuvée des Cadettes**

- *Grape Varieties:*
  Grenache 44%, Mourvèdre 28%,
  Syrah 28%
- *Average vine age:*
  90 years
- *Vineyard size:*
  5 hectares
- *Soil type:*
  Sand and quartzite stones
- *Production:*
  15,000 bottles

Finest Vintages:
2000, 1999, 1998, 1995, 1990, 1989

Château La Nerthe
Route de Sorgues
84230 Châteauneuf-du-Pape
Tel. (0033) 490 83 70 11
Château La Nerthe lies halfway
between Châteauneuf-du-Pape and
Sorgues, on the left as one goes
south. It is well signposted.
- *Owners:* Richard family
- *Director:* Alain Dugas
- *On-site sales:* 9–12 a.m., 2:30–
  5:30 p.m.
- *Visits:* Groups of 10, by appointment
- *Price:* ★★★

CHÂTEAU LA NERTHE

A marvelous vineyard location, allied with a tradition of good management and viticultural and wine-making innovation, have resulted in the long pre-eminence of La Nerthe among Châteauneuf-du-Pape's estates. Today it continues to benefit from the investment and the intelligent management necessary to ensure the production of great wine, and its wines are regularly among the most accomplished of the region.

The legacy of enlightened owners

The estate existed as far back as 1560, when it was known as Beauvenir and was the property of the Tulle de Villefranche family. By 1750 it covered 50 hectares, made wine, and its owners had already set up a network of agents, indeed its production was selling as far afield as London, Moscow, and America. Bottling was introduced on site in the ensuing years, and the writer Jullien, in his *Topographie de tous les vignobles connus* of 1822, called it a "vin de première classe."

La Nerthe's vineyards were destroyed by the dreaded phylloxera bug in the 1870s, and the Tulle de Villefranches sold the estate to Commandant Joseph Ducos. While all around him were replacing their decimated vineyards with fruit trees, Ducos, convinced that grafting Rhône vines onto phylloxera-resistant American rootstock was the answer, set about rebuilding his vineyard by that method. He was initially observed with disbelief, and then curiosity, by fellow growers, but was eventually imitated by them all. He conducted lengthy research into vine varieties, planting ten on his estate, and the results of his experiments were influential in the drawing-up of Châteauneuf-du-Pape's appellation laws in 1936.

After suffering extensive damage during the war and then a difficult postwar period the property was acquired in 1985 by the Richard family and entirely restored by Alain Dugas, who had studied with Dr. Dufays of Domaine de Nalys and who was appointed to run it and make the wine.

Expressing La Nerthe's *terroir*

A good number of the last century's traditions still stand today at La Nerthe, for they have long proved their value. Systematic destemming, followed by a light crushing and fifteen to eighteen days' vatting, were how the wine was made in 1860, and are more or less how it is made today. The multiplicity of vine varieties is essential to the balanced expression of La Nerthe's *terroir*, and the Grenache has thus never been particularly predominant in the blend. And then its marvelous site, its old vines, very low yields, and perfect grape ripeness all contribute to La Nerthe's quality.

Châteauneuf-du-Pape Cuvée des Cadettes

Dugas produces four wines: a very fine standard red and white Châteauneuf-du-Pape, and in favourable years a magnificent barrel-fermented white Clos de Beauvenir and the red Cuvée des Cadettes. The latter is made in wooden vat and aged in nothing but new oak barrels. Its impressive structure destines it for great longevity, and in the mouth it is very concentrated and ample, with a rich, spicy blackcurrant flavor and the toasted flavor of its new oak. This glorious wine, awarded three stars by the *Guide Hachette des vins* for its 1995 vintage, calls out for a haunch of venison.

RHÔNE VALLEY
A.O.C. Châteauneuf-du-Pape

- *Wine selected:*
  Châteauneuf-du-Pape red

- *Grape Varieties:*
  Grenache 70%, Mourvèdre 20%,
  Syrah 8%, Counoise/Muscardin/
  Vaccarèse 2%
- *Average vine age:*
  30 years
- *Vineyard size:*
  26 hectares
- *Soil type:*
  Clay and limestone
- *Production:*
  110,000 bottles

Finest Vintages:

2001, 2000, 1999, 1998, 1995, 1993,
1990, 1989, 1988, 1985, 1983, 1981

Clos des Papes
13 Avenue Pierre-de-Luxembourg
84230 Châteauneuf-du-Pape
Tel. (0033) 490 83 70 13
From the center of town head for
the Bédarrides-Sorgues crossroads,
and turn right in the Sorgues direction.
Clos des Papes is 300 m down on
the left.
- *Owner:* Clos des Papes–Paul Avril
- *Manager:* Vincent Avril
- *On-site sales:* 8–12 a.m., 2–6 p.m.
  (Fri. 5 p.m.)
- *Visits:* Yes
- *Price:* ★★

CLOS DES PAPES

Any listing of the finest producers of Châteauneuf-du-Pape invariably includes the Avril family and their Clos des Papes estate, for year in, year out, this father-and-son team make extremely good wine. What is more, their welcome is warm and their wines remain affordable.

Three centuries of wine makers

The Avrils were First Consuls and Treasurers of Châteauneuf-du-Pape from 1756 to 1790. Yet more importantly from the point of view of today's wine lover, over some three centuries they have been wine makers. They started bottling their produce very early on; a gold medal won in 1882 at the Avignon Fair attests to its quality at the time. The first wines to be sold under the name Clos des Papes appeared in 1896, both white and red selling for five francs a bottle, and Paul Avril, grandfather of the present Paul, registered the name as a trade mark in 1902. Recognizing the necessity of setting and safeguarding standards for his region's wines, Avril was the driving force behind a committee organized as early as 1911 to draw up basic production rules, which later on were to form the basis of the A.O.C. Since his days three generations have delighted the palates of wine lovers with many a fine vintage.

The advantages of a fragmented estate

Clos des Papes is a highly fragmented estate which counts eighteen parcels spread over the length and breadth of the appellation. A logistic disadvantage perhaps, yet since there is climatic variation between the different sectors it has the advantage of staggering the ripening of fruit—the northern part of the appellation can be up to ten days behind the southern part—enabling the harvesting of different parcels at peak ripeness. What is more, the fact that the grapes are grown in a wide diversity of soils and sub-soils also enhances the complexity of the wine. Clos des Papes, as one might suspect, is not simply a brand name but is one of the Avrils' vineyards; lying inside the grounds of the ruined château, it once formed part of the Papal estate.

The inescapable requisites of quality

Low yields and strict selectivity are the inescapable requisites for the production of quality wine, in the Avrils' view. To this end they take great steps to reduce the vine's natural productivity by severe pruning, debudding in the spring and green harvesting in July. Then once the harvest has started the fruit is examined and if necessary rejected either as it is cut, as it arrives at the trailer, or on the conveyor belt in the reception area.

The vinification which follows is thoroughly classic, taking place in enamel-lined vats at a relatively high temperature whichever color. The white wine is bottled without any wood contact, while the red is aged in *foudre* and cask for twelve to eighteen months.

Châteauneuf-du-Pape

The red Clos des Papes, so dark it seems black, develops a sumptuous, soft bouquet of morello cherries, cloves, and cinnamon after a few years in bottle, with an attractive smoky aspect. It is remarkable for its balance and harmony and the opulence of its flesh, which hides its tannic structure. Grilled red meats suit it down to the ground, indeed a barbecued rib of beef will show off its qualities to perfection.

RHÔNE VALLEY
A.O.C. Châteauneuf-du-Pape

- *Wine selected:*
  Châteauneuf-du-Pape

- *Grape Variety:*
  Grenache Noir
- *Average vine age:*
  15 and 70 years
- *Vineyard size:*
  8 hectares
- *Soil type:*
  Clay, limestone, sand
- *Production:*
  24,000 bottles

Finest Vintages:
1998, 1995, 1990

Château Rayas
Route de Courthézon
84230 Châteauneuf-du-Pape
Tel. (0033) 490 83 73 09
From the center of town head for
the Bédarrides-Sorgues crossroads,
and turn right in the direction of
Sorgues. Clos des Papes is 300 m
down on the left.
- *Owner:* Reynaud family
- *On-site sales:* No
- *Visits:* No
- *Price:* ★★★

CHÂTEAU RAYAS

There are few estates in France or indeed anywhere in the world which make a wine of such sublime, concentrated brilliance as Château Rayas. And there can be none which come near it for legend: so much has been written about this small, hidden, run-down property, its unorthodox methods and its eccentric proprietors, that the visitor, assuming he manages to find the place, may be forgiven a little apprehension.

A very unusual vineyard

As a wine estate Château Rayas is young. Its vineyards—some fifteen parcels, many surrounded by woods – were planted by Louis Reynaud in 1922, and are mostly north-facing. Intuition on the part of the young man? The vines as a result get both respite from excessive heat and a longer, gentler, ripening curve. They are composed of friable clay, limestone, and in some places sandy soils, without any of the smooth quartzite stones; rumor has it that Reynaud removed them all by hand. And in an appellation where thirteen varieties are permitted for red wines, Rayas uses but one—Grenache, which generally does not age well.

Father and son nurture a legend

Over the decades Rayas's reputation was forged by the eccentric Louis Reynaud, who held sway until his death at a ripe old age in 1978, when he was succeeded by his son Jacques, an equally exotic personage of great culture, intellect, and wine-making talent. The reclusive Jacques had no love of journalists and the warmth of his welcome was unpredictable—the estate is tucked away off the beaten track and visitors are discouraged—yet he made wines which mostly stood up brilliantly under the piercing spotlight of the world's wine critics.

A bachelor, he passed away in 1997, since when the estate has been run by his young nephew Emmanuel Reynaud, who shows all the signs of being capable of perpetuating the Rayas standards.

The apotheosis of Grenache Noir

Extremely low yields of 15–18 hectoliters per hectare, which would be regarded by many as excessive and unprofitable, have always been at the root of Rayas's quality. The almost over-ripe grapes, often with potential alcohol of 15°, are vinified slowly by thoroughly traditional methods, in cellars which belie the adage that fine wine can only be made in clean surroundings. The wine is then aged in a motley collection of old casks of various sizes, the contents of which are unhesitatingly refused inclusion into the *grand vin* if they are not utterly worthy. Stainless steel, thermoregulation, new oak—none of the trappings of the modern wine estate are to be found at Rayas.

Châteauneuf-du-Pape

Sporting its famous label and disdaining the bottle with the Papal emblem, Rayas is proud to be judged on its own intrinsic merits. Great breeding, extraordinary thickness and concentration, surprising refinement, it is the apotheosis of Grenache Noir. It speaks with waves of sumptuous, sweet flavor and a very consequent alcohol level, yet can be relied on for perfect balance and harmony. A *tour de force* by which others are judged, it needs a dozen years to develop its complexity, yet will last twice that in a good year. Truffled capon in a coarse salt crust makes a very successful accompaniment to Château Rayas at table. A toast to the Reynauds of this world!

RHÔNE VALLEY
A.O.C. Châteauneuf-du-Pape

• *Wine selected:*
  **Châteauneuf-du-Pape
  Cuvée Réservé**

• *Grape Varieties:*
  Grenache 95%, Syrah 5%
• *Average vine age:*
  70 years
• *Vineyard size:*
  1.3 hectares
• *Soil type:*
  Clay and limestone
• *Production:*
  Up to 4,000 bottles

Finest Vintages:
1998, 1995

Domaine de la Vieille Julienne
Le Grès
84100 Orange
Tel. (0033) 490 34 20 10
Follow the D68 northwards from
Châteauneuf-du-Pape in the direction
of Orange. At the intersection with the
D72 turn left; La Vieille Julienne is
1 km down the road.
• *Owner:* Daumen family
• *On-site sales:* By appointment
• *Visits:* By appointment
• *Price:* ★★

DOMAINE DE LA VIEILLE JULIENNE

The 1990s have witnessed much change at the La Vieille Julienne estate, which has coincided, as so often happens, with the handing over of responsibilities from a father to his son. In a short number of years Jean-Paul Daumen has reviewed a number of the estate's traditions and improved the wine considerably. La Vieille Julienne was always renowned for size and staying-power, but these days richness, complexity, and irresistible succulence are its major qualities.

A haven from the dreaded phylloxera

The estate, which came into being in the early eighteen century, takes its name from the Julienne family, its original owners. Daumen's family acquired it in 1905. At that time there were relatively few vines, yet somehow what there were mercifully escaped the depredations of the dreaded phylloxera. Initially the wine was made for the consumption of family and friends, but in the 1920s the step was taken to start selling it. Gradually demand from private customers for the wine in bottle grew, and by the 1950s the greater part of the production was being bottled. Today La Vieille Julienne finds its way to wine lovers all around the world.

Several essential changes

Grenache has always been the linchpin of this wine, indeed the centenarian plants which escaped the phylloxera are of that variety. Having observed the great quality of certain other Châteauneufs, Daumen knew when he took over in 1990 that there were several essential changes to be introduced. Perhaps the most important was the introduction of destalking, permitting a lengthier vatting period of some twenty-five days at controlled temperatures of 82–92°F (28–33°C), with the extraction of tannin, color, and aroma enhanced by pumping up and spraying the wine over the cap of solids (*remontage*) four times per day. Daumen ferments the different varieties individually, each in the company of an equal part of Grenache; that way he never has to pick a variety or a plot until it is perfectly ripe, and can carry out the stringent controls essential for quality.

After two rackings the wines are blended and then transferred to barrel. There were experiments with various proportions of new oak until 1995, since when a mix of wood of between one and four years' age has been used, as well as 50-hectoliter tuns. After some twelve to eighteen months' aging the wine is bottled in one go, without filtration. This quality *élevage* and the single bottling have been greatly instrumental in ridding the wine of its previous rusticity and solidness.

Châteauneuf-du-Pape Cuvée Réserve

The finest wine at La Vieille Julienne is made almost entirely with Grenache, from a scant yield of 20 hectoliters per hectare. The Cuvée Réserve, which is only made in exceptional years, is a wine of extraordinary depth and seduction, with a large tannic structure clothed in voluminous flesh and a refined flavor of spicy, cooked fruit with a vanilla backdrop. It is actually delicious young, yet is made for a decade's keeping, and will live far longer than that. This masterpiece is made for a stew of wild boar.

RHÔNE VALLEY
A.O.C. Châteauneuf-du-Pape

- *Wine selected:*
  Châteauneuf-du-Pape red

- *Grape Varieties:*
  Grenache Noir 60%, Mourvèdre
  15%, Syrah 15%, Cinsaut 5%,
  Others 5%
- *Average vine age:*
  50 years
- *Vineyard size:*
  63 hectares
- *Soil type:*
  Clay and limestone, quartzite stones
- *Production:*
  200,000 bottles

Finest Vintages:
2001, 2000, 1998, 1995,
1990, 1989, 1985

Domaine du Vieux Télégraphe
3 Route de Châteauneuf-du-Pape
84370 Bédarrides
Tel. (0033) 490 33 00 31
Domaine du Vieux Télégraphe lies off
the Châteauneuf-du-Pape-Bédarrides
road.
- *Owners:* Brunier family
- *On-site sales:* 8–12 a.m., 2–6 p.m.
- *Visits:* By appointment
- *Price:* ★★

DOMAINE DU VIEUX TÉLÉGRAPHE

The wines of Domaine du Vieux Télégraphe are looked upon by many as yardstick Châteauneuf-du-Pape, indeed it is by them that many foreigners discover the appellation, for 80 percent of the estate's sizeable production is exported to destinations around the world. The region could hardly have a finer ambassador. Recent years have seen the wine continue to excel, thanks to a lot of devotion and hard work.

A century of prosperity

The Brunier family can be proud of what they have achieved. The estate celebrated its centenary in 1998, and with faultless continuity has been passed down four generations: Hippolyte the founder, Jules, Henri, and now Frédéric and Daniel.

Prosperity has permitted expansion, not only of Vieux Télégraphe but also, in 1986, with the purchase of Domaine de la Roquette, another Châteauneuf-du-Pape estate of 28 hectares, and then in 1998 with Domaine Les Pallières, a Gigondas estate of great if somewhat fading reputation.

The dangers of routine

Vieux Télégraphe's eminence derives primarily from its vineyard site, a magnificent single block on the La Crau plateau in the appellation's south-eastern section. This vast, south-facing terrace of clay and limestone soil, covered with smooth, heat-reflecting quartzite stones and lying over a stratum of water-retaining impermeable red clay, is ideally suited to the climate's demands, and often serves as a model for viticultural experiments.

It is cultivated with the utmost respect by the Bruniers. Going further than simply being ecological in their practices, the brothers ceaselessly reflect on the why's and how's of all they do, and the effect on the grape-quality of their actions, for they have an acute awareness of the dangers of routine. Traditional treatments against fungal outbreaks are limited and targeted with precision, while the grape worm is combated by means of "sexual confusion," which involves diffusing the scent of the female *Eudemis* butterfly, its mother, in order that the male cannot find her.

Analysis of the grapes' needs

Low yields are viewed as essential, and are achieved by debudding in the spring and, if necessary, green-harvesting in July. Fruit quality is meticulously controlled during the harvest, and vinification then proceeds in a winery designed to move the raw material and then the wine by gravity, rather than pumping. Vinification is traditional yet, like vineyard operations, it is subject to analysis of the needs of the different grapes every year. It is ended with a protracted *élevage* and regular racking, permitting bottling without filtration.

Châteauneuf-du-Pape

In style the modern Vieux Télégraphe red is situated in between the truly long-term wines and those made for consumption young. Contrary to the structured, dense wines made before the mid-1980s, the accent is now on aroma and balance, and concentrated, juicy fruit which makes the wine delicious from youth onwards. Delicious aromas of black fruit, licorice, Provençal herbs, and garrigue perfume this generous wine, making it a fine partner for grilled red meats seasoned with herbs.

RHÔNE VALLEY
A.O.C. Gigondas

- *Wine selected:*
  Gigondas Cuvée Florence

- *Grape Varieties:*
  Grenache, Syrah
- *Average vine age:*
  30 years
- *Vineyard size:*
  9.91 hectares
- *Soil type:*
  Clay and limestone
- *Production:*
  12,700 bottles

Finest Vintages:
1998, 1996, 1995

Domaine Les Goubert
84190 Gigondas
Tél. : 04 90 65 86 38
Tel. (0033) 490 65 86 38
If heading southwards on the D7 from
Sablet, do not turn left into the village
of Gigondas, but take the small road
on the right just after the Vignerons de
Gigondas Cooperative. Les Goubert is
the second property on the left.
- *Owners:* Jean-Pierre & Mireille
  Cartier
- *On-site sales:* 9–12 a.m., 2–6 p.m.
  By appointment over the weekend.
- *Visits:* By appointment
- *Price:* ★★

DOMAINE LES GOUBERT

If the wines of Gigondas have made great strides forward in the last few decades it is thanks to growers like Jean-Pierre Cartier, the free-thinking innovator who is responsible for the destiny of the excellent Domaine Les Goubert. There is nothing frivolous made on this estate, for Cartier is unashamedly *pro-vin de garde* when it comes to red wine, and also makes deliciously full-flavored whites.

A wealth of different plots are united

Cartier was born into a family of *vignerons* which goes back many a generation—Goubert was the name of his mother's family—and by the time he was fourteen he was already helping out in the vineyard, listening and observing. By 1973, the year when his father left him 3 hectares, he had thoroughly solid notions not only of how to make wine but of the quality level he wanted to attain. From the outset he started bottling his produce and looking around for land in order to increase his production and be able to make a better living.

Today Jean-Pierre and Mireille Cartier own a splendid 23-hectare estate, made up of over forty parcels of vine on terraces or slopes in the communes of Beaumes-de-Venise, Lafare, Sablet and Séguret as well as Gigondas. This wealth of different plots comprises a lot of geological diversity, which, emphasized by Cartier's traditional methods of cultivation using neither chemical fertilizers nor insecticides, in turn brings great complexity to the finished wines.

Wine making *à l'ancienne*

Vinifications at Les Goubert could hardly be more traditional. The fruit for the red wines is mostly left on its stems and lightly crushed, and then loaded into concrete vats for *cuvaison*, which lasts for three to four weeks or more. Temperatures are allowed to rise to some 90°F (32°C) for better extraction, but if they look like rising further, since he has no cooling equipment Cartier controls them the way it was no doubt done by his forbears, by transferring the liquid to another vat overnight and then reuniting it with its marc the following day. After aging, the length of which depends on the wine and the vintage quality, there is *égalisation* of the different recipients and finally bottling, which is all done in one go. The white wines are made at 64–68°F (18–20°C) in either a mix of stainless steel and barrel or simply, in the case of the Viognier wine, ten-months' barrel.

Gigondas Cuvée Florence

In celebration of the birth of his daughter, in 1985 Cartier introduced a prestige wine of Grenache and Syrah, made from very low yields. Going against local practice he gave it a long aging in mainly new oak barrels. The result was a superbly successful wine, opulent and fleshy, of fascinating complexity in the mouth. Fortunately Florence's birth has since been celebrated with great regularity, and with particular distinction in 1995: 50 percent new oak, twenty-four months' aging, and bottling with neither fining nor filtration, this splendor breathes vanilla, violets, black fruit, and spice, in a supremely harmonious whole that finishes very, very long. It is well structured and will no doubt live at least twenty years. It deserves a flavorsome red meat or game at table, followed by some mature Gouda.

RHÔNE VALLEY
A.O.C. Gigondas

- *Wine selected:*
Gigondas Cuvée Valbelle

- *Grape Varieties:*
Grenache 70%, Syrah 30%
- *Average vine age:*
80 years
- *Vineyard size:*
4 hectares
- *Soil type:*
Clay and limestone
- *Production:*
12,000 bottles

Finest Vintages:
1998, 1996, 1995, 1989, 1985

Château de Saint-Cosme
84190 Gigondas
Tel. (0033) 490 65 80 80
When leaving the village of Gigondas
take the Route des Dentelles de
Montmirail. Saint-Cosme is well
signposted.
- *Owners:* Louis Barruol
- *On-site sales:* Yes
- *Visits:* No
- *Price:* ★★

CHÂTEAU DE SAINT-COSME

Louis Barruol is the heir to a fourteen-generation family tradition at the historic Château de Saint-Cosme, several hundred meters north of the village of Gigondas. Yet while the family are well known in the area the wine is little known on the international stage, for bottling on the estate has only recently recommenced. So pure and authentic are Barruol's wines, however, that Saint-Cosme is destined to become one of the great names of the southern Rhône.

A historic vineyard slope

Saint-Cosme is the most ancient estate in the region. Lying on the site of a Gallo-Roman villa which very probably already had its own vineyard, the estate's existence in 1416 is attested by a document mentioning the granting by Jean de Chalon, Prince of Orange, of "land for the planting of vines on the Saint-Cosme slope." The Barruols' ancestors acquired it in 1490, and at the end of the sixteenth century built a splendid residence over existing cellars.

The slope covers 15 hectares and is looked down on by the tenth-century chapel dedicated to Saint Cosme, who shares with Saint Damien the responsibility of patron saint of the parish. The site is perfect for viticulture, and the Grenache, Syrah, Mourvèdre, and Cinsaut vines are immaculately tended. Louis Barruol tries to maintain a high vine age of at least sixty years, for this, he tells one, is the key to quality, particularly when it comes to Grenache. Pruning is severe in order to maintain low yields (as low as 25 hectoliters per hectare) and harvesting is never started until the grapes become over-ripe.

Purity of fruit, expression of *terroir*

Barruol makes his wine without recourse to SO2 whenever possible in order to preserve the fruit's purity, and with minimum manipulation. Fermentation is conducted in concrete vats by the grapes' natural yeast, and maceration lasts some 40 days, with two sessions of foot-treading per day. Then the wine is transferred half to tank and half to cask (of which 50 percent are replaced annually) for a year's *élevage*, during which it is not racked, again to preserve the fruit's purity. At the end of the year it is bottled with neither fining nor filtration. The bottles then await purchasers in the estate's medieval cellars, which contain what are possibly the oldest fermentation vats in France, cut into the sandstone walls.

Gigondas Cuvée Valbelle

Whenever the end of the growing season permits harvesting at sufficient *surmaturité* Barruol makes a second Gigondas, which is a selection of the wines of the oldest vines. Valbelle is matured exclusively in casks, half of which are new, the remainder having already served several times. Again there is neither SO$_2$ nor racking. It is a dense wine, velvet of texture and extraordinarily rich, with a magnificent, smoky bouquet of pepper and ripe black fruit, and nuances of tobacco, leather, or game, depending on the vintage and age of the bottle. A magnificent triumph of old vines and non-interventionism! Stuffed shoulder of lamb with a mature Valbelle (or indeed the excellent Cuvée Classique) will send even the most *blasé gourmet* into raptures!

RHÔNE VALLEY
A.O.C. Gigondas

- *Wine selected:*
  Gigondas

- *Grape Varieties:*
  Grenache 80%, Syrah 15%,
  Mourvèdre 5%
- *Average vine age:*
  50 years
- *Vineyard size:*
  16 hectares
- *Soil type:*
  Clay and limestone
- *Production:*
  60,000 bottles

Finest Vintages:

2000, 1999, 1998, 1995, 1993, 1990,
1989, 1985, 1983, 1981

Domaine Saint-Gayan
84190 Gigondas
Tel. (0033) 490 65 86 33
Follow the D7 northwards towards
Sablet. Saint-Gayan is at the northerly
limit of the Gigondas appellation.
- *Owners:* G.F.A. de L'Oratoire—Roger
  Meffre family
- *On-site sales:* 9:00–11:45 a.m.,
  2:00–6:30 p.m.
- *Visits:* No
- *Price:* ★

DOMAINE SAINT-GAYAN

One of the oldest Gigondas estates is that of Saint-Gayan, which lies at the northern limit of the village's appellation, not far from Sablet. It is the property of Roger Meffre and his family, whose ancestors have been making wine there for nigh on four hundred years. Today Saint-Gayan is one of the greatest names in Gigondas.

At home in an arid environment

After half a century presiding over the destinies of Saint-Gayan, Roger Meffre retired in 1993, handing over responsibility for the running of the estate to his son Jean-Pierre and daughter-in-law Martine. The family possesses 16 hectares of Gigondas and a further 24 of Rasteau, Châteauneuf-du-Pape, Côtes-du-Rhône, and Vin de Pays, which provide them all told with some 1,500 hectoliters per year.

The Gigondas vineyards lie on the gently sloping plain around the house, where the soil is very poor and composed essentially of clay and limestone littered with stones from the Dentelles de Montmirail, with an important presence of compacted sand known as *safres* in places. The Grenache, Syrah, and Mourvèdre vines which hug the ground and struggle to prosper in this arid *terrain*, frequently blasted by the Mistral wind, are of a very respectable average age of fifty years, and there are also scattered bands of centenarian vines to be found.

A permanent and visible presence during harvest

The Meffres' Gigondas is one of the richest and sturdiest of the village. Not only is this high vine age a contributory factor to the wine's character, but moderate yields, attained by severe pruning, debudding, and then green harvesting where necessary, also play an essential role. Selection is of course necessary, obliging the Meffres like any serious vineyard owners to be permanently and visibly present during the harvest, failing which the tired pickers, backs aching, soon lose interest in discarding unripe or rotten grapes and cut anything and everything.

Vinified for maximum extraction

The Gigondas is fermented in stainless-steel and cement vats and macerated for a prolonged period of at least three weeks at a relatively high temperature for maximum extraction of its color, tannin, and aroma components. After *décuvage* the skins and pulp are pneumatically pressed and the press wine is added to the free-run wine. At that point the wines of the three varieties, which until then have been kept separate, are blended and spend the following two years in tank, followed by one year in *foudre*, before being bottled unfiltered in monthly sessions over the best part of the following year.

Gigondas

The Meffres' very conservative cellar practices result in a dense garnet wine with a powerful and heady bouquet of red fruit and pepper with a touch of *garrigue*, which requires a good few years to open up completely. In the mouth its density, concentration, power and structure are utterly impressive, and its finish is no less so. As the years roll by (for Saint-Gayan is one of the longest-living Gigondas) aromas of truffle, earth, and leather often emerge, making for a most enjoyable tasting. The complex and generous Saint-Gayan calls for a hearty game dish such as jugged hare, or duck with olives.

RHÔNE VALLEY
A.O.C. Gigondas

- *Wine selected:*
  **Gigondas Prestige
  des Hautes Garrigues**

- *Grape Varieties:*
  Grenache 80%, Mourvèdre 20%
- *Average vine age:*
  50 years
- *Vineyard size:*
  3.5 hectares
- *Soil type:*
  Clay and limestone
- *Production:*
  12,000 bottles

Finest Vintages:
1998, 1996, 1995

Domaine Santa Duc
Les Hautes Garrigues
84190 Gigondas
Tel. (0033) 490 65 84 49
The estate lies off the D80, between
the D7 and the D8.
- *Owners:* Edmond & Yves Gras
- *On-site sales:* Stock permitting
- *Visits:* By appointment
- *Price:* ★★

DOMAINE SANTA DUC

Until the mid-1980s few had heard of Santa Duc, an estate producing what was no doubt good wine but selling it all off in bulk, like many others, to the *négoce*. Then with a change of generation came a change of ambition, and very quickly the name got around and the wine started to be talked about and favorably reviewed. It is no surprise to note that today Santa Duc is one of the most highly rated Gigondas producers.

Respect for the vineyard environment
Santa Duc has now been in the Gras family for four generations. When the young Yves Gras took over from his father Edmond in 1985 he had definite ideas about his role as grower and about the type of wine he wished to make. The vineyard was where his time should be spent, he felt, since no good wine is made with anything less than top-quality fruit, and like many of his generation he was convinced that his vines would produce the finest fruit only if cultivated in as natural and ecological way as possible. Respect for the vineyard environment therefore dictates all Santa Duc's viticultural operations, and today neither insecticides nor chemical fertilizers are used, and treatments are only carried out if the crop would be at risk were they not, and then very sparingly; in short, *lutte raisonnée*, which proscribes the unthinking, routine use of chemical products.

Top-quality fruit only comes from low yields, so Yves goes out among the vines in July and enthusiastically lops off excess bunches. At harvest time he always waits until his crop is almost overripe before picking, for Grenache wines particularly need respectable alcohol levels, and fusses worriedly among his *vendangeurs* making sure that they are being sufficiently selective in the fruit they collect in their baskets.

The making of an authentic Gigondas
While Grenache naturally holds pride of place in his vineyard, Yves Gras cultivates a significant proportion of Mourvèdre, of which he is very fond, and some Syrah, for he is out to make "authentic" Gigondas, of the firm, tannic, and muscular sort, and these varieties contribute color, tannin, and bouquet to complement the Grenache's flesh and alcohol.

The family vineyards are very scattered, which makes for more complexity in the wines. Some are on the higher slopes, composed of poor sandy limestone, while the bulk are on flatter red clay below the village known as Les Hautes Garrigues. The former contribute finesse, elegance, and *terroir* character, growers tell one, while the latter give body, warmth, and bouquet.

Gigondas Prestige des Hautes Garrigues
Since 1989, in the finest years Yves Gras has produced a *cuvée* exclusively made from the Hautes Garrigues, which is a formidably rich, powerful, and structured wine of around 15°, made for long aging. This is made with selected Grenache and Mourvèdre, picked very late and vatted uncrushed without destemming, and then aged in new and one-year barrels for some eighteen months before bottling. Thick in extract it may be, but it is nevertheless as fresh as one could wish. Prestige des Hautes Garrigues is a great Gigondas, which may be served with jugged hare with truffles.

RHÔNE VALLEY
A.O.C. Vacqueyras

- *Wine selected:*
  Vacqueyras

- *Grape Varieties:*
  Grenache 98%,
  Syrah 2%
- *Average vine age:*
  30-70 years
- *Vineyard size:*
  6 hectares
- *Soil type:*
  Clay and limestone
- *Production:*
  16,000 bottles

Finest Vintages:
2000, 1998, 1996

Château des Tours
Quartier des Sablons
84260 Sarrians
Tel. (0033) 490 65 41 75
From Jonquières take the D950 towards
Sarrians. Take the second turning on
the left 100 m after crossing the
Ouvèze. The way to Château des Tours
is indicated thereafter.
- *Owners:* Reynaud family
- *On-site sales:* By appointment
- *Visits:* By appointment
- *Price:* ★★

CHÂTEAU DES TOURS

The Vaucluse village of Vacqueyras, which was granted its own appellation in 1990, does not have the reputation of nearby Gigondas, whose wines are generally rather finer and less rustic. Yet of the several estates which stand out, one in particular is worthy of close attention: Château des Tours, lying between Sarrians and Jonquières, is making progressively finer wine as its young owner accumulates experience, and its output may already be described as exceptional.

The winery is built

The young man in question is Emmanuel Reynaud, and when one knows that he is of the Reynaud dynasty of Château Rayas fame, all is explained. This is a family whose patriarch Louis long ago realized what was necessary to produce the best wine in the region, and passed down the message to his sons Jacques, who succeeded him at Rayas, and Bernard, Emmanuel's father.

Louis Reynaud acquired the Château des Tours estate (so named because of its small but very handsome twin-towered castle) just after the Second World War, as he did his other estate, Château de Fonsalette. He left it to Bernard, and for many years it produced a variety of crops which covered some 20 hectares of the 38 which comprise the estate; the grapes which were produced on the remaining land were taken to the cooperative. It was under the impulsion of the young Emmanuel, who had started working in 1980 beside his father, that a *cuverie* and cellars were built in 1989 and that the grape crop took on a different importance in the scheme of things.

Traditional methods and self-imposed discipline

Having worked for a while with his late uncle Jacques, Emmanuel had seen just how things are done at Rayas, and duly started applying equally strict discipline to viticultural practices on the Vacqueyras estate. The vineyard, like Rayas, is planted almost entirely with Grenache, and is run along thoroughly traditional lines. Very strict limitation of yields is at the heart of viticultural policy—20 hectoliters per hectare is the average production figure—and fruit is always harvested very late, just slightly overripe, again as at Rayas. Only so is it possible for such rich, concentrated, and aromatic wine to be produced.

All the bunches are left on their stalks for *cuvaison*, which takes place in stainless steel, and regular *remontages* help extract a maximum of color, aroma, and tannin from the cap of skins and stalks. Maturation takes place in concrete vats, with a few months' finishing in old wood, and the wines are then bottled with a light filtration.

Vacqueyras

Reynaud's progress during the 1990s has been very apparent, which bodes well for Rayas and Fonsalette as well as Tours, for since his heirless uncle Jacques's death he has found himself in charge of all three. Château des Tours, dense, rich, and magnificently aromatic, is destined to become highly *recherché*. It is capable of improving over ten to twelve years, or even longer in the best vintages, and accompanies all the regional specialities; mutton *daube* or beef *paupiettes* do very well.

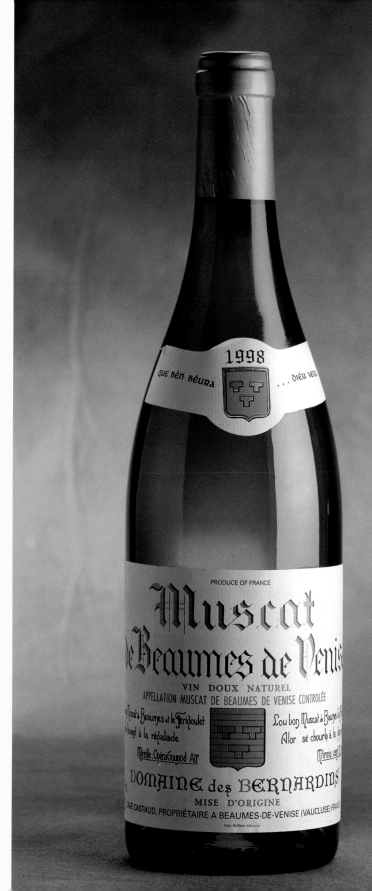

RHÔNE VALLEY
A.O.C. Muscat de Beaumes-de-Venise

- *Wine selected:*
  Muscat de Beaumes-de-Venise

- *Grape Varieties:*
  Muscat blanc à petits grains 75%,
  Muscat noir à petits grains 25%
- *Average vine age:*
  25 years
- *Vineyard size:*
  15 hectares
- *Soil type:*
  Sand and limestone
- *Production:*
  66,000 bottles

Finest Vintages:
2000, 1998, 1995, 1994, 1989

Domaine des Bernardins
Cave Castaud, 84190
Beaumes-de-Venise
Tel. (0033) 490 62 94 13
From the center of the village take the
road towards Lafare. Cave Castaud is
100 m down on the right.
- *Owners:* M. and Mme Castaud-
  Maurin & M. and Mme Hall
- *On-site sales:* 9–12 a.m., 2–5 p.m.
  (open until 6 p.m. in summer)
- *Visits:* No
- *Price:* ★

DOMAINE DES BERNARDINS

The pretty Vaucluse village of Beaumes-de-Venise has its very own vinous speciality, the sweet, aromatic Muscat de Beaumes-de-Venise. A handful of estates make and sell this *vin doux naturel* themselves, while the vast majority of the village's growers deliver their crop of Muscat grapes to the local cooperative. One of the handful, producing an excellent "old style" Muscat, is the Domaine des Bernardins.

The decline and renaissance of a local tradition

Like many villages in the area, Beaumes has made wine since Roman times, and in the 1870s its vineyards, like nearly all others, suffered the ravages of phylloxera, which almost consigned its long viticultural tradition to history. The production of *vin doux naturel* is thought to date back to the beginning of the nineteenth century, yet in the post-phylloxera decades, growers having planted other more profitable and less disease-prone crops, Muscat vines were a rare sight.

It was Louis Castaud of Domaine des Bernardins who first raised the alarm at the gradual disappearance of this village tradition, and thanks to whose efforts the wine won *appellation contrôlée* status in 1943. A *cave coopérative* was founded thirteen years later, and small growers could again hope to earn a living from Muscat. The surface area under that variety slowly began to increase.

At Les Bernardins Louis Castaud was eventually succeeded by his son Pierre, who retired in 1976 and handed over the estate to his sister and her husband, Jean Maurin. Today their own daughter and her English husband Andrew Hall are progressively taking over responsibilities.

Overripe grapes and halted fermentation

Nearly all Muscat de Beaumes-de-Venise is made from the Muscat blanc à petits grains. The grapes are picked when almost overripe, crushed, separated from their skins and then fermented in stainless steel at temperatures ranging from a little more than 68°F (20°C) to as low as 49°F (6°C). Domaine des Bernardins has always been the most traditional of the village's estates, using 25 percent Muscat noir à petits grains, which gives a fuller body and a more golden color than the Muscat blanc, and fermenting at 59–68°F (15°–20°C). The fermentation is halted by the addition of alcohol before all the sugar is fermented out, and the wine is then kept in vat for a few months before bottling and sale.

Muscat de Beaumes-de-Venise

The Domaine des Bernardins little resembles the run-of-the-mill "technological" Muscat made today. A fine amber-gold in color, heavy, rich, and rounded on the palate, its grapey aromas are somewhat dominated by its unctuous sweetness, and hints of almond and oxidation are also detectable. It needs several years in bottle to develop its bouquet and attain the ideal balance, and its makers claim it improves for up to twenty years. This Muscat is versatile at table, and proves a well-suited partner for *foie gras*, Roquefort cheese, and even chocolate dishes.

RHÔNE VALLEY
A.O.C. Lirac

- *Wine selected:*
  Lirac Cuvée La Reine des Bois

- *Grape Varieties:*
  Syrah 33%, Grenache 33%,
  Mourvèdre 34%
- *Average vine age:*
  40 years
- *Vineyard size:*
  25 hectares
- *Soil type:*
  Clay and silica
- *Production:*
  40,000 bottles

Finest Vintages:
2001, 2000, 1999, 1998

Domaine de la Mordorée
Chemin des Oliviers
30126 Tavel
Tel. (0033) 466 500 075
From Tavel's church take the Avignon
road. Take the first left, then left
again. Mordorée is on the left.
- *Owners:* Delorme family
- *On-site sales:* 8:00–12:00 a.m.,
  1:30–5:30 p.m.
- *Visits:* By appointment
- *Price:* ★

DOMAINE DE LA MORDORÉE

Until the 1980s the wines of Lirac had enjoyed little more than local popularity, as a result of the collective lethargy of the region's growers. In recent years however they have acquired wider renown thanks to the efforts of several estates, in particular Domaine de la Mordorée. La Mordorée has shown that the region is thoroughly capable of producing rich and flavorsome wines with some aging potential, and its convincing performance has been duly noted and appreciated by the world's critics and Rhône-wine lovers.

A viable estate is created

The estate's origins go back to 1974, when Francis Delorme's wife inherited some vines. Delorme, a businessman with his own firm, started learning about and making wine as a sideline. By 1986 he was ready to retire, and proposed setting up a commercial wine estate to his son Christophe, who accepted. Delorme sold his business and with the proceeds bought more vineyards, extended the existing wine buildings and his modernized wine-making equipment.

There followed a fruitful period of discussion, experimentation, and learning. Today, in order to grow top-quality grapes, the estate is run along thoroughly ecological lines: the technique of "sexual confusion" of the *Eudemis* butterfly to prevent the hatching of the grape worm is used; hedges have been planted around vineyard parcels to encourage the presence of the local fauna; grass is allowed to grow in the vineyards to favour deeper root-systems, reduce the vine's vigor, and provide biodiversity.

Respect for the soil and its micro-organisms and fauna is regarded by the Delormes as essential to healthy vines and thus juicy grapes.

For drinking young or laying down

Yields are kept extremely low, and the fruit is only picked when perfectly ripe. Vinification takes place in stainless steel and is preceded by total destalking, for the Delormes set out to make wines with supple, silky tannic structures which may be enjoyed from the first year, yet at the same time have decent aging potential. The different varieties are always fermented together for maximum aroma preservation, at around 86–90° F (30-32° C), with regular *remontages*. Once the period of fermentation and maceration has lasted long enough the better red wines are run off into barrel, in which they enjoy a judiciously judged *élevage* before being bottled, generally without filtration.

Lirac Cuvée La Reine des Bois

Referring to the *mordorée*, or woodcock, the red "Queen of the Woods" is a wine destined for laying down, and as such is only made in years when the Mourvèdre, contributing structure and color, is of sufficient quality. Dark, concentrated, and so fleshy that its soft tannin is barely perceptible, this is probably the finest red Lirac available today, and all the proof one could ask of the talent of Francis and Christophe Delorme. They have chosen the right direction and are pursuing it with single-minded determination. Stuffed veal's breast makes a persuasive suitor for *La Reine des Bois*.

RHÔNE VALLEY
A.O.C. Tavel

- *Wine selected:*
  Tavel

- *Grape Varieties:*
  Grenache 45%, Clairette 20%,
  Cinsaut 15%, Mourvèdre 10%,
  Bourboulenc 5%, Syrah 5%
- *Average vine age:*
  30 years
- *Vineyard size:*
  44 hectares
- *Soil type:*
  Sand and clay
- *Production:*
  270,000 bottles

Finest Vintages:
2001, 2000, 1998

Château d'Aquéria
30126 Tavel
Tel. (0033) 466 50 04 56
Internet: www.aqueria.com
From Tavel take the D4 towards
Avignon. Cross over the D976,
and continue for 800 m. The entry
to the estate is on the left, between
two large trees.
- *Owners:* Vincent & Bruno de Bez
- *On-site sales:* 8–12 a.m., 2–6 p.m.
- *Visits:* Yes
- *Price:* ★

CHÂTEAU D'AQUÉRIA

Tavel rosé has long enjoyed a reputation as France's best pink wine, with a full-bodied, dry and aromatic character very different to that of other French rosés. Whether the reputation is still merited is open to discussion, for the general standard today seems inconsistent and the wines too often lacking in body and typicity. The fault of modern enological science? One of the finest Tavels, and certainly the best known, is that made by the Olivier family on their large property Château d'Aquéria.

Demand from post-Prohibition America

Aquéria is an imposing and beautiful eighteenth-century house surrounded by its vineyard, one of Tavel's largest. It was acquired in the 1920s in a state of neglect by Jean Olivier, who refurbished it and laid the foundations of its fine reputation. Olivier's son-in-law Paul de Bez continued his work after his death, and since 1984 the estate has been run by de Bez's son Vincent.

Tavel has been very popular in the United States ever since the 1930s, a curious fact for which Jean Olivier may take all the credit. He, it appears, had a number of friends from New York and Boston who had visited his new estate and much enjoyed the wine. After the repeal of Prohibition in 1933 he sent them consignments, which were much appreciated by all their friends. Orders started coming back thick and fast, and Château d'Aquéria was one of the first French wines to be in regular demand from the newly reopened market. Demand for it and for Tavel in general has remained firm ever since.

Vinification by the *saignée* method

The Aquéria rosé is made by the *saignée* method, whereby it is macerated for a short period on its skins like a red wine, and run off them as soon as the required color has been attained. Fermentation then takes place in stainless-steel vats at a controlled low temperature of 64–68°F (18-20°C), which preserves aromatic freshness and reduces the risk of oxidation. The six grape varieties used are vinified two by two for greater aroma development, then blended together and aged for six months before bottling. When Vincent de Bez took charge he decided to block the malolactic fermentation, which changed the style towards crisper, less alcoholic wines from the mid-1980s. The wine nevertheless has all the power and flavor one would hope for from this appellation.

Tavel

With 44 hectares of its vineyard producing fruit for its Tavel, the Aquéria production seems positively industrial compared with that of other estates in the region. And yet, paradoxically, here quantity and quality go hand in hand, producing sufficient bottles of this attractive orange-tinted pink wine to satisfy Tavel-lovers around the world. Aquéria's quality lies in its fine balance between its 13 percent alcohol, its freshness and its depth of flavor, giving a wine which is thirst-quenching yet will complement dishes such as lamb cooked with herbs, *ratatouille* and oriental food perfectly. This is a rosé that can easily be enjoyed outside the summer-holiday period!

RHÔNE VALLEY
A.O.C. Côtes-du-Rhône-Villages

- *Wine selected:*
  Cairanne L'Ebrescade

- *Grape Varieties:*
  Grenache 60%,
  Syrah/Mourvèdre 40%
- *Average vine age:*
  40 years
- *Vineyard size:*
  4 hectares
- *Soil type:*
  Clay and limestone
- *Production:*
  10,000 bottles

Finest Vintages:
2000, 1999, 1998, 1995

Domaine Marcel Richaud
Route de Rasteau
84290 Cairanne
Tel. (0033) 490 30 85 25
At the traffic circle at the edge of the
village take the Vaison-la-Romaine
direction. Marcel Richaud's premises
are a few meters along on the left.
- *Owner:* Marcel Richaud
- *On-site sales:* Weekdays, 9–12 a.m.,
  2–6 p.m.
- *Visits:* By appointment
- *Price:* ★

DOMAINE MARCEL RICHAUD

The village of Cairanne is the source of much delicious wine, and is perhaps the finest of those Côtes-du-Rhône "named" villages which do not yet have their own *appellation contrôlée*. Indeed the fact that it does not is scandalous. A taste of Marcel Richaud's wine should convince even the most blinkered I.N.A.O. authority.

A break with family tradition

The short, silver-haired and voluble Richaud is not one for following the crowd. He forms definite ideas on things and follows them through, and it is this independence and intelligence as much as anything else that has brought him success. Born into a family who had been members of the cooperative back to his great-grandfather's time, Richaud decided while at school that that way would not be for him, and started making his own wine as soon as his schooldays were over in 1974.

He started off with rented vines, making the wine in a borrowed cellar. Lack of formal training was probably an advantage, for with an obvious feel for his vines and the different qualities that the different parcels of land could give, he gradually progressed in his wine-making, and was soon crafting wines of great purity, complexity, and class. As vintage succeeded vintage and the wine sold well he rented more land, then was in a position to buy some himself.

A duty to safeguard typicity

Success has not gone to Richaud's head. He finds it unhealthy that good growers are now lauded as artists, and reprehensible that so many, obsessed with earning critical success, lack the courage to make the sort of wine they really like, choosing instead to make highly extracted, heavily oaked "competition" wines. A grower has a moral duty to safeguard the typicity of his region and its wines, in order that the consumer, broaching a bottle far away, can imagine himself back there. He personally keeps a low profile, working hard in his vineyards, for only with intimate experience of them can one understand them, and thus obtain regularity in quality year after year, and progress even in the difficult years.

Delicious from the outset

Richaud likes to make wines which are good to drink from the outset, yet which at the same time have the wherewithal to improve in elegance and harmony. Perfect fruit is naturally a prerequisite, harvested only when it is properly ripe, and careful vinification by vineyard parcel and variety is nothing more than common sense. Unusually in the region, he does not like wood of any kind, and all his wines are made and then aged in cement vats. However, with typical open-mindedness, in early 1999 he was toying with the idea of acquiring some casks to see what they could contribute to the aging of his top *cuvée*, L'Ebrescade.

Cairanne L'Ebrescade

The land where Cairanne and its neighbor Rasteau rub shoulders is great viticultural terrain, and it is here that Richaud's oldest Grenaches grow, which form the basis of his *cuvée* L'Ebrescade. Supple in the mouth and richly fruity, a blend of plum, licorice, and spice with a subtle tannic structure, this *cuvée* has finesse and elegance in abundance, and is an eloquent demonstration of Marcel Richaud's way of thinking. Just the wine for filet of beef with *marchand au vin* sauce.

RHÔNE VALLEY
A.O.C. Côtes-du-Rhône-Villages

- *Wine selected:*
  Cairanne Haut-Coustias

- *Grape Varieties:*
  Mourvèdre 50%, Syrah 30%,
  Grenache 20%
- *Average vine age:*
  50 years
- *Vineyard size:*
  5 hectares
- *Soil type:*
  Clay and limestone
- *Production:*
  25,000 bottles

Finest Vintages:
1999, 1998, 1995, 1990

Domaine de l'Oratoire Saint-Martin
Route de Saint-Roman
84290 Cairanne
Tel. (0033) 490 30 82 07
From Cairanne take the road towards
Saint-Roman-de-Malegarde, and
follow it for 500 m.
- *Owners:* Frédéric & François Alary
- *On-site sales:* Yes
- *Visits:* 8–12 a.m., 2–7 p.m.
- *Price:* ★

DOMAINE DE L'ORATOIRE SAINT-MARTIN

Not for the Alarys a quiet life making good, saleable, easy-drinking Côtes-du-Rhône every year, which the Vaucluse climate indeed permits with not much effort from the grower. This is a family which is always striving for self-improvement, always trying out new ideas and methods in the pursuit of added complexity and personality. L'Oratoire Saint-Martin produces Cairanne and Côtes-du-Rhône of the quality of much more prestigious appellations with far more serious price tags.

Silkworms, madder, and the vine

Today Bernard Alary's sons Frédéric and François run L'Oratoire Saint-Martin, which is not to be confused with Domaine Alary, owned by Daniel and Denis Alary, the two being the result of the division of the one original estate in 1983. The Alary family tree attests to the family's presence in the Vaucluse *département* over ten generations, during which time they have had a number of occupations. In the second half of the nineteenth century the great-grandfather bred silkworms for the Cairanne silk factory, and cultivated not the vine but *garance*, the madder plant which was used for making the red dye which colored the French army's trousers during World War I. The invention of Nylon and the Army's decision to change the color of their trousers was a double blow, yet the great-grandfather nevertheless fortunately had his previous occupation of *vigneron* to fall back on.

Improving on a fine reputation

The estate's wines were always highly reputed in Bernard Alary's time, yet through their constant pursuit of greater quality Frédéric and François have made great strides. All 25 hectares of vineyard lie in the Cairanne commune. They are worked ecologically, with just very sparing use of organic manure, and all the necessary measures are taken to produce yields compatible with quality wine; indeed the very severe pruning, green harvesting, and leaf-stripping have given them a ten-year average production figure of 38 hectoliters per hectare, Cairanne and Côtes-du-Rhône *appellations* combined, whereas the law allows 42 and 50 hls/ha respectively.

The manually harvested crop is examined on a sorting table and then transferred by gravity to the open vats of concrete or stainless steel in which the red wines are to ferment. The whites go straight into oak barrels for their vinification. Since 1996 the property has been equipped with a *pigeage* machine mounted on overhead rails, and once the red fermentations are under way, by forcing the cake of solids down into the liquid the brothers have been able to achieve a better extraction of the wines' tannin and color.

Cairanne Haut-Coustias

Recent innovations include a white Viognier wine, and some Muscat à Petits Grains has been planted to blend with this eventually. A *vin de paille* of Marsanne or Clairette is also on the drawing-board. Choosing which of the estate's three Cairanne reds one prefers is not easy, yet the Haut-Coustias, made only in fine years, proclaims its quality loud and clear. Lightly toasted and redolent of leather, spice, and licorice, this is a splendid wine to serve with hare *à la royale*, or a lamb *ragoût* with thyme.

RHÔNE VALLEY
A.O.C. Côtes-du-Rhône-Villages

- *Wine selected:*
  Cairanne Cuvée d'Estevenas

- *Grape Varieties:*
  Grenache 80%, Syrah 20%
- *Average vine age:*
  30–100 years
- *Vineyard size:*
  2.5 hectares
- *Soil type:*
  Clay and limestone
- *Production:*
  8,000 bottles

Finest Vintages:
2000, 1999, 1998, 1995

Domaine Rabasse Charavin
La Font d'Estevenas
84290 Cairanne
Tel. (0033) 490 30 70 05
Follow the Rasteau road for 2 km,
then take the road on the left by the
bus shelter.
- *Owner:* Domaine Rabasse Charavin
  Couturier
- *On-site sales:* 8–11:30 a.m., 2–6 p.m.
  (Mon.–Fri.). Weekends (10 a.m.–
  7 p.m.) at La Maison Vigneronne,
  Place des Ecoles, Cairanne
- *Visits:* No
- *Price:* ★

DOMAINE RABASSE CHARAVIN

The fine reputation enjoyed by the village of Cairanne has been earned by families such as the Couturiers, growers who live for their land and its vines and devote all their energy and talent to transforming their fruit into the finest wine possible. Rabasse Charavin has long been one of the most reliable names in the Vaucluse, producing a fine range of wines of great character.

Unceasing efforts to ameliorate quality

Since 1984 the estate has been run by Corinne Couturier, a woman who excels at her work in what is largely a male-dominated business. Corinne learnt how to make wine from her father Abel, who instilled in her the essential notions of care for the vine and limitation of its yields. The estate's reputation was already established when Abel retired, but Corinne has consolidated it and devoted unceasing efforts to ameliorating the general quality even further; while her methods may by and large be described as traditional, the lady is not averse to trying out new ideas which could give interesting results.

Old vines for greater character

Rabasse Charavin is of a very respectable size, covering 68 hectares of which 60 were in production at the end of the 1990s. At the heart of the estate are the Cairanne vineyards, which cover 17 hectares; there are also 8 hectares in the neighboring village of Rasteau, and the remainder lie around Violès, several kilometers to the south. A noteworthy aspect of most of these vineyards is the high average age of their vines, which has the highly desirable effect of producing less but better-quality fruit, giving wine that is more intensely aromatic and also expresses the character of its terroir more forcefully. From the bottom of the range *vin de table*, which includes fifty-year-old Carignan, to the Cuvée Estevenas with its centenarian Grenache, there is not one of the eleven wines that could be accused of lacking personality.

Careful, intelligent wine making

The wines' intrinsic quality comes not only from the vineyard sites, but also from rigorous selection of the fruit during picking and on arrival at the winery, and subsequently from careful, intelligent wine making. The grapes are left on their stems for vinification and lightly crushed before vatting in concrete, and the different varieties and parcels are kept apart until after the malolactic fermentation, in order to be able to assess the finished wines better. The grapes having been left on their stems, *cuvaison* is relatively rapid, lasting four to eight days, with two *remontages* per day to extract color, aroma, and tannin. Then the wines are blended, and the finished products are aged, either in concrete or enamel-lined tanks, and eventually bottled without filtration.

Cairanne Cuvée d'Estevenas

A south-facing parcel at the top of clay and limestone slopes bears the fine fruit which is vinified as Cuvée Estevenas, the estate's greatest achievement. Concentrated and exhaling a splendid pepper-and-spice nose, with a spine of fine-quality tannin, Estevenas may be kept for a dozen years, and is best served from a decanter for maximum development of its bouquet, alongside any stewed and well-seasoned red meat.

RHÔNE VALLEY
A.O.C. Côtes-du-Rhône-Villages

- *Wine selected:*
  Côtes-du-Rhône-Villages Vieilles Vignes

- *Grape Varieties:*
  Syrah 60%, Grenache 40%
- *Average vine age:*
  Over 35 years
- *Vineyard size:*
  4 hectares
- *Soil type:*
  Sand and gravel
- *Production:*
  20,000 bottles

Finest Vintages:
1999, 1998, 1995

Château Saint-Estève d'Uchaux
Route de Sérignan
84100 Uchaux
Tel. (0033) 490 40 62 38
Château Saint-Estève d'Uchaux lies off the D172, which runs from Piolenc to Sérignan-du-Comtat, several kilometers from the latter.
- *Owners:* Français-Monier de Saint-Estève family
- *On-site sales:* Yes, except Sunday
- *Visits:* 9–12 a.m., 2–6 p.m.
- *Price:* ★

CHÂTEAU SAINT-ESTÈVE D'UCHAUX

Several kilometers north of Orange, in the gentle rolling countryside that constitutes the massif d'Uchaux, the cream-colored buildings which make up Château Saint-Estève d'Uchaux overlook the plain stretching away into the far distance. Saint-Estève has for several decades been at the forefront of local wine-making innovation, earning itself a solid reputation, a faithful clientele and a good number of medals in the process.

The most noble Rhône varieties

This estate has been the property of the Français family since 1809. The first century of its existence, we learn from John Livingstone-Learmonth in *The Wines of the Rhône*, was taken up with forestry, sheep farming and silk-worm rearing, and the vine was only planted in its soils at the beginning of the twentieth century.

The prime mover behind its progress in the domain of wine making was Gérard Français, who in the 1950s quickly doubled the vineyard area, renovated the wine buildings, and redesigned the cellars with a view to making and maturing a growing quantity of wine. He entrusted the running of the estate totally to his son Marc, who has proved a talented manager and innovative wine maker.

Today the estate comprises 30 hectares of Côtes-du-Rhône-Villages and 30 hectares of generic Côtes-du-Rhône, which are planted with the Rhône's noblest grape varieties: Grenache, Syrah, Cinsaut, and Mourvèdre for the red wines, Grenache Blanc and Roussanne for the whites. The estate also has 7 hectares of the white Viognier grape, of which Saint-Estève has become one of the acknowledged experts, thanks notably to its Vionysos wine.

Modernity in harmony with tradition

At Saint-Estève tradition rubs shoulders with modernity in the most relaxed fashion. Here the vines, cultivated naturally, are perfumed by the surrounding *garrigue*. The grapes are harvested at peak ripeness. They are then destalked, and in the case of the white wines lightly crushed and pneumatically pressed. The different white varieties are blended and vinification follows, at 62°F (17°C) in gleaming stainless-steel vats with temperature-control equipment, lasting some ten days. Saint-Estève's famous Viognier wine then enjoys a year's aging in vat before bottling. As for the black grapes, they are vinified variety by variety and parcel by parcel in stainless steel, and the quality of fruit dictates the type of aging they undergo. The estate never chaptalizes, nor does it use artificial yeast.

Côtes-du-Rhône-Villages Vieilles Vignes

Four red wines are produced, of which the most interesting is the Vieilles Vignes. Demand outstrips supply for this *cuvée*, from the oldest vines and best parcels, aged some twenty months in barrel and vat and bottled with less tampering than the other wines. Deeply fruity, succulent and fairly structured, this splendidly pure wine improves over a dozen years, after which it makes a fine partner for leg of lamb, perfumed with thyme.

RHÔNE VALLEY
A.O.C. Côtes-du-Rhône-Villages

- *Wine selected:*
  Rasteau Cuvée Confiance

- *Grape Varieties:*
  Grenache 80%, Syrah 10%,
  Mourvèdre 10%
- *Average vine age:*
  40–95 years
- *Vineyard size:*
  5 hectares
- *Soil type:*
  Clay and limestone
- *Production:*
  10,000 bottles

Finest Vintages:
2000, 1999, 1998, 1997

Domaine La Soumade
84110 Rasteau
Tel. (0033) 490 46 11 26
The estate lies on the D975, a couple
of kilometers outside the village.
- *Owners:* André Roméro
- *On-site sales:* 8:00–11:30 a.m.,
  2:00–6:00 p.m.
- *Visits:* Yes
- *Price:* ★★

DOMAINE LA SOUMADE

The Vaucluse *département* is not short of powerful, dense, tannic wines which need time to soften up and demonstrate their complexity, but very few match those of André Roméro of Domaine La Soumade for dimension and sheer depth of flavor. Roméro is self-taught and has a feel for extracting all that is best out of his carefully cultivated grapes; his wines, one could argue, have all the more personality for it.

Two centuries of family tradition

La Soumade has been in Roméro's family for two hundred years. With the panorama of the Dentelles de Montmirail and the mont du Ventoux making a splendid backdrop in the distance, the estate's 28 hectares are made up of a number of parcels, which lie on the gently sloping land below the village of Rasteau. The vines are cultivated à l'ancienne, the weeds being kept at bay by *labourage* and the soil being enriched only by the occasional organic treatment.

Terrain well suited to Grenache

Grenache Noir holds pride of place, as is to be expected, for the land around the village of Rasteau is recognized as singularly suitable for that variety, with Syrah and Mourvèdre playing principal supporting roles. These three together produce the two finest wines of La Soumade, the *cuvées* Prestige and Confiance. Yet a long list of other varieties such as Grenache Blanc, Cinsaut, Carignan, Clairette Rose and Blanche, Bourboulenc, Roussanne, and Muscardin, give Roméro fine raw material to make his Côtes-du-Rhône-Villages, rosé, and red and golden Vin Doux Naturel.

Their owner, an out-and-out claret fan, also has a couple of hectares of Cabernet-Sauvignon and Merlot; these of course are not authorized varieties in the Rhône Valley, and their wine has to be sold as Vin de Pays de la Principauté d'Orange.

Tradition without compromise

At the end of a year's attentive viticulture, once optimum ripeness is reached the harvest is carried out by hand, enabling pickers to discard any unripe, rotten, or generally substandard fruit. Roméro appreciating the uncompromisingly "traditional" style, the fruit is left on its stalks for fermentation; after a light crushing the fruit is fermented and macerated in stainless steel vats for twelve to fifteen days, with lots of *pigeage*. Then the wine is transferred to *foudre*, the press-wine is added, and a year's aging begins.

Rasteau Cuvée Confiance

The greatest wine produced at La Soumade is the Cuvée Confiance, a giant of a wine which is only made in the best years. Four-fifths very old Grenache, one-fifth Syrah, it is the product of the very oldest vines on the estate, which, aided by suitable vinification, impart extraordinary depth and aromatic complexity. Almost black and powerfully peppery on the nose, it has a wide flavor spectrum which encompasses primary black fruit, cinnamon and pepper spice, mineral, earthy nuances, and, as it ages, gamey flavors. This thick-set character has a tannic structure to match, and does require at least a decade in the cellar! Flavorsome food such as jugged hare is called for!

RHÔNE VALLEY
A.O.C. Côtes-du-Rhône

- *Wine selected:*
  Côtes-du-Rhône

- *Grape Varieties:*
  Grenache 50%, Cinsaut 35%,
  Syrah 15%
- *Average vine age:*
  15 and 70 years
- *Vineyard size:*
  10.5 hectares
- *Soil type:*
  Clay and limestone
- *Production:*
  28,000 bottles

Finest Vintages:
2000, 1999, 1998, 1995, 1990, 1989

Château de Fonsalette
84290 Lagarde-Paréol
Tel. (0033) 490 83 73 09
- *Owners:* Reynaud family
- *On-site sales:* No
- *Visits:* No
- *Price:* ★★

CHÂTEAU DE FONSALETTE

The vast 45,000-hectare appellation Côtes-du-Rhône produces wines of all qualities, from the light, fruity, carbonic-maceration liquids to far more serious beverages. Perhaps the most serious of them all, a great wine which proves just what is possible if one is determined enough, is the Reynaud family's Château de Fonsalette.

Louis Reynaud's second estate

The Reynaud dynasty is, of course, better known to Rhône-wine aficionados as owner of the great Châteauneuf-du-Pape, Château Rayas. Louis Reynaud purchased the 130-hectare Château de Fonsalette, at Lagarde-Paréol, in 1945.

At the time there were very few vines, and during the decade after the acquisition Reynaud did much experimentation with different varieties to see exactly which worked best in Fonsalette's soil. Pride of place, unsurprisingly, went to Grenache Noir, with Cinsaut and Syrah being chosen to play the supporting roles. White grapes were also planted, Reynaud opting for Grenache Blanc, Marsanne, Clairette, and Chardonnay. In all 12 hectares were planted, and the château remained surrounded on three sides by its huge park. The wines are made at Château Rayas, in more or less the same manner as their big brother and from yields only a little more generous.

Jacques Reynaud duly took over after his father's death in 1978, and during his lifetime made four different wines: a white Côtes-du-Rhône, never reputed for regularity but sublimely rich and complex in the best vintages; the red Fonsalette Côtes-du-Rhône; a red 100 percent Syrah wine; and a lighter red wine named La Pialade. Since his death in 1997 his nephew Emmanuel Reynaud has taken on the responsibility of producing these wines.

Grand wines from a humble appellation

The two principle Fonsalette red wines have absolutely nothing in common with the average run-of-the-mill Côtes-du-Rhône, and can proudly hold their heads high in the company of the Rhône Valley's finest. The Cuvée Syrah is made from what is left over of that variety after the Fonsalette has been blended; curiously there is even more demand for it than for the blended wine, and it is as good as most Hermitage. It should not be approached until it has had half-a-dozen years in bottle, at which stage it still has its sumptuous rich blackcurrant flavor yet has shrugged off its tannic structure to a degree. Better vintages will nevertheless keep for far longer. The third red, Pialade, does not have the same ambition, being made up of the other leftovers.

Côtes-du-Rhône

The "standard" Château de Fonsalette is a splendid wine, with a rich, intense, spicy flavor, substantial body, and an impressive structure. The grapes are picked, as they are for Château Rayas, on the point of overripeness, which, combined with the low yields and the great age of the vines makes for an extraordinary Côtes-du-Rhône, with great potential for improvement in bottle. The magnificent 1989 vintage, for example, after ten years was developing an amber hue and opening up nicely, yet was still some way from full maturity. Fonsalette, which makes a fine partner for game pie, naturally costs far more than other Côtes-du-Rhône, but is not expensive for what it is—a great wine.

RHÔNE VALLEY
A.O.C. Côtes-du-Rhône

- *Wine selected:*
  **Côtes-du-Rhône Ceps
  Centenaires "La Mémé"**

- *Grape Variety:*
  Grenache
- *Average vine age:*
  100+ years
- *Vineyard size:*
  2 hectares
- *Soil type:*
  Clay and limestone
- *Production:*
  5,000 bottles

Finest Vintages:
2000, 1999, 1998, 1995

Domaine Gramenon
26770 Montbrison-sur-Lez
Tel. (0033) 475 53 57 08
- *Owner:* Michèle Aubery Laurent
- *On-site sales:* By appointment
- *Visits:* No
- *Price:* ★★

DOMAINE GRAMENON

In these days of enology diplomas and high-tech vinification equipment, it would be interesting to see who could still make good wine if just left with his vines, a pair of secateurs, and a cellar equipped as in days gone by. The late Philippe Laurent would have been a sure-fire candidate for the gold medal. That was the way he worked while he was alive, and is the way his widow Michèle continues to work. The Laurent wines are of great quality and character, yet simply bear—it is difficult to believe it when savoring them—the modest Côtes-du-Rhône appellation.

The choice of independence

It must surely have been with great regret that the *négociants* E. Guigal and Paul Jaboulet Aîné learned in the late 1980s that Laurent was going solo, and would no longer be selling them his crop. Having bought his first 15 hectares of vines in 1979 this imposing, bearded man, born into a large wine-making family from Valréas, produced his first bottlings with his 1990 harvest, and made rapid progress. Today the name Gramenon is no longer a secret to serious Rhône wine lovers, and the estate's produce is avidly sought out by top restaurants and retailers for their lists.

Natural wines without artificial additives

"Le Vin en Liberté," branded on their corks, sums up the Laurent philosophy. Viticultural and wine-making methods are based on the knowledge that the vine, unsoiled by any artificial treatments, really can produce excellent, healthy fruit, as long as its natural productivity is curbed. There is no reason why this should not make superbly natural wine, as long as man does not tamper and intervene. It is simple enough as ideas go, yet numerous vignerons do not dare work without a safety net at every turn, to the inevitable detriment of their produce.

Low yields and old vines

Low yields and very old vines then are the cornerstone of Gramenon's reputation. When it comes to making the wine, Michèle assesses each year's crop and treats it as necessary—routine is out at Gramenon. The deliciously ripe fruit, carefully harvested by hand and checked for quality, may be a little or almost completely destemmed, and is fermented without any additives: musts are neither chaptalized nor acidified, nor is SO_2 used. Fermentations are carried out by the fruit's own yeast, and after long aging in old wood the wines are bottled with neither fining nor filtration. Throughout the process all movement of must and wine is by gravity, to protect its aromas.

Côtes-du-Rhône Ceps Centenaires "La Mémé"

The most concentrated and complex of the red wines which emerge from the Gramenon cellars is "La Mémé," made from a plot of centenarian Grenache plants. This thick, opulent, and rich nectar, pure and powerful, has a kirsch-type flavor which develops a smokiness with age that is memorable. A loin of lamb, grilled over dead vine wood, would accord it all the respect its venerable vines deserve!

LOIRE VALLEY
A.O.C. Savennières
Roche-aux-Moines

- *Wine selected:*
  **Savennières Roche-aux-Moines
  doux Chevalier Buhard**

- *Grape Variety:*
  Chenin
- *Average vine age*
  25 years
- *Vineyard size:*
  6.5 hectares
- *Soil type:*
  Siliceous clay and schist
- *Production:*
  2,000 bottles

Finest Vintages:
2000, 1997, 1996, 1995, 1990

Château de Chamboureau
49170 Savennières
Tel. (0033) 241 77 20 04
- *Owner:* Pierre Soulez
- *On-site sales:* Yes
- *Visits:* 10:00–12:30 a.m.,
  2:00–6:00 p.m.
- *Price:* ★★

CHÂTEAU DE CHAMBOUREAU

The picturesque Savennières appellation produces some of the Loire's most distinguished dry Chenin wines, of which the best have a firmness, structure, and fullness of flavor ensuring many years' improvement. The wines produced by Pierre Soulez at Château de Chamboureau are regularly among the finest examples.

A family affair

The family have owned the Chamboureau château and estate since 1949. Bought by Michel and Anne Soulez, it was left to their eleven children; today Pierre runs it, Hervé is responsible for the vineyard, and Hugues, a grandson, is the in-house enologist. Chamboureau lies within the Roche-aux-Moines appellation, one of Savennières's two *Grands Crus*. The Soulez family owns 8.5 of the 17 hectares of this wonderfully situated vineyard.

Geographical rather than varietal character

Its geological composition is of siliceous clay schist with volcanic debris—very poor, acid soil giving wines of great individuality. The aim being to bring out this *terroir* character in the wines, the Soulez viticultural methods are aimed at robust vine health through quasi-ecological cultivation, excluding any chemical treatments or pesticides. Weedkiller is out, indeed grass is grown between the rows of vines to limit the erosion, which is a problem in this sloping vineyard looking down on the Loire. And since the grass constitutes a rival to the vine for what nourishment there is in the top soil, the latter is obliged to bury its roots deeper; thus *terroir* character dominates the personality of the grape variety.

A return to the tradition of bygone days

Soulez harvests his grapes by successive passages through the vineyards, in order to pick only the fruit which has been attacked by *Botrytis cinerea* or has become sun-dried. The intrinsic richness of the juice then balances the natural austerity of the Chenin and the acid terrain, giving wines that, although they are eminently capable of the long haul, may be approached after several years.

The wines are fermented in barrels of french Vosges oak that have already been used several times. The use of small barrels represents a recent return to the tradition of bygone days, to which reference is made on the labels by the term Cuvée d'Avant. Fermentation is followed by aging with the occasional lees stirring, with no racking until the May after the harvest. Thereafter racking and fining achieve the necessary clarification, and bottling takes place in September.

Savennières Roche-aux-Moines doux Chevalier Buhard

Reviving another tradition that fell out of fashion, whenever Nature permits Soulez makes *demi-sec* or even sweet Savennières. The year 1997 was one such vintage: the harvest was picked during four tries, and certain selected grapes had a potential 19 percent alcohol. Fermented, their wine attained its balance at 13 percent with 6 percent potential, leaving 102 grams of unfermented grape-sugar. The result is a superbly rich, honeyed wine, light gold in color and with a mineral, very-ripe quince flavor on the palate. The Chevalier Buhard has a very long, complex finish, and is a highly original wine—a wine for sipping on its own, as Pierre Soulez puts it, *pour le plaisir*.

LOIRE VALLEY
A.O.C. Savennières Coulée de Serrant

• *Wine selected:*
Savennières Coulée de Serrant

• *Grape Variety:*
Chenin
• *Average vine age*
35 years
• *Vineyard size:*
7 hectares
• *Soil type:*
Schist
• *Production:*
20,000–25,000 bottles

Finest Vintages:
1999, 1997, 1996, 1995,
1990, 1989, 1988

Coulée de Serrant
Château de la Roche-aux-Moines
49170 Savennières
Tel. (0033) 241 72 22 32
The estate lies between Epiré and
Savennières, and is well signposted.
• *Owner:* Nicolas Joly
• *On-site sales:* 8:30–12:00 a.m.,
2:00-5:45 p.m.
• *Visits:* Yes (except Sundays and
bank holidays)
• *Price:* ★★★

COULÉE DE SERRANT

The magnificent Clos de la Coulée de Serrant has been under vine continually since it was planted by Cistercian monks in 1130, and its wine always considered rare and unique. French monarchs appreciated its qualities, as more recently have numerous critics such as the gastronome Curnonsky, who included it in his famous list of France's five finest white wines.

An unrivaled site

As a vineyard site, one cannot imagine how it could be improved: consisting of three steep parcels looking down on the Loire, it has poor, schistous soil affording both excellent drainage and humidity retention, and benefits from the moderating effect on its microclimate of the water.

The current custodian, Nicolas Joly, produces masterpieces of purity, harmony, and richness. Joly has gained himself a high profile (and initially much derision) by his unreserved adoption of biodynamic theory for his viticultural and wine-making activities. Thanks in large part to him, biodynamics are today becoming progressively more accepted and followed.

A natural remedy to a modern tragedy

The essential argument of biodynamics is that agricultural "progress" has destroyed many soils, which can hardly generate growth any more and have become dependent on chemical fertilisers, which are duly absorbed by the vine. Yet this source of growth is totally contrary to the notion of *appellation d'origine*. In days gone by the soil was fed, and the healthy vines expressed its character; today many soils are barren of life, the vines are artificially fed, and wine contains little geographical identity... and much impurity.

Exchanges between soil, water, air, light, and heat

Many are the remedies adopted by caring growers to renew the soil's micro-organic life, from *lutte raisonnée* (minor intervention) to biological treatments. Biodynamic theory goes further. Vines inhabit the earth, which is not simply the soil under our feet, but also the atmosphere around us, containing water, air, light, and heat; one can promote or destroy the constant exchange that life creates between these different elements, by using various composts and homoeopathic preparations to enhance the effect of each element and thus reinforce both the soil's life and plants' photosynthesis. Beyond our atmosphere the sun, moon, and stars also exert significant influence on the exchanges. The influence can be increased if the grower carefully chooses the most favorable days or times for each task.

In the vatroom, also, artificial aids and practices such as aroma yeast, settling, chilling, and temperature control are proscribed—proper agriculture renders unnecessary many common cellar acts.

Savennières Coulée de Serrant

Coulée de Serrant (like Joly's other wines) is quite obviously robustly healthy, with a wealth of aroma, sublime harmony and great *terroir*-bestowed individuality. Thanks to repeated racking during *élevage* it does not fear oxidation, indeed it benefits from being opened a day or more in advance; then, left open or recorked even if half-empty, it improves over several days (without refrigeration)! Served at 57–61°F (14–16°C) with pike in *beurre blanc* or lobster in sauce, one can understand why Curnonsky was so enthusiastic!

LOIRE VALLEY
A.O.C. Coteaux-du-Layon

- *Wine selected:*
Coteaux du Layon Cuvée Maria Juby
(50 cl bottle)

- *Grape Variety:*
Chenin
- *Average vine age*
35 years
- *Soil type:*
Schists, sandstone, carboniferous, clay
- *Production:*
Completely irregular!

Finest Vintages:
1997, 1996

Domaine Patrick Baudouin
49290 Chaudefonds-sur-Layon
Tél. : (0033) 241 78 66 04
Internet : www.patrick-baudouin-layon.com
- *Owner:* Patrick Baudouin
- *Wine-maker:* Patrick Baudouin
- *On-site sales:* Yes
- *Visits:* By appointment
- *Price:* ★★

DOMAINE PATRICK BAUDOUIN

Since the mid-1980s a number of perceptive and stubborn Coteaux-du-Layon growers have swum against the tide of increasing standardization and bureaucratic disinterest. Driven by the knowledge that their vineyards were capable of, but no longer producing, superb wine, they stripped away the bad habits of the late twentieth-century system and reverted to making the natural wines as of a century ago. One of the prime movers and most vocal dissidents, who is today producing wines of breath taking beauty, is the historian and vigneron Patrick Baudouin.

The spread of chaptalisation

Many are the problems which need addressing, of which chaptalization and lack of balance are perhaps the principal ones. Chenin is a versatile vine, producing all degrees of dryness and sweetness according to the climatic conditions of the vintage. In the nineteenth century growers took what nature gave them and made the best of it. Little by little subsequent generations started trying to produce sweet wine every year, which during difficult years obliged them to practise chaptalization—the addition of sugar to prolong fermentation and attain a higher percent of alcohol. Since the 1950s the practice has become widespread, yet it cannot produce wines of the richness obtained from sun-drying on the vine or from *Botrytis*. Harvesting by successive passages through the vineyard to pick all the fruit at just the right state of ripeness is absolutely essential, and has been a core element in the Layon's renaissance.

The quality of *Botrytis* is Patrick Baudouin's principal harvesting criterion; he picks small volumes of homogeneously botrytised grapes during numerous *tries*, and blends *tries* of similar qualities from different parcels to make up a *cuvée*.

The importance of balance

Another essential quality of *liquoreux* wines is balance, which requires the right level of acidity, alcohol, and residual sugar. The Chenin is admirably suited to sweet wine production due to its high natural acidity, which confers great freshness and delicacy. As for the alcohol, chaptalization and use of artificial yeast create lots of it, which would seem to be favored by the authorities: the minimum alcohol level required by the A.O.C. laws is 11 percent for a generic and 12 percent for a Coteaux-du-Layon-Village.

Yet that goes against nature: a wine with a high *Botrytis* sugar level ferments slowly and with difficulty, particularly if the yeast is natural, and stabilises more or less by itself at a low level of acquired alcohol, with little need for SO_2—and its balance is all the better for it. Some of the greatest Austrian, German, and Hungarian *liquoreux* are phenomenally rich yet have impeccable balance at half the obligatory Layon level of alcohol.

Coteaux-du-Layon Cuvée Maria Juby

Bearing out the cogency of his arguments, Baudouin's magnificently concentrated and pure Cuvée Maria Juby projects a gloriously fresh, powerful aroma of citrus peel and dried apricot, and caresses the palate with its sheer elegance and refinement; proof indeed, if it was needed, that nature is eminently capable of masterpieces, unaided. Incidentally, Maria Juby has a soft spot for poultry dishes prepared with spices.

LOIRE VALLEY
A.O.C. Coteaux-du-Layon

• *Wine selected:*
**Coteaux du Layon Sélection de
Grains Nobles**
(50 cl. bottle)

• *Grape Variety:*
Chenin
• *Average vine age*
30 years
• *Vineyard size:*
10 hectares
• *Soil type:*
Schist, pudding-stones, volcanic ash
• *Production:*
1,200–10,000 bottles

Finest Vintages:
2000, 1997, 1996, 1995

Domaine Philippe Delesvaux
Les Essards—La Haie Longue
49190 Saint-Aubin-de-Luigné
Tel. (0033) 241 78 18 71
• *Owners:* Philippe & Catherine
Delesvaux
• *On-site sales:* By appointment
• *Visits:* By appointment
• *Price:* ★★

DOMAINE PHILIPPE DELESVAUX

If the vast improvement in the general quality of Coteaux-du-Layon wines since the mid-1980s may be laid at the door of one single grower, Philippe Delesvaux could lay claim to the credit. His wines are textbook examples of purity, precision and harmony, and above all of naturalness. Fortunately many others have observed the success he has enjoyed and have since followed his example.

A challenge in perspective

Delesvaux's is a classic young-man-makes-good story. He left his native Versailles for Anjou to pursue his studies of mineralogy—his passion—fell in love with the region, and found a livestock and vineyard estate to run. He started work in 1978 and enjoyed looking after the forty cows, yet it was making wine which really started him thinking. The wine he was making there was sold off in bulk and was of limited interest. Yet bottles of his own produce, with his own name on the label... Now there was a challenge!

Obsessed with *grains nobles* and the *trie*

In 1982 he managed to find 3 hectares of vines to rent in the heart of the Coteaux-du-Layon area. The start was not easy: the vines were old and difficult to cultivate, and his wine-making facilities somewhat outdated. Yet Delesvaux's determination to produce great Coteaux-du-Layon, buttressed by the support of his wife Catherine, carried him through.

After two vintages of doing like everybody else he had an important flash of inspiration, and in 1985 decided to harvest his crop by successive passages through the vineyard, in order to pick all the grapes at maximum ripeness, or even after they

had been affected by noble rot. The crop came in at a potential 16.5 percent alcohol, which seemed enormous at the time. The couple realised that this was far better than their previous achievements, and local restaurateurs and experts agreed with them. From then on *grains nobles* and the *trie* became Delesvaux's obsession.

A staunch opponent of chaptalization

Today he has many highly-acclaimed wines behind him. His estate covers 14.5 hectares, and he has been able to invest in modern facilities and equipment to make the most of his raw material. The number of wines he makes each year varies, depending on nature's bounty, for Delesvaux is naturally a staunch opponent of chaptalization, just as he is of the use of artificial yeast. Each *trie* will be accepted and vinified for what it is, giving different *cuvées* ranging from the *sec* and the *demi-sec* to the *moelleux* and even *liquoreux*.

Coteaux-du-Layon Sélection de Grains Nobles

The Chenin grapes affected by *Botrytis* which made the 1997 Grains Nobles were harvested during the second and third *tries* of October and November 1997 at a potential 24.5 percent alcohol, and their wine attained its balance at 12 percent alcohol with no less than 212 grams of unfermented sugar remaining! This remarkable bottle is of course extremely sweet and rich, yet it is not in the least cloying, and has the great qualities of lightness, elegance and harmony on the palate. And what a phenomenally long, complex finish! With such richness and balance it will certainly last a half-century. Perfection such as this deserves sipping on its own, before or after a meal depending on one's inclinations, or with some *foie gras*...

LOIRE VALLEY
A.O.C. Coteaux-du-Layon Saint-Lambert

- *Wine selected:*
  Coteaux-du-Layon Saint-Lambert Ambroisie
  (50 cl bottle)

- *Grape Variety:*
  Chenin
- *Average vine age*
  10 years
- *Vineyard size:*
  1.2 hectares
- *Soil type:*
  Schist
- *Production:*
  900 bottles

Finest Vintages:
1997, 1996

Domaine Jo Pithon
Les Bergères
49750 Saint-Lambert-du-Lattay
Tél. : (00 33) 241 78 40 91
- *Owners:* Jo & Isabelle Pithon
- *On-site sales:* By appointment
- *Visits:* By appointment
- *Price:* ★★★

DOMAINE JO PITHON

Since he decided to stop producing bulk wine like everybody else and try his hand at the authentic, naturally rich variety, Jo Pithon has come a long way. Experience has engendered self-assurance and a readiness to take risks, enabling him to produce wines of stunning dimension. This generous, larger-than-life grower evidently relishes his work, and has been rewarded with well-merited success.

A rising of ambition

Despite having a *vigneron* grandfather, the young Pithon was not destined to become a grower himself. He attended agricultural school, yet came out simply with a strong urge to be his own boss. He decided to rent some vines and try his hand at making wine... and thus discovered a love of and a talent for the work. In 1978 he founded his own estate, and for the next twelve years did what just about everybody was doing, selling off his wine in bulk.

Then however came the change of orientation. Could it have been linked with his meeting Isabelle, and the end of his bachelor days? His first move was to invest in some barrels and start harvesting by *tries*, a decision that, in the glorious year of 1990, amply repaid the effort. However the following year was that of the terrible frost, a catastrophe for the Loire Valley, and the event made him decide to change the shape of his estate radically. From 14 hectares Pithon decided to trim it down to 4.5 by getting rid of a number of the lesser rented vineyards; his new aim was simply to concentrate on making Coteaux-du-Layon, of the very finest quality.

All-out measures to improve quality

He started spending much longer hours toiling among the vines to ensure higher-quality grapes, and worked to provide them with an ecological, chemical-free environment. These days a short pruning and subsequent debudding limits their eventual load to a very low six bunches per plant; leaf-stripping is carried out to ensure good aeration and reduced risk of rot, and also gives the bunches more sunlight, favoring greater ripeness.

And because it would be ludicrous to produce fine fruit and then pollute it during the vinification process, the wines are doped neither with artificial yeast, nor enzymes, nor sugar. Incredible as it may seem, the imposing residual sugar of Pithon's wines is entirely the result of noble rot or *passerillage*.

Coteaux-du-Layon Saint-Lambert Ambroisie

Like all his wines, Ambroisie, made from the most concentrated grapes in the Clos des Bonnes Blanches in the finest years, has a fine deep golden color. A first nosing detects enormous, somnolent richness, yet a couple of swirls liberate unexpected freshness and delicacy, and tasting then reveals a complex panoply of dried-fruit and spice aromas which envelop the palate. The degree of complexity and sweetness is stunning: in 1997 the harvest came in at 32 percent of potential alcohol, and the finished wine had 340 grams of residual sugar per liter! Yet, despite the wine's monumental sweetness, it is at the same time refreshing—proof of real viticultural and wine-making talent. This unforgettable wine is a treat sipped on its own, yet a little *foie gras* does enhance the experience!

LOIRE VALLEY
A.O.C. Coteaux-du-Layon Saint-Lambert

- *Wine selected:*
  Coteaux-du-Layon Saint-Lambert Clos des Bonnes Blanches
  (50 cl bottle)

- *Grape Variety:*
  Chenin
- *Average vine age*
  8 years
- *Vineyard size:*
  2 hectares
- *Soil type:*
  Schist
- *Production:*
  4,000 bottles

Finest Vintages:
1997, 1996, 1995

Domaine Ogereau
44 Rue de la Belle-Angevine
49750 Saint-Lambert-du-Lattay
Tel. (0033) 241 78 30 53
From Saint-Lambert take the direction
of Chemillé. Domaine Ogereau lies on
the right on the edge of the village.
- *Owner:* Domaine Ogereau
- *On-site sales:* 9–12 a.m., 2–7 p.m.
- *Visits:* Yes
- *Price:* ★★

DOMAINE OGEREAU

Vincent Ogereau is well known to lovers of Anjou wines for the exquisite quality of his produce, and a visit to his estate at Saint-Lambert-du-Lattay is highly advised. There the visitor can taste a complete range of wines: there are dry whites, a sparkling Crémant, rosés, and reds of great distinction, yet of course the jewels of the cellar are the very fine Coteaux-du-Layons.

The attentions of a noble fungus

The bearded, balding Ogereau trained at Bordeaux, and from 1982 worked with his father. Since 1989 he has been alone at the helm and has run the estate with masterly competence and feel. Every year he produces some 120,000 bottles from vines cultivated with absolute respect for their environment and well-being; viticulture is his passion, and perfectionism *de rigueur*. By limiting their yields he obtains intensely tasty, sweet grapes, and when the climatic conditions of warmth and humidity are met, his vineyard is also blessed with "nobly" rotten fruit which has enjoyed the attentions of the fungus *Botrytis cinerea*. With such excellent raw material the game is almost won!

A rich, waxy mouthful

Ogereau's two rosés are nicely crafted examples of their appellations. The Cabernet d'Anjou is particularly expressive: off-dry, its intense fruitiness, roundness, and sheer volume can surprise the uninitiated, for most wine sold under a appellation is more neutral; it is a delicious wine for the summer *apéritif* and for sweet and sour dishes. His red Anjou and Anjou Villages are harmoniously constituted, with a lot of extract and structure, and require a few years' softening up to develop the charm of which they are eminently capable.

The tasting starts becoming really exciting with the dry white Anjou. The result of successive *tries* of fourty-year-old vines, four-fifths Chenin and the remainder Sauvignon, the rich fruit is vinified both in barrel and vat and subsequently aged slowly on its lees for nourishment, to fatten it up and increase its complexity. The taster revels in the rich, waxy mouthful with its very fresh citrus aromas. Since 1995 Ogereau has produced a barrel-fermented dry white Cuvée Prestige, from grapes harvested when almost overripe. This sumptuous wine is that much fatter and richer, and needs more time to develop its bouquet. Finally come the wines which, one feels, really inspire their maker, the Coteaux-du-Layons.

Coteaux-du-Layon Saint Lambert Clos des Bonnes Blanches

Following a generic Coteaux-du-Layon Saint-Lambert of regularly excellent value for money come (depending on the year) a Cuvée Nectar and a Cuvée Prestige, both of great distinction. Finally, from the best-sited vines Ogereau makes limited quantities of the Clos des Bonnes Blanches, a *sélection de grains nobles* which is fermented and aged in new oak barrels. This is a wine of extraordinary richness, opulence even, yet its liquor is finely balanced by its mineral character, and its discreet but effective acidity; the over-riding impressions are of freshness and harmony. This delight must be enjoyed on its own, suggests Ogereau... it is really too sublime to be interfered with by alien flavors!

LOIRE VALLEY
A.O.C. Quarts-de-Chaume

- *Wine selected:*
  Quarts-de-Chaume

- *Grape Variety:*
  Chenin
- *Average vine age*
  30 years
- *Vineyard size:*
  5.3 hectares
- *Soil type:*
  Schist
- *Production:*
  8,000 bottles

Finest Vintages:
1999, 1997, 1996, 1990, 1989

Domaine des Baumard
8 Rue de l'Abbaye
49190 Rochefort-sur-Loire
Tel. (0033) 241 78 70 03
- *Owner:* SCEA Domaine des Baumard
- *On-site sales:* 10:00–12:00 a.m.,
  2.00-5.30 p.m. (except Sundays
  and Bank Holidays)
- *Visits:* Yes. Closed between
  Christmas and New Year's Day
- *Price:* ★★

DOMAINE DES BAUMARD

For credibility any list of the top producers of Anjou wines would have to include the Baumard family of Rochefort, who produce a fine array of nearly all the region's appellations, at a level of quality that is admirable. From the humblest to the most prestigious, these bottles are all benchmark examples.

A young man's heritage

The Baumards are one of the best known families of the region, having been established at Rochefort since 1634. The patriarch Jean, today retired, is an eminent figure, having been Professor of Viticulture at Angers and president of the Union of A.O.C Syndicates of the Loire as well as a much-admired wine maker. His son Florent took over responsibility for the estate in the mid-1990s, and has proved himself a grower and wine maker of great talent and sensitivity. A visit to the Baumards in their handsome seventeenth-century Logis de la Giraudière is a most agreeable and rewarding experience.

The fine-tuning of a house style

The Baumards are above all specialists of the sweet wines of Coteaux-du-Layon and Quarts de Chaume, and have long produced beautifully pure, rich and harmonious versions of these wines, favoring elegance and delicacy rather than the power and concentration of some. Jean Baumard diversified their vineyard holdings by investing in Savennières in the 1960s and developed a style of wine—dry, supple, fragrant, and good young—which was very different to the other producers' offerings of the time, and rapidly became very popular and a commercial success. Under Florent's influence recent vintages of all the wines seem to speak with a slightly more marked *terroir* accent.

Dehydration, concentration and noble rot

The *trie*, or passage through the vineyard to pick those grapes in a sufficiently concentrated state, is at the heart of the quality of Baumard wines. Some years, those with the necessary combination of heat and humidity, see the widespread appearance of *Botrytis cinerea*, causing the noble rot which dehydrates the grape, de-acidifies the juice and brings about the creation of glycerol. During other years however, if the end of the season is hot but dry, the overripe grapes wrinkle and dry out on the vine, giving highly concentrated juice with diminished malic acidity. This process is known as *passerillage*. In whichever of the two ways the grapes have been affected, harvesting by *tries* is essential to make the most of nature's bounty.

Quarts de Chaume

In its youth the Baumards' Quarts de Chaume is a brilliant pale gold, then takes on greenish and then amber nuances as the years pass; the Chenin's fresh, grapey aroma makes way for a fascinating potpourri in which quince, lime-blossom, peach, apricot, incense, wax, and honey can all feature, in proportions decided by the vintage. On the palate the sweetness is anything from gentle to powerfully concentrated, yet elegance and refinement always figure in the wine's profile. Does one enjoy it in the freshness of youth, the complexity of adulthood or the wisdom of advanced age? Whichever, hot Maroilles tart, Roquefort in puff-pastry and chicken-liver terrine provide unexpectedly eloquent accompaniments for this sumptuous wine.

LOIRE VALLEY
A.O.C. Quarts-de-Chaume

- *Wine selected:*
  **Quarts-de-Chaume
  Quintessence**

- *Grape Variety:*
  Chenin
- *Average vine age*
  25 years
- *Vineyard size:*
  12 hectares
- *Soil type:*
  Schist and sandstone
- *Production:*
  10,000 bottles

Finest Vintages:
1999, 1997, 1996, 1990, 1989

Château Bellerive
49190 Rochefort-sur-Loire
Tel. (0033) 241 78 33 66
- *Owners:* Serge & Michel Malinge
- *On-site sales:* Yes
- *Visits:* Yes
- *Price:* ★★

CHÂTEAU BELLERIVE

Many of those lucky souls who have tasted the magnificent Quarts-de-Chaume can thank Château Bellerive for the privilege. This splendid estate is one of the most important landholders, possessing no less than 12 of the 40 hectares of the appellation's surface, and makes nothing but Quarts-de-Chaume. It has long had a fine reputation for its extraordinarily sweet yet harmonious wine.

A tithe exacted on the lease-holder

Wine production around Chaume probably commenced in the eleventh or twelfth century. In the Middle Ages the fief belonged to the *Seigneurs de la Grande Guerche*, of Saint-Aubin-de-Luigné. At that time there was an arrangement known as *bail à complant* (planting lease), by which a seigneur would lend land to a grower, on the condition that he plant vines on it. A little later the flourishing vineyard would be divided into two equal parts, one reverting to the land-owner, the other remaining in the hands of the lease-holder, on condition of the payment of an annual tithe, a proportion of the harvest. Thus originated the Quarts-de-Chaume, a tithe which was defined precisely as "the quarter of the harvest hanging on the vines situated on the other side of the Coteau du Midi." This important precision, the choice of the sunniest plot, a gage of quality, served much later for delimiting the viticultural area of the A.O.C.

Splendid terrain for the Chenin

The Bellerive vines lie around the château and are situated in the centre of the appellation where the likelihood of the appearance of *Botrytis cinerea* is greatest. The vineyards are terraced, and the terrain there is very tough, containing fragments of schist and sandstone, and drains and warms up very well.

The Chenin vines are trained very low in order to gain maximum profit from the heat reflected by the soil, and are planted at a low density of five thousand plants per hectare in order to help along the ripening cycle. The vines are pruned very short to limit their productivity, and the yields are always below the A.O.C. maximum of 22 hl/ha.

After successive passages through the vineyard to pick grapes as they become sufficiently "nobly" rotten, each picking is gently pressed and the must then fermented slowly at a low temperature in barrel. The produce of different parcels is thereby kept separate, and the different wines are blended later. Maturation in oak follows, then bottling in September following the vintage.

Quarts-de-Chaume Quintessence

In exceptional vintages the richest part of the harvest is kept apart and bottled under the name Quintessence; this wine is somewhat more profound than the standard *cuvée*, yet it also is a model of harmony and balance. A lustrous deep gold in color, Quintessence has a stunningly complex flavor range of honey, and dried and crystallised fruit. The palate, very concentrated, reveals exquisite citrus nuances, which give an impression of lightness and delicacy. This great *cuvée* finishes very long, and one can only imagine that it is destined for a good half-century of splendor! Veritably, a wine fit for a seigneur! It marries well with fish such as salmon, turbot and brill in sauce, white meats, and blue cheese.

LOIRE VALLEY
A.O.C. Quarts-de-Chaume

- *Wine selected:*
  Quarts-de-Chaume
  (50 cl bottle)

- *Grape Variety:*
  Chenin
- *Average vine age*
  50 years
- *Vineyard size:*
  2.7 hectares
- *Soil type:*
  Carboniferous
- *Production:*
  7,000 bottles

Finest Vintages:
1999, 1997, 1996, 1995

Château Pierre-Bise
49750 Beaulieu-sur-Layon
Tél. : 02 41 78 31 44
- *Owner:* Claude Papin
- *On-site sales:* 8–12 a.m., 2–6 p.m.
- *Visits:* Yes
- *Price:* ★★

CHÂTEAU PIERRE-BISE

Wine should stimulate man's intelligence and engage him in reflection, reaction even. Like other art forms, it is a vector of communication; in an ideal world it excites his curiosity and incites him to try to understand its message, as written by its soil, environment and climatic characteristics. The veracity of that message is what drives Claude Papin as he makes his wines, which are recognized as being amongst the most authentic and rewarding produced in Anjou today.

Discovering Anjou's geological differences

Papin is self-taught, and method and analytical thought are no stranger to him. In 1959 his father acquired an abandoned vineyard, which he took over in 1974. From 1985 he became interested in developing the notion of terroir, and set out getting to know the minutest geological differences of Anjou's many vineyard slopes by consulting a geological map of the region and by tasting the grapes of each vineyard. His research deepened from 1992 when he collaborated with researchers from the Angers branch of the *Institut National de la Recherche Agronomique*.

A family of individual personalities

As a result of his painstaking work customers at Château Pierre-Bise can choose from a glittering family of wines, principally Coteaux du Layon, of individual personalities. The Pierre-Bise estate covers a lordly 53 hectares and is run along *lutte raisonnée* lines, even if the over-riding philosophy is one of natural (traditional) cultivation. Each parcel is cultivated as best befits its soil and microclimate; grass is allowed to overrun some, while in others it is

cultivated between every second row. Although the estate is not officially run under a biological regime the vines are protected by the use of oligo-elements, seaweed and pine oil, with total exclusion of insecticide.

Safeguarding the typicity

Besides severe pruning, Papin restricts the harvest of his vines by crop thinning, and always starts harvesting as late as possible, to obtain fruit of perfect ripeness or over-ripeness, depending on the wine. The wines made from late-harvested, botrytised grapes are naturally picked over successive *tries* lasting through to December, while even the red and rosé wines are picked as late as possible, by hand.

The produce of the different parcels is vinified separately, for there are terrains of schist, volcanic rock, and carboniferous soil, each of which leaves its imprint. To further protect individuality the juices undergo only a very light *débourbage*, thus safeguarding the families of yeast and ensuring lengthier fermentations.

Quarts-de-Chaume

As with all his wines, Papin's Quarts-de-Chaume is a model of purity, harmony, and restraint. Splendidly rich in natural sugar, opulent, and aromatically complex, its last word to the taster is nevertheless one of slightly bitter, mineral nervosité, demonstrating eloquently the nuances of the local geological dialect. The taster is left with a most favorable impression, for the words engage his intellect for a very long time. What a masterful wine, what talent of man and nature! *Foie gras* has a very valuable contribution to add to this conversation.

LOIRE VALLEY
A.O.C. Quarts-de-Chaume

• *Wine selected:*
Quarts-de-Chaume

• *Grape Variety:*
Chenin
• *Average vine age*
45 years
• *Vineyard size:*
5 hectares
• *Soil type:*
Schist and sandstone
• *Production:*
8,000–10,000 bottles

Finest Vintages:
1997

Château de Suronde
49190 Rochefort-sur-Loire
Tel. (0033) 241 78 66 37
Follow the D54 from Beaulieu towards
Saint-Aubin, and take the road on the
left just before the Telecom tower.
At the hamlet of Chaume take the
left fork, follow the road up and
around to the left, and at the red
fire hydrant take the vineyard track
on the right. The path leads down
to Château de Suronde.
• *Owner:* Francis Poirel
• *On-site sales:* By appointment
• *Visits:* By appointment
• *Price:* ★★★

CHÂTEAU DE SURONDE

A change of ownership has worked wonders for the wine of Château de Suronde, one of those favoured few properties lying in Anjou's extraordinary Quarts-de-Chaume vineyard. Thanks to his determination to produce the very finest wine possible, totally naturally and only from grapes seriously affected by *Botrytis cinerea*, Francis Poirel has in the space of a handful of years made a serious name for himself in the region. A taste of his wine is all that is needed to understand why.

Mid-life crisis and a change of direction

Francis Poirel came to wine making by choice, from the outside. Admittedly he had a grandfather who was a *vigneron* in the Côtes de Toul, and as the only grandson had often spent time with him when young, yet his experience of wine-making went no further than that! His working life had been spent in the fishing industry, yet as he entered his forties he found himself confronted with a mid-life crisis.

Poirel had a passion for wine and gastronomy. It must have needed little persuasion and encouragement on the part of his vigneron friends Mark Angeli, Philippe Alliet and others for him to enlist at Blanquefort's *lycée agricole* (secondary school for wine making) for a year's course in viticulture and making wine... after which came the rounds of the estate agents, the chuckles and the stock reply that smallish vineyard estates in Anjou did not come up for sale too often. Yet at the end of 1994 Château de Suronde came onto the market. Poirel did not hesitate.

Respect for future generations

As soon as he had settled in at the house, a charming architectural curiosity which clings to the slope as it runs down to the Layon, Poirel started work the way he meant to continue, running the vineyard along biological lines: not just for the quality of grapes he could harvest, but also out of respect for future generations—the weight of history and the transitory nature of each owner's presence is something of which he is very conscious. Every measure is taken to lighten the vines' load to five to seven bunches, starting with a severe pruning, then debudding, and a later crop-thinning if necessary, with leaf stripping to improve aeration and exposure to sunlight. It is no surprise to learn that Poirel operates more tries than most to pick his crop of Botrytised grapes, which are placed in small fifteen-kilo crates for transport to the press, in order to avoid premature crushing and oxidation.

Quarts de Chaume

Pressed slowly in a vertical press, the extraordinarily rich juice of the Quarts-de-Chaume slowly ferments in cask by the action of its own yeast, which find nothing but natural sugar to work on, for Poirel is absolutely opposed to chaptalisation of this sort of wine. Then for eighteen to twenty months the wine rounds out and develops, still in cask, before being bottled. The resulting nectar is splendidly sweet and concentrated and richly aromatic, with a splendid panoply of aromas of honey, spice, dried apricot, fig and date, and with citric overtones in certain vintages... It is also remarkably fresh, and enables one to appreciate the elegance, finesse and breed of its remarkable *terroir*. For the sake of variety, one could try serving it with pigeon roasted with tarragon... a surprisingly good combination! Fresh apricot *tarte Tatin* is also perfect.

LOIRE VALLEY
A.O.C. Bonnezeaux

- *Wine selected:*
  Bonnezeaux

- *Grape Variety:*
  Chenin
- *Average vine age*
  35 years
- *Vineyard size:*
  14 hectares
- *Soil type:*
  Phtanitic schist, quartz
- *Production:*
  46,000 bottles

Finest Vintages:
1999, 1997, 1996

Château de Fesles
49380 Thouarcé
Tel. (0033) 241 68 94 00
Internet: www.vgas.com
From Thouarcé take the Martigné-
Briand direction. 2 km on, turn left at
the firt junction. The entry is 800 m
along on the left.
- *Owner:* Bernard Germain
- *On-site sales:* 10 a.m.–6 p.m.
- *Price:* ★★

CHÂTEAU DE FESLES

The leading estate of Anjou's *Grand Cru* Bonnezeaux, certainly by size and many would say by quality, is Château de Fesles, which occupies a splendid position on a hilltop looking down over the Layon river. The vineyards of this property are very well sited, and it has always had an excellent reputation; today it is producing wines of extraordinary richness and power, for which one can thank its new owner, a man with the determination and means to exploit its potential to the full.

A portfolio of Anjou's greatest appellations

Bernard Germain inherits the experience and love for the winemaker's life of six generations of Bordeaux growers. His firm, Vignobles Germain et Associés, owns an impressive string of right-bank Bordeaux châteaux, and one can understand that he should have fallen for the fine Fesles estate, which would not be out of place in the Gironde lands he knows so well. When he bought it in 1996 the estate had recently enjoyed a total refurbishment, for the seller, the famous French *pâtissier* Gaston Lenôtre, had acquired it himself only a few years before. With it he also acquired several other properties in the region which had belonged to Lenôtre, giving him a portfolio of Anjou's greatest appellations.

Conditions conducive to grape ripeness

It is the slopes behind the château, looking down on the Layon, which give birth to the Bonnezeaux—the name is held by some to refer to the quality of the local ferruginous mineral water, by others to be of Celtic origin—while the vineyards on the plateau around the château are planted with the redgrape varieties, for they are much less prone to the development of *Botrytis*. Here the siliceous clay soils and the south-south-west exposure, combined with the region's mild climate and particularly low rainfall, form conditions highly conducive to grape ripeness.

Between five and seven successive pickings are carried out in order to gather all the harvest at the ultimate state of over-ripeness or noble rot. On arriving at the winery, constructed in 1991 by Lenôtre, the grapes are macerated for ten to twelve hours for extraction of aroma and acidity, gently pressed, left to settle at a low temperature and then fermented, trie by trie, in 400-liter barrels for one to two months. When the transformation is complete they are kept in barrel for ten to fifteen months in the splendid air conditioned cellars, and bottled when the time is deemed right.

Bonnezeaux

The perfectionism which imbues the vineyard and winery teams is all-apparent in the Château de Fesles Bonnezeaux, a wine of remarkable opulence, concentration and aroma which boasts the dimensions of a premier cru Sauternes, yet is of course stamped with the unique personality of Anjou's great Chenin grape. Its liqueur is fabulous, and its spicy, citrus peel *Botrytis* flavor very marked; yet such is the balancing acidity that the wine is absolutely harmonious, and indeed extremely elegant. It needs time to digest the new-oak flavor of its *élevage*, yet even young makes a highly eloquent partner for white meats and fish in creamy sauces, Roquefort cheese or unsugared pear tart, served hot.

LOIRE VALLEY
A.O.C. Bonnezeaux

- *Wine selected:*
  Bonnezeaux Le Malabé

- *Grape Variety:*
  Chenin
- *Average vine age*
  60 years
- *Vineyard size:*
  3 hectares
- *Soil type:*
  Schist
- *Production:*
  4,000-8,000 bottles

Finest Vintages:
2001, 1997, 1996, 1995,
1990, 1989, 1988, 1985

Domaine des Petits Quarts
La Douve
49380 Faye d'Anjou
Tel. (0033) 241 54 03 00
The estate is at the top end of the
village of Faye.
- *Owner:* Jean-Pascal Godineau
- *On-site sales:* 8–12 a.m., 2–6 p.m.
  (except Sundays and Bank Holidays)
- *Visits:* Yes
- *Price:* ★★

DOMAINE DES PETITS QUARTS

The real progress made in recent years in Bonnezeaux production may be accurately assessed by tasting the work of families such as the Godineaus of Faye d'Anjou, who go to great lengths to harvest fruit at a state of extreme "noble" rot, enabling them to produce wines of extraordinary richness and complexity. The wines made on this estate will no doubt be a revelation for any consumer who has not opened a bottle of Bonnezeaux for a few years!

A regular shower of medals

The Godineau family, one imagines, know the region as well as anyone: five generations ago they settled in the village of Bonnezeaux and started making wine, and in 1887 moved 800 meters west and founded their new estate Domaine des Petits Quarts in the commune of Faye d'Anjou. Today Jean-Pascal Godineau maintains the family tradition with great talent, as is witnessed by the regular shower of medals bestowed upon the estate at the annual Paris, Mâcon and Bonnezeaux competitions, and the *coups de cœur* and other attributions awarded by books such as the *Guide Hachette*.

Three essentials for producing fine Bonnezeaux

At sixty hectares the property is one of the largest in the region, and one of the most important Bonnezeaux producers, with sufficient land in the small 125-hectare appellation to enable Godineau to make several individual *cuvées*.

The three essentials for making the finest wine possible are respected: excellent *terroir*, low yields and advanced degrees of grape ripeness. The Chenin vines, many of which are of advanced age, are planted on steep south- and southeast-facing schistous slopes, which enjoy microclimatic conditions highly propitious to *passerillage* and the appearance of *Botrytis cinerea*. The yields of fruit produced are maintained at a very low average of fifteen to twenty hectoliters per hectare, where A.O.C. laws permit a maximum of twenty-five. And harvesting, which is naturally by hand and by successive pickings, takes place between 20th September and 25th November, or even finishes in December occasionally.

Once picked the harvest is rapidly pressed and vinified at a low temperature in both barrel and stainless steel vat. When the slow process is finished, the golden liquid is then bottled in the spring.

Bonnezeaux Le Malabé

The pride of the estate, its Le Malabé parcel, is fermented entirely in stainless steel, for Godineau feels that the use of barrels would be detrimental to the expression of the very marked personality of the gray and gray-green schist. This parcel is remarkably susceptible to the development of noble rot and *passerillage*, and up to seven tries are carried out in order to achieve maximum concentration of the raw material. The net result is an impressively rich, thick wine redolent of honeyed, toasted, and dried-fruit aromas, which has fine balance and a very long finish. How generous nature can be! Whether one enjoys it in the fresh fragrance of youth or the round complexity of age, Le Malabé is self-sufficient in a gastronomic sense; however, if one has a terrine of sweetbread or some *foie gras* or *pâté* nearby, they will certainly not detract from the pleasure!

LOIRE VALLEY
A.O.C. Anjou

- *Wine selected:*
  Anjou La Lune

- *Grape Variety:*
  Chenin
- *Average vine age*
  7–50 years
- *Vineyard size:*
  2.3 hectares
- *Soil type:*
  Sand, clay, carboniferous schist
- *Production:*
  7,000 bottles

Finest Vintages:
All recent vintages

Domaine La Sansonnière
49380 Thouarcé
Tel. (0033) 241 54 08 08
La Sansonnière is about 1 km outside
Thouarcé, on the Martigné-Briand
road.
- *Owner:* Mark Angeli
- *On-site sales:* No
- *Visits:* By appointment
- *Price:* ★★

DOMAINE DE LA SANSONNIÈRE

Anjou is gaining greatly by the arrival of Mark Angeli. As sometimes happens when men and women come to wine from outside, without any family wine-making tradition, the level of personal involvement is frequently greater, the inspiration and determination stronger than in established families. This young man loves and believes passionately in his adopted region, and is determined to help and carry along other like-minded youngsters with him, in the hope of improving its fortunes.

Inspiration from the past

After a course in wine making in Sauternes, Angeli moved into the Sansonnière estate in 1989. He was surprised to find that his instinct as a lover of Nature went against all the viticultural dogma he had been taught, and he gradually found himself demodernising the estate, preferring the way things were done in days gone by. He started cultivating the vineyards naturally, abhorring the chemical alternatives so widely used; he freed his vines from their training wires and stakes, preferring to leave them to sway in the breeze and grow upwards towards the sun; and he is progressively replacing his tractor with a horse, regretting the lack of emotion felt using the former. He even planted two parcels with ungrafted vines, one by the *en foule* method used before phylloxera and the advent of neat, orderly rows of vines. At forty thousand plants per hectare even a human has trouble moving through it! Finally by 1994 he was tending his vineyards by biodynamic principles, for the benefit of future custodians of his land.

The photograph of a specific terrain

Their intriguing geological diversity has incited him to produce an extended range of wines, each the photograph of a specific terrain. Cabernet Sauvignon produces particularly fine fruit in the Thouarcé region, and Angeli appreciates the possibilities of Grolleau Gris, yet it is Chenin which really excites him. For making liquoreux wines, naturally, but above all for its potential as a dry wine. Chenin is indestructible if one takes the necessary measures in the vineyard.

Wine making *à l'ancienne*

He harvests his crop at low yields, each and every variety by trie, and for the dry wines picks the Chenin when the grapes have turned golden, just before they shrivel.

The man makes his wine very much *à l'ancienne*, pressing the grapes very slowly in traditional vertical presses—which enable him to do without *débourbage*, the settling period in which so much goodness can escape—and then transferring them to 400-liter barrels to ferment, with no additives whatsoever save a minute amount of SO_2. Thereafter the yeast (and certainly not Angeli) dictate the length of *cuvaison* and *élevage*.

Anjou La Lune

So named by one of his workers because of its crescent shape, the La Lune parcel on the hill opposite the estate has a heterogeneous geological make-up giving a highly interesting dry wine of remarkable purity and definition. La Lune exudes harmony and elegance, and combines exquisite, ripe fruit and minerality while avoiding excessive fleshiness. It is a splendid demonstration of dry-fermented Anjou Chenin, and makes a fine partner for the simple nobility of grilled *langoustine*.

LOIRE VALLEY
A.O.C. Anjou-Villages Brissac

- *Wine selected:*
  **Anjou-Villages Brissac
  La Croix de Mission**

- *Grape Varieties:*
  Cabernet-Sauvignon 90%,
  Cabernet Franc 10%
- *Average vine age*
  20 years
- *Vineyard size:*
  7 hectares
- *Soil type:*
  Schist and quartz
- *Production:*
  20,000 bottles

Finest Vintages:
2000, 1997, 1996, 1995

Domaine des Rochelles
49320 Saint-Jean-des-Mauvrets
Tel. (0033) 241 91 92 07
The estate is on the edge of Saint-Jean-des-Mauvrets on the Juigné side.
If arriving from Juigné it is on the right,
after the Citroën garage.
- *Owners:* Jean-Yves & Anita Lebreton
- *On-site sales:* 9:00–12:00 a.m.,
  2:00–6:30 p.m.
- *Visits:* Yes
- *Price:* ★

DOMAINE DES ROCHELLES

Anjou's red wines are still a little-known quantity, the grapes that make them having in the past been used principally for the production of rosé. Only since the 1980s has there been any real impetus to make decent red, and even today the movement is hardly widespread. In explanation it must be said that many slopes are eminently better suited to Chenin than Cabernet; yet there are estates which have addressed the problem and made enormous progress, and offer Anjou rouge of great succulence, charm and ripe structure. The Lebreton family of Saint-Jean-des-Mauvrets is one.

An unrivalled fruity succulence

The family's property, Domaine des Rochelles, is today owned and run by Jean-Yves Lebreton and his wife Anita. At fifty hectares it is large, and enables them to make a complete range of wines, in which the stars are the Anjou-Villages Brissac reds, with elegant Coteaux de l'Aubance sweet whites following hard on their heels.

Hubert and Jean-Yves Lebreton have been instrumental in the general progress of the region's red wines, working with the enologist Didier Coutenceau both to achieve higher-quality grapes and to perfect vinification methods so as best to extract their rich fruitiness, tannic support and delicious aromas and transform them into balanced, harmonious and ripe wine. Lebreton has continued his father's diligent work, and today Domaine des Rochelles is reckoned by many the finest exponent of Anjou-Villages Brissac, thanks to methods which include natural vineyard practices including enherbement and picking the Cabernets when they are almost in a state of over-ripeness; that way it is possible to avoid the hard, tannic character of the variety which so often detracts from these wines' quality, and bring to the fore an unrivalled fruity succulence instead.

A splendid plot of schist and quartz

One part of the Rochelles estate, a seven-hectare parcel of schist and quartz lying between Saint-Jean-des-Mauvrets and Brissac, is particularly well suited to the Cabernet-Sauvignon vine, a fact which has prompted the Lebretons to make a *cuvée* almost exclusively from its produce, which is quite unusual in Anjou. The wine, La Croix de Mission, is vinified in stainless steel vats in order to preserve fruit purity and avoid the oxidation, not to mention oak flavor, which would come from aging in barrel. Fermentation and maceration of the wine last at least a month, giving good weight of fruit and structure, and bottling thereafter is carried out with minimal tampering.

Anjou-Villages Brissac La Croix de Mission

The end result is a wine of great distinction which merits a place in any wine lover's cellar: very dark in color, La Croix de Mission projects a sensual perfume of black fruit with a hint of licorice, and seduces the palate with its fleshy embrace and soft persistence. Certain vintages are a little more reserved than others when young, but all have great breed and personality. Grilled rib of beef provides the required simplicity and character for this fine wine.

LOIRE VALLEY
A.O.C. Saumur

- *Wine selected:*
  Saumur Les Cormiers

- *Grape Variety:*
  Chenin Blanc
- *Average vine age*
  30 years
- *Vineyard size:*
  3 hectares
- *Soil type:*
  Limestone
- *Production:*
  8,000 bottles

Finest Vintages:
2000, 1997, 1996, 1995

Château de Villeneuve
49400 Souzay-Champigny
Tel. (0033) 241 51 14 04
Château de Villeneuve lies next to the
church of Souzay, rising prominently
above the river.
- *Owners:* SCA Chevallier Père & Fils
- *On-site sales:* Yes
- *Tasting:* 9–12 a.m., 2–6 p.m., except
Sundays and bank holidays
- *Price:* ★★

CHÂTEAU DE VILLENEUVE

Passing through the gateway and contemplating the handsome Château de Villeneuve surrounded by its neatly tended vineyards, one could almost imagine oneself in Saint-Émilion... and indeed Cabernet Franc is no stranger here. But there is Chenin Blanc also. No, here we are a stone's throw from Saumur, and the estate looks down on the Loire. Here we are *chez* Jean-Pierre Chevallier, a leading producer who makes white Saumur and red Saumur-Champigny of very fine quality.

An exceptional white wine vineyard

The Chevalliers, a Souzay wine family, bought the property in 1969 and lovingly restored it to its present elegance. Jean-Pierre started work on the estate in 1982 after graduating at Bordeaux's Institut d'œnologie.

The vineyard enjoys an exceptional situation thanks both to its south-easterly orientation and its chalky soil, which gives wines of finesse and elegance. This land is admirably suited to the production of quality white wines, of which Chevallier has always been a great fan; indeed in days gone by the region made as much white as red, yet changing fashion was responsible for the increased production of the latter.

Environment-friendly viticultural practices

After his arrival Chevallier gradually introduced improvements in viticultural practice. In 1983 he stopped using fertilizer, then experimented with enherbement, letting grass grow in the vineyard. In 1985 he started thinning the crop, and to keep yields down to a level compatible with the highest quality, now removes all but six buds and eliminates *contrebourgeons*. Other refinements followed, yet it was not until 1993 that he was really happy with the wine he had made.

The experiments and innovations continue. Since 1998 he has addressed the problem of grape-worm by using the technique of *confusion sexuelle* in the vineyard. By saturating the air with the smell of the female *Eudemis* and *Cochylis* butterflies by means of hundreds of smell diffusers, male butterflies are disorientated and cannot find their partners. There is no coupling, no laying and hatching of eggs, and therefore no more destruction of grapes by *vers de la grappe*.

Ultra-ripe fruit for very rich wines

All these cares are lavished with the aim of harvesting ultra-ripe grapes, and even over-ripe grapes for certain *cuvées*, which Chevallier manages regularly. The high degree of potential alcohol means he does not need to chaptalise (the addition of sugar in order to prolong fermentation and obtain more alcohol), and in years when more than 55° F (13° C) is attained he produces a magnificent red wine from the Grand Clos which surrounds the château, and a superb white Les Cormiers.

Saumur Les Cormiers

Harvested by successive tries the sumptuously ripe Chenin grapes are vinified in a mix of new and one-year-old barrels, and then aged in barrel for the best part of a year. Following tradition there is no malo-lactic fermentation, which is as well given the opulence of the wine. Les Cormiers is magnificently rich and succulent, with a flavor range encompassing honeysuckle, white fruit and sometimes tropical fruit, yet it is fresh and dry on the palate, making it suitable company for delicacies such as asparagus tips with morels. Here is a wine which demonstrates the great progress of recent years!

LOIRE VALLEY
A.O.C. Saumur-Champigny

• *Wine selected:*
Saumur-Champigny
Les Rogelins

• *Grape Variety:*
Cabernet Franc
• *Average vine age*
15 years
• *Vineyard size:*
1 hectare
• *Soil type:*
Clay and limestone
• *Production:*
6,000 bottles

Finest Vintages:
1997, 1996, 1990, 1989

Domaine René-Noël Legrand
13 Rue des Rogelins
49400 Varrains
Tel. (0033) 241 52 94 11
From the Varrains church go down Rue
du Ruau, take the first left then the
first right, which is Rue des Rogelins.
• *Owner:* René-Noël Legrand
• *On-site sales:* By appointment
• *Visits:* By appointment
• *Price:* ★

DOMAINE RENÉ-NOËL LEGRAND

Quietly going about the business of producing the best possible wine with whatever Nature gives him every year, that, more than anything, is what interests René-Noël Legrand. He keeps a low profile, not being a natural communicator, and it is up to the wine lover to seek him out, pay him a visit and discover his wines. As indeed he should, for they are well worth the trouble of tracking down.

From father to son

The Legrand family has owned and cultivated parcels of land in one form or another in the region since the time of the Revolution. Ancestors were variously agricultural or vineyard laborers or coopers, and occasionally they acquired their own parcels and put them to viticulture, agriculture or livestock. Legrand's father made wine from 1947 to 1976, starting and finishing with an exceptional vintage, and René-Noël learnt everything from him. He took over in 1977... a dreadful vintage, he recalls, expressing the hope that he will not go out on one so awful!

Some very useful grass

The estate today covers fifteen hectares and is very fragmented, the parcels lying over the communes of Varrains, Chaintres, Chacé and Champigny. Legrand is an enthusiastic advocate of the *enherbement* method: the presence of ray grass and fescue grass in between the rows of vines is invaluable, since it contributes to reduced yields, and soaks up rain during the vintage, thus avoiding diluted grapes. What is more, it also pumps the nitrogen, a legacy of synthetic fertilisers, out of the soil. *Enherbement*, he reckons, is the greatest advance of the 1990s.

A cellar with a difference

Once harvested the crop is taken to the *chai*, a converted barn originally used for storing the straw for the horses, which forms one side of the courtyard of the Legrand premises. In it stand a handful of stainless steel vats, in which the fruit macerates and ferments over some three weeks. For the extraction of tannin, color and aroma which is so important to Legrand's wines, one is equipped with an *autopigeage* system, yet for reasons of cost the others use *remontage*, by pump and by compressed air. After that the wines enjoy long *élevage* in barrel in the underground tuffeau cellar reached by a descending ramp in the courtyard.

The cellar casts light on the way previous generations lived, and is well worth a visit: here there is a well, there a drinking-trough, here a bread oven, there a clothes-washing basin; there is a recess in which the pig was tethered, and another one for the horse. A shelf of 1893 *eau de vie* in pharmaceutical bottles catches the eye. And of course there are the barrels in which Legrand ages his wines.

Saumur-Champigny Les Rogelins

All his Champignys are rich in extract, and none more so than Les Rogelins, which therefore earns the benefit of being aged in oak, mostly new, over a long period. This is a gloriously dark, earthy wine redolent of red fruit and nuanced with spice, which has a significant tannic structure giving it potential for many a year's development. René-Noël Legrand may be a somewhat reserved character, but one can not say the same for his wines! Les Rogelins ideally calls for red meat or game—a haunch of venison cooked over a fire, for example.

LOIRE VALLEY
A.O.C. Saumur-Champigny

- *Wine selected:*
  Saumur-Champigny Marginale

- *Grape Variety:*
  Cabernet Franc
- *Average vine age*
  45 years
- *Vineyard size:*
  4 hectares
- *Soil type:*
  Turonian clay and limestone
- *Production:*
  12,000 bottles

Finest Vintages:
2001, 2000, 1997, 1996,
1995, 1990, 1989

Domaine des Roches Neuves
56 Boulevard Saint-Vincent
49400 Varrains
Tel. (0033) 241 52 94 02
The estate lies on the D93 on the
right between Varrains and the
Chacé turning.
- *Owner:* Thierry Germain
- *On-site sales:* By appointment
- *Visits:* By appointment
- *Price:* ★★

DOMAINE DES ROCHES NEUVES

Once he had moved north from Bordeaux to the Loire it did not take long for the young Thierry Germain to settle in on the estate he had acquired and start making fine wine. Soon the impressive quality of his Saumur-Champignys was noticed, and within a decade his reputation as one of the finest wine-makers was well and truly established. Red or white, the produce of Domaine des Roches Neuves shows its owner's sure feel for the potential of his harvest.

A great variety of soil nuances

When Germain bought the property, which has existed since 1850, it consisted of sixteen hectares of Cabernet Franc. Since then judicious purchases, including that of several hectares of Chenin Blanc, have increased its size to twenty-two hectares. One of the strengths of the estate is that its vineyard is made up of thirty-four parcels, spread over the communes of Varrains, Chacé, Saumur, Dampierre and Saint-Cyr. These present many nuances of the basic soil composition of clay and limestone lying over the *tuffeau* sub-soil, a calcareous rock harbouring grains of quartz and mica.

Each parcel expresses its character

Ninety per cent of a wine is made in the vineyard, the irrepressible Germain likes telling his visitors, and he and his team spend a great deal of the year seeing to the vines' well-being by attending to all the necessary tasks which biological viticulture demands. With so many different parcels to exploit Germain thrives on the challenge of letting each one express its character, and besides all the other painstaking viticultural cares the individual *terroirs* are given

voice through drastic yield limitation. Then once the beautifully ripe fruit has been carefully harvested by hand and minutely checked for quality, separate vinification of all the different parcels enables the personalities of the different wines to shine out.

The natural transformation of grape to wine

Respecting what Nature brings each year is what Germain's wine making is all about; none of the wines are contrived, for there is no artifice or cheating in the cellar, no chaptalization, no use of foreign yeast, no fining, no filtration... and above all the wine-making is unhurried. Three different *cuvées* of Saumur-Champigny are made, as well as small quantities of the sumptuous white Insolite, vinified in barrel *à la bourguignonne* from very low yields of Chenin grapes. Elegance and harmony characterise the basic red wine, which has good volume on the palate. The *cuvée* Terres Chaudes is altogether more dense and structured, with a powerful, spicy flavor and intense fruitiness. When the vintage produces fruit of sufficient quality Germain also produces Marginale.

Saumur-Champigny Marginale

The superb Marginale is as great a wine as is made anywhere with Cabernet Franc. Black to behold, it has a juicy, creamy black-fruit aroma and is fleshy and opulent on the palate, so much so that its significant structure is perfectly enveloped. Dominant aromas are sometimes mineral, sometimes grilled, and sometimes reveal nuances of licorice or peppermint... yet Marginale is always complex, suave and very hedonistic! Game pie accompanies this splendid wine very well.

LOIRE VALLEY
A.O.C. Saumur-Champigny

- *Wine selected:*
  Saumur-Champigny Les Poyeux

- *Grape Variety:*
  Cabernet Franc
- *Average vine age*
  40 years
- *Vineyard size:*
  2.7 hectares
- *Soil type:*
  Clay, limestone and flint
- *Production:*
  10,000 bottles

Finest Vintages:
1999, 1997, 1996, 1995, 1990, 1989

Clos Rougeard
15 Rue de l'Église
49400 Chacé
Tel. (0033) 241 52 92 65
- *Owners:* Foucault Frères
- *On-site sales:* Yes
- *Visits:* By appointment (maximum
  6 people)
- *Price:* ★★

Loire Valley, Chacé

CLOS ROUGEARD

Saumur Champigny was all the rage in Parisian bistros in the late 1980s, and the insipid and bland wines on offer did little for its image as a quality appellation and can hardly have endeared it to discerning wine lovers. That there is serious Saumur-Champigny, so serious that it can be ranked alongside France's greatest red wines, was and is not generally realised. The region owes a debt of gratitude to one family, the Foucaults of Chacé, for unwaveringly maintaining the wine's self-respect, and no less for setting an example for all the up-and-coming young stars of the region.

A simple affair of fine fruit and natural vinification

The Foucault family are proprietors of some 8 hectares of Saumur Champigny vineyard land, from which they produce three red wines under the Clos Rougeard label. The basic wine is called Clos Rougeard (which is actually not from one clos but from several parcels), and there are two other wines from the specified *lieux-dits* Les Poyeux and Le Bourg. Besides these they produce very limited quantities of white Coteaux de Saumur.

There is no secret formula for producing top-quality wine, the brothers Charly and Nadi modestly tell the visitor; all that is necessary is top-quality fruit and natural vinification. The Clos Rougeard wines are 100 percent Cabernet Franc (Cabernet Sauvignon and Pineau d'Aunis are technically allowed), and viticultural methods may be resumed as biological, with no use of synthetic products, severe yield limitation and harvesting only of perfectly ripe grapes.

From concrete to oak to glass

At the Foucaults' unostentatious premises the fermentation/maceration stage takes place in open concrete vats and lasts a very long four to six weeks, punctuated by a daily treading of the solids and pumping up and spraying of liquid over the floating cap, with the aim of extracting color, tannin and aroma. The free-run wine only is then transferred to barrel for aging.

The Le Bourg *cuvée* is aged in nothing but new oak barrels, while Les Poyeux is aged in one-year-old wood and the generic Clos Rougeard in two-year-old. The Foucaults' used barrels are supplemented with others from the Bordeaux *Premiers Crus* Châteaux Margaux, Latour and Haut-Brion. Finally when the time is right the wines are bottled. The operation is carried out by means of gravity simply, without filtration and without fining. After that bottles remain for a year or more on the Foucaults' premises before being released to their eager purchasers.

Saumur-Champigny Les Poyeux

After its eighteen to twenty-four months' aging, Les Poyeux is well equipped for a long and distinguished life. Its very dark color gives a hint of the rich *matière* waiting for tasting, which is succulent and fleshy, and noticeably tannic yet at the same time absolutely harmonious. Aromas of chocolate and prunes give way to nuances of coffee, tobacco and leather, depending on vintage characteristics, as it gets older... which it is eminently capable of doing! The magnificent Les Poyeux has all the refinement and breeding of a great Bordeaux. What to serve it with? Nadi Foucault unhesitatingly recommends the roast duck prepared by Jacky Dallais at his restaurant La Promenade, at Le Petit-Pressigny.

LOIRE VALLEY
A.O.C. Bourgueil

- *Wine selected:*
  Bourgueil Vaumoreau

- *Grape Variety:*
  Cabernet Franc
- *Average vine age*
  75–95 years
- *Vineyard size:*
  1.5 hectares
- *Soil type:*
  Clay and limestone
- *Production:*
  5,000 bottles

Finest Vintages:
2001, 2000, 1996, 1995,
1993, 1990, 1989, 1988

Domaine Pierre-Jacques Druet
7 Rue de la Croix-Rouge
Le Pied Fourrier
37140 Benais
Tel. (0033) 247 97 37 34
- *Owner:* Pierre-Jacques Druet
- *On-site sales:* Yes
- *Visits:* Yes
- *Price:* ★★

DOMAINE PIERRE-JACQUES DRUET

Youngsters wishing to set up in Touraine's red-wine country can take inspiration from the example set by Pierre-Jacques Druet. As a young man Druet decided he wanted to become a *vigneron*, and by dint of stubbornness and clearheaded vision, yet with little in the way of resources, rapidly started making some of Bourgueil's most pure and authentic wines. With time have come refinement and polish. These are splendid Bourgueils.

Wine studies and commercial experience

Druet, whose father was a wine trader, studied at the Beaune lycée viticole, and it was while helping out on friends' family estates in Burgundy that he saw the grower's life from close-up, and knew that he wanted above all else to be a *vigneron*. The secondary school was followed by studies at the universities of Montpellier and Bordeaux, and there followed some years selling wine-making hardware, notably the revolutionary Bücher press.

In 1980, after searching around, he and his wife Martine left the comfort of their well-to-do existence in Bordeaux and came to Bourgueil. At first things were hard: the fact that they were a mere few kilometers from his birthplace counted for nothing, in a region where outsiders are viewed with some suspicion...

Youthful dreams become reality

He had to rent everything: vines, cellars, a place to live, and got by at first with archaic material. In 1983, although he could not afford them, he bought three stainless-steel vats, made to a conical design of his own, in which he could properly vinify the wines of his different parcels. The following years saw much experimentation, for he is not the sort to follow tradition or wine school teaching unquestioningly, and much listening, gleaning the empirical experience of older growers of the village.

By the end of the decade other vats had joined the prototypes, the Druet domaine had expanded with more rented vines, and the family was well installed in a fine old Touraine house outside Benais. And, importantly, Druet had a long list of loyal clients. The backers who had ceded to the irresistible enthusiasm of the young man no doubt congratulated themselves on their perspicacity!

Bourgueil Vaumoreau

The separate vinification and bottling of his different parcels' crops has always been considered essential, and if the vintage is good enough Druet makes five different Bourgueil reds, a rosé, and a Chinon. All are picked by hand after a long wait for the grapes to become perfectly ripe, and each is vinified as best suits it... there is little that is routine in the Druet cellars.

In the very finest years the venerable vines of the small Vaumoreau parcel are bottled as such, producing a few thousand bottles of a splendour of huge dimensions, made for long keeping. Aged for thirty months in cask, black hued, immensely fleshy and rich, Vaumoreau has a formidable tannic structure, and a huge, rich concentration of fruit to go with it. It is a shame to consume a bottle of Vaumoreau before its tenth birthday, but after that hare *pâté* and a filet of pork *à l'agenaise* will tempt it out of its reserve.

LOIRE VALLEY
A.O.C. Bourgueil

- *Wine selected:*
  Bourgueil Le Grand Clos

- *Grape Variety:*
  Cabernet Franc
- *Average vine age*
  40 years
- *Vineyard size:*
  2 hectares
- *Soil type:*
  Siliceous clay
- *Production:*
  8,000 bottles

Finest Vintages:
1999, 1997, 1996, 1995

Domaine Yannick Amirault
5 Pavillon du Grand-Clos
37140 Bourgueil
Tel. (0033) 247 97 78 07
- *Owner:* Yannick Amirault
- *On-site sales:* 9–12 a.m., 2–7 p.m.
- *Visits:* Yes
- *Price:* ★

DOMAINE YANNICK AMIRAULT

Yannick Amirault is well known around Bourgueil and widely respected by his peers for the quality of his wine. There is nothing remarkable in the way he goes about producing them, and one can only deduce that it is a question of thoroughness and not tampering with Nature's work. It all sounds so easy!

The amalgamation of two family estates

The young Amirault took on his grandfather's vines in 1977, to which were progressively added those of his father Marcel as he started winding down his activities in preparation for retirement. All told the estate today covers sixteen hectares, five of which are in Saint-Nicolas-de-Bourgueil and the remaining eleven in Bourgueil itself.

Part is worked traditionally, to promote well-aired soils teeming with micro-organic life and to keep weeds at bay, while the steeper slopes are left unploughed and covered with grass, which limits the problem of erosion of the soils and also has the beneficial effect of acting as a brake on the vines' vigor. In case artificial products used. In no case are artificial products used.

Many of the vines are old: whereas thirty years of age is generally considered the prime of life, most of Amirault's are aged between fourty and sixty years; increasing age reduces a vine's vigor as well as increasing the quality of its juice. These vines are harvested by hand, generally at the beginning of October when they are splendidly ripe, with great selectivity to ensure that only perfect fruit finds its way to the vatroom.

Protection of the wines' natural qualities

The fruit is entirely destemmed before vatting, for the Cabernet Franc is sufficiently rich in tannin to provide all that is necessary for the wines' eventual balance if the *cuvaison* is suitably long. No artificial yeast are used, which would detract from the wines' authenticity, and the maceration and fermentation process is unhurried, with the occasional interruption for *pigeage*; some of the vats are equipped with *autopigeage* devices, but Amirault also treads by foot. The different parcels are always vinified separately.

Thereafter the wines are aged in oak, either in Bordeaux *barriques* acquired from Château Margaux or in 500-liter demi-muids for the less-rich wines. The duration depends on the quality of the vintage, but is generally between six months and one year. Finally the wines are bottled, without being filtered and without fining. This lack of interference in the vinification process goes a long way to explaining the quality of Amirault's wines.

Bourgueil Le Grand Clos

The Grand Clos is one of the longer-lasting, blessed as it is with rich fruit and a significant tannic structure, and is most impressive for the firm character it derives from its siliceous clay soil. Like all Amirault's wines, it does not seem excessively powerful, which may be attributed to its harmonious constitution, and it has a remarkable degree of charm and refinement for its appellation. Nevertheless it improves immeasurably if kept for a decade, and conducts itself admirably in the presence of hare stew.

LOIRE VALLEY
A.O.C. Chinon

• *Wine selected:*
Chinon Domaine Bernard Baudry

• *Grape Variety:*
Cabernet Franc
• *Average vine age*
35 years
• *Vineyard size:*
7 hectares
• *Soil type:*
Gravel, clay, and limestone
• *Production:*
30,000 bottles

Finest Vintages:
2001, 2000, 1996, 1995

Domaine Bernard Baudry
13 Coteau de Sonnay
37500 Cravant-les-Coteaux
Tel. (0033) 247 93 15 79
If heading from Chinon to Cravant, the
Baudry estate lies on the left just after
the Château de Sonnay, before
arriving in the village of Cravant.
• *Owner:* Bernard Baudry
• *On-site sales:* Yes
• *Visits:* By appointment
• *Price:* ★

DOMAINE BERNARD BAUDRY

Produced on either side of the Vienne river, the wines of Chinon vary from the light and fruity to serious, tannic wines for aging. Bernard Baudry has made his reputation with the latter style, although he also amuses himself making an excellent dry white wine and a succulent rosé. Thoughtful, meticulous and honest wine-making has gained him a loyal clientele who appreciates the unflamboyant, authentic character and marvellously pure and noble aromas of his various bottles.

From theory to practice

One of five children born into a Cravant wine-making family, Baudry studied wine making at the Beaune *lycée viticole* (secondary school for wine making) and started his working life in the company of the eminent Jacques Puisais as viticultural advisor at the Laboratoire de Tours. After five years he felt urge to put into practice what he was the teaching, resigned from his post in 1975 and rented two hectares of vines. From these modest beginnings the estate expanded in 1982, and has continued to do so as its owner, joined in 1999 by his son Matthieu, has taken on interesting vineyard parcels.

In perfect harmony with the soil

Baudry's vines grow in a variety of different types of terrain, enabling him to make a range of Chinons of different and marked personalities, which are sold by their place names rather than by fancy brand names.

As might be expected from an ex-viticultural advisor, he works hard to keep his vines in perfect harmony with their soil, and to that end the estate is quietly moving in the direction of *viticulture biologique*, although Baudry is not the sort to proclaim this. Keeping a close eye on the vines' well-being is very important, he insists, as is mastery of their yields; indeed an enormous amount of time is spent removing unwanted buds to reduce the dissipation of the soil's nutrients, and excess bunches are lopped off the vines in July if necessary.

Surveillance and non-intervention

Although the Chinon A.O.C. permits the inclusion of up to 10 percent Cabernet Sauvignon, Baudry uses nothing but Cabernet Franc, which is reckoned the ideal grape for the local soils. The harvest is entirely manual, enabling rejection of substandard bunches in the vineyard. Vinification is adapted to each *terroir*, and *surveillance* and *non-intervention* are the guiding principles. Wines are then aged in Baudry's smallish, impeccably-kept cellar in used casks, which he acquires from his friend Count Stephan von Niepperg of the Saint-Émilion Château Canon-La-Gaffelière.

Chinon Domaine Bernard Baudry

The Domaine Bernard Baudry *cuvée* is a blend of grapes grown in both gravel and calcareous clay terrains. A wine with medium-term aging potential, it is a fine demonstration of what Cabernet Franc is capable of if not permitted excessive yields and vinified slowly and naturally. Darkly colored, it is beautifully fragrant, with seductive aromas of violets and black fruit, and is richly fruity and succulent on the palate, with a fine tannic structure; its balance is impeccable, and its finish long. Once it has matured this textbook Chinon deserves to be served with a flavorful dish of meat or game: a haunch of venison, for example, is a fine choice.

LOIRE VALLEY
A.O.C. Chinon

- *Wine selected:*
  Chinon Clos de la Dioterie

- *Grape Variety:*
  Cabernet Franc
- *Average vine age*
  80 years
- *Vineyard size:*
  2.5 hectares
- *Soil type:*
  Clay and limestone
- *Production:*
  12,000 bottles

Finest Vintages:
2001, 2000, 1996, 1995,
1990, 1989, 1986, 1985

Domaine Charles Joguet
37220 Sazilly
Tel. (0033) 247 58 55 53
Internet: www.charlesjoguet.com
The estate is on the right of the
green, follow the signposts.
- *Owner:* Jacques Genet
- *On-site sales:* Yes
- *Visits:* 8:30 a.m.–12:30 p.m., 2:00–
  6:00 p.m.
- *Price:* ★★

DOMAINE CHARLES JOGUET

The Chinon estate with the highest profile is probably that of the artist Charles Joguet, and the splendid quality of its wines is borne out by their presence in many of France's greatest restaurants and the strong demand they enjoy on numerous export markets. Well-sited vineyards, perfectionism and the desire to produce wine which eloquently reflects its *terroir* result in a range of Chinons of great breed and class.

A young artist turns to wine-making

It was somewhat against the wishes of his parents, whose families had long made wine in the region, that Charles Joguet left Chinon college in 1949 and went up to Paris to take art lessons. Yet after his father's death in 1957 the young man returned home to help his mother run the estate. At the time, with the aid of a good wine maker and a horse and using modest equipment, they were able to keep their vines in reasonable shape and make good wine; however the great potential of their Clos de la Dioterie was not lost on them...

Strides forward in quality

Several people at the time gave Joguet invaluable advice, such as a local *vigneron* named Marcel Angeillaume who persuaded him to start bottling his production, another talented wine maker known as father Tafonneau and the highly-respected oenologist Jacques Puisais, and from 1962 he set about planting various parcels.

From the earliest days it appeared a heresy to him to blend young and old vines and different soil types, and he decided to make and market the produce of his different parcels separately, which was somewhat revolutionary at the time. The 1970s saw definite strides forward in quality: in

1973 Joguet started using small perforated crates instead of the traditional *hotte* for bringing in the harvest, and subjected his fruit to the delicate cares of Günter Amos's exceptional new destemming machine; the following year an electro-mechanical *pigeage* system, devised by Puisais, Guérin and Joguet, was put into service, and since that year all the wines have been made in stainless steel.

Continuity on the estate is assured

These and subsequent cares had their effect. Over the years the wines have shown splendidly pure, ripe fruitiness, fine tannic structure and great richness, and have a certain satiny polish which contributes to their great finesse.

Having surrounded himself with the talented duo of wine maker Michel Pinard, who arrived in 1983, and Alain Delaunay, who has run the estate since 1986, and having formed a *société civile d'exploitation agricole* with Jacques Genet in 1985 which enabled the expansion of the estate, Charles Joguet took well-earned retirement in 1997.

Chinon Clos de la Dioterie

Many young wine makers in the region cite Joguet's great Clos de la Dioterie 1989 as the wine which made them realize what potential lay in their soils... and how much work there was to be done. The combination of very old vines, very calcareous clay soil and the northerly orientation of the clos give a wine of extraordinary finesse, richness and fragrance, which really requires a dozen years in the cellar to reveal the extent of its complexity and harmony. Indeed Clos de la Dioterie is an inordinately harmonious wine, and partners a Challans duckling *en serviette* to perfection.

LOIRE VALLEY
A.O.C. Chinon

- *Wine selected:*
  Chinon Clos de l'Écho

- *Grape Variety:*
  Cabernet Franc
- *Average vine age*
  35–45 years
- *Vineyard size:*
  20 hectares
- *Soil type:*
  Clay and limestone
- *Production:*
  80,000 bottles

Finest Vintages:
2000, 1998, 1997, 1996,
1990, 1989, 1985, 1982

Maison Couly-Dutheil
12 Rue Diderot
37500 Chinon
Tel. (0033) 247 97 20 20
The tasting room is next to the Clos de
l'Écho, opposite the château.
- *Owner:* Couly-Dutheil
- *On-site sales:* By appointment
- *Visits:* Yes
- *Price:* ★★★

MAISON COULY-DUTHEIL

Over the twentieth century the Chinon families Couly and Dutheil have built up a fine estate and a thriving *négociant* business, which today provides a range of wines which are thoroughly dependable, and at the top end classics of their appellation. The size of the enterprise enables Couly-Dutheil to export all over the world, and Chinon wines could hardly have a better ambassador.

Four generations in the service of Chinon

Founded in 1910 by Baptiste Dutheil, the firm enjoyed great expansion while in the charge of René Couly and his wife Madeleine Dutheil, who acquired for it its finest vineyards in the 1950s. Today, in the hands of their sons Pierre and Jacques and grandson Bertrand, the aim for perfection and authenticity is resolutely maintained. The construction in 1989 of a fine new three-storey vinification centre has facilitated their task; besides contributing more space it enables better sorting and selection of incoming raw material, movement of musts and wines by gravity for better preservation of aromas, and affords more exact temperature control and thus mastery of fermentations.

A fine diversity of vineyard holdings

Couly-Dutheil is today proprietor of eighty hectares of prime Chinon vineyards—all in all a sizeable proportion of the two thousand hectares which make up the appellation—as well as seven hectares of Saumur and Saumur-Champigny, and vinifies the crop of a further fifty-five hectares. The Chinon estate is spread over the three Chinon *terroirs*: the sand and gravel land beside the Vienne, which gives uncomplicated light, fruity wines such as Les Gravières; the siliceous clay slopes and plateaus which produce more interesting wines of a certain finesse, such as the Domaine René Couly; and finally the clay and limestone slopes where the most serious Chinons come from, those with the greatest aging potential—notably the Clos de l'Écho and the Clos de l'Olive.

The Couly-Dutheils harvest everything by hand, and after sorting through the fruit in order to reject anything that is not first class, systematically destem and then without crushing give the fruit lengthy maceration and fermentation.

Chinon Clos de l'Écho

This splendid walled vineyard, lying north of Chinon and facing its castle, belonged to Rabelais' family, and earned its name from the echo sent back by the castle walls. Abandoned for many years to wheat production, it was purchased in 1952 by the Couly-Dutheil family and replanted the following year by René Couly.

Today it is undoubtedly one of Chinon's finest, a wine of great complexity, structure and aging potential derived from its calcareous clay soil. Vinification is adapted to the quality of the vintage and raw material, with fermentation and maceration lasting up to two months and long aging in barrel. The result is a dark, rich wine of splendid dimension and aromatic complexity. Lighter vintages drink well after a handful of years, and prove surprisingly attentive to rabbit terrine, while the greater ones deserve putting away for many a year, to develop sumptuous bouquets of undergrowth, tobacco, truffle and game. When mature they appreciate the complex savor of a haunch of venison.

LOIRE VALLEY
A.O.C. Chinon

- *Wine selected:*
  Chinon Coteau de Noiré

- *Grape Variety:*
  Cabernet Franc
- *Average vine age*
  20 years
- *Vineyard size:*
  3 hectares
- *Soil type:*
  Clay and limestone
- *Production:*
  10,000 bottles

Finest Vintages:
2000, 1997, 1996, 1995

Domaine Philippe Alliet
L'Ouche-Mondé
37500 Cravant-les-Côteaux
Tel. (0033) 247 93 17 62
- *Owner:* Philippe Alliet
- *On-site sales:* By appointment
- *Visits:* By appointment
- *Price:* ★

DOMAINE PHILIPPE ALLIET

One of the brightest stars in the Chinon wine-making fraternity is an elusive, hard-working perfectionist who quietly gets on with making some of the appellation's most refined wines, by the name of Philippe Alliet. His estate is small and the amounts produced modest, yet these bottles are well worth taking the time it takes to track down, for they are very classy indeed.

The influence of different soils

Alliet's are wines of finesse rather than body, which may be explained at least in part by the composition of the soils on which the vines lie, for the bulk of the estate is planted in the gravel land below Cravant. As any lover of Médoc and Graves wine knows, gravel is fine for viticulture, being a poor provider of nutrition for the vine and affording a degree of heat retention and excellent drainage... and imparting that prized quality, finesse. Alliet's finest parcel on the other hand, the Coteau de Noiré above the town of Chinon, is of clay and limestone, which generally gives more body and muscle. However even this wine is not as robust as many, for the techniques of the wine maker are not without influence on the final wine!

A courageous decision is taken

Alliet and his wife started out in 1978, cultivating vines which had belonged to his grandfather and others which they rented. The year 1989 marked a turning-point in the business, when they completely changed their working methods in order to attain a higher level of quality. They put an end to the regular sprayings of weedkiller, pesticide and other chemical products and took to ploughing and working the land by machine and hand, ecologically, and at the same time started making concerted attempts to limit their vines' production; they also started waiting longer before harvesting, and picking by hand, which enabled them to sort the fruit as they went, giving raw material of a far higher standard to make into wine. A giant leap had been undertaken...

Refinements in the cellar

Refinements were (and still are) introduced in the cellar. The crop is totally destemmed, then macerated and fermented in cement vats with morning and evening *pigeage* during the fermentation, for some three to four weeks. The wine is then run into barrel for the malolactic fermentation. After trial runs the Alliets found that this gives a less violent marriage between wine and wood, that the oak flavor is better integrated, and that the wines gain in finesse. Thereafter they are aged for twelve months or more and bottled unfined and unfiltered. The oak barrels used are either new or are one-wine-old barrels from Château Margaux's cellars.

Chinon Coteau de Noiré

The Coteau de Noiré produces a dark wine of great richness, depth and complexity. It has good structure and the firmness of its *terroir*, yet so intelligent is Alliet's treatment of the grapes that the taster is struck by its finesse and harmony, and indeed its breed. Here is proof of great attentiveness in the vineyard and intelligence in the vatroom and cellars! Lighter vintages marry well with pigeon pie, richer ones with a saddle of hare.

LOIRE VALLEY
A.O.C. Vouvray

- *Wine selected:*
  Vouvray Le Marigny moelleux

- *Grape Variety:*
  Chenin
- *Average vine age*
  50 years
- *Vineyard size:*
  3 hectares
- *Soil type:*
  Clay and limestone
- *Production:*
  4,000 bottles

Finest Vintages:
2000, 1997, 1996, 1990

Domaine des Aubuisières
32 Rue Gambetta
37210 Vouvray
Tel. (0033) 247 52 61 55
- *Owner:* Bernard Fouquet
- *On-site sales:* 9:00–12:00 a.m.,
  2:30–6:00 p.m.
- *Visits:* Yes
- *Price:* ★★

DOMAINE DES AUBUISIÈRES

There is no secret to making top-quality Vouvray, insists the down-to-earth Bernard Fouquet, one simply has to spend time in the vineyard. Only by doing so can one avoid the pitfalls proffered from time to time by nature and Touraine's capricious weather and bring in a good crop to be vinified. The proof that Fouquet runs his vineyards from close-up is found in each bottle leaving his premises, which contains Vouvray of irreproachable quality.

A young man sets up on his own

Fouquet's father had a vine nursery business, providing him with a ready source of grafted plants for his vineyards as well as a source of revenue. However the nursery business did not interest Bernard, who was far more interested in making wine. He looked around for some vines of his own to buy, found some, and had the great fortune also to find cellars available for rental nearby, which he equipped for the job in hand. From 1982 he was making his own wine, putting into practice the lessons he had learned at the viticulture-enology school he had attended after leaving college, and started off selling most of his production in bulk.

A clientele is built up

By 1988 he had built up something of a clientele and was marketing his wine in bottle. As luck would have it a well-known English high-street retail chain placed an order that year—and indeed remains a loyal customer to this day. Then, thanks to excellent press reviews of his 1988, 1989 and 1990 vintages, his telephone started ringing with regularity, and other foreign importers wanted to buy his wine. The ball was rolling! His father finally took retirement and Bernard Fouquet moved into the family cellars, from which he operates today.

Adapting to rapidly-changing circumstances

Since then there has been no looking back. Yet success has not much changed his way of doing things: he remains an *homme du terrain*, and regards today's technology with a certain mistrust, for it is easy to place too much reliance on it; those growers who prefer to rely on their computers rather than their own observations to tell them when things need doing in the vineyard and the *chai* are heading for trouble!

The essential thing for a *vigneron* is to produce top-quality fruit, insists Fouquet. The more concentrated the grape juice, the easier it is to make good wine... which is why it is essential, despite the difficulties, to harvest selectively by a number of visits to the vineyard. And the Vouvray grower must be able to adapt very rapidly, for in one week things can change dramatically, dictating whether one makes *sec*, *demi-sec* or *moelleux* wine.

Vouvray Le Marigny moelleux

Le Marigny is one of the finest clay and limestone vineyards in Vouvray, giving Fouquet some splendid raw material with which to make a sumptuous *moelleux* when conditions permit. Dried fruit, honey, and spice dominate on the nose of the superb 1996, while the palate displays concentrated *Botrytis* sweetness, a perfect degree of acidity and an underlying chalky mineral element. All in all, Le Marigny is a masterly display of finesse and harmony, to be savored on its own, or with morels in puff-pastry or some Bleu des Causses cheese.

LOIRE VALLEY
A.O.C. Vouvray

- *Wine selected:*
  Vouvray moelleux

- *Grape Variety:*
  Chenin
- *Average vine age*
  35 years
- *Vineyard size:*
  12 hectares
- *Soil type:*
  Siliceous clay
- *Production:*
  20,000 bottles

Finest Vintages:
1997, 1996, 1995, 1990, 1989

Domaine du Clos Naudin
14 Rue de la Croix-Buisée
37210 Vouvray
Tel. (0033) 247 52 71 46
From the centre of Vouvray take the
road towards Vernou. Rue de la Croix-
Buisée is the first on the left, and Clos
Naudin is signposted.
- *Owner:* Philippe Foreau
- *On-site sales:* 8:30–12:00 a.m.,
  2:00–6:30 p.m.
- *Visits:* Yes
- *Price:* ★★

DOMAINE DU CLOS NAUDIN

The Loire Valley is fortunate in having a number of estates which have always produced top-quality wine, unostentatiously maintaining standards throughout the difficult times and showing that their region is capable of great things. One is the Vouvray estate Domaine du Clos Naudin. There Philippe Foreau quietly goes about his work producing masterpieces of harmony and elegance, just as his grandfather Armand and father André did in their day. Clos Naudin is, and always has been, a source of quintessential Vouvray.

Regular hard work in the vineyard

Since taking over responsibilities in 1983 Philippe Foreau's working week has changed little from that of his forebears. Much time is spent among the vines, which all grow in the siliceous clay soil known locally as *perruches*. The work is physically demanding but essential if one is to produce grapes of the highest order. The Chenin is a great vine variety, capable of producing wines of rare distinction, but equally capable of producing liquid of little character if one does not limit its vigor and look after it properly. Therefore the yearly cycle always starts with a severe pruning to limit yield. After that every year is different, and with Touraine's unpredictable weather there is never the same routine in the vineyard.

A very tricky decision

What is constant is the respect for the vineyard environment: ploughing and very limited distribution of organic compost are preferred to weedkiller and fertilizer, obliging the vines to bury their roots deeply for nutrients and bringing out the specific character of each parcel. Nature alone decides how concentrated the grapes will become each year, and Foreau's experience and fine judgement generally manage to identify the right moment to pick correctly. With luck the end-season will be sunny and picking will take place over a number of *tries*, enabling the production of *demi-sec* and *moelleux* wines.

Respect for Nature's bounty

In the cellars also there is total respect for nature's bounty. After a delicate squeeze by pneumatic press —in 1976 André Foreau, in a rare display of innovation, was the first in Vouvray to acquire this technology—the juice is run into three hundred-liter barrels to ferment. There is no use of artificial yeast, no chaptalization, and a bare minimum of SO_2. In the Foreaus' splendid *tuffeau* cellars the temperature is low, fermentations slow, and the wood old but well maintained. And whatever the style of wine, it is bottled before the summer, for more than six months in wood diminishes the Chenin's personality.

Vouvray moelleux

Foreau's wines are all about harmony, as might be expected from someone who abhors extravagance. The complexity and sheer class of his *moelleux* is something every wine lover owes it to himself to experience. On the nose and in the mouth beautifully pure aromatic nuances of peach, greengage, blood orange, apricot, and honey are just some of those which jostle for the taster's appreciation. No two vintages are alike: some are sweeter, fleshier, more opulent, others are leaner, more austere, more cerebral... yet all are a joy to taste, on their own, well chilled, or with *tarte Tatin* or some other sweetmeat.

LOIRE VALLEY
A.O.C. Vouvray

• *Wine selected:*
Vouvray Le Haut-Lieu demi-sec

• *Grape Variety:*
Chenin
• *Average vine age*
30 years
• *Vineyard size:*
9 hectares
• *Soil type:*
Clay and limestone
• *Production:*
40,000 bottles

Finest Vintages:

2000, 1999, 1998, 1996,
1995, 1989, 1988

Domaine Huet
11–13 Rue de la Croix-Buisée
37210 Vouvray
Tel. (0033) 247 52 78 87
• *Owner:* Gaston Huet
• *On-site sales:* 9–12 a.m., 2–6 p.m.
• *Visits:* By appointment
• *Price:* ★

DOMAINE HUET

Gaston Huet is now retired, after a long and distinguished career as grower, member of the INAO, long-time mayor of Vouvray and successful adversary of governmental plans to lay a TGV railway line through Vouvray's best vineyards. He also, incidentally, produced some of Vouvray's landmark vintages, in 1945, 1947, 1959... Wines which are still extraordinarily fresh, complex, and impeccably balanced. His son-in-law Noël Pinguet is now maintaining this fine estate's reputation with consummate talent.

A change to biodynamics

Huet started making wine in 1929, at a time when his family owned one parcel, Le Haut-Lieu. In 1953 he acquired Le Clos du Bourg and added Le Mont to the family holdings five years later. These three parcels constitute the bulk of the estate today, which covers thirty-five hectares.

Pinguet started vinifying the wines in 1976. Like many a young grower he wondered about the state of the vineyard soils, and in 1987 was persuaded to try running a small plot the biodynamic way. By the following year all insecticides and other synthetic products had been banished, and a balanced ecological environment had been recreated in which the natural predators soon appeared again. Treatments against vinous maladies were limited to copper sulphate, sulphur powder, and preparations based on nettles, horse-tail and yarrow; and soil enrichment was limited to one ton per hectare of a home-made mixture of cow dung and straw, spread at the moment of winter ploughing. The results were soon to be seen, and from 1990 Pinguet put the whole estate under a biodynamic regime.

The benefits of the Huet biodynamic adventure speak for themselves: the vineyards hum with life and are conspicuously healthy, the vines are naturally less productive, and the fruit is ready for picking a good week earlier than on other estates. Yet for Pinguet it is a tool and certainly not a religion; and it was not, as on some estates, adopted for show, with limited conviction but great fanfare.

Tank, barrel or chestnut *muid*

Harvesting is carried out painstakingly by successive tries, in order to overcome the problem of uneven ripeness and botrytization. The musts are neither yeasted nor chaptalized, and are fermented in tank, barrel or old chestnut *muid* (hogsheads barrel). The fermentation of the wines with residual sugar is stopped by racking and adding a small amount of SO2. As is traditional in Vouvray, the malolactic fermentation is avoided.

Vouvray Le Haut-Lieu demi-sec

The *demi-sec* style as made by Noël Pinguet is regularly a textbook example of its type: bright gold with a noticeable green tinge, it has an enticing floral fragrance with a suggestion of quince and pears when young, then often develops a certain waxiness and honeyed aspect after a few years. It is ample, succulent and harmonious on the palate, and has a mineral side which adds a little weight to the frivolity of its seductive charm. This *demi-sec* is a delight at any time of day or night, and may be served with sweetbreads or *œufs en meurette*—as prepared in the region, with Vouvray wine—for a real treat.

LOIRE VALLEY
A.O.C. Montlouis

- *Wine selected:*
  Montlouis sec Rémus

- *Grape Variety:*
  Chenin Blanc
- *Average vine age*
  70–80 years
- *Vineyard size:*
  13 hectares
- *Soil type:*
  Siliceous clay over limestone
- *Production:*
  7,000–15,000 bottles

Finest Vintages:
1998, 1997, 1996, 1995

Domaine de la Taille aux Loups
8 Rue des Aîtres — Husseau
37270 Montlouis-sur-Loire
Tel. (0033) 247 45 11 11
The Hamlet Husseau lease off the
D751. From Amboise, pass the
aquarium and take the first on the left,
1 km further on. On arriving in
Husseau, the estate is on the right.
- *Owners:* Blot family
- *On-site sales:* Yes
- *Visits:* Yes
- *Price:* ★

DOMAINE DE LA TAILLE AUX LOUPS

When in a short space of time three of Montlouis' growers reached retirement age without successors, it was natural that local wine broker Jacky Blot should learn about it. As it happened Blot had long harboured a yearning to make his own wine rather than deal in others', and arrangements were reached. In 1988 Domaine de la Taille aux Loups was founded. Over the course of its short existence some remarkably accomplished wines have been made.

The potential of some fine old vines

Blot knew that the vineyards offered were old and contained no clones, and were therefore potentially the source of very fine fruit. From the start he cultivated them by *lutte raisonnée*, ploughing the soil (very rare in the neighborhood) instead of using weedkiller and other chemical products, reducing soil enrichment to the occasional organic manuring, pruning the vines severely, and training them by the *gobelet* shape as opposed to the widely-used *guyot*, which gives high yields and is better suited to red wines. By taking such measures yields have been kept down over the years to a very modest average of thirty-five hectoliters per hectare, and the wines are redolent of *terroir* character.

Sorting tables in the vineyard

Wine is made in the vineyard and not in the cellar, Blot is fond of telling visitors. He delays harvesting as much as possible, and generally starts when others are in full swing or have even finished. Several pickings are carried out, in order to harvest bunches or even parts of bunches at optimum ripeness. The bunches are placed in shallow containers to avoid any crushing, and are then taken to mobile sorting tables in the vineyard. The sorting enables classification into three categories of fruit: the unripe or rotten which will be rejected, the ripe, and the "nobly" rotten. If one wants to find Jacky Blot, locate the tables—he does not move from them during the entire harvest!

Lengthy fermentation in cold tufa cellars

For fruit which has passed its examination, it merely remains to press it softly in a pneumatic Bücher, let it settle for twenty-four hours and then lodge it in the Bordeaux barriques bought second-hand from Château d'Yquem or the traditional 600-liter demi-muids. Fermentation can then follow its lengthy course in the cold tufa cellars, by the action of the grapes' own yeast... and never aided by chaptalization, for a genuine reflection of the year's climate is sought. After which several rackings and a light fining, and then blending of the different barrels. Then, in the Burgundian manner, long aging on the wine's fine lees with *bâtonnage*, and bottling in the autumn of the year following the harvest.

Montlouis sec Rémus

Aged for a year in equal proportions of new and one-year oak, the dry but very rich Rémus is a very eloquent testimony to Blot's talent, a stunning mix of freshness, fleshiness, and refined, ephemeral aroma. Its great concentration on the palate destines it unreservedly for the table, next to a plate of sweetbread for instance, and its acidity (well hidden in the fleshy folds) and length indicate great potential for development in bottle. With wines like this, Montlouis is destined to become very fashionable! Serve it from a carafe, at 52–53°F (11–12°C).

LOIRE VALLEY
A.O.C. Sancerre

- *Wine selected:*
  Sancerre Galinot

- *Grape Variety:*
  Sauvignon Jaune
- *Average vine age*
  40 years
- *Vineyard size:*
  0.8 hectares
- *Soil type:*
  Flint
- *Production:*
  7,000 bottles

Finest Vintages:
2000, 1998, 1997, 1996, 1992,
1990, 1987, 1985, 1982

Domaine Gitton Père & Fils
Chemin de Lavaud
18300 Ménétréol-sous-Sancerre
Tel. (0033) 248 54 38 84
Internet: www.gitton.fr
Once one arrives at Ménétréol the
estate is well signposted.
- *Owners:* Gitton family
- *On-site sales:* Yes
- *Visits:* By appointment
- *Price:* ★

DOMAINE GITTON PÈRE & FILS

Vinifying and bottling separately every interesting parcel one possesses must complicate life a great deal for any wine maker, yet that has always been the Gitton way of doing things. For the casual wine drinker, a visit to the firm's large premises at Ménétréol is a revelation. There he will be shown that Sancerre is not simply the crisp, fruity, thirst-quenching liquid many imagine it to be, but can display a very wide range of aromatic characteristics reflecting geographical origin. No doubt he will want to buy some, for Gitton wines are first class.

A fine estate is pieced together

The firm was founded in 1945 by Marcel Gitton with a half-hectare of land, and over the years has grown as Gitton and his son Pascal, who runs the firm with his Australian wife Denise today, have acquired many plots of land in the best *climats* around Sancerre and Ménétréol, selected for the diversity of their soils. The plots are composed of many different forms of limestone, as well as flinty siliceous soil. Today the Gittons' Sancerre vineyards cover 27 hectares, to which are added 7.5 hectares of Pouilly and Pouilly-sur-Loire, and, since 1989, 13 hectares of Côtes-de-Duras at their Château Lafon, one hour's drive east of Bordeaux.

A range of wines to surprise

Ripeness is very important in the Gitton scheme of things, and organic viticulture coupled with low yields help attain it with greater ease and regularity. Old vines are treasured, for they naturally contribute less fruit, yet of a greater quality; the Vigne du Larrey parcel, for example, was planted between 1947 and 1956, and Galinot in 1959. The fruit is picked on the point of overripeness, when its juice is charged with sugar, or even after it has been affected by *Botrytis cinerea*, giving high potential alcohol.

Wine making is non-interventionist and unhurried. Not only different parcels but also fruit from vines of different ages and different rootstock are vinified apart. Then, whether it is in demi-muid or stainless steel, wines are aged for a long while before bottling, in order to gain fat and richness from their fine lees. The result is a range of wines that are not only aromatically very original and varied but also low in acidity and rich, fleshy, and succulent—in short, very likely to surprise the drinker whose Sancerre experience is limited to the unexceptional!

Sancerre Galinot

The magnificent 80 ares of the east-facing Galinot vineyard owned by the Gittons, situated at 230 meters' altitude on a 25-degree slope, give birth to a sumptuous wine with interesting aging possibilities. The mere sight of its rich golden yellow color, more akin to that of a great Burgundy than a Sancerre, tells the taster that he has something special in his glass. And indeed on the palate this wine stuns with its richness, fleshiness and depth of flavor, with its honeyed, waxy, pears-and-spice aroma. Galinot deserves several years in bottle to round out, and will partner many a dish with talent: grilled lobster, chicken in a coarse salt crust, filet of salmon with braised vegetables. What bliss!

LOIRE VALLEY
A.O.C. Sancerre

- *Wine selected:*
  Sancerre La Bourgeoise

- *Grape Variety:*
  Sauvignon Blanc
- *Average vine age*
  50 years +
- *Vineyard size:*
  4.3 hectares
- *Soil type:*
  Siliceous
- *Production:*
  23,000 bottles

Finest Vintages:
2000, 1999, 1998, 1996, 1990

Domaine Henri Bourgeois
Chavignol
18300 Sancerre
Tel. (0033) 248 78 53 20
Internet: www.bourgeois-sancerre.com
Proceed through Chavignol to the top
of the village. The Henri Bourgeois
shop is on the left, the offices further
down on the left.
- *Owner:* Henri Bourgeois
- *Director:* Jean-Marie Bourgeois
- *On-site sales:* Yes
- *Visits:* By appointment
- *Price:* ★

DOMAINE HENRI BOURGEOIS

Making good wine involves paying attention to a host of small details, Jean-Marie Bourgeois explains to his visitors; if there is a weak link in the chain the end result suffers. The meticulous approach certainly pays off, for the many wines made by the Chavignol firm Henri Bourgeois, which are exported to destinations all around the world, are fine ambassadors.

The growth of an important business

Ten generations of Bourgeois have tended vines and brought their harvest into the family cellars at the top end of the village of Chavignol, which is also highly reputed for its Crottin de Chavignol goat's cheese. Indeed every second door seems to lead into one of the family's cellars, which is understandable when one learns that by tradition each generation adds a new cellar to the family holdings! The business underwent great growth under Henri Bourgeois, who had 2 hectares in 1950 and with his sons patiently built up his landholdings to their impressive current size of 65 hectares. Today the firm's destinies are in the hands of the businesslike yet very hospitable Jean-Marie, aided by his sons and a not insignificant workforce.

A host of small details

The details start in the vineyard, which is run along *lutte raisonnée* lines, with the use of the "sexual confusion" technique to reduce grape worm. Yields are kept to sensible levels by debudding and green harvesting, and once picked the crop is transported to the vatroom with all speed: the interval between picking and the first vinification operations never exceeds 1.30 hours.

A magnificent new four-story winery enables the transfer of all liquids by gravity. The different parcels and *terroirs* are vinified separately. Many of the wines need little if any chaptalization, for effective work in the vineyard enables the fruit to gain at least a degree of alcohol. Use of SO_2 is avoided whenever possible during the wine-making process, CO_2 being preferred to protect against oxidation. After the end of fermentation wines are aged on their fine lees until bottling between February and September in the following year. Finally, one last detail: labeling and packing. Each bottle is visually checked to ensure that its presentation is up to the standard of its contents.

Sancerre La Bourgeoise

The firm produces several top-of-the-range white wines, of which La Bourgeoise is probably the best known. Made from old vines planted on siliceous soils, this wine is fermented 60 percent in stainless steel and 40 percent in oak (one-third of which is new) and then aged on its lees with *bâtonnage* for seven to eight months. After a few more months it is bottled, then left for at least a year before sale. La Bourgeoise is an athlete in peak form: lithe and concentrated yet without an ounce of excess flesh, very refined and perfectly balanced, it has a sumptuous flinty, spicy flavor and great length. This wine, which develops very well over a decade, is a fine partner for sea-perch roasted with fennel, or cold jellied chicken with tarragon. But there is nothing to stop one simply enjoying it while nibbling some Crottin de Chavignol!

LOIRE VALLEY
A.O.C. Sancerre

- *Wine selected:*
  **Sancerre Vendange
  du 21 Octobre 1997**

- *Grape Variety:*
  Sauvignon Blanc
- *Average vine age*
  20 years
- *Vineyard size:*
  1.5 hectares
- *Soil type:*
  Clay and limestone
- *Production:*
  5,000–7,000 bottles

Finest Vintages:
1996, 1990, 1989

Domaine Lucien Crochet
Place de l'Église
18300 Bué
Tel. (0033) 248 54 08 10
From Sancerre follow the D955 towards
Bourges 4 km, then turn right into the
center of Bué. Continue until arriving
in the Place de l'Eglise.
- *Manager:* Gilles Crochet
- *On-site sales:* Yes
- *Visits:* No
- *Price:* ★★

DOMAINE LUCIEN CROCHET

Crochet is a name well known to lovers of Sancerre, and the village of Bué, which lies off the Bourges road several kilometers south of the town, is where one finds nearly all of that tentacular family of growers. The largest and no doubt best-known estate is Domaine Lucien Crochet, the producer of white wines of remarkable harmony and finesse and red wines of great distinction.

A sure touch for quality

Now that Lucien himself is officially retired (yet when if ever does a retired *vigneron* really let go of the reins?) his son Gilles, having graduated in enology at Dijon, is in charge and displaying a sure touch for encouraging top-quality fruit out of his vines and vinifying it with intelligence and understanding.

The firm's 36 hectares are principally situated around Bué, but are also around Sancerre itself, Crézancy and Vinon—none of which are very far away, thankfully, since bringing in the crop quickly is of great importance. As befits a leading estate, all fruit is hand-picked, enabling selectivity in the vineyard. Once back at base the whole bunches of Sauvignon are gently crushed by pneumatic press and their juice chilled and left to settle for eighteen-forty-eight hours, depending on the vintage and the use to which they will be put. Vinification is then carried out in stainless steel vats over twenty to fifty days, and racking is retarded in order to allow wines to feed off their lees and gain in fat and complexity. Bottling takes place in June or September, preceded by a light fining and filtration.

Preserving a long tradition

The red Sancerres made by the Crochets deserve special mention. With them they are reviving a long tradition, for it was red wine which made the area's reputation and brought it durable prosperity until the destruction of the vineyards by phylloxera at the end of the nineteenth century, after which growers replanted with Sauvignon Blanc.

The Pinot Noir crop is destemmed and vatted for fifteen to twenty days with daily *pigeage* and *remontage* for extraction of color, tannin, and aroma. Aging then takes place in both oak and stainless steel for twelve to sixteen months until the wines are ready to be bottled. The regular *cuvée*, La Croix du Roy, is well colored, succulent and rich, while the Cuvée Prestige LC, made only in the best years, is even darker, dense, complex, and structured for a decade or more's development. It is well capable of looking its Côte d'Or cousins in the eye without blushing.

Sancerre Vendange du 21 Octobre 1997

As he occasionally does in exceptional years, ten days after the end of the 1997 harvest Crochet sent his team out to pick the Sauvignon grapes in four parcels which had been left to become more concentrated by *passerillage*. Fermented and aged 75 percent in stainless steel and the remainder in new oak barrels, this dehydrated crop has produced a wine of enormous finesse with a nose combining floral and fruit nuances. Rich yet perfectly dry on the palate, it is ample and harmonious thanks to its impeccable alcohol/acidity balance, and has a long, intense finish. In short just the wine to serve with shellfish cooked with spices, white meats with morels and cream sauce, *foie gras*, or to enjoy on its own, for a moment of delicious hedonism!

LOIRE VALLEY
A.O.C. Sancerre

- *Wine selected:*
  Sancerre Cuvée Edmond

- *Grape Variety:*
  Sauvignon Blanc
- *Average vine age*
  60–80 years
- *Vineyard size:*
  10 hectares
- *Soil type:*
  Marl over kimmeridge clay

Finest Vintages:
2000, 1999, 1996, 1995, 1990, 1989

Domaine La Moussière
SCEA Alphonse Mellot
1 Rue Porte-César
18300 Sancerre
Tel. (0033) 248 54 07 41
Internet : www.a-mellot-sancerre.com
- *Owner:* Alphonse Mellot
- *On-site sales:* Yes
- *Visits:* By appointment
- *Price:* ★★

DOMAINE LA MOUSSIÈRE

That the wines of Sancerre can constitute serious rivals to France's most prestigious appellations is an idea which some would find far-fetched. Yet this proposition is put beyond any doubt by a visit to the cellars of the Alphonse Mellots, where both whites and reds of superlative quality are produced.

A moral obligation

Alphonse Mellot is driven by an unshakeable belief, shared by his son Alphonse, in the potential of Sancerre's magnificent vineyard land and the moral obligation of each grower to produce the very best wine possible. His splendid La Moussière estate is run along thoroughly organic lines, with unremitting working of the soil to promote its micro-organic life and to oblige the vines to bury their roots ever deeper. Contrasting with his parcels, a vineyard tour reveals the sad reality of the compacted soil of numerous neighboring plots, an unmistakable indication of the widespread maltreatment of the soil by the use of weedkiller.

A fervent defender of Sauvignon

For many years Mellot has been trying to persuade his fellow growers that the appellation would benefit from the establishment of a system of *crus*, to give it greater credibility on the world's wine stage. This cultivated, warm-hearted, and generous man has as role-model Burgundy's Côte d'Or, yet he is a fervent defender of Sauvignon, which is so often perceived as good for nothing but light fruity wines. As proof of the grape's capabilities, friends visiting the firm's labyrinth of beautiful vaulted cellars may be invited to taste one or two "exercises de style" such as a magnificently rich, sweet, Sauternes-style wine made from botrytised grapes, or a remarkable Vin Jaune-style wine to rival many a bottle from the Jura.

Extreme measures for quality

Extreme care goes into the making of the La Moussière wines. Low yields favor early ripening, and thus save Mellot the need to chaptalize. All fruit is hand-picked, extreme measures are used to protect the fruit in transit, and a stringent, second selection process is exercised before vinification.

Four wines are made, all of which are of remarkable quality: the La Moussière, in both red and white versions, is aromatic, ripe and succulent, with splendid balance and great elegance. The red *cuvée* Génération XIX, inaugurated by Mellot fils in 1995, is a splendid, well-colored wine of fine bouquet and great finesse, with a tannic structure enabling significant development in bottle. All wines reflect the climatic character of their vintage, making for fascinating vertical tastings.

Sancerre Cuvée Edmond

The oldest Sauvignons produce Cuvée Edmond. Fermented in new oak, this sensual wine is perfectly balanced, with no excess fat and just the right acidity. The absolute ripeness of the fruit gives the wine slightly tropical aromas in most vintages, and one can detect a slight spiciness in years when *Botrytis cinerea* affected some of the crop, such as 1997. Cuvée Edmond ages well over a decade, and is a splendid table companion for braised sweetbreads, or even turbot supreme, which is poached and served with oysters.

LOIRE VALLEY
A.O.C. Pouilly Fumé

- *Wine selected:*
  Pouilly Fumé Silex

- *Grape Variety:*
  Sauvignon
- *Average vine age*
  50 years
- *Vineyard size:*
  2.2 hectares
- *Soil type:*
  Siliceous clay
- *Production:*
  10,000 bottles

Finest Vintages:
2000, 1999, 1996, 1995

Domaine Didier Dagueneau
Le Bourg
58150 Saint-Andelain
Tel. (0033) 386 39 15 62
- *Owner:* Didier Dagueneau
- *On-site sales:* By appointment
- *Visits:* By appointment
- *Price:* ★★

DOMAINE DIDIER DAGUENEAU

Pur Sang, Astéroïde, Silex, Buisson Renard, Chailloux. The mere names of the wines and their eye-catching packaging tell the consumer straight away that these are no run-of-the-mill Pouilly Fumés, and this impression is amply confirmed on tasting. Since the mid-1980s the wines of Didier Dagueneau have been making waves, giving critics and consumers an exciting glimpse of the heights to which Sauvignon Blanc can aspire. Today Dagueneau is without question the leading grower in the region, and the paltry fifty thousand bottles which leave his premises every year are snapped up by top restaurants, retailers, and connoisseurs.

A young man with convictions

Dagueneau has got where he is by the strength of his own convictions. The scion of a local wine family, he was sacked by his father and obliged to set up on his own in 1982. He starting working with oak barrels several years later, and was soon producing wines of great accomplishment. Certain traditionalists said they were not real Pouilly Fumés. His non-conformist personality did little harm to his public relations: the long unkempt hair, bushy beard and an intense look which reputedly earned him the sobriquet "wild man of Saint-Andelain", made Dagueneau eminently newsworthy, not to mention his passion for dogs and sledding.

Recognition and success progressively followed, and in 1989 he was in a position to have new wine-making premises built in Saint-Andelain, giving him much-needed space and enabling him to pursue his ideas and perfect his techniques.

Authenticity and perfection

What does Dagueneau have that others do not? No doubt rare wine-making intuition, and certainly great rigor. Authenticity and perfection have always been his goals. Following a severe pruning at the beginning of the year, no less than three months are spent painstakingly debudding the vines by his conscientious vineyard workers in order to achieve grapes of the finest quality. When the ripening cycle is complete, harvesting is carried out by hand, enabling selectivity of what is picked and what is discarded or left for picking later.

The new wine-making facilities, designed around Dagueneau's vinification methods, use gravity to move liquids and enable him to work without the least compromise or restriction. After fermentation the wines are aged in a handsome barrel cellar containing both demi-muids and *cigares*, the latter a small, elongated barrel made expressly for Dagueneau. The cellar is kept cold to limit the interaction between wine and oak, and avoid the wines taking on too much of the wood's flavor.

Pouilly Fumé Silex

No other silex wines have the firm, austere authority of the Dagueneau offering, an intense, smoky character of great richness, perfect harmony, and impressive length. Disciplined it may be, yet it caresses the palate with its innate charm, indeed the quality of the raw material sings out! The magnificent Silex is in all probability capable of improving over two decades, yet it is altogether irresistible young. Scallop carpaccio is a suitable table mate.

LOIRE VALLEY
A.O.C. Pouilly Fumé

- *Wine selected:*
  Pouilly Fumé Baron de L.

- *Grape Variety:*
  Sauvignon
- *Average vine age*
  40–50 years
- *Vineyard size:*
  100 hectares
- *Soil type:*
  Kimmeridge marl, siliceous
- *Production:*
  120,000 bottles

Finest Vintages:
1996, 1995, 1990, 1989

De Ladoucette
Château du Nozet
58150 Pouilly-sur-Loire
Tel. (0033) 386 39 18 33
- *Owner:* Patrick de Ladoucette
- *On-site sales:* By appointment
- *Visits:* By appointment
- *Price:* ★★★

De Ladoucette

For many years de Ladoucette has been the Pouilly Fumé standard-bearer, exporting its wines all over the world and introducing generations of novice wine drinkers to the pleasures of Sauvignon in its central-Loire interpretation. The region owes much to the firm, which has had an undeniable impact on demand and sales and been the catalyst of much progress.

The extraordinary growth of a family business

This modern success story can be attributed to one young man, Baron Patrick de Ladoucette, who took over the family estate at the tender age of twenty-one in 1972. It had a good reputation and was run at the time by a manager who had been in charge ever since the young man's father had emigrated to Argentina just after the war.

Ladoucette however was not for sitting on the family laurels and envisaged things on a different scale. He invested large sums in updating the wine-making facilities and equipment: temperature-controlled stainless-steel fermentation vats, glass-lined storage vats and a bottling line were some of the principal acquisitions which enabled him to start producing supremely aromatic, crisp, modern Pouilly Fumé, in sizeable quantities. And since the bottles had to be sold, the young man set about the task with energy and talent. Soon it was necessary to start buying raw material to supplement his own production in order to meet demand.

A luxury *cuvée* is born

Since then prosperity has brought diversification: the firm now also produces Sancerre, Vouvray, Chinon, and Bourgueil, has taken over the Chablis producer Albert Pic, and has even invested in California's Napa Valley. The equipment has been renewed again, and great care is lavished on the estate, which lies around the fabulous turreted, fairy-tale Château du Nozet, constructed in 1850 by the architect Viollet-le-Duc for de Ladoucette's forbear Comte Lafond, who was the governor of the Bank of France.

The vineyards are splendidly situated, and the oldest vines in the two best parcels, both on the famous Saint-Andelain slope, are the source of the firm's finest wine, Pouilly Fumé Baron de L. This was inaugurated in 1973 and was France's first "luxury" *cuvée* of Sauvignon, an innovatory stroke of genius from the young proprietor that showed growers what was possible if one raised one's sights a bit and deviated from the traditional way of doing things.

Pouilly Fumé Baron de L

Stringent selection of the raw material and the subsequent juice, use of gravity to move liquids, slow fermentation followed by aging on the wine's lees, little racking, no fining and only light filtering. such are the cares with which this splendid paradox of delicacy and concentration is produced. Richly complex of aroma, round, ample, and intensely flavored on the palate, and leaving in its wake a magnificently long, complex flavor trail, Baron de L is a model of harmony, elegance and breed. This aristocrat likes nothing but the full attention of those in his company. Yet he is not averse to the unschooled interruptions of a *tartare de saumon*, or a scallop carpaccio.

LOIRE VALLEY
A.O.C. Pouilly Fumé

- *Wine selected:*
  Pouilly Fumé Château de Tracy

- *Grape Variety:*
  Sauvignon
- *Average vine age*
  25 years
- *Vineyard size:*
  30 hectares
- *Soil type:*
  Kimmeridge limestone,
  siliceous clay
- *Production:*
  200,000 bottles

Finest Vintages:

2000, 1996

Château de Tracy
Tracy-sur-Loire
58150 Pouilly-sur-Loire
Tel. (0033) 386 26 15 12
The château sits above the small
village of Tracy. One cannot miss it!
- *Owner:* Comtesse d'Assay
- *Manager:* Comte Henry d'Assay
- *On-site sales:* By appointment
- *Visits:* By appointment
- *Price:* ★

CHÂTEAU DE TRACY

The "other" château producing Pouilly Fumé, which has a slightly lower profile yet makes wine of splendid purity and authenticity, is Château de Tracy, which dominates the village of the same name at the northern end of the appellation. This is the senior Pouilly estate in historical terms, having been the scene of viticulture for some six centuries.

Scots in the service of Charles VII

Château de Tracy belongs to the Comtesse d'Estutt d'Assay, whose family have resided on the spot since the sixteenth century. The family was originally from Scotland: the Stutts of Lagan crossed the Channel to serve Charles VII against the occupying English in the fifteenth century, and were rewarded with lands in Assay in the Berry region, acquiring Château de Tracy later on through marriage.

Wine growing was mentioned on a parchment as early as 1396. It continued in the eighteenth and nineteenth centuries, when there were 50 hectares under vine. The vineyard was abandoned after the 1929 crisis, until being replanted in the 1950s by Count Alain d'Assay, the late husband of the Countess. Today it covers 30 hectares, lying on the coteaux of Tracy and of Vilmoy, and is run by their son Henry.

Stimulating the vine's natural resources

Quality is the guiding principle on the estate, and Henry d'Assay and his team are permanently looking for ways to improve their work. In the mid-1990s great advances were made when they adopted a *conduite intégrée* strategy, with the aim of using and stimulating the vineyard ecosystem's natural resources and mechanisms. Since then phytopharmaceutical products have been used only when there is no other solution, and then only in minimal doses. Insecticide is no longer used and phytosanitary treatments have been halved in four years, giving the rewarding sight of the insects' natural predators once more in the vineyard. Working the soil naturally and enriching it with home-made organic compost has increased the soils' micro-organic life and the vines' natural resistance.

Vinification rendered more natural

By reducing foliage around the bunches, the ripeness and condition of the grapes has been improved, enabling the Count to cease or greatly reduce chaptalization of musts. Low yields have also played an important part in the ripening cycle.

Interventions during the wine-making process have also been refined and reduced. The wine's lees are now stirred for the initial six months of aging, imparting richer flavor and consistency. Fining and filtration have been reduced, cold stabilization has been largely ceased, and selectivity of the vats going to make up the Château de Tracy wine has become more rigorous.

Pouilly Fumé Château de Tracy

All these measures today give a wine which is intensely aromatic, ripe, and pure, a splendid expression of Sauvignon from these historic vineyards. The exquisite fragrance, a mix of citrus and exotic fruit, gunflint and a touch of smokiness, is absolutely faithful to its origins; and the wine's harmony is total, the richness and ripeness of the fruit proving a perfect counterbalance to the wine's natural acidity. Château de Tracy is best drunk several years after the vintage, with a plateful of oysters or some fresh salmon cooked *en papillote*.

ALSACE
A.O.C. Alsace Grand Cru

- *Wine selected:*
  Riesling Geisberg
  Vendange Tardive
  Grand Cru

- *Grape Variety:*
  Riesling
- *Average vine age:*
  40 years
- *Vineyard size:*
  1.5 hectares
- *Soil type:*
  Clay and limestone
- *Production:*
  1,500 bottles

Finest Vintages:
1997, 1995, 1989, 1988

Domaine André Kientzler
50 Route de Bergheim
68150 Ribeauvillé
Tel. (0033) 389 73 67 10
André Kientzler's estate lies on the
Route des vins between Ribeauvillé
and Bergheim.
- *Owner:* André Kientzler
- *On-site sales:* By appointment
- *Visits:* By appointment
- *Price:* ★★

DOMAINE ANDRÉ KIENTZLER

The fairytale village of Ribeauvillé, which has long been a preferred tourist destination, is surrounded by some of Alsace's finest vineyards, marl and sandstone slopes of a quality which has been recognized and exploited since at least the mid-eighth century. These soils are ideal for that noble among nobles, the Riesling, and in the hands of a grower named André Kientzler the soil/grape coupling gives wines of extraordinary refinement, precision, and elegance.

Authenticity at the expense of fashion

The jewels of the 11-hectare Kientzler estate are his holdings in the village's three splendid *Grands Crus*, Geisberg, Kirchberg, and Osterberg. Drawing on the know-how of the five preceding generations and employing viticultural methods enabling these *terroirs* to assert their personality in the grapes, Kientzler makes wines of pure authenticity in which geographical identity is privileged above all; he does not view the achievement of residual sugar as very important, contrary to most in Alsace today, and as a result his wines are often a little austere and have less charm than others when young. It is with bottle-age that they become really irresistible.

The eternal quest for quality

His father and the previous generations made their wine in the cramped family cellars in the center of the village, yet with the logistical problems caused by the increasing tourist frequentation of Ribeauvillé's narrow streets, and the impossibility of finding extra space in the village in which to work, Kientzler took the decision to move out in 1972. Since then he has enjoyed a splendidly functional and roomy winery and home among the vines.

In the vineyards and subsequently in his new cellars he allows himself no compromise in the never-ending quest for quality. Eschewing chemical products inasmuch as is possible, he keeps the vineyards totally or partially grassed over, depending on their steepness, and goes out of his way to limit the vines' yields to levels compatible with the highest quality. As a rule he picks his crop fairly early, preferring pure fruitiness and rapier-like acidity to the richness of higher sugar levels. All picking is done by hand, enabling draconian selectivity of the fruit before it finds its way to the vatroom.

Riesling Geisberg Grand Cru Vendange Tardive

The small clay and limestone terraces of the south-facing Geisberg slope are particularly well-suited to the Riesling. Occasionally, despite relatively early harvesting, the severe selection throws up a small amount of overripe fruit with which Kientzler can make a Vendange Tardive.

A fine deep gold in color, this wine has a splendidly pure nose suggesting crystallized grapes and citrus fruit, with a slight smokiness. On the palate the attack is rich, the density and concentration magnificent, and the harmony between sugar and acidity remarkable—a triumph of athletic opulence. On the dry side of off-dry, this superb Riesling, besides being a delight to sip on its own, is a marvelous accompaniment to pan-fried *foie gras* or sweet and sour dishes, suggests Kientzler. The wine can improve over many years, and benefits from being decanted.

ALSACE
A.O.C. Alsace Grand Cru

- *Wine selected:*
Grand Vin de l'Altenberg de Bergheim
Grand Cru

- *Grape Varieties:*
Riesling 70%,
Gewurztraminer/Tokay Pinot Gris
30% (approximately)
- *Average vine age:*
15-20
- *Vineyard size:*
1.5 hectares
- *Soil type:*
Clay, limestone, sandstone
- *Production:*
3,000 bottles

Finest Vintages:
2000, 1999, 1998, 1997, 1995

Domaine Marcel Deiss
15 Route du Vin
68750 Bergheim
Tel. (0033) 389 73 63 37
- *Owner:* Jean–Michel Deiss
- *On-site sales:* Yes
- *Visits:* 8–12 a.m., 2–5 p.m.
(Monday-Friday)
- *Price:* ★★★

DOMAINE MARCEL DEISS

His convictions concerning the importance of the notion of *terroir* have led Jean-Michel Deiss, one of Alsace's most gifted wine makers, to produce a magnificent range of single-vineyard wines, and taking the idea further, to produce a multi-variety wine in the hallowed Altenberg de Bergheim vineyard which, not being a single-grape wine, was of course ineligible for the *Grand Cru* AOC under 1970s wine legislation. Yet the quality of the wine and the evident sense of his convictions, which in reality demand nothing more than a return to the ancestral practices of days long gone, have stimulated official willingness to reassess the rules.

Early proponents of the single-vineyard wine

The Deiss estate was founded by Marcel, father of Jean-Michel, in 1949, and today covers 27 hectares, the jewels of which are parcels in the *Grands Crus* Altenberg de Bergheim, Mambourg and Schoenenbourg, as well as seven other quality *lieux-dits*. The Deiss family started making and marketing individual wines from their various parcels long before it became the trend, and the expression of *terroir* in a wine is the pivotal point of the family philosophy.

Capturing the nuances of *terroir*

The geological subtleties of each parcel can only be captured by obliging vines to bury their roots deep down in the subsoil; if they are allowed a lazy existence, as in vineyards treated with chemical fertilizer, their roots will spread horizontally and they will feed in the topsoil, and only varietal character will flavor the wine. All the efforts of Deiss and his team are therefore spent ensuring vine roots go downwards: plots are toiled by hand, and even pickaxes are used to break roots foolhardy enough to loiter near the surface; the vines are rarely fed compost, and when they are, it consists of the specially prepared substances recommended by the biodynamic precepts which Deiss progressively adopted from 1997 onwards; and the vines are planted extremely densely, at ten thousand per hectare (indeed even twelve thousand in the Mambourg parcel), creating competition for the nutrients to be found in the subsoil and acting as a natural brake upon their vigor. The plants also undergo a draconian pruning at the beginning of the year with the aim of limiting their yields to levels compatible with the highest quality.

Grand Vin de l'Altenberg de Bergheim

Since 1994 Deiss has produced a "Grand Vin" from a mixture of varieties grown together in the Altenberg vineyard, acting on his conviction that *terroir* is better served if not limited to a single variety, which is nothing more than a return to the past practice of complantation. Surprisingly, when different varieties are grown together their ripening cycles are identical, and at similar yields attain the same degree of potential alcohol.

Grand Vin de l'Altenberg de Bergheim is a wine of great refinement and delicacy, subtlety even, of tantalizing lemon, spice and rose-petal aroma, nuanced with caramel and honey; yet it is rich, ample in body, lively in acidity, and absolutely harmonious. It blossoms more readily if poured into a decanter, and is a delight to sip on its own, or with a Bresse chicken prepared with honey.

ALSACE
A.O.C. Alsace Grand Cru

- *Wine selected:*
**Gewurztraminer Fürstentum
Vendanges Tardives**
Grand Cru

- *Grape Variety:*
Gewurztraminer
- *Average vine age:*
30+ years
- *Soil type:*
Stony
- *Production:*
4,600 bottles

Finest Vintages:
2000, 1999, 1997, 1996, 1995

Domaine Paul Blanck
32 Grand'Rue
68240 Kientzheim
Tel. (0033) 389 78 23 56
Internet: www.blanck.com
- *Owner:* Domaine Paul Blanck
- *On-site sales:* 9:00–11:45 a.m.,
1:30–6:00 p.m. (5 p.m. Sat.). Closed
on Sundays and bank holidays
- *Visits:* Yes
- *Price:* ★★★

DOMAINE PAUL BLANCK

In true Alsace tradition the Blanck dynasty has been making wine since time immemorial. The business is a veritable family affair today, and seemingly set for a long future in the hands of coming generations. The family produces an extended range of wines of very high quality from their splendid holdings around their village of Kientzheim and in the vicinity.

A profusion of *Grands Crus* and *lieux-dits*
The Blancks can trace their lineage back to Hans Planck, born in 1591, who acquired his first vines in 1610. They already owned a parcel of the Schlossberg vineyard in the first half of the eighteenth century, and have been established at Kientzheim since the beginning of the nineteenth. Since then the estate has been greatly extended and now comprises land over eight communes, giving them great variety in their raw material and an insurance policy against the risks of frost and hail. Besides the parcel of Schlossberg splendid south-facing vineyard of terraces and granitic soils there are parcels in four other *Grands Crus*, totaling in all an impressive 12 hectares: Fürstentum, Mambourg, Sommerberg, and Wineck-Schlossberg; and in four *lieux-dits*: Patergarten, Altenbourg, Grafreben, and Rosenbourg.

A change of generation
Following the example of Paul Blanck, who with other growers formulated the guidelines for viticulture and vinification of Schlossberg in 1927, Bernard and Marcel, his sons, played an important role in the creation of the Alsace Grand Cru appellation in 1975, of which the first beneficiary was Schlossberg, that same year. Finally, in 1985 the cousins Frédéric and Philippe Blanck, the sons of Bernard and Michel, took over responsibilities for production and marketing.

Wines for every occasion
The Blancks' aim is to provide a range of wines perfectly representative of their grape varieties and *terroirs*, which show well at the dining table. Working in large cellars lined with stainless-steel vats and *foudres*, Frédéric, the wine maker, makes three levels of wine: the generics, what they term *vins de fruit*, which are made for easy drinking, and which will hopefully seduce the novice into a deeper brush with the Alsace experience; the *vins de pierre*, in which the characteristics of the various named sites are brought out, giving another dimension to the fruitiness; and the late-harvested wines, which are a demonstration of the wonders of nature: rare, opulent, exuberant wines for the special occasion.

Gewurztraminer Fürstentum Vendanges Tardives
It was Marcel Blanck who clamored for the recognition of Fürstentum, a steep, hot, south-facing slope in which Mediterranean-type flora thrive. In its marl/sandstone/limestone soil the Gewurztraminer produces wine of great finesse and aromatic power, reaching Vendanges Tardives maturity with easy regularity. The 1997, relatively dry on the palate, has an intense bouquet of rose-petal and pineapple, with a splendid concentration of spicy flavor on the palate and enough acidity to balance its alcohol and give the wine freshness. It signs off with a splendidly long, slightly smokey finish, and is a wine to please the most exacting Alsace aficionado. Serve it from a decanter, suggest the Blancks, with natural goose livers.

ALSACE
A.O.C. Alsace Grand Cru

- *Wine selected:*
  Riesling Rangen de Thann
  Clos Saint Urbain
  Grand Cru

- *Grape Variety:*
  Riesling
- *Average vine age:*
  40 and 15 years
- *Vineyard size:*
  2 hectares
- *Soil type:*
  Volcanic, sedimentary
- *Production:*
  6,000 bottles

Finest Vintages:
2000, 1998, 1997, 1996, 1995, 1993

Domaine Zind-Humbrecht
4 Route de Colmar
68230 Turckheim
Tel. (0033) 389 27 02 05
- *Owners:* Léonard & Olivier Humbrecht
- *On-site sales:* 10–12 a.m.,
  2:30–6:00 p.m. (by appointment)
- *Visits:* By appointment
- *Price:* ★★★

DOMAINE ZIND-HUMBRECHT

Just how far is it possible to go in expressing the multiple geological nuances of Alsace's best *terroirs* through the juice of the region's noble grape varieties? For the answer there is perhaps one domaine which provides a greater portfolio than all others, that every year provides a magnificent selection of wines nuanced by the latest vintage's climatic particularities. For many Zind-Humbrecht is the ultimate Alsace estate.

A magnificent estate is built up

Though the Humbrechts have been making wine since 1620, the estate as we know it had its origins in the amalgamation of two family estates, brought about on the occasion of the marriage of Léonard Humbrecht to Geneviève Zind in 1959. Today stretching over 40 hectares it is one of Alsace's largest; Rangen, Hengst, Goldert, Brand—the estate is well endowed in *Grand Cru* land, thanks to Léonard Humbrecht's astute acquisitions over the years, and also comprises other parcels of superlative quality, notably Herrenweg, Rotenberg, Clos Jebsal, Clos Hauserer, and Clos Windsbuhl.

The champion of yield limitation

The disciplined cultivation of these parcels is at the root of Zind-Humbrecht's pre-eminence. The vines are densely planted and pruned mercilessly to restrict their productivity, and spared subjection to chemical products. Indeed the owners have adopted biodynamic precepts in certain parcels. Over the course of the years Léonard Humbrecht has been untiring in his efforts at promoting yield limitation;

the maximum permitted in the *Grands Crus* should not be 70 hectoliters per hectare, believe the Humbrechts, but half that quantity.

A very particular vineyard slope

The jewel in the crown of this estate could well be its 5.5 hectares of the Rangen de Thann vineyard. The excellence of this, Alsace's most southern vineyard, has been recognized since the Middle Ages: unique in Alsace for its ruddy-brown carboniferous soil of volcanic rock and sandstone sediment, andesite and volcanic tufa, it faces due south, has a 70-degree slope, which makes terracing necessary for viticulture, and lies above the small river Thur, which spares its lower part the inconvenience of spring frosts and provides humid conditions attractive to the *Botrytis cinerea* fungus.

Riesling Rangen de Thann Clos Saint-Urbain

Having let the *terroir* express itself fully through natural viticulture, Olivier Humbrecht then leaves the grapes well alone during fermentation, obstinately refusing to prefilter, to chaptalize, to add yeast, to fine, and so on. The result is one of the most powerful, racy, and rich Rieslings in existence. Rather austere in its first years, it fills out and becomes progressively more eloquent over time; whatever the style—in 1998 the grapes attained *surmaturité*, with some *Botrytis*; the following year all sugar was fermented out—it amply repays a dozen years' patience or more. Pan-fried fresh duck's liver draws the Rangen into conversation without fail, while lobster *à l'américaine* really engages its attention!

ALSACE
A.O.C. Alsace

- *Wine selected:*
Riesling Clos Ste.-Hune

- *Grape Variety:*
Riesling
- *Average vine age:*
40-50 years
- *Vineyard size:*
1.3 hectares
- *Soil type:*
Calcareous marl
- *Production:*
6,000 bottles

Finest Vintages:
2000, 1998, 1996, 1995,
1990, 1989, 1985, 1983

Domaine F.E. Trimbach
15 Route de Bergheim
68150 Ribeauvillé
Tel. (0033) 389 73 60 30
Domaine Trimbach is opposite the
cemetery on the Bergheim road.
- *Owners:* Trimbach family
- *On-site sales:* 9–12 a.m., 2–5 p.m.
- *Visits:* Yes
- *Price:* ★★★★

DOMAINE F. E. TRIMBACH

Not for nothing does the Ribeauvillé family firm F. E. Trimbach have a worldwide reputation, for it makes some of the very finest Alsace; lean, racy wines for the connoisseur which develop beautifully with time, wines which are stripped to the bare essentials, enabling their purity and class to shine through without the distraction of the residual sugar needed by so many others. Riesling, that most noble of Alsace varieties, is the Trimbach speciality.

Twelve generations in the service of Alsace

The family can trace its existence in Alsace back to 1626, the year Jean Trimbach arrived in Riquewihr. Successive generations all devoted their working lives to wine, as growers, coopers or otherwise, but it was Frédéric-Émile who really established the Trimbach reputation outside the region in the late nineteenth century. His son Théodore moved the business to Ribeauvillé, and it is the latter's great-grandsons Pierre and Jean, the twelfth generation, who run the business today, the former taking care of the wine-making, the latter of public relations.

Brand names and absurd regulations

Over the years the family has pieced together a fine estate which today covers 27 hectares, spread over six villages. They have for years bolstered their own production with bought-in grapes, working in close collaboration with a hundred-odd growers, buying nothing which is not of irreproachable quality. The estate comprises parcels in the three *Grands Crus* Geisberg, Osterberg, Mandelberg and the entire 1.38 hectares of Clos Ste.-Hune, a particularly remarkable parcel lying in the heart of the *Grand Cru* Rosacker, as well as other parcels of village land.

Despite these prestigious holdings it has never been Trimbach policy to market wines as *Grand Cru*. They prefer to make blends with brand names: their superb *cuvée* Frédéric-Emile, for instance, is sourced in both Geisberg and Osterberg, and their top Gewurztraminer goes by the name Cuvée des Seigneurs de Ribeaupierre. The top wine Clos Ste. Hune, on the other hand, is a single-cru wine, yet they cannot claim the *Grand Cru* AOC for it, because absurd regulations forbid the use of the AOC if it is owned in its entirety by one firm! The firm could label it Rosacker Grand Cru, but given the relative ordinariness of the *cru* compared with the clos lying within it, that would be pointless!

Riesling Clos Ste. Hune

In the opinion of many connoisseurs Clos Ste. Hune is quite simply the finest dry Riesling wine made anywhere in the world. It represents the quintessence of the house style of purity, richness, and reserve, and is generally very austere in its youth, for which reason the firm only sells it when it has had at the very least three years in bottle. Always a very mineral wine, it reacts to the passage of time in various ways depending on the vintage, taking on a wax, resin, petrol, balsamic, or spice character, while at the same time its fruit rounds out and becomes richer, and its finish lengthens and intensifies. Clos Ste.-Hune has great innate harmony and enormous class, and adores the company of the finest products of sea and river: turbot, sole, perch, lobster.

ALSACE
A.O.C. Alsace

- *Wine selected:*
**Gewurztraminer
Sélection de Grains Nobles**

- *Grape Variety:*
Gewurztraminer
- *Average vine age:*
30 years
- *Vineyard size:*
12 hectares
- *Soil type:*
Clay and limestone
- *Production:*
2,000–8,000 bottles

Finest Vintages:
2000, 1997, 1989

Hugel & Fils
68340 Riquewihr
Tel. (0033) 389 47 92 15
Internet: www.hugel.com
Hugel's premises lie in the heart of
the oldest, most picturesque part of
Riquewihr.
- *Owners:* Hugel family
- *On-site sales:* Yes
- *Visits:* Monday to Friday midday,
by appointment
- *Price:* ★★★★

HUGEL & FILS

For many years the family firm Hugel & Fils of Riquewihr has been Alsace's most unswerving and loyal champion in all the countries where fine wine is drunk. Yet it has not been just the Hugels' globe-trotting promotional endeavours that have made the yellow label famous around the world, for the different bottles all regularly provide excellent drinking.

Established in 1639

His forebears had already been established in Alsace for several centuries when Hans Ulrich Hugel started his own wine-making business in 1639. His son built a fine house in the rue des Cordeliers, and progressive generations carefully tended their vines, pressed their grapes and made wine, gradually acquiring an excellent reputation. In 1902 Frédéric Émile Hugel moved the business to the premises that they occupy today in the center of the pretty village.

Growers and men of action

By the beginning of the twentieth century, however, Alsace's wine industry was in depression after the successive attacks of oidium, mildew, and Phylloxera, and its vineyards planted with inferior hybrids favored by its German masters. Frédéric Émile was one of the small band of determined growers who decided that something had to be done, and with Alsace once more under French sovereignty after World War I, pioneered the planting of the noble varieties we know today.

His son Jean carried on improving the wines, and Jean's sons Georges, Jean, and André were among the first to produce the Vendanges Tardives and Sélection de Grains Nobles styles, and worked hard to formulate and get passed into law the texts that have defined and protected these wines since 1984. Now it is the thirteenth generation of Jean-Philippe, Marc, and Étienne who face the challenge of ensuring Alsace's and Hugel's continuing prosperity in the face of ever-improving foreign competition.

Careful, hands-off vinification

Hugel today owns 26 hectares, which include one-third of Riquewihr's *Grand Cru* Sporen and a large chunk of its Schoenenbourg, and also buy in the produce of 115 hectares belonging to other growers. At the root of the wines' quality are low yields, hand-picking, use of free-run wine only, and careful, hands-off vinification without additives. And when the wine is not up to scratch the firm does not hesitate in selling it off in bulk.

Gewurztraminer Sélection de Grains Nobles

By chance Hugel's 350th anniversary coincided with a superlative vintage in which record sugar levels were attained by unprecedented *Botrytis* development. The last Gewurztraminer grapes in the Sporen vineyard were picked on November 9th, and this, the resulting wine (the Hugels do not put vineyard names on their labels), reached its equilibrium at 13.35 percent with 153 grams of residual sugar per liter. After a decade in bottle it has developed a rich amber-gold hue, and its intense, concentrated, honeyed bouquet, with the varietal spiciness and the tanginess of the *Botrytis* adding tonus to the richly overripe flavor, is memorable. It is splendidly smooth and sweet on the palate, and perfectly balanced by its acidity. Remarkably long and complex on the finish, it is best enjoyed on its own if one is to appreciate fully this wine's exceptional quality.

ALSACE
A.O.C. Alsace

- *Wine selected:*
  Tokay Pinot Gris
  Quintessence de Grains Nobles

- *Grape Variety:*
  Tokay Pinot Gris
- *Vineyard size:*
  1 hectare
- *Soil type:*
  Calcareous marl
- *Production:*
  400 bottles

Finest Vintages:
2000, 1998, 1997, 1996, 1995

**Domaine Weinbach – Colette Faller
et ses Filles**
Clos des Capucins
68240 Kaysersberg
Tel. (0033) 389 47 13 21
- *Owners:* Colette, Catherine &
  Laurence Faller
- *On-site sales:* 9–12 a.m., 2–6 p.m.
  (except Sundays)
- *Visits:* No
- *Price:* ★★★★

DOMAINE WEINBACH-COLETTE FALLER ET SES FILLES

The historic Weinbach estate, lying just outside the village of Kaysersberg, is one of Alsace's finest. Its owners, Madame Colette Faller and her daughters Catherine and Laurence, produce a range of wines of great elegance, finesse, and breed: the basic generic wines are as good as many growers' more select wines, and the rarer top-of-the-range *cuvées* are very memorable bottles, with great potential for improvement over time. Behind the unmistakeable Weinbach labels (complicated masterpieces of calligraphic art!) lie some of Alsace's most exquisite wines.

Three ladies safeguard a historic reputation

Before the French Revolution the estate was a monastery and housed an independant branch of Franciscan monks known as Capucins, who were very active growers and wine makers. The buildings lay next to a walled vineyard, and buildings and vineyard have since become known as Clos des Capucins, a fact which is advertised by a special neck label on bottles of the Fallers' wine.

Having passed into lay hands after the Revolution, the estate was acquired by the brothers Théodore and Jean-Baptiste Faller in 1898. Théo Faller of the succeeding generation, late husband of Colette, was responsible to a great degree for hoisting the estate to the position it occupies today, yet after his death in 1979 his widow resolutely filled his shoes, raising the reputation even higher and even enlarging the estate.

The magnificent vineyards of Kaysersberg

The estate is large by Alsacian standards, covering 26 hectares around Kaysersberg and Kientzheim.

While the 5.2-hectare Clos des Capucins might be said to be the jewel in the Weinbach crown, the family are also the proud owners of 8 hectares of the famed Schlossberg vineyard, the first vineyard to be officially classified *Grand Cru* in 1975. There are also parcels in two other *Grands Crus*, yet whether from that vineyard category or from less prestigious slopes, the generally high quality of all the grapes brought in at harvest-time is indicative of the talent and perfectionism of the Fallers.

All the Alsace vine varieties are grown, with Riesling taking up the lion's share of the vineyards—the Schlossberg soils are particularly well suited to it—and Gewurztraminer also occupying a large proportion of the estate. Viticultural methods may be described as biological, with high plantation density, and green harvests contributing to the achievement of that rarity in Alsace, low yields.

Tokay Pinot Gris Quintessence de Grains Nobles

The Tokay Pinot Gris vine is remarkably susceptible to the attentions of *Botrytis cinerea*, and on occasion the Fallers are able to make the glorious Quintessence. To fête its one hundred years of existence, Domaine Weinbach marketed the Cuvée du Centenaire, the result of one *trie* of entirely *Botrytis*-affected grapes from the *lieu-dit* Altenbourg. Fermented in wood by the action of indigenous yeast, this extraordinary wine is memorable for its concentration, aromatic complexity, and excellent acidity. A masterpiece of spicy, opulent richness, it will certainly last decades. It is perhaps best enjoyed on its own, in humble appreciation of Nature's great bounty!

JURA
A.O.C. Côtes-du-Jura

- *Wine selected:*
  Côtes du Jura Vin Jaune

- *Grape Variety:*
  Savagnin
- *Average vine age:*
  35 years
- *Vineyard size:*
  6 hectares
- *Soil type:*
  Clay and limestone
- *Production:*
  6,500 *clavelins*
  (The traditional Vin Jaune bottle,
  the *clavelin*, contains 62 cl.)

Finest Vintages:
1994, 1990, 1989, 1988, 1985

Château d'Arlay
Route de Saint-Germain
39140 Arlay
Tel. (0033) 384 85 04 22
Internet: www.arlay.com
From Arlay take the Saint-Germain-lès-
Arlay direction; the château is at the
edge of the village, on the right.
- *Owner:* Comte Alain de Laguiche
- *On-site sales:* 9–12 a.m., 2–6 p.m.
  (by appointment on Sundays)
- *Visits:* Yes
- *Price:* ★★

CHÂTEAU D'ARLAY

The Jura region, nestling between the Bresse plain east of Burgundy and the Alpine foothills, is a hiker's delight of forests, limestone cliffs, rivers, and lush pasture, and boasts wines to match its dramatic scenery: splendidly original drinks made with vine varieties some of which are seen little if at all elsewhere. The region's most prestigious estate, and one of its best wine producers, is Château d'Arlay, a *monument historique* situated ten kilometers north of Lons-le-Saunier.

A thousand years of turbulent history

As far back as the ninth century a fortress was built on the Arlay hill, which dominates the surrounding countryside, and a castle was built on the spot. An estate progressively built up around it in the Middle Ages by the Counts of Chalon-Arlay, Princes of Orange. Destroyed, rebuilt, it has witnessed the turmoil of a thousand years' history during which it passed through the hands of English, Spanish, and French royalty, yet has never been sold during the course of its existence.

The estate was inherited by Count Renaud de Laguiche through his marriage with a daughter of the De Vogüé family. Like others in the region its vineyards had shrunk to a fraction of their pre-phylloxera size, and in 1960 he set about replanting and making a successful business of it. Since 1995 his son, Count Alain, has presided over its destinies.

A curious regional wine-making tradition

The Arlay hill is indeed a splendid site for viticulture. Its subsoil is of limestone and rich marl, and the vines—Pinot Noir, Trousseau, Poulsard, Chardonnay and Savagnin—are planted on the southern slope and enjoy long hours of sunlight and protection from the northern winds.

At Château d'Arlay the whole gamut of the region's specialities are produced, including of course a Vin Jaune. This wine, Jura's crowning glory, is only produced in the better vintages, those when an Indian summer enables the Savagnin to develop some 14–15 percent potential alcohol. The particularity of the wine lies in its *élevage*: once fermented it must be left in old barrels for at least six years without any topping up to replace the proportion of wine which evaporates. A thin layer of yeasts forms on its surface (what is known in sherry-making as *flor*), which imparts a special flavor and prevents the wine from turning into vinegar.

Côtes du Jura Vin Jaune

This is the only white wine which benefits inestimably from being served relatively warm, at 62–64°F (16–18°C). Deep golden in color, the Château d'Arlay's bouquet is always complex and multi-faceted, invariably nutty yet also spicy, with aromas of raisins and other dried fruit, resin, ginger, and as it gets older, coffee, wild mushrooms, and truffle. Like all Vin Jaune it is bone-dry and slightly bitter to taste, yet this one is both very rich and remarkably refined, with good balancing acidity and a remarkably long finish.

It is a gourmet's dream: Bresse fowl with cream and morels, cooked in Vin Jaune, is the classic accompanying dish, yet this wine gets on famously with almost everything that the sea produces, as it does with snails cooked in garlic, *foie gras* and mountain cheeses. Arlay's Vin Jaune is certainly one of France's greatest wines.

JURA
A.O.C. Château-Chalon

• *Wine selected:*
  Château-Chalon

• *Grape Variety:*
  Savagnin
• *Average vine age:*
  20 years
• *Vineyard size:*
  4 hectares
• *Soil type:*
  Clay and limestone
• *Production:*
  6,000 bottles
  (The traditional Vin Jaune bottle,
  the *clavelin*, contains 62 cl.)

Finest Vintages:
1995, 1993, 1992, 1990, 1988, 1983

Domaine Jean Macle
Rue de la Roche
39210 Château-Chalon
Tel. (0033) 384 85 21 85
• *Owner:* Domaine Jean Macle
• *On-site sales:* 9:00–12:00 a.m.,
  2:30–7:00 p.m. (by appt. on Sundays)
• *Visits:* Yes
• *Price:* ★★

DOMAINE JEAN MACLE

The most prestigious appellation in the Jura is Château-Chalon, which applies exclusively to Vin Jaune produced around the villages Domblans, Menétru-le-Vignoble, Nevy, Voiteur, and the hill-top Château-Chalon itself. This wine, rated one of France's five greatest white wines by Curnonsky, the *prince des gastronomes*, is recognized as having exceptional finesse and delicacy. A tasting in Jean Macle's cellars in Château-Chalon certainly bears out this theory.

The past glories of an ancient vineyard

Vines have been grown around Voiteur since time immemorial, and according to Pliny the Younger and Martial the wines were much appreciated by the Romans. The history of the village of Château-Chalon is inextricably linked with that of its Abbey, whose Abbesses saw to it that the wine's reputation was held high throughout the Middle Ages. Legend has it that they imported some Tokay vines from their sisters in Hungary, and that these, thriving in the region, with time became the Savagnin. The Revolution unfortunately saw them stripped of their lands, which were then dispersed.

A special soil and microclimate

Château-Chalon earned the right to its own appellation in 1936 thanks to its special soil, a blue-gray marl, in which are mixed the stony debris of the dominating cliff, contributing to the warming of the microclimate and thus the ripening of the grapes. Its microclimate is also an important influence on the wine's quality: the cliff itself, which is particularly high for the region, protects the vines from the north and east winds, and the vineyards, which slope at up to 45 degrees, receive long hours of sunlight. Their steepness obliges the growers to use caterpillar-tracked vehicles and to counter erosion by carrying soil back up the slopes, and in many places the vines are cultivated on terraces.

Arduous toil on the steepest slopes

The Macle family produce two wines on their 12-hectare estate, a Côtes-du-Jura of exceptional quality and the Château-Chalon itself, which is only made in the better years. The family's vineyards are amongst the steepest in the area, and are cultivated more or less biologically, with tilling four or five times a year.

The 4 hectares of Château-Chalon Savagnin are harvested around All Saints' Day, often after the first frosts which stabilize the sugar in the grapes. The crop is destemmed before pressing and fermented in enamel-lined stainless-steel vats. The wine is then transferred into the 228-liter barrels in which it is to spend over seven years maturing, and slowly evaporating.

Château-Chalon

Lighter in color than most, Jean Macle's Château-Chalon is also less obviously impregnated by the taste of *jaune*, and offers the taster a formidably complex aroma range and superb concentration and harmony on the palate. A wine of remarkable refinement and finesse, it finishes with great length and over the years becomes gently rounder and smoother, its nutty, spicy, or burnt flavors becoming more pronounced. A splendid match for fresh or pan-fried *foie gras*, or the local speciality of *poularde au vin jaune*, followed, of course, by some Comté cheese.

PROVENCE
A.O.C. Bandol

- *Wine selected:*
  Bandol red

- *Grape Varieties:*
  Mourvèdre 90%, Grenache 10%
- *Average vine age:*
  25 years
- *Vineyard size:*
  30 hectares
- *Soil type:*
  Clay and limestone
- *Production:*
  100,000 bottles

Finest Vintages:
2000, 1999, 1998, 1996,
1995, 1990, 1989

Château de Pibarnon
410 Chemin de la Croix-des-Signaux
83740 La Cadière-d'Azur
Tel. (0033) 494 90 12 73
From the A50 exit no. 11 "La
Cadière/Le Beausset", take the La
Cadière direction, for approximately
300 m, then take the second road on
the left and follow the signs for 4 km.
- *Owners:* Éric & Henri de Saint-Victor
- *On-site sales:* Yes
- *Visits:* 9–12 a.m., 2–6 p.m. (Mon.–Sat.)
- *Price:* ★★

CHÂTEAU DE PIBARNON

In past centuries Bandol and the Mourvèdre grape made wines which graced the highest tables, and recent years have at last seen the fine quality so appreciated by Louis XV in evidence again, thanks to the work of a handful of perfectionist estates. A glass of Château de Pibarnon conclusively demonstrates this: here is a wine of harmony, refinement, and class, displaying all the *grandeur* of a great Bordeaux, with a light Provençal dialect for good measure.

A pioneering spirit and unfailing optimism

Pibarnon's greatness is the combination of a human adventure and a geological rarity. Count Henri de Saint-Victor embarked on the adventure when, at age fifty-two, he gave up his successful business in Paris to buy the property, having fallen in love with its wine but knowing nothing of wine making. At the time it had only a few hectares of vineyard, and the Count set about enlarging his new property with digger and bulldozer, carving terraces out of the calcareous soil. A pioneering spirit, unfailing optimism, and resolute determination were at work.

Soils unique in the region

The hill on which Pibarnon's vineyard parcels are scattered is unique in the region for its geological make-up, a fact to which the wine owes its uniqueness. An enormous upheaval during the emergence of the Alps threw up some Triassic limestone, several hundred million years older than the soil it was to cover. This highly calcareous soil, very different to the granite and other soils predominant in the region, and the hill's altitude of 300 meters, explain Pibarnon's great elegance and aromatic finesse, and its approachability younger than most of its peers. What is more, the subsoil is highly moisture-retentive, sparing the vines stress and arrested ripening in very dry years.

A protective amphitheater of terraces

The splendid semi-circular amphitheatre of terraces provides ideal ripening conditions for the difficult Mourvèdre, and protection from the Mistral. Most vineyard tasks are carried out by hand, and vines are limited to a yield of fiver bunches each by green harvesting. Picking by hand provides the opportunity for a serious selection of the raw material.

The wine-making is traditional, with three weeks' vatting and daily *pigeage* to obtain a dark color and a long potential lifespan. The wine is then matured in large oak barrels for eighteen months or more, with up to fourteen rackings to air the Mourvèdre and rid it of its excessive pungency.

Bandol red

Exceptionally for a great Bandol, Pibarnon drinks well young, when its stone-fruit, blackberry, and violet aromas are purely, intensely seductive. Yet after a half-dozen years it is an infinitely more complex and rewarding wine, showing black fruit and licorice, then undergrowth, truffle, and spice. Always soft and silky, its structure and freshness keep it magnificently alert for many a year. Immature it goes well with veal, lamb, pigeon and duck; mature, it expects more talkative companions, such as venison, hare, *foie gras*, and almost anything associated with truffles.

PROVENCE
A.O.C. Bandol

- *Wine selected:*
  Bandol red

- *Grape Varieties:*
  Mourvèdre 95%, Grenache 5%
- *Average vine age:*
  30 years
- *Vineyard size:*
  19 hectares
- *Soil type:*
  Clay and limestone
- *Production:*
  60,000 bottles

Finest Vintages:

2000, 1999, 1998, 1995, 1990

Château Pradeaux
676 Chemin des Pradeaux
83270 Saint-Cyr-sur-Mer
Tel. (0033) 494 3 210 21
From the centre of Saint-Cyr drive to
the ZAC des Pradeaux (business park),
drive through it and turn left into the
chemin des Pradeaux. The estate is
signposted.
- *Owner:* EARL Château Pradeaux
Les Héritiers de Comte Portalis
- *On-site sales:* 10–12 a.m., 3–6 p.m.
  Closed Sunday
- *Visits:* No
- *Price:* ★

CHÂTEAU PRADEAUX

For a good while now Château Pradeaux has been one of the top Bandol estates, making wine that is generally considered a reference for excellence in the region, wine which exemplifies the true character and demonstrates the quality potential of the Mourvèdre grape when cultivated in this particular part of France. More than others Pradeaux needs time to develop its bouquet in bottle and to digest its imposing tannic structure. When mature, it is a memorable and unmistakeably great wine.

The Portalis family inheritance

The estate is the property of the Portalis family, who acquired it in 1752 when it was inherited by Jean-Marie-Étienne Portalis, one of Napoleon's ministers, co-author of the Code civil and author of the Concordat. During the Second World War Countess Arlette Portalis moved with her mother from Paris to the estate, which at the time was run by a manager and worked by two share-croppers, producing olives as well as grapes. The Countess became thoroughly involved in running the estate and making the wine, and replanted the vineyard, which had been ransacked by occupying troops, largely with Mourvèdre. Since 1983 the estate's fortunes have been the business of Cyrille Portalis, her nephew and adopted son, and his wife Magali. Cyrille trained at Beaune's *lycée viticole* (secondary school for wine making), and has taken on his responsibilities with great talent and a strong resolve to perpetuate Pradeaux's traditions and hand them on to future generations.

A vineyard refreshed by a permanent sea breeze

The estate covers 26 hectares, of which 21 are planted with vines. The soils are mainly limestone, with some clay, and because of the sea's proximity the vineyard is permanently subject to sea breezes, which is suspected to have a beneficial influence on the wine's finesse. The vineyard is worked manually and mechanically, the only treatments used being sulphur, to counter oïdium, and copper sulphate, to counter mildew. Indeed the sea breeze proves a veritable boon in maintaining vine health and avoiding the necessity of any treatments. Low yields are one of the imperatives, indeed at Pradeaux the grapes are generally harvested at 28–32 hectoliters per hectare, much lower than the authorized 40 hl/ha.

A team of some ten locals picks the ripe grapes, which are then lightly crushed and put into ciment vats. The grapes are left on their stalks, for Mourvèdre stalks are considered not to impart unripe grassy flavors, and the tannin they contribute is not to be wasted: the aim after all is to make wines with twenty years' improvement potential or more. A long maturation of three to four years in the traditional large barrels then rounds off the wine and develops its characteristics. Bottling, without any filtering of the wine, is the last step.

Bandol red

Rigid, unforthcoming, and charmless it may be when young, but what change a dozen years in bottle brings! Gradually a complex aroma range of leather, spice, thyme, tobacco, torrefaction, and many other nuances develops, each vintage having its particular facets. The one constant, which becomes progressively more evident with time, is the wine's remarkable harmony. And equally impressive, is its splendid freshness, even after twenty years in bottle. Mature vintages are a revelation for those not in the know. Roast pheasant or a saddle of hare are admirable accompaniments for this remarkable wine.

PROVENCE
A.O.C. Bandol

- *Wine selected:*
  Bandol La Tourtine

- *Grape Varieties:*
  Mourvèdre 68%, Cinsaut 15%,
  Grenache 17%
- *Average vine age:*
  33 years
- *Vineyard size:*
  6.5 hectares
- *Soil type:*
  Clay and limestone, stone
- *Production:*
  10,000 bottles

Finest Vintages:
2000, 1999, 1998, 1996, 1995

Domaine Tempier
Le Plan-du-Castellet
83330 Le Castellet
Tel. (0033) 494 98 70 21
The estate is in Le Plan-du-Castellet,
behind the school.
- *Owners:* Peyraud family
- *Director:* Daniel Ravier
- *On-site sales:* Yes
- *Visits:* 9–12 a.m., 2–5 p.m.
- *Price:* ★★

DOMAINE TEMPIER

For many, Bandol is synonymous with Domaine Tempier, for its exotically named Migoua, Tourtine, and Cabassaou *cuvées*, and their predecessor the Cuvée Spéciale, have long been regarded as ultimate expressions of the region's grapes and vineyards; and more significantly, its late owner, Lucien Peyraud was largely responsible for dragging the region to its feet after the 1939–1945 war. Nowadays Tempier shares the headlines with a handful of other estates, to the greater benefit of the consumer, yet it remains one of France's greats.

Phylloxera and a changing economic climate

The Tempier family have been making wine in Bandol since at least 1834, and in the pre-phylloxera days the Mourvèdre, a grape of Spanish origin, was widely planted. However after the decimation of their vineyards by the aphid, which first appeared in France in the Bandol town of Ollioules, the growers opted for planting more productive varieties. The burgeoning market, its attainability thanks to the new rail links, and the economic hardships of the 1930s, combined to make quantity and reliability most desirable characteristics in a vine variety for growers. The low-yielding, late-ripening, classy Mourvèdre virtually disappeared.

Champion of the Mourvèdre

Lucien Peyraud married Lucie Tempier just before the war, and they created the estate we know today. Peyraud was convinced that Bandol's future lay with Mourvèdre, set about persuading other growers to adopt it, was instrumental in getting it officially recognized as the principal grape of the region, and in getting a yield limitation set, when the Bandol AOC rules were formulated in 1941.

From small beginnings the Peyrauds acquired the splendid Le Castellet hillside vineyard La Tourtine in 1951, and subsequently Migoua, at Le Beausset, and other vineyard land around Le Plan-du-Castellet, bringing their estate to its current size of 30 hectares. Peyraud progressively handed over control to his sons Jean-Marie and François, now retired, and following the initial wine, "Cuvée Classique," came "Cuvée Spéciale" in 1968, and from 1979 individual bottlings of La Tourtine and Migoua. With the evolution of the range, the place given to Mourvèdre became progressively greater, culminating in the 100% Mourvèdre Cabassaou, from a one-hectare parcel of Mourvèdre vines on the lower, steeper part of La Tourtine.

Bandol La Tourtine

All the Tempier wines need a certain amount of time to develop, for they are unmistakably "traditional" wines. La Tourtine generally requires a minimum dozen years to soften up and start displaying its magnificent aromatic range, indeed owners of bottles should beware of opening them before the wine has emerged from its lengthy closed-up period! Grilled meat, *tapenade*, pepper, scorched earth, tobacco, these are the intriguing aromas a mature Tourtine develops, yet its underlying rich fruitiness long remains, and its rich fleshy mouthfeel vindicates Lucien Peyraud's intense lobbying of yesteryear for low yields. Mature, La Tourtine deserves a quality meat, prepared simply, to enable its complex character to express itself fully, a fillet of lamb *en croûte*, for example.

PROVENCE
A.O.C. Bandol

- *Wine selected:*
  Bandol red

- *Grape Varieties:*
  Mourvèdre 90%, Grenache 10%
- *Average vine age:*
  38 years
- *Vineyard size:*
  8 hectares
- *Soil type:*
  Clay and limestone
- *Production:*
  40,000 bottles

Finest Vintages:

1999, 1998, 1996, 1995, 1993,
1990, 1989, 1985, 1983, 1982

Château Vannières
Chemin Saint-Antoine
83740 Bandol
Tel. (0033) 494 90 08 08
Internet: www.chateauvannieres.com
From La Cadière-d'Azur take the D66
towards Saint-Cyr-sur-Mer. Two km
further, take the turn on the right,
which leads to Château Vannières.
- *Owner:* Éric Boisseaux
- *On-site sales:* Yes
- *Visits:* 8–12 a.m., 2–6 p.m.
- *Price:* ★★

CHÂTEAU VANNIÈRES

More than one taster has compared the greater Bandol red wines with fine claret, for, like Pauillac, Saint-Julien, and Margaux, certain lands in this Provençal appellation are capable of producing bottles of great finesse, harmony and complexity. Château Vannières is very much a case in point; a fine vineyard and a dedicated owner make this estate the source of splendid wines which are capable of improving in bottle over a dozen years or more.

Land long known for its viticultural quality

Vannières, which lies between La Cadière-d'Azur and Saint-Cyr-sur-Mer, has a long history. The estate can be traced back to the end of the sixteenth century, when the Abbey of Saint-Victor gave some land known as Les Vannières to Sieur de Lombard, the seigneur of Le Castellet. The existing, very un-Provençal château (built by a Scotsman) was constructed over the original cellars in the nineteenth century. The estate was acquired in 1957 by the grandfather of the present incumbent Éric Boisseaux, who learned his wine making both at Vannières and on the family's small estate at Beaune. The 35-hectare vineyard lies in one unfragmented block, which is unusual in the appellation, around the château. It is south- and west-facing and is protected from the cold winds by the Massif de la Sainte-Baume. The soil is principally composed of marl and limestone.

Measures to obtain prime-quality fruit

Boisseaux and his team go to great lengths to ensure that the vineyard yields prime-quality fruit. Chemical products are out, and of course Bandol's dry climate naturally reduces the incidence of cryptogamic ailments. Yields are kept well within the AOC maximum of 40 hectoliters per hectare by severe pruning. As the end of the growing cycle arrives, extreme attention is paid to the grapes' ripening and the choice of the optimum moment for harvesting; as the critical moment approaches, daily analyses of the fruit of each parcel for acidity, sugar, and also color and tannic richness are carried out.

The harvest is done by hand, with different varieties and parcels kept separate. Faithful to his Burgundian origins, Boisseaux likes to tread his grapes, so the fruit is macerated in ancient open vats, with the quality of the harvest dictating duration and amount of treading. Vinification then takes place in *foudre* for 70 percent of the wine and *barrique* for the remainder. Only before the fermented wines are ready for maturation are the different varieties and parcels blended. Maturation lasts some eighteen months, with several rackings to air the wine and separate it from its lees. It is then bottled without filtering.

Bandol red

Once bottled the Château Vannières Bandol is ready to confront the passage of time, and the many vintages stretching back over two decades on sale at the estate demonstrate just how capable of this it is. Full-bodied and rich, smooth and harmonious on the palate, after a few years it acquires splendid complexity, its beautiful initial cedary fragrance developing nuances reminiscent of leather, game, spice, truffles; each vintage has its personality. An immature Vannières harmonizes well with lamb roasted with Provençal herbs; with mature vintages however one can serve richer dishes: a haunch of venison, for example, accompanied by a wild mushroom gratin.

PROVENCE
A.O.C. Bellet

- *Wine selected:*
  Bellet Baron de G white

- *Grape Varieties:*
  Rolle 95%, Chardonnay 5%
- *Average vine age:*
  35 years
- *Vineyard size:*
  1.5 hectares
- *Soil type:*
  Sand, limestone, stone
- *Production:*
  5,000–6,000 bottles

Finest Vintages:
2000, 1999, 1998, 1997, 1996

Château de Bellet
440 Chemin de Saquier
Quartier Saint-Roman
06200 Nice
Tel. (0033) 493 37 81 57
Once in the quartier Saint-Roman, look
for the Saint-Roman-de-Bellet church;
the Chemin de Saquier is 500 m past
it on the left as one heads away from
Nice. The entrance to the château
is 500 m along on the left.
- *Owner:* Ghislain de Charnacé
- *On-site sales:* By appointment
- *Visits:* No
- *Price:* ★★

CHÂTEAU DE BELLET

At 39 hectares the Bellet appellation is one of France's smallest, and most people are more likely to have read about its wines than to have drunk them, for very few bottles travel far from their birthplace in the hills above Nice. The most important estate, in both historical and vinous terms, is Château de Bellet, which produces wines of all three colors, delicious and most original.

Last defenders of a Provençal appellation

All credit is due to the few remaining Bellet *vignerons* for hanging on and continuing to make wine in economic circumstances which must pose a permanent dilemma for them, such is the voracious demand for land for development only one tenth of the authorized Bellet vineyard land is now planted with vines. Here, unfortunately, any renaissance of the appellation is out of the question.

Château de Bellet is the property of Ghislain de Charnacé, whose mother Rose de Bellet, a descendant of the Barons de Bellet, inherited it and put it back on its feet with her husband Bernard de Charnacé. Since Ghislain, the younger son, has been running it, he has been a stalwart defender of this unique appellation, going out of his way to preserve its indigenous grapes varieties and typicity, and resisting the siren call of easy, modern, standardized wine production. His dedication and hard work have made the estate the standard-bearer of the appellation today.

A healthy climate for indigenous vines

The château itself was built in the sixteenth century, and has been much modified since then. Its 8 hectares of vineyards are perched on the hill overlooking the Var river (opposite the long-vanished La Gaude vineyard), and contain Braquet and Folle Noire vines for the red and rosé wines, supplemented by a little Grenache, and Rolle vines, with a smattering of Chardonnay, for the whites. The various vineyard plots are cultivated ecologically, and the maritime/alpine climate and the altitude of some 250 meters duly play their part in keeping down the incidence of the vine's usual ailments.

Bellet Baron de G white

Ghislain de Charnacé produces two white wines, one made in vat and the other, "Baron de G", fermented in oak barrel. Both show just how fine a variety the Rolle is: known in Italy and Corsica as Vermentino, this variety retains a good degree of acidity and aroma in hot climates, and makes fresh, interesting wine of body and succulence. It can be vinified in wood with success, as the "Baron de G" demonstrates, and has the wherewithal to gain in personality over the years.

When young the aromas of the oaked-vinified wine are reminiscent of tropical fruit, yet once emerged from its shell the mature wine is softer, well-rounded and showing an attractive, honeyed side, which enables many a successful pairing with local dishes: spiced scallops, for example, the iodine nature of which harmonizes very well with the honeyed finesse of the "Baron de G." This wine may be hard to find, but is well worth the effort.

385

PROVENCE
A.O.C. Palette

- *Wine selected:*
  Palette white

- *Grape Varieties:*
  Clairette 80%, Grenache Blanc 8%,
  Ugni Blanc 8%, Muscat Blanc 4%
- *Average vine age:*
  60 years
- *Vineyard size:*
  7.5 hectares
- *Soil type:*
  Calcareous rocks
- *Production:*
  35,000 bottles

Finest Vintages:
2000, 1998, 1996, 1991, 1990, 1988

Château Simone
13590 Meyreuil
Tel. (0033) 442 66 92 58
From Aix take the N7. Once past the
Pont des Trois-Sautées the estate is
signposted.
- *Owners:* Rougier family
- *On-site sales:* 9–12 a.m., 2–6 p.m.
- *Visits:* No
- *Price:* ★★

CHÂTEAU SIMONE

There are but two estates lying within the Provençal appellation Palette, just outside Aix-en-Provence. Château Simone is the best known and makes wines of all three colors. They are very distinctive, for they owe little to modern wine-making trends and technologies and are made with unusual proportions of various southern French grapes. Unusually for a southern estate the white wine is arguably the most distinguished of the three, and in this age of standardised varietal wines is one of France's most interesting offerings.

An unusual vineyard

Vines have been cultivated there since Roman times. Whoever first recognized the suitability of the site for viticulture knew his business: the vineyards lie on the north-facing slopes of the Montaiguet hills facing the montagne Sainte-Victoire, and are hemmed in by forests and the river Arc. The resulting moderate temperatures, protection from the strong winds of the region, humidity from the forests and the river and the very stony *calcaire* de Langesse rock, all contrive to make this an unusually fine vineyard in the arid Provençal countryside.

Venerable plants and rare grape varieties

The owners of Château Simone are the Rougier family, who acquired the estate from a lady named De Simon over two centuries ago. Preservation of old vines, and little-known local varieties at that, respectful cultivation and traditional wine-making are the methods favored by the Rougiers, and they account for the quality and originality of the wines. After destruction by phylloxera the vineyards were replanted in 1891, and some parcels still contain these plants, which are still producing fruit today! The average age of the remainder of the vineyard is an impressive sixty years, which provides natural yield regulation. The wines are made from a whole panoply of varieties: besides southern grapes such as Grenache Noir, Mourvèdre, Syrah, Cinsaut, and Carignan for the red and rosé, there are also Muscat de Hambourg and Cabernet-Sauvignon, and a sprinkling of the almost-extinct Provençal varieties Manosquin, Théoulier, and Castet; Clairette is the principal grape of the white wine, supported by Ugni Blanc, Grenache Blanc, Muscat Blanc, and a little Picpoul and Sémillon.

Palette blanc

The grapes are picked by hand and checked for quality then and on arrival at the *chai*. The white wine is fermented in small wooden vats by the grapes' own yeast at a not particularly low 68°F (20°C) and aged for one year in *foudre* then one year in barrel (it is made for development in bottle, and primary fruitiness is not required). The wine is bottled unfiltered.

It combines floral and fruity aromas with a hint of oakiness when young, and is most elegant. As the years pass it often acquires touches of cedarwood, herbs, and nuts, and becomes richer, rounder and more complex. It eventually becomes deep gold in color, yet is remarkable for its freshness, balance and good acidity, all of which are a testament to the quality of the vineyard site and environment. This splendid and original wine is excellent with most fish dishes, in sauces lightly perfumed with *Provençal* herbs.

PROVENCE
A.O.C. Vin de Pays des Bouches-du-Rhône

- *Wine selected:*
  Domaine de Trévallon red

- *Grape Varieties:*
  Cabernet-Sauvignon 50%, Syrah 50%
- *Average vine age:*
  25 years
- *Vineyard size:*
  15 hectares
- *Soil type:*
  Limestone
- *Production:*
  50,000 bottles

Finest Vintages:
1999, 1998, 1996, 1995,
1991, 1990, 1989

Domaine de Trévallon
13103 Saint-Étienne-du-Grès
Tel. (0033) 490 490 600
Internet: www.trevallon.com
From Saint-Rémy-de-Provence take
the D99 towards Tarascon, then turn
left onto the D27 towards Les Baux.
Turn right at the second crossroads.
Two kilometers further there is a
Narrow Road sign announcing Avenue
Notre-Dame-du-Château. The dirt road
leading to Trévallon is 50 meters past
the sign, on the left.
- *Owner:* Éloi Dürrbach
- *On-site sales:* Yes
- *Visits:* By appointment only
- *Price:* ★★★

DOMAINE DE TRÉVALLON

One would have difficulty finding more inhospitable vineyard *terrain*, and yet, proving conclusively that the vine performs better in poor soil, one has to search hard to find greater wine. Over the quarter century of its existence Domaine de Trévallon, near Saint-Rémy-de-Provence, has produced wines which have progressively gained in stature and are today sought out by wine lovers around the world. Trévallon is an original, and any cellar worthy of the name should hold a few bottles of its wine.

A vineyard dynamited into existence

The property was bought in 1955 by René Dürrbach, painter, sculptor, and friend of Picasso, as a family home to which he and his wife could get away from the bustle of the Côte d'Azur. René ruminated on the possibility of making a great wine in this forbidding landscape, however it was his son Éloi, a twenty-three-year-old student of architecture in Paris, who decided in 1973 to found a vineyard, and gave up his studies to go and live on the property.

Creating the vineyard was no mean task, for the *garrigue* and limestone-covered hills forming the Val d'Enfer, or Valley of Hell, in which the property lies, had to be literally blasted by dynamite to create land in which vines could be planted. In the winter of that year some plots were ready.

No compromises for a self-taught wine maker

The young Dürrbach had read that Dr Guyot, in his 1868 book *Étude du vignoble de France*, considered that a blend of Cabernet-Sauvignon and Syrah could produce remarkable wines in the region, and set about planting these varieties, eschewing the ubiquitous Grenache. From the start he worked without recourse to artificial viticultural aids, and aimed for very low yields, to produce wine of concentration and character. As vintages succeeded each other they progressively gained in finesse and polish, and by the mid-1980s Trévallon was well established.

Initially the wine was sold under the AOC Coteaux d'Aix-en-Provence, Les Baux-de-Provence, yet in 1995 the authorities decided that more than 30 percent Cabernet-Sauvignon in a Les Baux wine was unsuitable, despite the Trévallon example overwhelmingly proving the contrary. Dürrbach refused to change his wine, at the cost of seeing it demoted to Vin de pays des Bouches-du-Rhône. Sales, needless to say, were not affected.

Domaine de Trévallon red

Darkly colored, concentrated, splendidly and compellingly aromatic, Trévallon is a full-throttle wine combining the elegance of a great Pauillac and the dimension of a Hermitage, colored with the herbs, spice, and heat of its extraordinary Provençal birthplace. It is a great wine to which no taster can remain impervious. Certain vintages are actually delicious in their first years, yet the greater ones, such as the 1998, 1995, and 1990 will surely enjoy thirty-year lifespans; the more mature and complex they become, the less seasoned and less rich the dish should be, to give full scope to the wine's magnificent bouquet. Fillet of duck with figs is an excellent match.

LANGUEDOC-ROUSSILLON
A.O.C. Limoux

- *Wine selected:*
Limoux Les Aigles

- *Grape Variety:*
Chardonnay
- *Average vine age:*
20 years
- *Vineyard size:*
2.5 hectares
- *Soil type:*
Clay and limestone
- *Production:*
25,000 bottles

Finest Vintages:
1999, 1998, 1997

Domaine de l'Aigle
11300 Roquetaillade
Tel. (0033) 468 31 39 12
- *Owner:* Jean-Louis Denois
- *On-site sales:* By appointment
- *Visits:* By appointment
- *Price:* ★★

DOMAINE DE L'AIGLE

The great progress accomplished in recent years by many appellations of the Languedoc-Roussillon region can be verified by tasting the excellent bottles now available on the market. Limoux, south of Carcassonne, has always had a certain reputation for its sparkling wines and still wines traditionally made from the Mauzac grape. Today however some still Chardonnay wines from this white-wine AOC are emerging that turn the notion that the Midi can only produce red wine on its head. Domaine de l'Aigle in particular makes wines to convince even the most sceptical.

A stress-free life in the mountain vineyards

Jean-Louis Denois created the estate in 1989. It lies around the picturesque village of Roquetaillade at the feet of the Pyrenees, at the southwestern extremity of the Languedoc. Here the climate is in essence Atlantic, and this allied with the altitude of the vineyards (up to 450 meters above sea-level) affords cool conditions in which vines can live a stress-free life, develop the necessary acidities, and produce wines of balance and finesse. The Haute Vallée region has calcareous clay soils where the Chardonnay, Pinot Noir, and Merlot thrive, and the soils at l'Aigle are of particularly pure clay, a cold soil-type especially appreciated by the Chardonnay.

Cultivated for richness and authenticity

At l'Aigle viticultural methods are respectful of the environment and the plants, with treatments used only when necessary, and with absolutely no use of trace-leaving weedkillers, strong pesticides, nor chemical fertilizer. The various parcels are left partially or totally grassed-over in order to reduce the vines' vigor and productivity, and are only occasionally fertilized, with vegetal compost. The vines are trained high to limit the effects of spring frosts, and are planted at a density of five thousand plants per hectare. The grass and the plant density create a competitive situation where the vines are obliged to bury their roots deeply in the quest for sustenance, bringing the *terroir* characteristics that much more forcefully to the wines.

Limoux Les Aigles

The "Cabane de l'Aigle" vineyard is harvested by successive pickings from the end of September to mid-October, as the grapes become overripe. The first, middle, and last juices of the pressing are kept separate, and only the first, the purest, is used for Les Aigles. A long fermentation in 500-liter demi-muids ensues, with neither chaptalization nor acidification to enhance the wine, followed by a year's aging on its lees with frequent lees-stirring before eventual bottling.

The freshness and breed of this wine are light years away from the heavy whites generally made in the Midi. A scintillating light golden yellow in color, the wine has an exquisitely fragrant, floral nose, and a surprisingly rich attack on the palate. Richly opulent, yet without excess thanks to its remarkable acidity, it is tangy, intense, and thoroughly modern, a seeming combination of all that is best in Chardonnay of the New World and the Old, and signs off with a long, concentrated finish. Les Aigles is a remarkable wine, which merits the attentions of lobster, *à l'américaine* or simply grilled on a spit.

LANGUEDOC-ROUSSILLON
A.O.C. Coteaux-du-Languedoc

- *Wine selected:*
  **Coteaux-du-Languedoc
  Côte Dorée**

- *Grape Variety:*
  Syrah
- *Average vine age:*
  40 years
- *Vineyard size:*
  7 hectares
- *Soil type:*
  Limestone
- *Production:*
  15,000 bottles

Finest Vintages:
2001, 2000, 1999, 1998, 1995

Domaine L'Aiguelière
2 Place du Square-M.-Teisserenc
34150 Montpeyroux
Tel. (0033) 467 96 61 43
The estate is at the entry to the village
if arriving from Gignac, or at the exit if
arriving from Clermont-L'Hérault.
- *Owners:* Commeyras
- *On-site sales:* Yes
- *Visits:* 8–12 a.m., 2–6 p.m.,
  by appointment
- *Price:* ★★

DOMAINE L'AIGUELIÈRE

The village of Montpeyroux, in the Midi's Hérault département, has been producing some startlingly good wines in recent years, and a mention of the name now produces an interested reaction from many a wine lover on the lookout for quality at a reasonable price. One of the names to have emerged recently and rapidly made a reputation for itself is that of Domaine L'Aiguelière, an estate producing deliciously sensual, rich bottles which are now in great demand.

Between plain and mountain

The village is situated on a natural juncture of low plain and mountain, and is marked by the traces of long-forgotten battles and migrations. The vine quickly established itself here, for Montpeyroux lies at 300 meters' altitude at the northern limit of the Mediterranean climatic influence, where the cool of the Cévennes starts to be felt. Here, in the fragmented, heterogeneous soils it could thrive.

L'Aiguelière was founded in 1987 by Aimé Commeyras and his family, long-established vine-growers in the region, and the enologist Pierre-Louis Teissedre. Their aim was to produce really special wine, and Commeyras and Teissedre set about selecting parcels of old vines from among the family's holdings, those planted on the best land and liable to complement each other. Some contained Syrah and Grenache, which Commeyras had planted years before, trying even then to push back the ramparts of tradition. First results exceeded expectations, and expansion followed; the estate today consists of nineteen parcels covering 25 hectares, spread over three geologically different zones. Producing such differing yet complementary raw material has been a fundamental aspect of the Aiguelière wines' quality.

Individual grape and vineyard vinifications

The vineyards are naturally protected by the cold, dry winds blowing down from the Cévennes, and no treatment other than Bordeaux mixture and SO_2 is necessary for obtaining healthy, ripe grapes of the highest quality. Only organic manure is used to nourish the vines, and only sparingly, in order not to increase their yields. Harvesting, naturally, is carried out by hand, with selection and rejection in the vineyard of anything unripe or damaged. The enologist then has the task of vinifying all the different varieties, from the nineteen parcels, separately, and ultimately of blending them.

Temperature-controlled stainless-steel vats are used, and the grapes are macerated and fermented on their stalks for fifteen to twenty-eight days. Then comes the delicate art of blending, maturation in barrel, and finally the decision of when the wine is at its peak and may be bottled.

Coteaux-du-Languedoc Côte Dorée

The prestige wine Côte Dorée is made from sixty-year-old Syrah vines grown in a particularly sun-drenched parcel, and matured in new oak barrels for ten months. Deeply colored and highly aromatic, this impressive wine is a revelation to those who encounter it for the first time, thanks to its heady bouquet of blackcurrant, licorice, spice, and cloves the subtle touch of vanilla that captivates the senses, its sensual, fleshy mouth-coating presence on the palate, and its long, long finish. This is a delicious advertisement for an up-and-coming wine region, to enjoy with a fine game dish such as haunch of venison with cranberries.

LANGUEDOC-ROUSSILLON
A.O.C. Coteaux-du-Languedoc

- *Wine selected:*
  Coteaux-du-Languedoc red

- *Grape Varieties:*
  Grenache, Syrah, Mourvèdre; one
  plot containing the 13 Châteauneuf-
  du-Pape varieties
- *Average vine age:*
  28 years
- *Vineyard size:*
  27 hectares
- *Soil type:*
  Clay, limestone, sandstone, silica
- *Production:*
  52,000 bottles

Finest Vintages:
2000, 1999, 1998, 1996, 1995

Prieuré de Saint-Jean-de-Bébian
Route de Nizas
34120 Pézenas
Tel. (0033) 467 98 13 60
Internet: www.bebian.com
From Pézenas take the N113 towards
Montpellier, then the D30 towards
Nizas. The Prieuré is 2.5 km along that
road.
- *Owners:* Chantal Lecouty & Jean-
  Claude Le Brun
- *On-site sales:* Yes
- *Visits:* 10 a.m.–12:30 p.m., 3:30 –
  6 p.m. (summer). By appointment
  (rest of the year)
- *Price:* ★★

PRIEURÉ DE SAINT-JEAN DE BÉBIAN

For many years Prieuré de Saint-Jean-de-Bébian has been one of the foremost Languedoc estates, producing glorious wine which has set others thinking, and certainly acting as one of the catalysts for the impressive renewal of the region. This is one of those thoroughly dependable estates which routinely take the necessary measures to ensure quality year after year.

The senior estate of the Languedoc

We cannot be sure if there were vines when there was a Roman villa on the site, but monks arrived here in the eleventh century, and an 1152 document relates that they were already constituting a sizeable vineyard estate. The monks remained until they were dispossessed during the French Revolution, after which the estate was auctioned off as state property. Alain Roux inherited it in 1975 and overhauled it, replanting the vineyard with Syrah, Mourvèdre, and Grenache, and also planting one parcel with all thirteen Châteauneuf-du-Pape varieties. Yet at the same time he carefully safeguarded the existing old Mediterranean Cinsaut and Carignan vines.

Then in 1994 Roux sold the estate to Chantal Lecouty and Jean-Claude Le Brun, who had sold off their magazine group, which included *La Revue du vin de France*, to become wine makers. The new owners set out with the intention of continuing Roux's work of producing Mediterranean wines of the highest quality.

Factors and measures for an exceptional wine

The Bébian vineyard lies in the foothills of the Cévennes. It is very fragmented, and consists of twenty-eight plots, all arid and stony, geologically varied, and south- or southwest-facing. The vines are almost all the result of *sélection massale*, and come from the most reputable sources—Chave for the Syrah, Rayas for the Grenache, Tempier for the Mourvèdre—and are planted at up to 5,500 vines per hectare, the maximum for the Languedoc. They are not subjected to systematic treatments, are fertilized with organic manure, and are pruned as short as possible, with the aim of harvesting very low yields. The average yield here is 25 hectoliters per hectare.

The different varieties are all fermented independently, all except the Syrah and some Grenache on their stalks, and maceration lasts four to eight weeks with regular *remontage* and *pigeage* for maximum extraction of aroma, color, tannin, and acidity. The Syrah and Mourvèdre are transferred to barrel for the second, malolactic fermentation, then the wines are matured in barrel, blended, and bottled without filtering.

Coteaux-du-Languedoc red

The numerous grape varieties and *terroirs*, and the extreme pains taken to produce prime quality grapes, result in a wine unlike any other. Combining power and elegance, Bébian is richly, intensely aromatic, smooth and harmonious, and very long on the finish. This is unmistakeably a wine to let develop over the years in bottle. Its blasts of blackberry, pepper, Provençal herbs, and leather, slightly toasted, enable it to sit alongside dishes as varied as *daube provençale*, *tagine* or wild boar stew. This is a cold-weather wine, one of France's finest.

LANGUEDOC-ROUSSILLON
A.O.C. Rivesaltes

• *Wine selected:*
Rivesaltes Cuvée Aimé Cazes

• *Grape Variety:*
Grenache Blanc
• *Average vine age:*
50 years
• *Vineyard size:*
4 hectares
• *Soil type:*
Stony clay
• *Production:*
12,000 bottles

Finest Vintages:
1976, 1973, 1963

Domaine Cazes
4, rue Francisco-Ferrer — BP 61
66602 Rivesaltes Cedex
Tel. (0033) 468 64 08 26
Internet: www.cazes-rivesaltes.com
Rue Francisco-Ferrer is opposite the
cemetery as one leaves the village in
the Narbonne direction.
• *Owners:* André & Bernard Cazes
• *On-site sales:* Yes
• *Visits:* By appointment
• *Price:* ★★★

DOMAINE CAZES

I f there is one name with which the Roussillon is associated more than any other, it is probably that of the Cazes family. Over the course of its century of existence the family has built up a huge 160-hectare estate, developed a wide range of wines, and exported to markets all over the world, and been showered with medals in recognition of their quality. Yet despite this splendid commercial success the family do not sit on their laurels, preferring to reassess, refine and innovate regularly.

Expansion and modernization

The estate was founded at the beginning of the twentieth century, and made great strides between the 1930s and 1950s under the management of Aimé Cazes, a remarkable and widely respected man who handed the estate over to his sons in 1976, and passed away in December 2000 several months before his centenary. Since then André and Bernard have maintained the impetus set by their father, enlarging the estate and modernizing it in order to ensure continued quality, investing in new wine-making technology, refining vineyard techniques and maintaining a highly competent team.

Diversity of soils and grape varieties

There is never a quiet moment on this estate. Lying around Rivesaltes and Salses-le-Château some 30 kilometers from the Spanish border it has highly varied soils, which has enabled the successful cultivation of many vine varieties and thereby an extended product range. Viticultural methods are continuously being re-evaluated: the brothers (christened "les frères dynamite" by *Le Point*) were the first to start using weedkiller, for example, and subsequently the first to abandon it and go back to traditional working of the soil. Since 1996 they have run the vineyard in accordance with biodynamic precepts.

As might be expected with over a dozen varieties, the harvest starts early, in mid-August, when certain white grapes such as Chardonnay, Macabeu, and Muscat à petits grains attain perfect ripeness. It goes on through mid-October when at last the Grenache, which has to attain 14 percent potential alcohol for the Rivesaltes wines, may be picked. Thereafter all sorts of different vinification paths are followed, depending on the wine.

Rivesaltes Cuvée Aimé Cazes

The estate is best known for its Muscat de Rivesaltes, a wine of impeccable quality and great character, which has surely initiated many a wine-lover into the mysteries of *vins doux naturels*. Yet the culmination of this style of wine chez Cazes is the Rivesaltes Cuvée Aimé Cazes, a magnificent wine dedicated to the memory of their father. It was inaugurated with the vintage 1963, marketed in 1983, and continued with the 1975, marketed in 1995. The 1976 follows on, after twenty-two years maturing in oak *foudres*, which, incidentally, involves the loss of two-thirds of the volume, the "angels' share," through evaporation!

This sublime wine is made with Grenache Blanc. Smooth, ample, and heart-warming, its long maturation has given it magnificent aromatic complexity: bitter oranges, figs, dried apricots, roast hazelnuts, cinnamon, nutmeg, and an extraordinarily long finish. Best served at 59°F (15°C) in a large glass, it is enhanced by *foie gras*, desserts flavored with eastern spices, or a good Havana.

LANGUEDOC-ROUSSILLON
A.O.C. Côtes-du-Roussillon-Villages

- *Wine selected:*
  Côtes-du-Roussillon-Villages Muntada

- *Grape Varieties:*
  Syrah 60%, Carignan 30%, Grenache 10%
- *Average vine age:*
  Between 8 and 100+ years
- *Vineyard size:*
  15 hectares
- *Soil type:*
  Limestone, schist and marl subsoils
- *Production:*
  9,000 bottles

Finest Vintages:

2001, 2000, 1999

Domaine Gauby
Le Faradjal
66600 Calce
Tel. (0033) 468 64 35 19
From Perpignan pass through Baixas, taking the D18 to Calce. The estate is at the entry to the village, signposted.
- *Owners:* Ghislaine & Gérard Gauby
- *On-site sales:* No
- *Visits:* By appointment only
- *Price:* ★★★★

DOMAINE GAUBY

N o wine region could wish for greater ambassadors than the Gaubys, who must surely rank among France's most perfectionist growers and wine makers. The wines from this estate are stunning, and the proof of the quality level that can be attained in the most southern parts of France will surprise many an unsuspecting, uninitiated wine drinker.

Respect for the ecosystem

Domaine Gauby, which is a short drive northwest of Perpignan, was founded in 1985 by Gérard and Ghislaine Gauby, with vines rented and owned around the village of Calce. The couple's son Lionel is now working with them on the estate, lending extra arms and energy, which are most welcome when the aim is to practice a totally natural, painstaking viticulture without recourse to any modern labor-saving chemical aids or technology.

Indeed this estate is operated on biodynamic lines, with utmost respect for the eco-system: here the numerous vineyard parcels are intermingled with fields of cereal crops and surrounded by hedges, and the countryside teems with natural life. Heed is paid to planetary movements, and the various vineyard and cellar operations can thus be carried out at the most propicious moment.

The estate is home to a good number of vine varieties of all ages. Thanks to mechanical cultivation and only occasional organic nourishment, their root systems must dig deep underground, which enables the vines to resist drought and soak up the mineral character of the various soils.

Mineral character and pure fruit

The harvest at Domaine Gauby is a drawn-out affair, stretching from mid-August through to the end of September, as the different varieties all in their own time reach perfect ripeness. Extreme care is taken when picking to keep only the finest bunches. In the cellars the guiding principle is close surveillance but no interference.

The bunches of white grapes are gently pressed and their juice fermented by the indigenous yeast, and the wines are then matured on their lees, with little lees-stirring. The results are remarkable: rich, smooth on the palate, fleshy yet with good acidity, and perfectly fresh. Coming from a corner of France not known for producing decent white wine they, even more than the reds, reveal the talent of the Gaubys. The black grapes are destemmed, macerated for a few days, then fermented in vat, with gentle extraction of matter and minimal use of SO2. The red wines are then matured in both vat and barrel, and are blended and bottled with neither fining nor filtering.

Côtes-du-Roussillon-Villages Muntada

Since 1998 the fruit of some centenarian Carignans and Grenaches has been added to the Syrah to produce the top wine, Muntada, and its intensity, harmony and class are breathtaking. Concentrated and silky on the palate, it has a fine, ripe tannic structure, and a pure, intense fruitiness which is irresistible. This delicious wine can be enjoyed in its youth, yet those who prefer to wait will no doubt congratulate themselves on their foresight as they wallow in the sumptuous, rich bouquet of the mature vintage. Served with some pigeon or young boar roasted on a spit, Muntada has lots to talk about.

LANGUEDOC-ROUSSILLON
A.O.C. Vin de Pays de l'Hérault

- *Wine selected:*
  Mas de Daumas Gassac Blanc de Blancs

- *Grape Varieties:*
  Petit-Manseng 30%, Viognier 30%, Chardonnay 30%, Chenin, Sercial and 10 others 10%
- *Average vine age:*
  10 years minimum
- *Vineyard size:*
  13 hectares
- *Soil type:*
  Limestone
- *Production:*
  50,000 bottles

Finest Vintages:

2001, 2000, 1998, 1995, 1994, 1992, 1988, 1986, 1985, 1982, 1980

Mas de Daumas Gassac
Haute Vallée du Gassac
34150 Aniane
Tel. (0033) 467 57 71 28
Internet : www.daumas-gassac.com
Mas de Daumas Gassac lies off the D32 half-way between Gignac and Aniane, and is signposted.
- *Owners:* Véronique Guibert de la Vaissière
- *On-site sales:* Yes
- *Visits:* 10–12 a.m., 2–6 p.m.
- *Price:* ★★

MAS DE DAUMAS GASSAC

In these days of strong and increasing worldwide demand for fine wine, one would imagine that all the best vineyard land in France is already identified and planted; it would seem unlikely that a wine estate capable of producing truly great and original new wines could be created from scratch. Yet the extraordinary Mas de Daumas Gassac of the Hérault region is one such. The bulk of its production is red, yet it also produces a white of great quality and originality.

A remarkable discovery

The creator of Mas de Daumas Gassac is the charismatic Aimé Guibert. In the 1970s Guibert, who knew little of wine, acquired the mas as a family home. He happened to know Henri Enjalbert, an eminent professor of geography at Bordeaux University. During a visit Enjalbert noticed the estate's soil, a remarkable and rare type, he advised his host, capable of producing wines of exceptional quality. Encouraged by his friend, Guibert (never a man to back away from a challenge) started learning about wine and wine making, planted parcels of land, and persuaded the celebrated Bordeaux enologist Émile Peynaud to advise him on making his wine. Within a few years the wines were surprising all who tasted them.

An exceptional and rare *terroir*

Enjalbert's intuition had been well founded. The soil, an accumulation of glacial dust deposited by the wind, is remarkable for its depth, drainage, poverty in vegetal matter, and richness in oxide minerals. The microclimate also is remarkable: the Haute Vallée du Gassac is exceptionally cool for this sun-scorched region, affording the vines repose at night and thus finer-balanced fruit; what is more the winery lies over two cold underground streams which provide permanently cool conditions, enabling slow, protracted fermentation, and the attainment of wines of finesse and aromatic delicacy. The vineyard parcels face north. Guibert went out of his way to protect the surrounding *garrigue*, planting small plots of vines so that the smells of the countryside should flavor the wine. Low yields, organic cultivation methods, and the use of uncloned vines were all part of his scheme.

Mas de Daumas Gassac Blanc de Blancs

He planted many varieties including some alien to the region. The cocktail of grapes which makes up the white Daumas Gassac produces a highly aromatic wine, the range and richness of which is emphasised by skin maceration at $41°F$ ($5°C$) lasting some eight days, before slow fermentation in stainless steel and a four to eight weeks' sojourn in new oak. Nuances of apricot, pear, and violets reveal the presence of Petit-Manseng and Viognier, then the rich utterances of Chardonnay make themselves heard, with a light accent of the *garrigue*. What an intriguing wine! An original aperitif, it also sits easily alongside asparagus or aubergine dishes, or any fish or white meat dishes prepared with Mediterranean vegetables.

Delicious in the fragrant fruitiness of youth, it develops very interestingly over the years. After ten years in bottle the 1990 vintage had developed a fine golden yellow hue and a honeyed, stewed-apple flavor, with a subtle, refined nutty aspect coloring the long finish. Better young or old? A question of individual taste.

LANGUEDOC-ROUSSILLON
A.O.C. Corbières

- *Wine selected:*
  Corbières Cuvée Romain Pauc

- *Grape Varieties:*
  Carignan 60%, Grenache 20%, Syrah
  10%, Mourvèdre 10%
- *Average vine age:*
  45-90 years
- *Vineyard size:*
  11 hectares
- *Soil type:*
  Stony
- *Production:*
  37,000 bottles

Finest Vintages:
1999, 1998, 1995

Château La Voulte-Gasparets
11200 Boutenac
Tel. (0033) 468 27 07 86
From Boutenac take the D61 to
Gasparets, and pass through it. La
Voulte-Gasparets is straight ahead.
- *Owner:* Patrick Reverdy
- *On-site sales:* Yes
- *Visits:* 9–12 a.m., 2–6 p.m.
- *Price:* ★

CHÂTEAU LA VOULTE-GASPARETS

The land around Boutenac has long been recognized for its exceptional aptitude for viticulture, and today much of the best Corbières produced comes from estates in the vicinity. One of the best known is the historic Château La Voulte-Gasparets, which has been winning awards in the *Concours générale agricole de Paris*, the *Concours des grands vins de France* at Mâcon and other national competitions with impressive regularity since 1905. This estate makes wines of all three colors, and its exceptional Cuvée Romain Pauc is well worth looking out for.

A highly individual vineyard site

La Voulte-Gasparets lies on a terrace of ancient alluvial soil with an important quartz content, on which lie a large number of quartzite *galets roulés*, pudding-stones similar to those found in Châteauneuf-du-Pape. Well drained and facing east and south, the land enjoys strong, intense sunlight and heat, which the stones duly amplify.

In the fifth century a Gallo-Roman nobleman named Consentius planted vines and olive trees on the site of the estate, and built a splendid villa in which to live. Through the ninteenth and twentieth centuries up until today it has remained in the hands of a single family; today Patrick Reverdy, of the fifth generation, is at the helm, seconded by his son Laurent and nephew Jean-Marc Bergès. Lack of continuity is not a problem here!

Carignan's finest hour

The family has always remained faithful to the mainstay grapes of Corbières, Carignan, and Grenache; the former robust and structured, the latter fine and delicate. The two are ideal partners, yet the recent introduction into the vineyard of varieties such as Syrah and Mourvèdre, in limited quantities, has undeniably added a little extra dimension to the wines. The arid environment renders many of the treatments of more northerly vineyards unnecessary, and the vines' roots find the sustenance they need deep under the surface, aided just occasionally by a dose of organic fertilizer. The harvest is picked by hand at perfect ripeness, at yields well below those authorized by the AOC regulations.

The most elderly vines, planted for the most part in 1905 in a choice sector where the stones are particularly abundant and the sunlight most intense, are used for the production of the *cuvée* named after Reverdy's great-grandfather Romain Pauc.

Corbières Cuvée Romain

Proving that, contrary to the long-held view, Carignan is capable of producing excellent wines as long as its yields are kept well down, Romain Pauc has won many a rave review, and been dubbed *Cru Exceptionnel*, *Grand Cru* and the like by wine publications. Its intense licorice-and-spice bouquet, mouth-coating flavor, fleshy texture and harmonious constitution make it a most memorable wine, and a worthy inclusion in any genuine wine-lover's cellar. Most definitely a "food" wine, it drinks splendidly with local preparations such as mutton *daube* and rabbit in chocolate sauce, and with the local Laguiole cheese.

SOUTHWEST FRANCE
A.O.C. Monbazillac

- *Wine selected:*
  Monbazillac Cuvée Madame
  (50 cl bottle)

- *Grape Varieties:*
  Muscadelle 50%, Sémillon 45%,
  Sauvignon 5%
- *Average vine age:*
  40 years
- *Vineyard size:*
  9.2 hectares
- *Soil type:*
  Clay and limestone
- *Production:*
  4,900 bottles

Finest Vintages:
1999, 1998, 1997, 1996, 1995, 1994

Château Tirecul La Gravière
24240 Monbazillac
Tel. (0033) 553 57 44 75
From Monbazillac take the Pomport
road, and once past the cemetery take
the first right (a signboard indicates
the estate). The cellars are 300 m
down on the right.
- *Owners:* Claudie & Bruno Bilancini
- *On-site sales:* Yes
- *Visits:* Monday-Friday 9:00–12:00
  a.m., 2:00–5:30 p.m. Otherwise
  by appointment
- *Price:* ★★★★

CHÂTEAU TIRECUL LA GRAVIÈRE

Monbazillac has long had a reputation for good, reliable sweet wine, yet there has never been anyone making what one could unhesitatingly describe as "great", wine capable of attracting the attention of critics and connoisseurs and winning their undivided praise. Yet that is no longer true: since the mid-1990s Château Tirecul La Gravière, under the inspired ownership of Claudie and Bruno Bilancini, has been making wine of outstanding quality, on a level with the greatest names of the more prestigious appellations.

A haven for *Botrytis cinerea*

The Bilancinis have been at Tirecul La Gravière since mid-1992. The estate lies in the center of this ancient wine region, which for centuries exported its produce to many countries and found its way onto the highest tables. The vines are on the famous "Côte Nord" of Monbazillac, which has been recognized for its quality since the seventeenth century. They face north and east, enjoying a slow ripening cycle and the preservation of complexity and aromatic finesse in their juice. The vineyard has a significant slope, giving good drainage, and the orientation, combined with the abundance of clay in the soil, favors the autumnal mists so indispensable to the development of *Botrytis cinerea*.

Mixed planting of venerable vines

Faithful to local tradition the Muscadelle is the principal grape, with Sémillon in attendance and Sauvignon in a minor role. Muscadelle is appreciated for its aromatic range and its freshness, while Sémillon contributes opulence, roundness, and fleshiness. The average age of the Bilancinis' vines is fourty years, yet some plots contain ninety-year-olds. The different varieties are intermixed in the vineyard: that was the practice when the older vines were planted, and current replanting continues to respect this complantation.

As with all great sweet wines, the harvest is carried out progressively by *tries* (sweeps) as the grapes become sufficiently shriveled by *Botrytis*. Picking generally lasts six weeks, from mid-October through to the end of November. Yields vary between seven and twelve hectoliters per hectare.

Monbazillac Cuvée Madame

The precious crop is treated with utmost care once picked, and there is no mechanized manipulation in the cellar. After a slow, gentle pressing the juices are run off by gravity, spend one night settling, and are then transferred to oak barrel for fermentation. This can last until June for the richest lots of must. Then follows maturation, also in oak naturally, for up to two years.

The magnificent quality of the shriveled grapes, and the painstaking, natural vinification, shine through in the wine. Cuvée Madame—and to only a slightly lesser degree the standard *cuvée*—attracts the eye with its glorious full gold color, then caresses the taster's palate with its magnificent smooth, rich texture, its finesse, and its very complex bouquet of apricot, orange, dried fruit, and cinnamon, subtly rounded off with classy oak nuances. The aromas are superbly pure, the balance is impeccable, and the finish is very, very long. What a revelation! Drink Cuvée Madame with goose *foie gras*, pan-fried or grilled, or young lacquered pigeon with spice, suggest the Bilancinis.

SOUTH-WEST FRANCE
A.O.C. Gaillac

- *Wine selected:*
  Le Vin de Voile

- *Grape Variety:*
  Mauzac Roux
- *Average vine age:*
  45 years
- *Vineyard size:*
  2 hectares
- *Soil type:*
  Clay and limestone

Finest Vintages:
1992, 1987, 1981

Robert Plageoles & Fils
Domaine des Très Cantous
81140 Cahuzac-sur-Vère
Tel. (0033) 563 33 90 40
- *Owners:* Robert & Bernard Plageoles
- *On-site sales:* 8–12 a.m., 2–6 p.m.
  (Sundays by appointment)
- *Visits:* By appointment
- *Price:* ★★

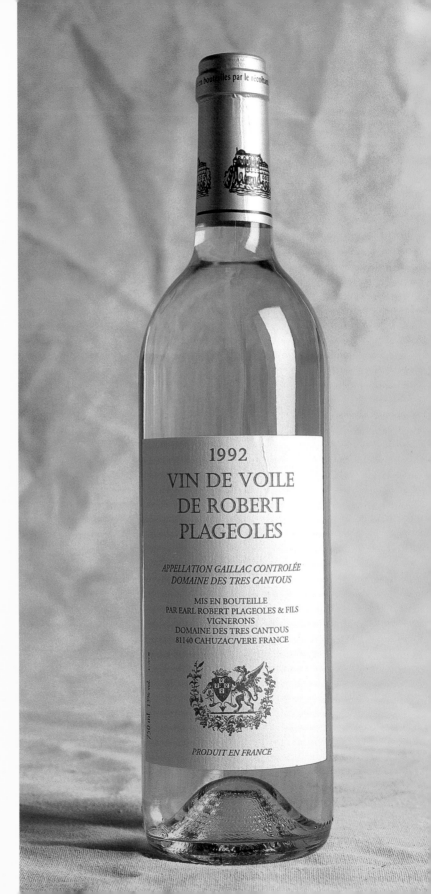

ROBERT PLAGEOLES & FILS

The ancient wine region of Gaillac, some fifty kilomèters northeast of Toulouse, could so easily have forgotten its past and opted to make the sort of bland, fruity mass-market wines which are guaranteed to sell easily. Yet the Gaillacois are tenacious and proud of their traditions, and none perhaps more so than Robert Plageoles and his family. Their dedication as purveyors of Gaillac authenticity is born out by a range of highly original wines.

Two excellent vineyard estates

The Plageoles family have been making wine since 1820 on their Très Cantous estate at Cahuzac-sur-Vère, and acquired a second property, Roucou Cantemerle, at Castelnau-de-Montmiral, in 1963. The first covers 8 hectares of the clay and limestone Coteaux de Salettes slopes, while the second covers 7 hectares and lies on different terrain, the siliceous clay of the plateaux du Montmiralais. These two excellent and different vineyards, cultivated by hand by their owners, are the site of what they describe as the "ampelographic safeguarding of autochthonal vines."

Guardians of historical vine plants

The Mauzac vine, widely used in Gaillac, has pride of place in the vineyards, which in fact contain four sub-varieties (*vert, roux, rose, and gris*) of Mauzac Blanc which give remarkably different wines. While this variety has never been at risk, another variety championed by Plageoles, the Ondenc, certainly has: famous in days long gone by but almost relegated to history over the last two centuries, it has been resuscitated by Plageoles, who makes the much-acclaimed sweet Vin d'Autun with it. Duras (with Mauzac probably the oldest Gaillac variety), Prunelart (a variety of Cot highly esteemed in the Middle Ages), Lenc de l'El, Mauzac Noir, and Braucol, as well as the better-known Muscadelle, Syrah, and Gamay, these are the other inhabitants of the Plageoles vineyards.

A reflection of the year's climate

Adapting to each year's climatic cycle and making the most of it, Plageoles and his son Bernard produce every style of white wine, from dry through *doux* to out-and-out *liquoreux*, this last with grapes which are usually *passerillés*—left to dry on the vine when overripe—although the nobly-rotting *Botrytis* fungus occasionally shows up in the vineyard. Characterful red wines and a sparkling wine complete the production.

Le Vin de Voile

Another ancient local custom which Plageoles perpetuates is that of making an oxidative wine. When the vintage permits—the grapes must have sufficient acidity and not be excessively ripe, yet also have a good alcohol level—he produces small quantities of what he has named Le Vin de Voile. This dry wine is matured for seven years with no topping up of the barrel, which is possible because a voile or layer of yeast forms on the surface of the wine after a while, protecting it from bacterial attack. Vin de Voile, a cousin of Vin Jaune and dry sherry, shares their oxydo-reduction character and balsamic and nutty aromas, and has innate liveliness and great finesse. Its potential for improvement is formidable, easily spanning twenty to fifty years. This wine shows very well in the company of trout served with morel sauce or, suggest the Plageoles, seventeenth-century delights such as *coq en croûte comme à Gaillac, cigalade de poulpes, lapinade de presbytère* or *la Vauréenne*.

SOUTHWEST FRANCE
A.O.C. Madiran

• *Wine selected:*
Château Montus XL

• *Grape Variety:*
Tannat
• *Average vine age:*
22 years
• *Vineyard size:*
85 hectares
• *Soil type:*
Pudding stones and gravel over clay
• *Production:*
6,000 bottles

Finest Vintages:
1996, 1995

Alain Brumont
S.A. Domaines et Châteaux d'Alain
Brumont
32400 Maumusson-Laguian
Tel. (0033) 562 69 74 67
Internet: www.brumontalain.com
Alain Brumont is based at Château
Bouscassé, which lies (well
signposted) on the edge of
Maumusson.
• *Owner:* Alain Brumont
• *On-site sales:* Yes
• *Visits:* Yes
• *Price:* ★★★★

ALAIN BRUMONT

Who had heard of Madiran and Pacherenc-du-Vic-Bilh wines twenty years ago? Very few people outside the region of Béarn where they are made. Today however some of these wines are mightily impressive, and are increasingly sought out by those who wish to get away from the wines of better-known regions and try something different. This rehabilitation can be attributed above all to one man, Alain Brumont, now the most successful and probably the best-known grower in the southwest of France.

A young man with a vision

Brumont is the archetypal self-made man, who through his courage, vision, and obstinacy has dragged the ancient Madiran wine region into the twenty-first century, and turned a moribund wine-making tradition into a thriving and profitable activity for many. Born into a family which had grown maize and made wine for generations, he started working young in the fields and vineyards of the family estate, Bouscassé. In the late 1970s he discovered what great wine was all about during a visit to the Médoc, and returned home fired with a desire to make some himself, and what is more to make it with Madiran's own Tannat grape, which everyone was ripping up at the time.

The struggle rewarded

He managed to scrape together the means to acquire a nearby dilapidated property called Montus. Single-handedly he planted the vineyard, built the cellars, and subsequently started making his wine—the way he felt it should be made, from low yields, picked by hand, and aged in oak, which earned him not a little derision from the locals. Its quality was quickly recognized by those who tried it, and then, when the wine beat the Bordeaux first growths in a blind tasting, interest and demand went wild. Montus was elected Gault et Millau's wine of the decade, and Brumont was able to view the future more serenely.

Whites worthy of the reds

Not being one to sit on his laurels, Brumont turned his attention to white wines and started making Pacherenc-du-Vic-Bilh (Madiran's white-wine appellation) as well. Having honed their qualities over the years, Brumont today makes a sumptuous dry Pacherenc at Montus from the local Petit Courbu grape, which is destined to become very *recherché*, and sweet Pacherenc from Petit-Manseng at Bouscassé.

Château Montus XL

Forty months in new 400-liter barrels—very few wines are capable of withstanding such treatment and emerging with perfect balance, yet the XL is and does. A monument of richness, opulence, and class, it is held upright by a magnificent structure of ripe tannin and imposing acidity, lovingly envelopped in its succulent, ample flesh. With complex aromas of spice, cloves, and black fruit when young and a remarkably long, intense finish, XL is undeniably one of the world's greatest red wines. It will keep for two to three decades, and should be reserved for one's best friends, for drinking with roast wild duck, accompanied by some of Monsieur Brumont's famous Tarbes beans.

SOUTH-WEST FRANCE
A.O.C. Madiran

- *Wine selected:*
  Madiran

- *Grape Varieties:*
  Tannat 90%, Cabernets 10%
- *Average vine age:*
  30 years
- *Vineyard size:*
  45 hectares
- *Soil type:*
  Clay and limestone, clay and gravel
- *Production:*
  120,000 bottles

Finest Vintages:
2001, 2000, 1998, 1997, 1995

Château d'Aydie
64330 Aydie
Tel. (0033) 559 040 800
Internet: pierre-laplace.com
From the Aydie church, take the
Diusse-Garlin direction. The entrance
is on the left, just after the château,
which is on the right.
- *Owners:* Vignobles Laplace
- *On-site sales:* Yes
- *Visits:* 9–12:30 a.m., 2–7 p.m.
- *Price:* ★

CHÂTEAU D'AYDIE

The best Madirans today are those which successfully counterbalance the dense, structured austerity natural to the Tannat grape with the polish, elegance, and harmony which comes from painstaking vineyard work, and to which the modern palate has become attuned. The Laplace family have been making this sort of Madiran for quite a while now, and their Château d'Aydie is a yardstick example.

Keeping the flame alight

Château d'Aydie, bought by the late Frédéric Laplace, was for many a year the only name of note in a region which, despite its glorious history, went through almost terminal decline as a result of phylloxera and the economic hardships of the first half of the twentieth century. As recently as the 1970s nearly all the remaining growers sold their crop to the local cooperative, yet the Laplaces started bottling quite early on, and were an inspiration to others who felt the urge to go it alone. Frédéric Laplace was succeeded by his son Pierre, and today Pierre's four children are looking after the business.

The true character of Madiran

Aydie is a splendid estate of sloping vineyard parcels spread around a handsome château, with the Pyrenees providing a fine backdrop. The subsoil of this land, which lies in the heart of the appellation, is composed of clay and gravel, and large pudding-stones lie on the surface, or in places there is fine gravel. This is the most typical soil of the appellation. In dry years the roots will thrive on the cool of the clay deep down, while in damp years these sandy, stony soils provide excellent drainage.

Frédéric and Pierre were known in their time as pioneers, and in the same spirit the younger generation continue reviewing working practices and trying out new ideas. Tannat is given pride of place in the wines, and the vines are densely planted in order to stimulate competition amongst them and thus reduce yields, which are further reduced when necessary by a green harvest in July. Ripening is aided and aeration promoted by leaf stripping, and erosion is tackled and competition again stimulated by letting grass grow around every other row. These and other actions have one aim, that of harvesting fine, overripe, flavorsome grapes through which the land can express itself.

The technique of *microbullage*

In the cellars also the Laplaces continually work hard to improve their wines. With Patrick Ducourneau the family have perfected the technique of *microbullage*, which is a way of giving wine maturing in vat contact with the air, as wines in barrel have through the pores of the wood. This procedure helps ripen the color and tannin of a wine. Another new technique, that of separating the wine from its lees and stirring and oxygenating them for several weeks before reuniting the two, gives wine greater volume, substance, and roundness.

Madiran

The Château d'Aydie is a textbook example of modern Madiran, giving the taster authentic density, structure, and power and at the same time silkiness, harmony, and a certain elegance. This rich, complex wine has a very attractive flavor of black fruit, cinnamon, cloves, and vanilla, a fine close-grained texture and a long finish. It is ideally suited to local cuisine: the tannin of the wine and the fat of the duck or goose dish engage each other on one side, leaving the splendid aromas to succeed each other across center stage, displaying their charms and seducing the taster.

SOUTH-WEST FRANCE
A.O.C. Jurançon

- *Wine selected:*
  Jurançon Noblesse du Temps

- *Grape Variety:*
  Petit-Manseng
- *Average vine age:*
  25 years
- *Vineyard size:*
  7 hectares
- *Soil type:*
  Clay
- *Production:*
  18,000 bottles

Finest Vintages:
2001, 2000, 1999, 1998, 1996, 1995

Domaine Cauhapé
Quartier Castet
64360 Monein
Tel. (0033) 559 21 33 02
From the centre of Monein take the
Navarrenx road, follow it for roughly
4 km, then take the Cardesse road
on the left and follow the signs.
- *Owner:* Henri Ramonteu
- *On-site sales:* Yes
- *Visits:* Yes
- *Price:* ★★

DOMAINE CAUHAPÉ

Highly prized in days long gone by, the wines of Jurançon suffered serious decline as a result of the ravages of phylloxera and the economic and social upheavals of the first half of the twentieth century. Barely maintaining even a local reputation they needed a champion, a pioneer to resuscitate them in a form capable of attracting the attention and appreciation of modern wine lovers. It might be unfair to give all the credit to one man, but Henri Ramonteu of Domaine Cauhapé might be said to be responsible.

A climate conducive to excellent quality

The foothills which start rolling to the Pyrenees from just south of the market town of Pau are blessed with a climate conducive to making dry and sweet white wines of excellent quality. The moderating Atlantic influence and regular sunshine provide conditions in which the grapes can ripen properly, and the relative altitude of the vineyards, the frequent Indian summers, and the warm wind that blows up from Spain enable the grapes to shrivel on their stalks; their juice concentrated by this *passerillage*, they are capable of making highly sweet wines of splendid quality. One can easily understand how in the past they were considered in the same breath as Sauternes and the finest Loire wines, and enjoyed the patronage of Pau's son Henry IV, who was famously baptized with Jurançon and garlic, and England's Charles II.

A period of intense experimentation

The Ramonteu family acquired Domaine Cauhapé in 1957, at a time when there were only 4 hectares of vineyard, planted principally with Gros-Manseng,

the variety more suitable for the production of dry wines. Henri started making wine in the early 1980s, and contact with luminaries such as Denis Dubourdieu stimulated his ambitions and saw the start of experiments: stainless steel, pre-fermentation maceration, temperature control, lees contact, and indeed many other techniques were tried out. Soon he was producing dry wines of stunningly precise aroma and complexity, thoroughly modern, original, racy, and absolutely irresistible.

The logical progression was to plant quantities of the finer Petit-Manseng, and turn his hand to sweet wines. From 1988 he started using barrels to mature and subsequently even ferment them, and became obsessed with harvesting late, by successive *tries* (sweeps). Today at Cauhapé the two Mansengs, in a variety of different expressions, give three dry wines and four sweet wines of a quality which has made wine lovers and other growers alike sit up and take note.

Jurançon Noblesse du Temps

Less famous than Ramonteu's award-winning Quintessence, his Noblesse du Temps is the result of the second and third *tries* of Petit-Manseng around the beginning of December. Fermented and aged for eighteen months in new oak, this is a gloriously rich, honeyed wine that is rendered all the more complex by the multiple flavors of *élevage* in oak. Unbelievably smooth and displaying inordinate finesse, it caresses the palate with its silky concentration, with a raciness which prevents its sweetness becoming excessive. This is a long-term wine, for savoring alongside pan-fried fresh *foie gras*.

SOUTH-WEST FRANCE
A.O.C. Jurançon

- *Wine selected:*
  Jurançon Uroulat

- *Grape Variety:*
  Petit-Manseng
- *Average vine age:*
  20 years
- *Vineyard size:*
  4 hectares
- *Soil type:*
  Siliceous clay with pudding-stones
- *Production:*
  15,000 bottles

Finest Vintages:
2000, 1999, 1998, 1996, 1995, 1994

Clos Uroulat
Quartier Trouilh
64360 Monein
Tel. (0033) 559 21 46 19
- *Owners:* Charles & Marie Hours
- *On-site sales:* By appointment
- *Visits:* By appointment
- *Price:* ★

CLOS UROULAT

Only two wines are made by Charles Hours on his Clos Uroulat estate, but what splendors! One is a dry white, the other a sweet white, and both are made in a modern style favoring elegance, purity, and harmony, packed with flavor yet with no undue flamboyance. These are textbook Jurançons, as the estate's customers are fully aware, and few visitors leave the premises, one imagines, without at least a small purchase loaded into the car trunk. Hours, a relative newcomer to wine making, is a master of his craft.

A change of career

The estate, lying outside the town of Monein in the western sector of the delimited Jurançon appellation region, was acquired by its owner in 1983. He had no wine-making experience, yet his family did have links with wine, for his grandparents had run a vine nursery, and other family members had vines in Jurançon. Indeed he chose an estate adjacent to two other properties owned by the family. When he acquired it only half of the 7 hectares were planted, yet that situation did not last very long. The vineyards contain the classic varieties of the region, Petit-Manseng, and Gros-Manseng, and a little Courbu.

The warm wind does its work

They are well situated on southeast-facing clay and marl slopes, which contain large amounts of smooth calcareous pudding-stones perfect for regulation of the water input over the growing season. The vines are trained three meters high by the local *hautain* method, which reduces the risks associated with the spring frosts so frequent in the region. Viticultural methods are as organic as possible, and can be resumed by what is generally known as *lutte raisonnée*.

Harvesting is carried out by hand from mid-October onwards, when the Courbu and Gros-Manseng are picked and vinified to make the dry white Cuvée Marie. Harvesting of the Petit-Manseng carries on into November as the successive pickings bring in the grapes and bunches that have become sufficiently dehydrated to be vinified. This *passerillage* is the work of the *foehn*, the warm wind which blows over the Pyrenees, bringing about the evaporation of the water in the juice and subsequent concentration of the grape's sugar and acidity.

Jurançon Uroulat

Once picked the fruit is gently crushed in a pneumatic press without delay, and the juice left to settle by gravity. Thereafter the fermentation and aging take place in oak barrels over some eleven months. For the dry wine some 10 percent of the barrels are renewed each year, while the sweet Uroulat gets roughly 25 percent, the vintage quality dictating the exact amount.

The dry Cuvée Marie is a splendidly rich, concentrated wine with good balancing acidity, which is ideally drunk alongside food. It represents great quality at a fraction of the price of a Meursault or a Pessac-Léognan. Charles Hours is best known though for his sweet Uroulat, a lovely plump yet fresh wine of impressive dimensions and superb length, which thanks to its fine acidity develops well in bottle. Its exquisite floral aromas and subtly exotic character are absolutely irresistible, and it is a treat enjoyed on its own. Uroulat also partners lightly spiced oriental dishes remarkably well.

SOUTH-WEST FRANCE
A.O.C. Cahors

- *Wine selected:*
  Cahors Le Cèdre

- *Grape Variety:*
  Malbec
- *Average vine age:*
  30-40 years
- *Vineyard size:*
  13 hectares
- *Soil type:*
  Clay and limestone
- *Production:*
  48,000 bottles

Finest Vintages:
2000, 1999, 1998, 1996

Château du Cèdre
Bru
46700 Vire-sur-Lot
Tel. (0033) 565 36 53 87
Once in the centre of Vire-sur-Lot
the estate may be found by following
the signs.
- *Owners:* Pascal & Jean-Marc
  Verhaeghe
- *On-site sales:* Yes
- *Visits:* 9–12 a.m., 2–6 p.m. (Mon.–Sat.)
- *Price:* ★★

CHÂTEAU DU CÈDRE

The devastation caused by phylloxera and then the frosts of 1956 together almost wiped out wine production in the historic Cahors region, there remaining only 1 percent of the mid-nineteenth-century vineyard by the 1960s! Today, fortunately, it is enjoying a renaissance, thanks to a handful of growers who are making the most of its fine vineyard terrain and to a market that is ready to pay them sensible prices for their pains. The most sought-after wine today is perhaps that of Château du Cèdre, which over the last fifteen years has risen from anonymity to prominence under the impulsion of the two young Verhaeghe brothers. This estate now counts as one of the finest in the entire southwest of France.

A Flemish family in southwest France

It all started when the Flemish Verhaeghe family fled to France during World War I in 1915. They remained for fifteen years before returning to Belgium, but one Verhaeghe decided to stay on, got married and settled in the village of Boulvé, where he farmed and grew vines. His son Charles married and moved to Vire-sur-Lot, and in his turn became a vine grower and wine maker. It was he who created the estate, on vineyard land devasted by the frosts several years before.

His sons Pascal and Jean-Marc duly studied wine making, the former in Burgundy and California, the latter in Bordeaux, and joined their father, who retired in 1993. The 1990s saw a number of modifications to working practices, and the wines quickly became noticed.

A richer, more concentrated crop

Nothing really revolutionary was started at Château du Cèdre, simply measures recognized as necessary by many young wine makers today: ecological viticultural methods avoiding weedkiller and chemical fertilizers, yield reduction by serious pruning, leaf stripping for greater sun exposure and air circulation, harvesting of the grapes on the verge of overripeness. These disciplines are still not widely practiced in the region, and the Auxerrois (the Côt of the Loire, the Malbec of Bordeaux) and Tannat grapes of Cahors can give wines singularly lacking in charm if not perfectly ripe.

In the cellars the Verhaeghes aim at softness, richness, and harmony. They promote very gentle extraction of the grapes' matter through long vattings and limited *pigeage*, malolactic fermentation and finely-judged maturation in new oak barrels. The reflection and the efforts of the brothers have paid handsome dividends.

Cahors Le Cèdre

Introduced in 1996, the Le Cèdre is surely the finest Malbec wine in France. Black as ink, soft and remarkably sensual for the grape, it is creamy and concentrated on the palate, with a rich black-fruit and licorice flavor rounded off by the subtle vanilla backdrop imparted by its oak-aging. Its ample flesh envelops the ripe tannic structure, and the whole has fine balance and great class, and finishes with very good length. A lifespan of at least two decades may be expected for this superlative wine, which rejoices in the company of local goat's cheeses such as Rocamadour and Cabécou, grilled meats, and all the region's methods of preparing duck.

CHAMPAGNE
A.O.C. Champagne

- *Wine selected:*
  Grande Cuvée
  (Multi-Vintage)

- *Grape Varieties:*
  Pinot Noir 45–50%, Chardonnay
  30–35%, Pinot Meunier 15–20%
- *Reserve wines:*
  40%
- *Aging on lees:*
  6 years
- *Dosage:*
  6 gms/liter

Krug
5 Rue Coquebert
51100 Reims
Tel. (0033) 326 84 44 20
Rue Coquebert leads off boulevard
Lundy. Krug is a few meters along, on
the left-hand side.
- *Owner:* L.V.M.H.
- *Chairman & Managing Director:*
  Rémi Krug
- *On-site sales:* No
- *Visits:* By appointment
- *Price:* ★★★★

KRUG

If there is one name that can be said to sum up all that is best in Champagne, a name synonymous with consistent perfectionism and unremitting excellence, that name must be Krug. The small family firm on rue Coquebert makes wines of enormous complexity, smooth richness, and great longevity, which are regularly demanded and hedonistically savored by the world's wine lovers.

The house of Krug is founded

In 1841 a young German *émigré* named Johann-Josef Krug married an English girl in Paris. His brother-in-law, who was head of the Jacquesson champagne firm, gave him a job, but by 1843 Krug was itching to go into business for himself. He rented cellars in the center of Rheims and rapidly made a fine reputation for himself as a blender of champagnes. In 1846 he gained French nationality and changed his name to Jean-Joseph.

Ever since, successive generations of Krugs have always respected the founder's exacting ground rules, which is one explanation for the relentless continuity of quality. What is more, the family members have always been entirely ensconced in the production of the house's champagnes. Blending is today carried out by family teamwork: the two brothers Henri and Rémi and their children all participate actively.

In the late 1960s Paul Krug sold a majority share-holding to Rémy Martin in order to consolidate the firm's finances and give it the wherewithal to develop. That enabled a program of vineyard acquisitions to start, which included the small, walled Clos du Mesnil. In 1999 LVMH acquired Krug. Rémy Martin and subsequently LVMH have had the good sense to leave the family's wine-making well alone, and have approved the gradual handover to the young generation, which is in transition. This link-up between family firm and multinational is beneficial to all concerned.

Fermentation in barrel

Krug is probably the only major house today to ferment all its wines in small barrels, which provides the creamy thickness that characterizes its wine. After the transformation the wine is periodically racked in order to separate it from its lees. When the family gets down to blending they use a significant quantity of mature reserve wines, drawing on the impressive resources they have built up; this is where the Krug *savoir-faire* comes into play. Then when the second fermentation is over, wines are matured on their lees for at least six years before disgorging and sale.

Grande Cuvée

Krug's Grande Cuvée, a 'multi-vintage', represents four-fifths of the house's production and is a veritable work of art. It is full-bodied, with a slightly austere woodiness which requires a few years to soften up, and has a suave creamy richness, discreet prickle and great aromatic complexity. Not the least of its qualities is its very long and intense finish.

Its balance and complexity make it absolutely delicious on its own, yet like all great wines it really deserves to be drunk with food, and the world's most talented chefs fall over themselves to concoct dishes around Grande Cuvée. A relatively simple one to which it is well suited is Bresse chicken, truffled and roasted. A sumptuous combination!

CHAMPAGNE
A.O.C. Champagne

• *Wine selected:*
Cristal
(Vintage)

• *Grape Varieties:*
Pinot Noir 55%–60%,
Chardonnay 40%–45%
• *Aging on lees:*
6 years
• *Dosage:*
11 gms/liter

Finest Vintages:
1994, 1990, 1989, 1988,
1985, 1983, 1982

Louis Roederer
21 Boulevard Lundy
51100 Reims
Tel. (0033) 326 40 42 11
Boulevard Lundy stretches between
Place Aristide-Briand and Place de
la République. Roederer's offices are
on the left if coming from the Place.
• *Owner:* Claude Rouzaud
• *Managing Director:* Jean-Claude
Rouzaud
• *On-site sales:* No
• *Visits:* 10–12 a.m., 2–4 p.m., by
appointment and with
recommendation only
• *Price:* ★★★★

LOUIS ROEDERER

The revered house of Louis Roederer has a fine history, and has long enjoyed a reputation for producing benchmark champagne. Today it has the rare privileges of still being a family firm and of being relatively independent with regard to grape supplies, due to its own magnificent vineyard holdings.

A bright young man's inheritance

Louis Roederer was founded in 1776 by a Monsieur Dubois and his son. Following the younger Dubois' tenure it subsequently passed into the hands of Nicolas Schreider. This gentleman, having no offspring, hired his eighteen-year-old nephew Louis Roederer to second him, and was so impressed with the young man that he bequeathed him the firm when he died in 1833.

Roederer was indeed highly talented, and set about developing export markets, principally in Russia, America, and England. With the help of his German salesman Herr Krafft, very soon his champagne was being savored by the upper echelons of Russian society—Tsar Nicolas I was himself an appreciative customer. At the time of Roederer's inheritance the firm was selling some one-hundred thousand bottles per year, but by the time of his death in 1870 over two million bottles were sold around the world!

A crystal champagne for the Czar

Roederer's son, also named Louis, carried on his father's work, and it was he who had to satisfy Tsar Alexander II's request in 1876 for his wine to be visibly different from that drunk by his subjects. The young man promptly designed a special crystal bottle, in which all shipments destined for the Tsar were subsequently bottled. The Czar's cellarman came to Reims every year to help blend his master's

wine, and Cristal was in all likelihood the forerunner of luxury champagnes.

The young Roederer died prematurely in 1880, and the firm subsequently passed to his sister, then to her son Léon Olry-Roederer, and his wife Camille. Today Jean-Claude Rouzaud, their grandson, is at the helm.

A wealth of reserve wines

The quality of Roederer champagnes can be attributed in part to the fruit of the house's vineyards. Thanks to the foresight and good financial management of successive heads of the house, Roederer today owns 494 acres (200 hectares) wines in *Grand* and *Premier Cru* sites in the three principal vineyard areas. The house has also built up a fine cellar of reserve wines, which in general spend some five years in wooden tuns before being pressed into service, eventually making up eight to twelve percent of the blend.

"Cristal"

The legendary Cristal bottle, having disappeared at the moment of the Russian Revolution, was reintroduced in the 1930s by Camille Olry-Roederer, widow of Léon. Through the glass one may admire its brilliant full gold color, and, once poured, its wealth of very small bubbles. On the nose Cristal is complex, with a range of aromas including hazelnuts, pears, *brioche*, fresh bread... The palate is very refined, combining elegance and richness, with great freshness. And once swallowed, the wine has great length.

Cristal is a marvelous champagne, which can be drunk with many a dish. Jacques Puisais, in *Le Goût juste*, suggests serving it with crab salad with walnut oil, decorated with a smattering of mussels; caviar served with Cristal is also a treat!

CHAMPAGNE
A.O.C. Champagne

- *Wine selected:*
  Cuvée Louise
  (Vintage)

- *Grape Varieties:*
  Pinot Noir 40%, Chardonnay 60%
- *Aging on lees:*
  8 years
- *Dosage:*
  6 gms/liter

Finest Vintages:
1990, 1988

Pommery
5 Place du Général-Gouraud
51100 Reims
Tel. (0033) 326 61 62 63
From the center of Rheims head along
Boulevard Pasteur then Boulevard
Henri-Vasnier, which leads into Place
du Général-Gouraud.
- *Owner:* LVMH
- *Chairman & Managing Director:*
  Jean-Marie Lefèvre
- *On-site sales:* Yes
- *Visits:* By appointment
  (Tel. [00 33] 626 61 62 56)
- *Price:* ★★★★

POMMERY

The house of Pommery, like several other renowned champagne firms, owes its initial development and success to a widow. With great flair, self-assurance, and determination, Louise Pommery built up the firm over thirty years and established it in foreign markets. Today she is commemorated by the firm's luxury *cuvée*, one of the finest of its kind.

Business acumen and strong convictions

In 1856 Louis Pommery went into partnership with Narcisse Greno, a talented wine merchant in need of a financial backer. However a mere two years later Pommery died, and Greno encouraged his thirty-nine-year-old widow Louise, who had until then not been involved in the enterprise, to take her husband's place. Louise Pommery rapidly revealed great business acumen and strong convictions, and decided on two major changes: they were to forget Greno's red-wine business and start producing champagne, and priority was to be given to building up export markets, notably that of Great Britain. Adroit in character assessment, the widow promptly employed one Adolphe Hubinet as her agent, and from 1861 this talented salesman had enormous success in selling Pommery and gaining a solid reputation for the firm.

At home Pommery and Greno rapidly enjoyed great prosperity, and after the Franco-Prussian War (1870–1872) she found new and far larger premises on the butte Saint-Nicaise, under which lay 120 chalk pits which were ideal for conversion into champagne cellars. Above ground she ordered the construction of the eye-catching conglomeration of buildings that are still in place today.

A decade of great fulfilment

This transitory period did not prevent the firm from making some innovative wines, such as the first completely Brut champagne, sold without any dosage, or a Nature Vin Brut, or Pommery Nature 1874, which were received with great enthusiasm. The year 1879 witnessed the marriage of the widow's daughter to Comte Guy de Polignac, a member of one of the oldest and most noble families in the land.

The widow passed away in 1890, at the age of seventy-one. Successive generations of De Polignacs inherited and ran the firm until it was bought in 1979 by the Gardinier family and then sold in 1984 to the conglomerate BSN. In 1991 BSN decided to part with its champagne interests, and sold Pommery to the luxury-goods group LVMH. Nevertheless, a De Polignac still holds a key position today: Prince Alain, the widow's great-great-grandson, makes the wines.

Louise

Lightness, delicacy and freshness, these are the Pommery hallmarks, which are achieved in part by the extreme care taken in handling the raw material and musts before fermentation. The quintessence of this style may be found in the white and rosé *cuvées* named after the widow.

The white Louise 1988, a wine of great finesse and distinction, is made with Pinot Noir from the firm's Ay vineyard and Chardonnay from its Avize and Cramant holdings. It subtly combines delicate and refined floral aromas with a silky texture and good weight on the palate. Its great delicacy makes Louise a great champagne for sipping on its own, but it is also particularly well-suited to dishes built around red mullet.

CHAMPAGNE
A.O.C. Champagne

- *Wine selected:*
  Comtes de Champagne
  (Vintage)

- *Grape Variety:*
  Chardonnay
- *Aging on lees:*
  8 years
- *Dosage:*
  10 gms/liter

Finest Vintages:
1990, 1989, 1988, 1985, 1982

Taittinger
9 Place Sainte-Nicaise
51100 Reims
Tel. (0033) 326 85 45 35
From the center of Rheims head along
Boulevard Pasteur, then Boulevard
Victor-Hugo, which leads into Place
Saint-Nicaise.
- *Owner:* Taittinger
- *Chairman & Managing Director:*
  Claude Taittinger
- *On-site sales:* Yes
- *Visits:* By appointment
- *Price:* ★★★★

TAITTINGER

The house of Taittinger has only existed since 1931, yet due to vineyard acquisitions in fine sites, exacting wine-making, and an innovative style owing much to the Chardonnay grape, it has gained world-wide renown. The hallmarks of Taittinger wines are finesse, refinement, aromatic complexity, and exquisite freshness.

An outsider invests in Champagne

Just after the World War I, Pierre Taittinger, from a family of bankers and politicians from Lorraine, bought the beautiful Château de la Marquetterie and its vineyards, just south of Épernay. Despite having no wine background, he had faith in the future of champagne and started buying up other vineyard parcels, which in the depressed conditions of the time were selling very cheaply. In 1931 Forest-Fourneaux, a small Rheims house founded in 1734 and based in the Château des Comtes de Champagne, came on the market. Taittinger seized the opportunity, acquiring in a single stroke more vineyards, another prestigious address, and a certain historical prestige.

François Taittinger succeeded Pierre at the head of the firm in 1942. He continued the firm's policy of investing in vineyards, and in the 1950s acquired the house of Irroy. By the time Claude Taittinger took over in 1960 the firm had a huge estate covering 617 acres (250 hectares), centered around the *Grand Cru* localities of Verzenay, Mailly, Ambonnay, Bouzy, Cramant, and Avize, which today supplies fifty percent of the house's needs.

The family decided in the mid-1970s to limit production to four million bottles and invest their capital elsewhere. They acquired the Loire sparkling-wine houses Bouvet-Ladubay and Monmousseau and founded a wine estate in California. They have also invested in luxury hotels and other businesses unrelated to wine.

The innovative genius of Taittinger

Up until the inter-war period, champagnes were almost always made with healthy quantities of Pinot in the blend, and as a result were heavier and more powerful than they are today. However Chardonnay played an important role in Taittinger's plans, and from the start he gave it pride of place, creating blends of infinitely greater subtlety and finesse than were available at the time. These characteristics came to epitomize the house style.

Art also has played a role in Taittinger's production since 1983, the year the Taittinger Collection was launched. The firm has commissioned artists such as Arman, Vasarely, Masson, and Lichtenstein to decorate exceptional vintage *cuvées*. The fact that they are produced in tiny quantities has made these bottles eminently desirable collectors' items.

Comtes de Champagne

The luxury *cuvée* Comtes de Champagne was created in 1957. It is made entirely from Chardonnay grown in *Grand Cru* localities on the Côte des Blancs. With this *cuvée* the Taittingers pay their respects to the champagne tradition, maturing it in wood, and disgorging it *à la volée* (by hand, literally with a bang). Its elegant, fresh nose is followed by a silky, ample mouthful and a very long finish. This magnificent wine can be profitably laid down for a decade or two, and expresses itself very eloquently in the company of seafood and fish dishes in sauce: braised salmon with sorrel sauce is perfect.

CHAMPAGNE
A.O.C. Champagne

- *Wine selected:*
  La Grande Dame
  (Vintage)

- *Grape Varieties:*
  Pinot Noir 62.5%,
  Chardonnay 37.5%
- *Aging on lees:*
  7 years
- *Dosage:*
  8 gms/liter

Finest Vintages:
1995, 1993, 1990, 1989, 1988, 1985

Veuve Clicquot-Ponsardin
12 Rue du Temple
51100 Reims
Tel. (0033) 326 89 54 40
From Place Aristide-Briand head along
Rue Jean-Jacques-Rousseau. Rue du
Temple is the second on the right.
- *Owner:* LVMH
- *Chairman & Managing Director:*
  Cécile Bonnefond
- *On-site sales:* Yes
- *Visits:* By appointment
- *Price:* ★★★★

VEUVE CLICQUOT-PONSARDIN

The history of the house of Veuve Clicquot-Ponsardin is littered with courageous exploits, inspired gambles, and determined personalities. None more so than the widow herself, who was certainly one of the people most instrumental in developing the world's taste for champagne. The house standards have always been of the very highest order.

The young widow asserts herself

When François Clicquot, the twenty-seven-year-old head of the Clicquot champagne business, died in 1805, his widow Nicole-Barbe Ponsardin resolved to carry on his work. Her family disapproved, because at the time women did not go into business, yet closing down was unimaginable, and she had a reasonable grasp of the business. She made their talented traveling salesman Louis Bohne a partner, took on a Monsieur Fourneaux to make the champagne, borrowed money, and set about continuing François' development of foreign markets. It was a very courageous decision for a young lady in her time.

The Russian market is won

Madame Clicquot decided from the start to concentrate the firm's energies in Russia. Despite the hazards of the times—the English maritime blockade of France, the Napoleonic Wars, and the Russian embargo on French goods—by cloak-and-dagger maneuvring, coded communications, inspired gambles, and much risk, she managed to get large quantities of champagne through to the thirsty Russian market, and became the toast of Russian society. Eventually exports were more or less limited to one single destination, and Klikofskoë was in such demand that in 1825 sales there totaled two-hundred fifty thousand bottles.

Bohne died in 1821, yet Madame Clicquot had the good fortune of finding another gifted young German, Edouard Werle, who went on to serve the firm loyally for half a century. Werle was unhappy with the firm's dependence on the Russian market and gradually developed others—England, Germany, America, and even the hitherto-ignored domestic one—and his painstaking work was largely responsible for the worldwide renown which the house has enjoyed ever since.

Madame Clicquot died in 1866 at the venerable age of eighty-nine, leaving Werle the firm and some of her vineyards. His descendants succeeded him, and over the decades built up huge vineyard holdings with the house's profits. In 1978 the firm bought the Canard-Duchêne house, then in 1986 the Veuve Clicquot group joined forces with the Louis Vuitton Moët-Hennessy luxury goods group, which owns it today.

La Grande Dame

The house style is personified by its excellent Brut Carte Jaune (Yellow Label), a rich and full-flavored champagne. However its greatest wine is undoubtedly La Grande Dame. This magnificent champagne is made with nothing but *Grand Cru* fruit. The 1990 vintage has a very refined, fruity nose, with touches of grilled almonds and hazelnuts. On the palate it is ample, creamy and concentrated, harmoniously balanced and fresh, with great length. It calls for the most refined of food: caviar, a fillet of sea-perch, truffled Bresse chicken... these are but several possibilities, yet whatever the choice, a meal in the company of La Grande Dame is an unforgettable experience.

CHAMPAGNE
A.O.C. Champagne

- *Wine selected:*
  Cuvée Paradis
  (Vintage)

- *Grape Varieties:*
  Chardonnay 65%, Pinot Meunier
  20%, Pinot Noir 15%
- *Aging on lees:*
  6 years
- *Dosage:*
  12 gms/liter

Alfred Gratien
30 Rue Maurice-Cerveaux
51200 Epernay
Tel. (0033) 326 54 38 20
Head uphill along rue Maurice-
Cerveaux. Alfred Gratien is past Marne
& Champagne, on the right.
- *Owner:* Gratien, Meyer, Seydoux
  Holding
- *Director:* Alain Seydoux
- *On-site sales:* Yes
- *Visits:* By appointment
- *Price:* ★★★

ALFRED GRATIEN

Hidden away in the back-streets of Épernay, Alfred Gratien is one of Champagne's most traditional and perfectionist houses. This firm is still family-owned and resolutely independent, and goes about making its champagnes now in very much the same way, one imagines, as it did 130 years ago: with no short cuts and no frills, simply much devotion and pride.

Alfred Gratien sets up his twin operations

In 1864 the twenty-three-year-old Gratien, a native of Richelieu, south of Chinon, founded a sparkling wine business in Saumur. As if that were not enough, the same year he founded a champagne business in Épernay. He took into partnership an Alsacien named Jean Meyer, and it was Meyer who assumed control of the two firms on Gratien's premature death at the age of forty-four. Meyer was succeeded by his son Albert, who ran the firm for some forty years until his death in 1965, and Albert was followed by his son-in-law, Éric Seydoux. Today, following their father's retirement, operations are in the hands of Alain and Gérard Seydoux. But this is not the only family devotedly serving the firm: in the cellar also, the position of *chef de cave* has been held by three generations of Jaegers, and Jean-Pierre Jaeger's son is already awaiting his turn...

The most traditional of wine-makers

The Gratien style is similar to that of Krug, which is not surprising considering that the two families are closely related. The firm owns no vineyards and can therefore be as selective as it likes at harvest time. It buys in all three major zones, in the best localities.

Like Krug, Gratien use a significant amount of Pinot Meunier in their blends, making a mockery of the general theory that this is a poor, rapidly-aging variety; it is very useful for the Gratien style of wine, contributing body and structure, although a little Pinot Noir is also necessary for its finesse.

Since the grapes are picked in widely-scattered areas, they are pressed rapidly in press-houses in the vineyards, in order to avoid the slightest skin color tingeing the clear juice, before being transported to Gratien's premises in tanker-trucks. After cold clarification, all wines are fermented in 205-liter *champenois* oak barrels, and are not permitted a malolactic fermentation, in order to maintain the characteristics of the grapes and the *terroirs*. These rich and acidic base wines then undergo their second fermentation, and are thereafter left to mature on their lees for very long periods before manual disgorging and sale.

Cuvée Paradis

The Cuvée Paradis, a vintage wine although no year is advertised on the bottle, is very complete, and personifies the house's style, which is all about fullness of body and elegance of fruit. Its color is medium-gold with green tinges, and it has a fine, delicate *mousse*. It has a rich attack and is fat, concentrated, and complex on the palate, with flavors of *brioche*, vanilla, and red fruit. Once swallowed, it has a long and refined finish, with all the complexity of flavor it had in the mouth. Cuvée Paradis is definitely a wine for savoring with food, a noble crustacean for instance, or pike-perch braised in champagne.

CHAMPAGNE
A.O.C. Champagne

- *Wine selected:*
  Blanc de Blancs
  (Vintage)

- *Grape Variety:*
  Chardonnay
- *Aging on lees:*
  7 years
- *Dosage:*
  7 gms/liter

Finest Vintages:
1990, 1989, 1988, 1985

Billecart-Salmon
40 Rue Carnot
51160 Mareuil-sur-Ay
Tel. 00 33 326 89 54 40
Follow the D1 from Ay to Mareuil and
head into the village. Billecart-Salmon
on the left is in the middle of the
village.
- *Owners:* Billecart family
- *Director:* François Roland-Billecart
- *On-site:* Yes
- *Visits:* By appointment
- *Price:* ★★★

BILLECART-SALMON

The house of Billecart-Salmon, situated in the quiet village of Mareuil-sur-Ay, has a long tradition of perfectionist wine-making. It is that rare bird, the family-owned house which has always managed to remain independent, and the Billecart family are justly proud of that fact, and of the quality of their wines.

Two families go into partnership

The Billecart and the Salmon families both had vineyards, and were both selling their products to the big champagne houses, when Nicolas-François Billecart married Élisabeth Salmon in 1818. Élisabeth brought him 14 hectares of vines in dowry, which prompted him to start making his own wine, in partnership with his brother-in-law Louis Salmon.

The time was right, foreign markets were ripe for champagne, and very soon Billecart-Salmon wines were selling very well in the United States, Eastern Europe, and Russia. By 1858, when Nicolas-François died and was succeeded by his son Charles, the firm had long-enjoyed great prosperity. Suddenly disaster struck: Billecart-Salmon's American agent went bankrupt, and it was subsequently found that he had been regularly cheating the firm out of significant sums of money. Somehow the Billecart-Salmons managed to face up to this setback, but it was a long uphill struggle. Then came the economic depression, hard on the heels of the World War I, and the firm found itself obliged to sell off its vineyards. Gradually, by steadfastly adhering to the family goal of quality, the firm once more prospered. Successive generations followed one another, and today François Roland-Billecart is at the helm.

Aromatic purity and freshness

Even when the firm's vineyard holdings were at their most substantial, Billecart-Salmon bought in grapes. Today the vast majority of their grapes comes from growers with whom they have long-term contracts, whose families have in many cases been supplying to the firm for over thirty years. The average rating of grapes purchased is 96%.

Only the *cuvée*, the first pressing of the grapes, is used. The family takes great steps to avoid any risk of oxidation during the wine-making process, for what it seeks above all is aromatic purity and freshness. This is achieved by a *double débourbage* —a prolonged settling of all the year's musts at a low temperature before fermentation; by fermenting all the different musts individually and above all slowly, at a low temperature; and by cooling the wine again after fermentation for further clarification.

These measures give base wines of superb, steely purity, which may then be transformed into champagnes for long-term keeping. They are relatively light and delicate, but also complex and rich, due primarily to the prolonged fermentation.

Blanc de Blancs

One of the house specialities is its Blanc de Blancs—in fact a paper dated 1850, laying out the essentials for making this style of wine, has been found in the family archives. Chardonnay grapes from Cramant, Le Mesnil, and Avize are used to make this vivacious, flowery, and elegant *cuvée*, which deserves a noble crustacean for its ultimate rendezvous: lobster fricasseed in champagne makes an excellent choice.

431

CHAMPAGNE
A.O.C. Champagne

- *Wine selected:*
  Spécial Cuvée
  (Non-Vintage)

- *Grape Varieties:*
  Pinot Noir 60%, Chardonnay 25%,
  Pinot Meunier 15%
- *Reserve wines:*
  10%
- *Aging on lees:*
  3 years
- *Dosage:*
  8 gms/liter

Bollinger S.A.
16 Rue Jules-Lobet
51160 Ay
Tel. (0033) 326 89 54 40
From Epernay take the Ay road
through Magenta. Turn left (just
before the overhead bridge) down
Boulevard Charles-de-Gaulle, and
continue straight ahead. At the end,
turn left; Bollinger is on the right.
- *Chairman & Managing Director:*
  Ghislain de Montgolfier
- *On-site sales:* 9–12 a.m., 2–5:30 p.m.
- *Visits:* By appointment
- *Price:* ★★

BOLLINGER

One of the great names in Champagne, a byword for style, authenticity, and quality, is that of Bollinger. This establishment is one of a dying breed—the large family-owned firm—and its wines, made slowly by traditional methods, never fail to satisfy. They are ordered by discerning consumers the world over, for Bollinger is synonymous with excellence.

The Admiral and the salesman

In 1829 Admiral Comte Athanase-Louis-Emmanuel de Villermont engaged a young German Champagne salesman, Joseph Bollinger, to make and market champagne from the produce of his vineyards around Ay and Cuis. From the outset Bollinger's name was used for marketing the wine, and he did extremely well, gaining the firm a solid reputation. In 1837 he married the Admiral's daughter, then three years later he inherited the firm following his father-in-law's death.

After his death at the ripe old age of eighty-five, his sons Joseph and Georges took over. The two proved adept at opening up foreign markets, notably those of America, and to England, where the firm became the official purveyor of champagne to the royal household. Since then the firm has passed down through the generations of Bollinger descendants, and today all the key positions are held by cousins.

A leading role for the Pinot Noir

Bollinger champagnes, made principally from the Pinot Noir grape, are made exclusively from first pressings. The musts destined for the Spécial Cuvée are generally fermented in small stainless-steel vats, while those destined for vintage wines carry out the process in 205-liter oak barrels. Reserve wines are drawn from the barrels, and are matured for at least five years in magnums stopped with corks, with varieties, growths, and years remaining unmixed, enabling the most subtle fine-tuning during blending. As befits top-quality champagne, after the second fermentation the wines are left to mature on their lees for far longer than is obligatory, in general three years in the case of non-vintage and five or six years in the case of vintage wines. Finally, dosage is minimal, thanks to the richness and breed of the wines.

Two house specialities

Two of the Bollinger range are house specialities: R.D. (recently disgorged) vintage champagnes, which are left on their lees for longer than usual before *dégorgement*, and therefore have extraordinary richness and aromatic complexity combined with perfect freshness when they reach the consumer; and Vieilles Vignes Françaises, made from two small plots of Pinot Noir vines at Ay and Bouzy which never suffered the phylloxera epidemic. The vines are grown by the old method *en foule* (massed together, not in rows), and in great years several thousand bottles of this wine are produced unblended; a unique, rich, and powerful champagne.

Spécial Cuvée

Bollinger is happy to be judged by its basic champagne, the non-vintage Spécial Cuvée, of which the family is proud. This is a rich and full-bodied wine made from the three champagne grape varieties, from sources nearly all rated *Grand* or *Premier Cru*. The Spécial Cuvée, which is superior to many a luxury blend, is essentially an aperitif champagne, yet its robustness stands it in good stead in the company of *foie gras*, or chicken *gigolettes* served with morels (*gigolettes de volaille aux morilles*).

CHAMPAGNE
A.O.C. Champagne

- *Wine selected:*
  Grand Millésime
  (Vintage)

- *Grape Varieties:*
  Pinot Noir 38%, Chardonnay 62%
- *Aging on lees:*
  7 years
- *Dosage:*
  11 gms/liter

Finest Vintages:
1996, 1993, 1989, 1985

Gosset
69 Rue Jules-Blondeau
BP 7
51160 Ay
Tel. (0033) 326 56 99 56
Internet: www.champagne-gosset.com
From Épernay take the Ay road
through Magenta. Turn left (just
before the overhead bridge) down
boulevard Charles-de-Gaulle, and
right at the first junction. Gosset is
on the right.
- *Owner:* Domaines et Cuvées de
  Prestige
- *Chairman & Managing Director:*
  Béatrice Cointreau
- *On-site sales:* 8–12 a.m., 2–6 p.m.
  (5 p.m. Fri.)
- *Visits:* By appointment only
- *Price:* ★★★

GOSSET

One of the very finest champagnes that is made today comes from a house at Ay founded over four centuries ago, in an era when the wines of Ay and Beaune were rated as the kingdom's best and fought it out for a place on the tables of French and foreign monarchs. Whether Pierre Gosset had royal clients we do not know, but after all this time Gosset champagnes continue to perpetuate the Ay tradition of quality, and are present in many of the world's most prestigious restaurants, not to mention the French President's Élysée Palace and the French Senate.

The oldest wine house in Champagne

Pierre Gosset made still red wines, for this was fully a century before the invention of champagne, and he founded a firm to market them in 1584. His descendants duly moved with the times and adapted their skills to champagne-making, and the firm grew in size over the years as the result of their dedicated management and wine-making skills.

Albert Gosset, of the thirteenth generation, passed away in 1991 and was succeeded by his sons. Two years later they sold the firm to the Max Cointreau family, proprietors of the Cognac house Domaine Pierre Frapin. The two families being driven by the same quality-orientated philosophy, the wines continue to be made in the same traditional manner.

The importance of high-quality base wines

The quality of Gosset champagnes comes from the quality of their base wines, on which they rely, and the quality of these lies in the firm's adherence to traditional methods and in its selectivity in choosing its raw material. Grapes are drawn from a large palette of *Grand Cru* and *Premier Cru* sources, and only the first pressings are used.

Fermentation takes place both in vat and in wood, and the wines are not permitted a malolactic fermentation, for they are destined for a long life and need the raciness and the purer fruitiness of malic acidity. Absolutely no concessions are made to modern economic imperatives as far as the wines' aging goes, for all wines lie on their lees for far longer than is habitual in other houses. When the time is right, riddling and disgorging are both carried out by hand, and the wines need little or no *liqueur de dosage* because of the richness acquired over their long maturation.

Grand Millésime

The grapes that went into the Grand Millésime 1996 were sourced from sixteen localities almost all of which are classified *Grand Cru*. After vinification and *prise de mousse* in the house's traditional manner, it spent seven years sur lattes—three years is the legal minimum, five years is normal for quality champagne—feeding off and enriching itself on its lees, before being prepared for market. And that certainly shows in the glass.

Great finesse, intensity, concentration of flavor, utter refinement... All these qualities contribute to make this a memorable bottle for great occasions, which merits a savory dish of guinea-fowl *suprême* cooked in champagne. This is also one of the rare wines to go well with eggs: the pairing of scrambled eggs with caviar and Gosset 1996 is delicious!

CHAMPAGNE
A.O.C. Champagne

- *Wine selected:*
  Grand Vin Signature
  (Vintage)

- *Grape Varieties:*
  Pinot Noir 50%, Chardonnay 50%
- *Aging on lees:*
  9 years
- *Dosage:*
  4.5 gms/liter

Finest Vintages:
1993, 1990, 1988

Jacquesson & Fils
68 Rue du Colonel-Fabien
51530 Dizy
Tel. (0033) 326 55 68 11
Leave Épernay by the Rheims road and
turn right at the Hotel Campanile
traffic circles. Cross one traffic light,
and continue for a few yards.
Jacquesson is on the right.
- *Owners:* Chiquet family
- *Directors:* Jean-Hervé & Laurent
  Chiquet
- *On-site sales:* 8–12 a.m., 1:30–5:30
  p.m. (4:30 p.m. Fri.)
- *Visits:* By appointment
- *Price:* ★★★

JACQUESSON & FILS

There are light, fruity, party champagnes, and—diametrically opposed—there are the Jacquessons of the champagne world: connoisseurs' champagnes, made by craftsmen to exacting standards, using traditional methods, which become progressively more eloquent with age. Jacquesson is a major champagne house.

The champagne served at Napoleon's wedding

The house was founded in 1798 by Claude Jacquesson and his son Memmie. It made a name for itself very rapidly, and the champagne became a favorite of Napoleon I, who served it at his wedding to the Archduchess Marie-Louise of Austria, and took stocks with him on his military campaigns. A mere twelve years after the founding of the house, the Emperor honored it with a visit in order to present the Jacquessons with a gold medal, the highest award of the time for commercial achievement.

The invention of the wire muzzle

Memmie's son Adolphe was soon working at his father's side. Adolphe Jacquesson was a creative soul who invented a number of devices to improve efficiency and safety in the cellars; however his greatest contribution to the industry was the wire muzzle which replaced string for stopping corks flying out of bottles, and the metal capsule which prevents the muzzle digging into the cork.

By 1867 the firm's sales had reached the one million mark, but after Adolphe's death they regressed significantly. In 1920 the firm was acquired by Léon de Tassigny, who managed to stop its decline, then in 1974 Jean Chiquet bought it. Today Chiquet's sons Jean-Hervé and Laurent run Jacquesson with love and talent, maintaining the low-volume "hand-made" traditional approach that gurantees the champagnes' continuing great quality.

"Nothing less than perfection"

The Chiquets' recipe for quality starts in the vineyard: the grapes they grow and buy come from prestigious localities with very high ratings; they are picked at nothing less than perfect ripeness, and gently pressed with much expertise; only the juice of first pressings is normally used, yet even the first fifty to seventy-five liters of this is discarded to guarantee cleanliness and purity.

After clarification, 40 percent of every harvest is fermented in oak barrels in order to produce the controlled oxidation which alone can give the rich and vinous flavors sought by the Chiquets; and all wines are aged for very long periods to enhance their rich complexity and roundness. After disgorging they therefore need little or no *liqueur de dosage*.

Grand Vin Signature

There is not a top-of-the-range wine at Jacquesson, for at its level each is a masterpiece. The superb Grand Vin Signature is a wine many producers would be proud to have as their prestige *cuvée*: the 1990 vintage, produced from fruit of an average rating of 99.2% on the *échelle des crus*, was vinified and aged in oak *foudres* for nine to ten months before blending and bottling with only a light fining prior to its *prise de mousse*, and is a wine of impressive richness and complexity, and remarkable freshness. Its fine, honeyed bouquet of dried fruit and toast is sumptuous, it is smooth and seductive on the palate, and it finishes long and intense. This is a most elegant bottle, and a fine match for chicken *gigolettes* served with morels.

CHAMPAGNE
A.O.C. Champagne

- *Wine selected:*
  Grand Siècle
  (Non-Vintage)

- *Grape Varieties:*
  Pinot Noir 45%, Chardonnay 55%
- *Aging on lees:*
  8 years
- *Dosage:*
  12 gms/liter

Laurent-Perrier
32 Avenue de Champagne
51150 Tours-sur-Marne
Tel. (0033) 326 58 91 22
Follow the D1 from Mareuil-sur-Ay
to Tours-sur-Marne. Laurent-Perrier
is on the right just before leaving
the village.
- *Owners:* De Nonancourt family
- *On-site sales:* Yes
- *Visits:* By appointment (no groups)
- *Price:* ★★★★

LAURENT-PERRIER

The fifth largest champagne firm is based not in Rheims, nor in Épernay, but in the village of Tours-sur-Marne. There Laurent-Perrier practices with great dexterity the fine *champenois* art of blending, and make wines which inspire great loyalty among the firm's admirers.

A widow builds up sales

Even if it is an old champagne house, Laurent-Perrier is a modern success story. The firm was founded in 1812 by a cooper named Laurent. On his death he was succeeded by his son Eugène, who was married to Mathilde-Émilie Perrier. When Eugène died in 1887, widow Laurent-Perrier decided to carry on her husband's work, and set out to develop foreign markets for her wine. She encountered great success, particularly in Great Britain, and by 1914 the firm was selling six hundred thousand bottles per year. However the First World War hit the business badly.

On the brink of disappearance

Madame Laurent-Perrier died in 1925, and there followed a period of slow but inexorable decline, to the point where in 1938 the firm was to be closed. Suddenly, out of the blue, came another widow: Marie-Louise de Nonancourt, born Lanson, who knew the industry well and determined to rescue the firm.

Things began to look up until the world plunged again into war. By the time peace was declared there remained a mere twelve thousand bottles in the cellars. Madame de Nonancourt had passed away, and her son Maurice, who had inherited the firm, had died in captivity. It looked as if the firm's fate was sealed... unless Maurice's brother Bernard could do something.

The triumph of Bernard de Nonancourt

The firm's recovery, conceived and executed by the man known affectionately in the champagne industry as "Big Bernard", has been remarkable. In the two decades following the war, sales climbed to one million bottles per year, and the next three decades saw that figure multiply by seven. This energetic and determined man created a holding company which today owns Salon, Delamotte, Joseph Perrier, and De Castellane, and the group's combined sales are now in excess of ten million bottles per year. Having reached retirement age— though apparently not yet particularly inclined to take it—de Nonancourt is training his daughters Alexandra and Stéphanie, who will eventually inherit the family group.

Grand Siècle

The firm's top-of-the-range wine, Grand Siècle, is a Bernard de Nonancourt invention. This exquisite *cuvée* is, as its label used to put it, a 'marriage of vintages', although the firm did break the rule by marketing a 1988 version and then a 1990. Fruit used for this wine is exclusively *Grand Cru* and exclusively from excellent vintages, and this fact explains in part the wine's utter refinement, breeding, and finesse. Add to that another essential ingredient—perfectionist vinification and inspired blending by Alain Terrier—plus a healthy helping of time to develop its aromatic qualities in the cellar, and one has a sublime lacy liquid of toasted honeysuckle and vanilla flavors. On its own, or served with poached turbot and oysters in champagne sauce, or a simple panful of mussels and mushrooms, Grand Siècle is exquisite.

CHAMPAGNE
A.O.C. Champagne

- *Wine selected:*
  Dom Pérignon
  (Vintage)

- *Grape Varieties:*
  Pinot Noir 42%, Chardonnay 58%
- *Aging on lees:*
  6 years
- *Dosage:*
  10 gms/liter

Finest Vintages:
1990, 1988, 1985

Moët & Chandon
20 Avenue de Champagne
51200 Epernay
Tel. (0033) 326 51 20 00
The avenue de Champagne leads off
the place de la République. Moët &
Chandon is the first large building on
the right.
- *Owner:* LVMH
- *Chairman & Managing Director:*
  Jean-Marie Laborde
- *On-site sales:* Yes
- *Visits:* By appointment only
- *Price:* ★★★★/★★★★★

MOËT & CHANDON

It is said that a bottle of Moët & Chandon is opened somewhere in the world every two seconds. With its omnipresence on the world's wine-retail shelves and copious advertising around the world, Moët & Chandon is without doubt the best-known brand in the world. Yet, paradoxically, despite its vast production the house manages to maintain a very high level of quality.

A prestigious friend and client

The Moët phenomenon started with a grower named Claude Moët, who started making wine and selling it as least as early as 1743. Moët's son, Claude-Louis-Nicolas, joined him in the enterprise, and they were very successful; the firm's client list soon included many of the famous names of the time. Claude-Louis-Nicolas eventually left the firm to his son Jean-Rémy, a friend of Napoleon, who became a frequent visitor.

The benefits of this friendship were not long in coming: after 1804, when Napoleon was proclaimed Emperor of France, a period of fantastic social and commercial success opened up for the firm, during which many of Europe's crowned heads and European statesmen paid visits enjoyed the firm's champagne. In 1816 Jean-Rémy Moët's daughter married Pierre-Gabriel Chandon de Briailles. After sixteen more years of extraordinary commercial expansion and renown, he took, well-earned retirement and handed over control of the company to his son Victor and to his son-in-law Pierre-Gabriel Chandon. The Moët & Chandon brand was born.

From family firm to multinational

Long years of prosperity followed, and by the beginning of the 1960s Moët was one of the largest family-owned firms in France. In 1962 its shares were introduced on to the Paris Stock Market. A number of operations subsequently took place, including the acquisition of the Ruinart and Mercier champagne houses and Christian Dior Perfumes, a merger with Hennessy Cognac and numerous vineyards investments around the world. Then in 1987 the firm associated itself with the Louis Vuitton company to form the world's largest luxury-goods group.

Quantity and quality

Thanks to its fabulous prosperity the firm built up an enormous vineyard holding, which today covers 772 hectares. Yet so great are its sales that today its vines supply a mere quarter of the house's needs. Curiously, despite its enormous annual production, high standards are still maintained, as is born out by a tasting of the Brut Imperial non-vintage, named after Napoleon, which is always well-marked in blind tastings for its cleanness, freshness, elegance, and balance.

Dom Pérignon

The prestige brand of the house, which is treated as a separate entity, is named after the famous monk. The white Dom Pérignon is a scintillating combination of elegance, breeding, freshness, and balance, with, when young, complex and intense floral aromas, which are gradually superseded by those of crystallized fruit, nuts, and *brioche*. A suitable homage to the great monk. Dom Pérignon ages well over the years, and its age dictates whether it is best drunk *en apéritif* or whether it has a personality better married with food. A mature vintage is set off to perfection by a salad of *langoustines*, or turbot in *hollandaise* sauce.

CHAMPAGNE
A.O.C. Champagne

- *Wine selected:*
Blanc de Blancs Grand Cru
(Vintage)

- *Grape Variety:*
Chardonnay
- *Aging on lees:*
8 years
- *Dosage:*
4 gms/liter

Finest Vintages:

1996, 1995, 1990, 1989,
1988, 1985, 1982, 1981

Jacques Selosse
22 Rue Ernest-Vallé
51190 Avize
Tel. (0033) 326 57 53 56
From Épernay take the D40 to Avize.
To visit Jacques Selosse it is advisable
to park in Place Léon-Bourgeois—
pass the lycée viticole on the left
down the Rempart du Midi, and take
the first turn on the left, which leads
into the property.
- *Owners:* Corinne and Anselme
Selosse
- *On-site sales:* Yes
- *Visits:* By appointment
- *Price:* ★★

JACQUES SELOSSE

Occasionally, thoughtful young men start off their wine-making careers with ideas which run contrary to local traditions. If their ideas are well thought-out and their conviction is strong enough, so much the better; they produce wine which ranges from the interesting, to the thought-provoking, to the thoroughly innovative. That is admirable. It is these headstrong men who push forward the frontiers of creativity, who build new traditions. Anselme Selosse is one such man.

A young thinker inherits an estate

Jacques Selosse founded the family estate, based at Avize, just after the Second World War, and forged himself a fine reputation for his Blanc de Blancs. He was succeeded by his son Anselme in 1980. The young Selosse had studied wine-making not in Champagne but in Beaune, and the way he saw the Burgundians vinifying their white wines profoundly influenced his conception of making Blanc de Blancs champagne.

Adopting the Burgundian approach

Selosse's viticultural habits were from the start thoroughly ecological, as might be expected of a thinker. Yields are kept very low, and Selosse decides when to harvest by observing the color of pips, which indicates physiological maturity, and by chewing skins, to assess aromatic development.

Once the grapes have been pressed, musts are run off into 228-liter barrels, one tenth of which are new, for fermentation. There is no temperature control, and fermentations are left to pursue their own rhythm. The lees are stirred up every week during winter, every month during summer, following the practice at Meursault, for maximum richness and fatness of texture. Malolactic fermentations are blocked naturally by the wines' high natural acidity, which is attained by avoiding mineral potassium in composts. Selosse is the only producer in Champagne to use a solera system, better known for making sherry, for his non-vintage Origine.

After bottling and *prise de mousse*, the wines enrich themselves over long periods on their lees, being occasionally shaken to keep the lees in suspension, and, when they are ready, are disgorged by hand. Dosage is always minimal, and for this Selosse uses fructose, liqueur made from grape-sugar, as opposed to saccharose. This practice is highly controversial, as the fructose can be made from grapes grown anywhere in the world.

Blanc de Blancs Grand Cru

The Selosse vintage wines are generally made from two parcels at Avize containing vines over fifty years old. Bottled without fining or filtration, after *prise de mousse* these wines lie on their lees for roughly eight years, and are only sold when considered ready to drink.

In the mouth they are rich and complex, with a well-integrated structure. Exquisite dried fruit flavors are discreetly backed up with vanilla, and the wine is creamy, thick and very long. This is the artist in full flow: a memorable champagne, which calls for food. Anselme Selosse would suggest scallops cooked in olive oil, but other possibilities are legion.

CHAMPAGNE
A.O.C. Champagne

- *Wine selected:*
  Fleuron
  (Vintage)

- *Grape Variety:*
  Chardonnay
- *Aging on lees:*
  5 years
- *Dosage:*
  6 gms/liter

Finest Vintages:
1996, 1995, 1990, 1989, 1985, 1982

Pierre Gimonnet & Fils
1 Rue de la République
51530 Cuis
Tel. (0033) 326 59 78 70
Leave Épernay in the direction of
Sézanne, and follow the D40 towards
Cramant and Avize. At the entry of
Cuis a large sign annonces the way to
Pierre Gimonnet—50 meters further
on the right.
- *Owners:* Gimonnet family
- *Directors:* Olivier & Didier Gimonnet
- *On-site sales:* Yes
- *Visits:* No
- *Price:* ★★

PIERRE GIMONNET & FILS

The Gimonnet firm is a rarity in the Champagne region in having a unique policy of producing vintage wines in every year except for really poor ones, which reflect, in the manner of Bordeaux wines, the qualities of each vintage. Gimonnet wines are benchmark Blancs de Blancs.

Pierre Gimonnet extends his horizons

The family have lived at Cuis and grown vines for over two hundred years, but until the hard times of the 1930s their work was finished once they had sold their fruit to the champagne houses. However Pierre Gimonnet, unable to find a buyer for his produce in 1935 and 1936, by necessity started wine making himself, and this very rapidly became the *raison d'être* of the family's activities, despite the fact that Blanc de Blancs champagnes were almost unknown at the time.

The family holdings are at Cuis, classified *Premier Cru* with a 95% rating, and Cramant and Chouilly, classified *Grands Crus*, and make up an impressive 26 hectares. The vines have a high average age of forty years, thus giving juice of exceptional quality, two parcels at Cramant— La Terre des Buissons and Le Fond du Bateau— were last replanted in 1911 and 1913.

A wide range of vintage Champagnes

The Gimonnet range includes several types of vintage *cuvées* which have different names depending on their vocation. One, Gastronome Brut, is made for drinking young, and thus uses much of the produce of average years; it is a blend of *Premiers* and *Grands Crus*. Fleuron Brut corresponds more to the traditional notion of a vintage champagne, being made only in great years.

Spécial Club Brut is made principally from Cramant fruit of over forty years old. It is marketed in the reproduction eighteenth-century bottle of the Club de Viticulteurs Champenois, having spent at least five years maturing on its lees. Last, but certainly not least, the *cuvée* named Œnophile Maxi-Brut, which is non-vintage and made in limited quantities, is aged for at least seven years on its lees, and is sent out to market without dosage; an excellent wine more reminiscent of a Côte d'Or Chardonnay with bubbles than a champagne.

The pursuit of excellence

The quest for perfection which fires the Gimonnets is permanent. The juices of vines of different localities, plots and ages are vinified separately in small vats, and whenever possible are not chaptalized – which is ambitious in a region as northerly as Champagne; malolactic fermentations are systematic; wines are clarified by chilling, with just one light filtration before *tirage*; and dosage is minimal—between six to eight grams of sugar per liter for a Brut.

Fleuron

The Fleuron is aged for over four years before dosage. It is always a blend of Premiers and Grands Crus, since Cuis vines have the highest acidity of any on the Côte des Blancs, and are indispensable for balance in very ripe years. Fleuron 1990 has rich and intense honeyed and mineral flavors and is full-bodied, with great freshness and purity. It is a magnificent wine, marvelous on its own, but it could also be served a dish of character, such as sweetbread *cassolettes* with shrimps.

CHAMPAGNE
A.O.C. Champagne

- *Wine selected:*
  Salon
  (Vintage)

- *Grape Variety:*
  Chardonnay
- *Aging on lees:*
  12 years
- *Dosage:*
  3 gms/liter

Finest Vintages:
1995, 1990, 1988, 1985, 1982

Salon
5 Rue de la Brèche-d'Oger
51190 Le Mesnil-sur-Oger
Tel. (0033) 326 57 51 65
Follow the D10 down the Côte des
Blancs to Le Mesnil-sur-Oger and turn
right up Grande-Rue. At the top turn
right, then turn left into rue de la
Place. Drive up past the mairie, then
turn right into rue de la Brèche-d'Oger.
Salon is some 50 meters along on the
left, discreetly identified by a small
brass plaque.
- *Owners:* Laurent-Perrier group
- *Chairman:* Didier Depond
- *On-site sales:* Yes
- *Visits:* By appointment
- *Price:* ★★★★★

SALON

Regarded by many connoisseurs as the *crème de la crème* of great champagnes, Salon is rarely seen and even more rarely enjoyed, for little of it is produced and it is very costly. It is more akin to great Burgundy than champagne, for it is always the product of one grape-variety, one *cru* and one year— its makers describe it not as champagne but as "simply a great wine... with bubbles".

The dream of Eugène-Aimé Salon

Salon's story is that of one man, Eugène-Aimé Salon—the son of a champenois cartwright—who as a youth went off to Paris, found a job in the fur trade and quickly rose to fame and fortune. He was an aesthete, and, dissatisfied with the quality of existing champagnes, he dreamed of producing his own, an unblended champagne of pure Chardonnay—a totally innovative concept at the time. He bought his vineyard, situated in Le Mesnil-sur-Oger, at the bottom of the slope next to the church, where the balance between sugar and acids is best.

The myth of Salon spreads

The first recorded vintage was the 1911, and successive vintages so enraptured Salon's many friends that they urged him to make the champagne available to them. He therefore created the Salon firm in 1921 to satisfy their demand. This was the *belle époque*, and soon the wine was to be found on many of the most select tables, and was the house champagne at Maxim's, in its heyday.

Eugène-Aimé Salon died in 1943 and the firm was inherited by his grand-nephew, who subsequently sold it to the Dubonnet-Cinzano group, which was taken over by Pernod-Ricard in 1978. In 1988 Salon Champagne came under the wing of the champagne firm Laurent-Perrier, as did its immediate neighbor, Delamotte.

Ever since the first vintages, its creator's ground-rules have never been slackened: it is only made in the very finest years, from the first pressings of grapes; malolactic fermentation is usually avoided, for the wine needs high acidity to balance its structure and complexity over many years; it is aged on its lees for between eight and twelve years; riddling is carried out by hand over approximately nine weeks, and disgorging is manual and to order, just prior to shipping. Finally, dosage is always extremely restrained.

Salon

A tasting of different vintages demonstrates just how they benefit from bottle-age. Tasted in October 1997 the Salon 1990, still *sur lattes* and thus undosed, had a pale gold color with glints of green, a fine *mousse*, and combined ripe fruit, richness, great refinement, and structure on the palate. Salon 1988 had a very classy creamy attack, and great richness, but also rather austere wood aromas. It has very great potential and may be laid down for many years. Finally Salon 1976, that its *mousse* of tiny bubbles and golden yellow color, had magnificently complex torrefied aromas which for a while tried to mask a great mature Chardonnay wine. Paradoxically these tertiary aromas were livened up by great freshness. It had a wonderfully long finish.

When mature, this great wine needs to be served at 50–54° F (10–12° C), and allowed to breathe. Depending on the vintage and its age, one can accompany it with oysters, caviar, *coquilles Saint-Jacques, foie gras...*

APPENDICES

Sales Outlets

UNITED STATES

Bacchus Imported Ltd.
1801-D Portal St
Baltimore, MD 21224
Tel. (001) 410 633 0400

Classic Wine Imports
99 Rivermoor St
Boston, MA 02132
Tel. (001) 617 469 5799

**Commonwealth
Wine & Spirits**
20 Middlesex Rd
Mansfield, MA 02048
Tel. (001) 508 261 9300

**Diageo Château
& Estate Wines**
800 Third Ave
New York, NY 10022
Tel. (001) 212 572 1360

European Cellars
236 West 27th St, Suite 801
New York NY 10001
Tel. (001) 212 924 4949

Grands Crus Imports Inc.
704 Forman Rd
Souderton, PA 18964
Tel. (001) 215 723 2033

Grape Expectations Inc.
1091 Essex Ave
Richmond, CA 94801
Tel. (001) 510 412 5969

Kermit Lynch
1605 San Pablo Ave
Berkeley, CA 94702
Tel. (001) 510 524 1524

Kysela Père & Fils
130 Windy Hill Lane
Winchester, VA 22602
Tel. (001) 540 722 9228

Louis Latour Inc.
45 Mitchell Bvd, Suite 14
San Rafael, CA 94903
Tel. (001) 415 479 4616

Martin Scott Wines
198 Marcus Ave, Suite E117
Lake Success, NY 11042
Tel. (001) 516 327 0808

Newcastle Imports
1004N 29th Ave North, Suite B
Myrtle Beach, SC 29577
Tel. (001) 843 448 9463

Pinnacle Wine Company
345 Underhill Bvd
Syosset, NY 11791
Tel. (001) 516 921 9005

Rosenthal Wine Merchant
Select Vineyards
PO Box 658, Rt 83
Shekomeko, NY 12567
Tel. (001) 518 398 1800

Stacole Co., Inc.
1003 Clint Moore Rd
Clint Moore Plaza
Boca Raton, FL 33487
Tel. (001) 561 998 0029

GREAT BRITAIN

Corney & Barrow
12 Helmet Row
London EC1V 3TD
Tel. (0044) 20 7539 3200
www.corneyandbarrow.com

Farr Vintners
19 Sussex St
London SW1V 4RR
Tel. (0044) 20 7821 2000
www.farr-vintners.com

Fine and Rare Wines Ltd.
124–128 Barlby Road
North Kensington
London W10 6BL
Tel. (0044) 20 8960 0404
www.frw.co.uk

Fortnum & Mason
181 Piccadilly
London W1A 1ER
Tel. (0044) 20 7734 8040

Gauntleys
4 High St
Nottingham NG1 2ET
Tel. (0044) 115 911 0555

Harrod's
Knightsbridge
London SW1X 7XL
Tel. (0044) 20 7730 1234

H & H Bancroft
1 China Wharf
Mill Street
London SE1 2BQ
Tel. (0044) 87 0444 1700

Lea & Sandeman
170 Fulham Rd
London SW10 9PR
Tel. (0044) 20 7244 0522

Louis Latour Ltd.
7a Grafton St
London W1X 3LA
Tel. (0044) 17 1409 7276

Nickolls & Perks Ltd.
37 High St, Stourbridge
West Midlands DY8 1TA

Tel. (0044) 13 8439 4518 and
(0044) 13 8437 7211
www.nickollsandperks.co.uk

Oddbins (main office)
31–33 Weir Road
Wimbledon SW19 8UG
Tel. (0044) 20 8971 3448
www.oddbins.com

Richard Kihl Ltd.
Slaughden House
140-144 High Street, Aldeburgh
Suffolk IP15 5AQ
Tel. (0044) 17 2845 4455
www.richardkihl.ltd.uk

Richards Walford
Hales Lodge
Pickworth, Stamford
Lincs PE9 4DJ
Tel. (0044) 17 8046 0451

Savage Selections Ltd.
The Ox House
Market Place, Northleach
Gloucestershire GL54 3EG
Tel. (0044) 14 5186 0896

Seckford Wines
Dock Lane, Melton
Suffolk IP12 1PE
Tel. (0044) 13 9444 6622
www.seckfordwines.co.uk

Thorman Hunt
4 Pratt Walk, Lambeth
London SE11 6AR
Tel. (0044) 20 7735 6511

Valvona & Crolla
19 Elm Row
Edinburgh EH7 4AA
Tel. (0044) 13 1556 6066
www.valvonacrolla.com

La Vigneronne
105 Old Brompton Rd
London SW7 3LE
Tel. (0044) 20 7589 6113

Yapp Brothers Ltd.
Mere
Wiltshire BA12 6DY
Tel. (0044) 17 4786 0423

FRANCE

Caves Augé
116 Blvd Haussmann
75008 Paris
Tel. (0033) 145 22 16 97

Caves Estève
10 Rue de la Cerisaie
75004 Paris
Tel. (0033) 142 72 33 05

La Cave à Millésimes
180 Rue Lecourbe
75015 Paris
Tel. (0033) 148 28 22 62

Cave du Moulin Vieux
4 Rue Butte-aux-Cailles
75013 Paris
Tel. (0033) 145 80 42 38

Les Caves du Roy
31 Rue Simart
75018 Paris
Tel. (0033) 142 23 99 11

Les Caves Taillevent
199 Rue du Faubourg-Saint-
Honoré
75008 Paris
Tel. (0033) 145 61 14 09

Fauchon
26 Place de la Madeleine
75008 Paris
Tel. (0033) 147 42 91 10

La Grande Épicerie
38 Rue de Sèvres
75007 Paris
Tel. (0033) 144 39 81 00

Hédiard
21 Place de la Madeleine
75008 Paris
Tel. (0033) 143 12 88 88

Inno Montparnasse
35 Rue du Départ
75014 Paris
Tel. (0033) 143 20 69 30

Juveniles
47 Rue de Richelieu
75001 Paris
Tel. (0033) 142 97 46 49

Lafayette Gourmet
48 Blvd Haussmann
75009 Paris
Tel. (0033) 142 81 25 61

Legrand Filles & Fils
1 Rue de la Banque
75002 Paris
Tel. (0033) 142 60 07 12

Millésima
87 Quai de Paludate
BP 89
33038 Bordeaux
Tel. (0033) 557 80 88 08
www.millesima.com

**Les Marchés aux Vins
Pérardel**
Ave Charles-de-Gaulle
21200 Beaune
Tel. (0033) 380 24 08 09

Le Repaire de Bacchus
31 Ave de l'Opéra
75001 Paris
Tel. (0033) 153 29 97 97

Les Vins du Terroir
34, Ave. Duquesne
75007 Paris
Tel. (0033) 140 61 91 87

BELGIUM

Vins Francis Bernard
Passage Linthout 39
1200 Brussels
Tel. (0032) 27 35 88 80

HOLLAND

Accounter Plazza
Gal & Gal Administration
PO Box 5030
1520 EA Wormerveer
Tel. (0031) 75 65 18 572

D.R. Trading Utrecht B.V.
Rocsoord 17
3508 AE Utrecht
Tel. (0031) 30 232 11 23

P. de Bruijn
Bijleveldsingel 25
6521 An Nijmegen
Tel. (0031) 24 322 93 01

Sauter-Wijnen Courtage
Fregatweg 46B
6202 Maastricht
Tel. (0031) 43 36 37 7999

GERMANY

A. Segnitz & Co. Gmbh
Postfach 10 15 06
28015 Bremen
Tel. (0049) 03 81 30 37

Ste. Marcus Cordier Gmbh
Galileo-Galilei Strasse 16
55129 Mainz (Hechtsheim)
Tel. (0049) 61 31 80 95

**La Petite France—
Weinhandel**
Burg Buschdorf
Buschdorfer Strasse 1
53117 Bonn
Tel. (0049) 228 68 74 38

Vinea
Moerser Strasse 304
47228 Duisburg
Tel. (0049) 20 65 896 31

Concise Glossary

A.O.C. or *Appellation d'Origine Contrôlée:* term guaranteeing the authenticity of a wine's origin, type, and adherence to local wine-making rules

bâttonage: lees stirring; the process of stirring the wine during *élevage* to keep the lees in suspension in the wine, which increases aromatic quality and roundness in the wine

breed: grape quality based on *terroir* characteristics

climat: plot of land in a vineyard; primarily a Burgundian term

clos: vineyard surrounded by walls

chapitalization: the addition of sugar in order to prolong fermentation and obtain more alcohol during vinification

débourbage: the settling of pressed white grape juice for approximately twenty-four hours before vinification

disgorging: the process of expelling the sediment from champagne after riddling

échelle des crus: classification of Champagne wines by percentage scale

élevage: a wine-making term for the maturing of a wine after fermentation and before bottling, which includes the process of aging wine in barrels

enherbement: the ecological practice of cultivating grass between vine rows to produce higher quality grapes and to avoid soil erosion

foudres: large wooden vat or barrel

lees: sediment left in a vinification vat or a barrel

liqueur de dosage: the liqueur added to champagne in the final operation before the wine is sent to market, which determines whether it will be *brut, demi-sec,* or *sec*

lutte raisonnée: literally, minor intervention; the philosophy of avoiding the use of chemical products except when necessary

must: grape juice that is unfermented or in the process of fermenting

négociant: a wine wholesaler, distributor, and—notably in Burgundy—a property that makes wine in large quantities from its own and brought-in grapes

noble rot: vernacular term for the *Botrytis cinerea* fungus that covers grape bunches, producing ideal conditions for sweet wines

passerillage: the process of drying-out grapes on the vine, which produces highly-concentrated juice

pigeage: the extraction in red wine vinification of the grapes' best qualities (color, aroma, tannin, acidity) by traditional treading or modern technology

prise de mousse: the attainment of champagne bubbles as a result of the second in-bottle fermentation

terroir: the multifaceted growing environment of a particular vineyard, including the soil composition, microclimate, altitude, and local weather

riddling: the act of gradually turning and tilting sparkling wine bottles over several weeks in order to accumulate all sediment in the neck of the bottle, where it is later frozen and disgorged

sélection de grains nobles: a sweet, rich white wine made from nobly rotten grapes, which have been harvested in *tries*

tries: successive passages through a vineyard to pick all the fruit at the ideal state of ripeness

vendages tardives: late harvest

vieille vignes: old vines

vigneron: a vine grower and wine maker

vin jaune: a dry, oxidized wine made from Savagnin grapes

vin de paille: a sweet white wine made from grapes that have been dried in the sun on straw mats

à la volée: a method of removing yeast sediment from champage by hand

Bibliography

Jean-François Bazin, *Le Vin de Bourgogne*, Paris: Hachette, 1996.

Bruno Boidron, *The Little Book of Bordeaux Wines*. Paris: Flammarion, 2001.

Clive Coates, M.W., *Grands Vins—The Finest Château of Bordeaux and Their Wines*, London: Weidenfeld & Nicolson, 1995.

Clive Coates, M.W., *The Vine* (monthly), London, various editions.

Collombet, François, *Flammarion Guide to World Wines*. Paris: Flammarion, 2000.

Thierry Desseauve, *The Book of Wine*. Paris: Flammarion, 2001.

Michel Dovaz, *Châteauneuf-du-Pape* (from Le Grand Bernard des Vins de France collection), Boulogne, France: Jacques Legrand, 1992.

Patrick Forbes, *Champagne: The Wine, the Land and*

the People. London: Victor Gollancz Ltd., 1972.

Anthony Hanson, *Burgundy* (2nd edition). London: Faber and Faber, 1995.

Guy Jacquemont and Gérard Guicheteau, *Le Grand Livre des vins de Loire.* Paris: Éditions du Chêne, 1992.

Hugh Johnson, *Wine Companion* (2nd edition). London: Mitchell Beazley, 1987.

Hugh Johnson and Francis Robinson, *The World Atlas of Wines*. London: Mitchell Beazley, 2001.

Daniel Le Conte des Floris, Eric Riewer, Tamara Thorgevsky, Pierre-Emile Durand, *The Little Book of Wines*. Paris: Flammarion, 2001.

Marc-Henry Lemay, *Bordeaux et Ses Vins*, (15th edition). Bordeaux: éditions Féret, 1995.

John Livingstone-Learmonth, *The Wines of the Rhône* (3rd edition). London: Faber and Faber, 1992.

Remington Norman, *The Great Domaines of Burgundy* (2nd edition). London: Kyle Cathie Limited, 1996.

Remington Norman, *Rhône Renaissance*. London: Mitchell Beazley, 1995.

Richard Olney, *Romanée-Conti*, Paris: Flammarion, 1991.

La Revue du Vin de France, Revue du Vin de France SA, Levallois-Perret, various editions.

Tom Stevenson, *The World Sotheby's Wine Encyclpedia*. London: Dorling Kindersley, 2001.

Tom Stevenson, *The Wines of Alsace*. London: Faber and Faber, 1993.

Paul Strang, *Wines of South-West France*, London: Kyle Cathie Limited, 1996.

Roger Voss, *Wines of the Loire*, London: Faber and Faber, 1995.

Index

Acknowledgments

The author would like to express his gratitude to all the growers and estate managers for the warm welcome and hospitality extended to him during the preparation of this book, for the time devoted to answering his questions, and for very kindly providing him with the necessary documentation and a bottle to be photographed.

Photo credits

Daniel Czap: front cover photograph and pages 110, 114–150, 154–170, 174–184, 190–202, 206–286, 418–424, 428–432, 438, 442, 446.
Jean-Pierre Dieterlen: pages 8–76, 80–84, 88, 90, 94, 96, 98, 100, 102, 106, 108.
Vincent Lyky: pages 78, 86, 92, 104, 112, 152, 172, 186, 188, 204, 288–416, 426, 434, 436, 444.

Editor: Jean-Jacques Brisebarre

Art director: Thomas Brisebarre

Editorial assistant: Geneviève Le Dilosker, Juliette Neveux

Layout: Florence Guex, François Leclerc

Proofread by Christine Schultz-Touge

Published simultaneously in French as *Les plus grands vins de France*
© Archipel studio, 2002
Created and produced by Archipel studio
10, rue Louis-Bertrand - 94200 Ivry-sur-Seine

English-language edition
© 2002 Flammarion

ISBN: 2-0801-0893-X
FA0893-02-VIII
Dépôt légal: 09/2002

Printed in Italy